P9-CMF-921

L. S. Woodhull, M.D.

THE PRAYER-BOOK

OF

QUEEN ELIZABETH.

The Ancient and Modern Library of Theological Literature.

THE PRAYER-BOOK

OF

QUEEN ELIZABETH.

The Ancient and Modern Library of Theological Literature.

Lawrence S. Woodhull,
Maundy Thursday 1898.

THE PRAYER-BOOK

105055

OF

QUEEN ELIZABETH

1559

*TO WHICH ARE APPENDED SOME OCCASIONAL
FORMS OF PRAYER ISSUED IN HER REIGN*

THE WHOLE PRINTED FROM ORIGINALS IN THE BRITISH
MUSEUM, AND OTHER PUBLIC LIBRARIES

With an Historical Introduction

GEN. THEO. SEMINARY
LIBRARY
NEW YORK

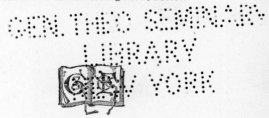

LONDON
GRIFFITH FARRAN & CO.
NEWBERY HOUSE, 39 CHARING CROSS ROAD

105085

Lit
2000
1559
1890
c.3

GEN THEO SEMINARY
LIBRARY
NEW YORK

HISTORICAL INTRODUCTION.

WITH the death of King Edward VI., the Reformed Liturgy of the Church of England came, for the time being, to an end. The elections which followed the accession of Mary were favourable to her party ; Cardinal Pole was invited to England as Papal Legate, two members only of the House of Commons, out of 360, voted, and that silently, against his proposal of reunion with Rome. On St Andrew's Day 1554, the reconciliation was formally made at Westminster, and the Roman Mass was restored. The history of the Reformed Liturgy is continued indeed in the " History of the Troubles at Frankfort," the controversy which was carried on abroad among the English refugees and the Continental Reformers. Within both these were those on one side who were bent on still further Protestantising the Prayer-book, and on the other the moderates. This chapter in the history of Religion, however, forms no part of our present subject. Worse troubles followed in England. Mr Froude holds that in spite of the apparent spontaneousness of the English reunion, the people were at least indifferent on the subject and that the whole proceeding was hollow (Froude, v. 416-500). The indifference was changed into a more active feeling by the Marian persecution, the result of which has been that from that day to this the Roman Catholic religion has been associated in the popular English mind with tyranny and revolting cruelty. The death of Mary (Nov. 17, 1556) was felt as a relief by the nation, and the accession of her sister Elizabeth was hailed with joy.

Elizabeth's first efforts were all directed towards the maintenance of peace in religion. The Mass, as by law established, was celebrated at her coronation, though the Londoners had already shown unmistakably their hatred for it, and the Protestant clergy, coming out of their hiding places, began to read the Edwardian service again, and an English Litany was used in the Royal Chapel. That Litany is given in the present volume, pp. 1-6. Cecil put forth enquiries among the leaders of the different parties as to the course to be taken with respect to the National Religion (See Froude, vi. 124-5). The result showed that there was no longer such hope as there had been of unity. Gardiner and even Warham before him had consented to the doctrine of the Royal supremacy, combined with Roman dogma, and the policy of Henry VIII. had rested on this. But now the Marian bishops were uncompromising in their desire to maintain things as they were, and the Protestant divines were for the most part hot Zwinglians. They had passed beyond Luther and even Calvin. But there was a large secular party, who agreed with neither, and of these the greater number would have preserved the Roman system, simply on the ground that the people, at any rate in the country, would prefer this. " The Catholics," they said, " are in a majority in every county but Middlesex and Kent." The Queen herself was opposed to both extremes. Her views were probably like those of her father, and she certainly would have preferred her brother's first Prayer Book to the second (Froude, vi. 115). She was bent now on setting the religion of the country on a basis which should be national and not Zwinglian. Cecil's queries had pointed to the restoration of the book of 1549, but the answers of the Protestant divines were hostile. Thus Dr Guest, afterwards Bishop of Rochester, one of the most moderate, who took the lead in consequence of Archbishop Parker's illness, even proposed to leave open the posture of the communicants at reception. The steps taken all indicate the caution with which the Queen and her Council found it needful to proceed. Thus on December 27, 1558, a Proclamation was issued, addressed to the Lord Mayor of London, in which all preaching was forbidden. It allowed the Gospel, Epistle, and Ten Commandments to be read in English, but without exposition, and commanded that no other form of public worship should be used except that by law received, or the Litany at present used in her Majesty's Chapel, and the Lord's Prayer and Creed in English, until consultation may be had by Parliament. Nevertheless, it is certain that the zealous Protestants continued to preach in churches [Zurich Letters, pp. 21, 57], and to use the Edwardian Prayer Book.

The result of the queries of Cecil and the deliberations of the divines appointed to consider the great question, was that the second Book of Edward was adopted as the basis of the new Liturgy. When it was sent up by them to the Queen's Secretary, Guest wrote an explanatory letter explaining why. Ceremonies once taken away, he said, ought not to be restored. If a surplice was sufficient for baptizing, preaching, and praying, it should suffice for the Communion. Non-communicants ought to depart before the consecration. Prayers for the Dead should not be used, because it appears to make for sacrifice. The Prayer at Consecration, " Hear us, O merciful Father," &c. [A. and M. L. Edition, p. 203], was omitted, because Petition is no part of Consecration, Christ in instituting having made no petition but only a thanksgiving. The old use of the Church was to stand at reception, but kneeling was lawful, and therefore the posture should be left to men's own choice.

This indicates the principles upon which the Protestant party acted. But these did not, as we have seen, commend themselves to the Queen. Nor in all probability did they to Archbishop Parker. Had they been carried out, there would have been no chance of their acceptance with those, who, though they were no friends of the Papal power, were also not prepared to cast in their lot with the destructives of Geneva and Zurich.

The result was a compromise. The book was accepted, but with certain significant and important modifications. Mr Gladstone has admirably put the matter as follows :—" Had the divines had their way, there might at once have been a conflict with the whole Roman Catholic party, a crisis in the foreign policy of the country, possibly a war, both civil and foreign. Apart from any ritualistic and theological leanings of the Queen, she did what the national safety and unity evidently required. The spirit of nationalism, generally dominant under Henry VIII., had given way first in one direction under Edward VI., apparently without reserves, then in the other direction with some reserves, to political interests and passions. In her it found a restorer and a champion. Elizabeth admitted the Protestant claim in the gross, but admitted it with serious discounts. Yet those discounts were adjusted with extraordinary skill." (*Nineteenth Cent.*, Nov. 1888, p. 767).

The book thus modified was presented to Parliament, and a new Act of Uniformity, passed April 28th, 1559, enacted that it should be used from and after St John Baptist's Day. The Queen, in her zeal, so far broke the law, that she anticipated this date, and ordered it to be read in her chapel on Sunday, May 12. And on the day appointed, out of the whole body of 9,400 clergy, only 189 refused to conform.

This book is presented to the reader in the present volume, but with this slight difference from those of King Edward in the same series, that the Epistles and Gospels are not given in full. They will be found in the preceding books, and the printing of them at length would have necessitated enlarging the size and price of the volume.

We have now to note the differences between the Second Book of King Edward and that before us. Less than two pages of print will cover them all, and yet, as we have said, they are of great importance. The first, and by far the most weighty, will be found on page 41, the famous " Ornaments Rubric." The reader comparing this with that at page 29 of 2 King Edward, will see the vast difference. The " accustomed place of the Church, chapel, or chancel," is substituted for the place where " the people may best hear." And the prohibited vestments, " alb, vestment and cope," are restored. Mr Gladstone, remarking on the drawing up of this measure, is of opinion that it was intended to conciliate the rural districts, where there is every reason to suppose it would at the time be popular. And he adds, with a moderation and straight-forwardness which will commend themselves to all unprejudiced minds, " I am not aware of any evidence to show that it was ever

enforced against unwilling clergymen, or that it supplied a pro-
minent topic for the controversies of the day.   In the matter of
clerical habits, these turned mainly on the use of the surplice.   It
was as much as the Queen and Government could do to hold this
narrower ground with success against the determined opposition
of the Puritans in mass, and the leanings of a large proportion of
the bishops.   But they did hold it; and the experience of the
Cromwellian and Restoration periods shows that they rightly
gauged the general tendencies of the nation, which did not favour
a naked Protestantism, they suffered the ornaments rubric to lie
partially dormant, but they kept it in force, and they sternly resisted all attempts to alter the Prayer Book in the sense of the
Swiss Reformation."

The next change to note is the omission of the petition in the
Litany against "the tyranny of the Bishop of Rome and all his
detestable enormities."   Compare 2 Edward, p. 42, and present
vol., p. 55.   No doubt the devout feeling of Christian people
would acquiesce in this omission.   There are also a few additional
words in the suffrage for the Queen.   The addition of the prayers
for the Queen and Clergy at pp. 59 and 60, and a few other variations, are also to be noted.

More important is the difference in the words of administration
in the Holy Communion.   The words in the first book of Edward
had been totally different from those in the second.   Elizabeth's
book took them both (p. 103), and to this day they so remain.
And lastly, in this service the "kneeling rubric" of 2 Edward (p.
172) was omitted in Queen Elizabeth (p. 106).   In the Ordinal,
"the Oath of the King's Supremacy (2 Edward, p. 223) becomes
"the Oath of the Queen's Sovereignty" (Elizabeth, 165), and the
alteration of the opening words of the oath itself has much signifi-
cance as indicating the desire for peace and charity.

Before the new Prayer Book was two years old some alterations
were made in the Calendar, not of great importance (*cf.* pp. 21-40
with pp. 185-205).   The Puritans were from the first eager to bring
the book into fuller harmony with their own views, and in 1566 a
Bill was brought into Parliament with that intention.   It was frustrated by the Queen laying it down that such a bill cannot pass
without approval of Convocation.   But so much was conceded to
them that certain "Advertisements" were issued in 1566.   The Act
of Uniformity, after repeating the Ornaments Rubric, had gone on
to say, "until other order shall be therein taken by authority of
the Queen's Majesty with the advice of her Commissioners . . . or
of the Metropolitan of this realm."   And now these Advertisements declared that the surplice was sufficient, and, by consequence, the alb, vestment, cope were so far set aside.   They were
not abolished, for the Ornaments Rubric remained.   And the
Advertisements did not become law; the Queen connived at them,
but they had no statutory authority, and they did not satisfy the

Puritans. But they went far to lead to the disuse of the vestments, though certainly in a few cases there are proofs of their continuance.

Following the Prayer Book will be found in the present volume a collection of " Godly Prayers " (p. 147). So far back as the days of Henry VIII. the Reformers had provided books of private devotion for the people, following herein the *Horæ* of previous days. The Primers of Henry VIII. and Edward VI. were such volumes ; there were many editions varying more or less in detail. And the Godly Prayers before us are one form of these. They were not, therefore, a part of the Liturgy, but almost from the beginning were bound up with some editions of it ; not with the folios, which were specially prepared for church use, but with smaller editions. At a later date was added another collection of private prayers, composed by the exiles abroad at the time of the Marian persecution. And with these were bound up the Metrical Psalms of Sternhold and Hopkins (" The Old Version ") with musical notation.

The Appendices to the present volume require a few words. After the New Calendar of 1561, of which we have already spoken, they comprise Occasional Forms drawn up for special occasions in the course of Elizabeth's reign, and are of great historical interest. There are many more of these, which are little more than repetitions with variations ; we have selected the most characteristic, and those connected with the most important events of this wonderful reign.

That at p. 206 is the commonest of all the forms which were drawn up at the visitation of the Plague which in the 16th and 17th centuries desolated England from time to time. The form before us was drawn up by Grindal, Bishop of London, in 1563. The plague of that year was brought hither by the English Army from Havre, the French Protestants having put us in possession of that district.

Appendix IV. (p. 217) owes its origin to the attack upon Malta by the Turks, who, it will be remembered, were then the terror not only of Eastern Europe, but of the Mediterranean. Malta was at this time in possession of the Knights of St John of Jerusalem, and, one might almost say, the fate of Southern Europe depended on their being able to hold it. There is another form, which we have not given, of thanksgiving for their success against the invaders, and also for the defeats of the same barbarians in Hungary.

Appendix V., " The Prayer " was occasioned by the rising of the Earls of Northumberland and Westmoreland, on behalf of the Queen of Scots, in November 1569. (See Froude, ix., ch. 52.) A homily was put forth " against disobedience and wilful rebellion," to which this prayer was appended.

The form of prayer for the anniversary of the Queen's Accession, p. 227, is interesting as being the first of the kind which we have.

Such forms were begun at the Reformation and have been continued until now. It is noteworthy that James II. commanded the bishops to compose one for his accession, which was founded on this. It is said that the first of these services was drawn up by Cooper, Vice-Chancellor of Oxford, afterwards Bishop of Winchester, in 1567.

Appendix X. was written at a time when the nation was dreading the Spanish Invasion, and also afflicted with a dearth.

Appendix XI. marks the period when the Armada was almost in sight. The form was originally drawn up in 1572, but was reissued by the Archbishop (Whitgift) with alterations and additions on July 10th, 1588. Nine days later the great fleet was visible off the Lizard.

This form is appropriately followed (p. 254) by the Thanksgiving for the defeat of the Armada. Probably there was never before, or since, such a burst of joy and devout thanksgiving as that which England poured forth then. The first public service was held at Paul's Cross, August 20th. They followed everywhere in a few days.

Appendix XIII. (p. 258). Henry IV. of France was fighting the League. Elizabeth sent four thousand men to his assistance, as well as "a greater sum than, as he declared, he had ever seen before." There are two or three of these forms of prayer belonging to the year 1589-90. The present is of the latter date. There is another form for the Plague which was again heavy in 1593, twenty thousand persons dying in London.

Appendix XIV. Occasioned by Spanish machinations against the Queen's life, and the treasons of her fugitive Roman Catholic subjects in the Netherlands.

Appendix XV., XVI. Philip II. was making fresh preparations against England, in consequence of which the English Government took the aggressive, and a powerful fleet was sent to Cadiz in 1596, and captured it on the 21st June.

Appendix XVII. Philip next planned a descent on Ireland, and the fleet which Elizabeth sent against him is the subject of this service.

Much of the information given in this Introduction is taken from Mr Clay's admirable edition of the Elizabethan Liturgy, published by the Parker Society, but is supplemented from later works on the same period. Every form, however, here given, has been collated with the originals in the libraries of the British Museum, Lambeth Palace, and Cambridge University.   W. B.

January 1890.

THE LITANY AND SUFFRAGES
1558.

O GOD, the father of heauen : haue mercie vpon vs miserable synners.

O God the father of heauen : haue mercye vpon vs miserable synners.

O God the soonne, redemer of the worlde : haue mercie vpon vs miserable sinners.

O God the sonne, redemer of the worlde : haue mercie vpon vs miserable sinners.

O God the holy ghoste, procedyng from the father and the soonne : haue mercie vpon vs miserable synners.

O God the holy ghost, procedyng from the father and the soonne : haue mercie vpon vs miserable sinners.

O holie, blessed, and glorious Trinitie, three persons and one God : haue mercie vpon vs miserable sinners.

O holy, blessed, and glorious Trinitie, three persons and one God : haue mercie vpon vs miserable synners.

Remembre not lorde our offences, nor the offences of our forfathers, neither take thou vengeaunce of oure synnes : spare vs good Lorde, spare thy people, whom thou hast redemed with thy moste precious bloud, and be not angry with vs for euer :

Spare vs good lorde.

From all euill and mischief, from synne, from the craftes and assaultes of the deuill, from thy wrathe, and from euerlastyng dampnacion :

Good lorde deliuer vs.

From al blindnes of hart, from pride, vanglorie, and hipocrisy, from enuie, hatred, and malice, and all vncharitablenes :

Good Lorde delyuer vs.

A

From fornication, and al other dedly sinne, and from al the deceites of the worlde, the fleshe, and the deuill :
Good Lorde delyuer vs.

From lightnyngs and tempests, from plague, pestilence, and famine, from battaill, and murder, and from sodain death :
Good Lorde deliuer vs.

From all sedition and priuie conspiracie, from the tiranie of the bisshop of Rome, and all his detestable enormities, from al false doctrine and heresie, from hardnes of harte, and contempte of thy worde and commaundemente :
Good Lorde deliuer vs.

By the misterie of thy holy incarnacion, by the [1] holy natiuitee and circumcision, by thy baptisme, fasting and temptacion :
Good lorde deliuer vs.

By thyne agonie and bloudye sweate, by thy crosse and passion, by thy precious death and buriall, by thy glorious resurrection and ascention, and by the cominyng of the holie ghost :
Good lorde deliuer vs.

In all tyme of our tribulation, in all time of our wealth, in the houre of death, and in the daie of iudgement :
Good Lorde deliuer vs.

We sinners dooe beseche thee to heare vs, O lorde God, and that it maie please thee to rule and gouerne thy holie churche vniuersall in the right waie :
We beseche thee to heare vs good lorde.

That it may please the to kepe Elizabeth thy seruaunte our Quene and gouernour :
We beseche thee to heare vs good lorde.

That it maie please the to rule her harte in thy faithe feare and loue, and that she maie alwayes haue affiaunce in thee, and euer seke thy honor and glorie :
We beseche thee to heare vs good lorde.

That it maie please thee to be her defender and keper, giuing her the victory ouer al her enemies :
We beseche thee to heare vs good lorde.

That it maie please thee to illuminate al bisshops, pastours and ministers of the Churche, with true knowledge and vnderstandyng of thy worde, and that bothe by their preachyng and liuing thei may set it forth and shewe it accordingly :
We beseche thee to heare vs good lorde.

[1 Most probably, a misprint for, thy.]

That it maie please thee to endue the lordes of the counsaill, and al the nobilitie with grace, wisedome, and vnderstanding :
We beseche thee to heare vs good lorde.

That it maie please thee to blesse and kepe the magistrates, giuyng them grace to execute iustice, and to maintain truth :
We beseche thee to heare vs good lorde.

That it maie please thee to blesse and kepe all thy people :
We beseche thee to heare vs good lorde.

That it may please the to give to all nacions vnitie, peace, and concorde :
We beseche thee to heare vs good lorde.

That it may please the to giue vs an harte to loue and dreade thee, and diligently to liue after thy commaundementes :
We beseche thee to heare vs good lorde.

That it may please the to giue all thy people encrease of grace, to hear mekely thy woorde, and to receiue it with pure affection, and to bryng forthe the fruites of the spirite :
We beseche thee to heare vs good lorde.

That it maie please thee to bryng into the waie of truthe all soche as haue erred, and are deceiued :
We beseche thee to heare vs good lorde.

That it maie please thee to strengthen soche as do stande and comfort and helpe the weake harted, and to raise vp them that fall, and finally to beate doune Sathan vnder our fete :
We beseche thee to heare vs good lorde.

That it maie please the to succoure, helpe, and comforte all that bee in daunger, necessitee and tribulation :
We beseche thee to heare vs good lorde.

That it maie please the to preserue all that trauaill by lande or by water, all women laboring of child, al sicke persons and yong children, and to shew thy pitie vpon all prisoners and captiues :
We beseche thee to heare vs good lorde.

That it maie please thee to defende, and prouide for the father-lesse children and widowes, and al that be desolate and oppressed :
We beseche thee to heare vs good lorde.

That it maie please thee to haue mercie vpon all men :
We beseche thee to heare vs good lorde.

Tha it maie please thee to forgiue our enemies, persecutors and sclaunderers, and to turne their hartes :
We beseche thee to heare vs good lorde.

A 2

THE PRAYER-BOOK OF QUEEN ELIZABETH, 1558.

That it maye please thee to giue and preserue to our vse the kindly fruites of the earth, so that in due tyme we maie enioye theim :

We beseche thee to heare vs good lorde.

That it maie please the to giue to vs true repentaunce, to forgiue vs all our sinnes, negligences and ignoraunces, to and[1] endue vs with the grace of thy holie spirit, to amend our liues accordyng to thy holy worde :

We beseche thee to heare vs good lorde.

Sonne of God : we beseche thee to heare vs.
Sonne of God : we beseche thee to heare vs.

O lambe of God, that takest awaie the sinnes of the worlde :
Graunt vs thy peace.

O lambe of God, that takest awaie the sinnes of the worlde :
Haue mercie vpon vs.

O Christ heare vs.
O Christ heare vs.

Lorde haue mercie vpon vs.
Lorde haue mercie vpon vs.

Christ haue mercie vpon vs.
Christ haue mercie vpon vs.

Lorde haue mercie vpon vs.
Lorde haue mercie vpon vs.

Our Father whiche art in. &c.
And suffer vs not to be led into temptation.
But deliuer vs from euill. Amen.

Versicle. O lorde deale not with vs after our sinnes.
Answere. Neither rewarde vs after our iniquities.

Let vs praie.

O GOD merciful father, that despisest not the sighing of a contrite hart, nor the desire of soche as be sorowful, mercifully assist our praiers, that wee make before the in al our troubles and aduersitees, whensoeuer thei oppresse vs : and graciously heare vs, that those euils, whiche the craft and subtiltee of the deuill or man worketh against vs, be brought to nought, and by the prouidence of thy goodnes thei maie bee dispersed, that we thy seruaunts beyng hurte by no persecutions, maie euermore giue thankes vnto thee in thy holy churche : through Jesu Christ our Lorde. Amen
O Lorde arise, helpe vs, and deliuer vs for thy names sake.

[1 Misprint for, and to.]

O God, wee haue heard with our eares, and our fathers haue declared vnto vs the noble workés, that thou didst in their dayes, and in the old time before them.

O Lorde arise, helpe vs, and deliuer vs for thyne honour.

Glory bee to the father, and to the sonne, and to the holy ghost. As it was in the beginnyng, is now, and euer shall be, worlde without ende. Amen.

From our enemies defende vs, O Christ.

Gratiously loke vpon our afflictions.

Pitifully beholde the douloure of our harte.

Mercifully forgiue the sinnes of thy people.

Fauourably with mercie hear our praiers.

O Sonne of Dauid, haue mercie vpon vs.

Bothe now and euer vouchesafe to heare vs, O Christ.

Graciously heare vs, O Christ.

Graciously heare vs, O lorde Christ.

Versicle. O Lorde let thy mercie be shewed vpon vs.
Answere. As we do put our trust in thee.

¶ *Let vs praie.*

WE humblie besech thee, O father, mercifully to looke vpon our infirmitees, and for the glorie of thy name sake tourne from vs those euilles that we moste righteuosly haue deserued. And graunt that in all our troubles, wee maie put our whole trust and confidence in thy mercy, and euermore serue the in holines and purenes of liuyng, to thy honoure and glorie through our onely mediatoure and aduocate Jesus Christ, our Lorde. Amen.

O GOD, whose nature and propertie is, euer to haue mercie and to forgiue, receiue our humble peticions : and though we be tied and bound with the chaine of our synnes, yet let the pitifulnes of thy greate mercie lose vs : for the honour of Jesus Christes sake, our mediatour and aduocate.

ALMIGHTIE and euerlastyng God, whiche onely workest greate marueiles, sende doune vpon our Bisshops and curates, and all congregations committed to their charge, ye helthfull spirite of thy grace, and that thei maie truely please thee : Poure vpon them the continuall dewe of thy blessyng : graunt this, O Lorde for the honour of our aduocate and mediator Jesus Christ. Amen.

GRAUNT we beseche thee, O Almightie God, that we in our trouble put our whole confidence vpon thy mercie that wee against all aduersitie bee defended vnder thy protection : graunt this, O lorde God, for our onely mediateur and aduocate Jesus Christes sake. Amen.

☞ *A Praier of Chrisostome.*

ALMIGHTIE God, whiche hast giuen vs grace at this time with one accorde, to make our common supplications vnto thee, and doest promise that when twoo or three bee gathered together in thy name, thou wilte graunte their requestes : fulfill now, O Lorde, the desires and peticions of thy seruauntes, as maie be moste expedient for them : grauntyng vs in this worlde, knowledge of thy truth, and in the world to cum, life euerlasting.　Amen.

❡ THE

BOKE OF COMMON PRAIER,

AND ADMINISTRATION

OF

THE SACRAMENTES, AND OTHER

RITES AND CEREMONIES IN

THE CHURCHE OF

ENGLAND.

Londini in Officina
Richardi Graftoni
Cum priuilegio Regie Maiestatis.
Anno. 1559.

❧ THE CONTENTES OF THIS BOOKE.

D AN ACTE FOR THE UNIFORMITIE OF COMMON

PRAIER, AND SERUICE IN THE CHURCH, AND THE ADMINIS-TRACION OF THE SACRAMENTES.

WHERE at the death of oure late Soueraigne lord King Edward the sixt, there remained one vniforme order of common seruice and prayer, and of the administracion of Sacramentes, Rites, and Ceremonies, in the churche of Englande, whiche was set furth in one booke entituled : The booke of cōmon prayer, and administracion of Sacramentes, and other Rites and ceremonies in the churche of Englande, aucthorised by Act of Parliament, holden in the fift and sixt yeres of our saied late Soueraigne lorde kyng. Edward the sixte, intituled : An acte for the vniformitie of Common prayer, and administracion of the Sacramētes, the which was repealed and taken away by acte of parliament, in the first yere of the raygne of our late Soueraigne Ladye Quene Marye, to the great decaye of the due honour of God, and discomfort to the professours of the trueth of Christes religion :

Be it therefore enacted, by the aucthoritie of this present parliament, that the sayde statute of repeale, and euery thing therein conteined, onely concerning the sayde booke, and the Seruice, administracion of Sacramentes, Rites, and Ceremonies, conteined or appoyncted, in, or by the saide booke shalbe voyde and of none effecte, from, and after the feaste of the Natiuitie of S. John Baptist, next commyng. And that the sayde booke, with the ordre of seruice, and of the administracion of Sacramentes, Rites and Ceremonies, with the alteracion, and addicions, therein added and appoynted by this estatute, shall stande, and be from and after the sayde feaste of the Natiuitie of Sainct John Baptist, in full force and effect, according to the tenour and effect of this estatute, any thing in the aforesayde statute of repeale to the contrary notwithstanding.

And further be it enacted by the quenes highnes, with the assent of the lordes and commons, in thys present Parliament assembled, and by aucthoritie of the same, that all and synguler ministers, in any cathedrall, or paryshe church, or other place within thys realme of Englande, Wales, and the marches of the same, or other the quenes dominions : shall from, and after the feaste of the Natiuitie of Saynct John Baptist next comming, be bounden to saye and use the Matins, Euensong, celebracion of the Lordes supper, and administracion of eche of the Sacramentes, and all their Common and open prayer, in suche ordre and fourme, as is mencioned in the sayde booke, so aucthorised by Parliament in the sayde .v. and sixte yere of the raygne of king Edward the sixt, with one alteracion or additiō of certayn Lessons to be vsed on euery Sonday in the yere, and the fourme of the Letanie altered and corrected, and two Sentences onely added in the deliuery of the Sacrament to the cōmunicantes, and none other, or other wyse. And that if anye maner of persone,[1] Vicare, or other, whatsoeuer minister that ought or shoulde syng or saye common prayer mencioned in the sayde booke, or minister the Sacramentes, from and after the feaste of the Natiuitie of Sainct John Baptiste nexte commyng, refuse to vse the sayde common prayers, or to minyster the Sacramentes in suche Cathedrall or paryshe Churche, or other places, as he shoulde vse to minister the same, in such ordre and fourme, as they be mencioned and set foorth in the sayde booke : or shall wilfully or obstinately standynge in the same, vse anye other Ryte, ceremonye, ordre, fourme, or maner of celebrating of the Lords supper opēly or priuely, or Mattins, Euensong, adminis-tracion of the Sacramentes, or other open prayers, then is men-cioned and set foorth in the sayd booke [*Open prayer in and throughoute this Acte, is mente that prayer whiche is for other to come vnto, or heare, eyther in Common Churches, or priuie Chap-pelles, or Oratories, commonlye called the Seruice of the Churche*], or shall preach, declare, or speake any thyng in the derogacion or deprauing of the sayd booke, or any thyng therein conteyned, or of any part thereof, and shalbe thereof lawfullye conuicted, according to the lawes of this realme, by verdicte of .xii. men, or by hys owne confession, or by the notorious euidence of the facte, shall lose and forfeyte to the Queenes hyghnesse, her heyres and successours, for hys fyrst offence, the profite of all his spiritual benefices or pro-mocions, comming or arysyng in one whole yere next after this conuiction. And also that the persone so conuicted, shall for the same offence suffer imprisonment by the space of .vi. monethes, without baile or mainpryse. And if any suche persone, once conuicte of anye offence, concernyng the premysses, shall after hys fyrst conuiction eftsones offende, and be thereof in fourme afore-sayd lawfully conuict : that then the same person shall for his second offence suffer imprisonment by the space of one hole yere, and also shall therefore be depriued, *ipso facto*, of all his spiritual promotions. And that it shalbe lawfull to all patrons or donors of all and singuler the same spirituall promocions, or of any of them, to present or collate to the same, as though the person and persons so offending wer dead ; and that if any such person or persons, after he shalbe twise conuicted in fourme aforesayd, shal offend agaynst any of the premysses the thyrd time, and shalbe thereof in fourme aforesayd lawfully conuicted : That then the person so offending, and conuycted the thyrd tyme, shalbe depriued, *ipso*

[1 Person *or* parson : rector.]

facto, of all his spirituall promocions, and also shall suffer imprisonment during hys lyfe.

AND if the person that shall offend, and be conuicte in fourme
aforesayde, concernyng any of the premisses, shall not be bene-
ficed, nor haue anye spirituall promotion : That then the same
person so offending and conuict, shall for the fyrst offence suffer
imprisonment during one hole yere next after his sayde conuiction,
without bayle or maynepryse. And yf anye suche person, not
hauynge anye spirituall promotion, after his firste conuiction, shall
eftsones offende in anye thynge concernynge the premysses, and
shal in fourme aforesayd be therof lawfully conuicted : That then
the same person shall for his secōde offence, suffer imprysonment
durynge hys lyfe.

And it is ordeyned and enacted by the aucthoritie abouesayde,
that yf any person or personnes whatsoeuer, after the sayde feaste
of the Natiuitie of Saincte John Baptyste nexte commynge, shall in
any Enterludes, Playes, Songes, Rymes, or by other open wordes,
declare or speake anye thinge in the derogation, deprauynge or
despysynge of the same booke, or of anye thynge therin conteyned,
or anye parte thereof, or shall by open facte, deede, or by open
threatnynges compell or cause, or otherwyse procure or mayntayne
anye Pars, Vonycar, or other Mynister, in anye Cathedrall or paryshe
Churche, or in Chappell, or in anye other place to synge or saye
anye commen and open prayer, or to minister anye Sacramente
otherwyse, or in anye other maner and forme then is mencioned
in the sayde booke, or that by anye of the sayde meanes shall vn-
lawfully interrupt or let any parson, vycar, or other minister, in
anye Cathedrall, or paryshe Churche, Chappel, or anye other place
to synge or saye common and open praier, or to minister the
Sacramentes or anye of them, in suche maner and fourme, as is
mencioned in the sayde booke : That then euerye suche parson [1]
beynge thereof lawefully conuicted in fourme aboue sayde,
shall forfeyte to the Quene oure Soueraygne Ladye, her heires and
successours, for the fyrste offence a hundredth markes. And yf
any parson or parsons, beynge once conuicte of anye suche offence
eftsons offende againste anye of the laste recyted offences, and
shal in fourme aforesayde be thereof lawfullye conuicte. That
then the same parson so offendinge and conuicte, shall for the
seconde offence forfeyte to the Quene oure Soueraigne Ladye, her
heyres and successours, foure hundredth markes. And yf anye
parson after he, in forme aforesayde, shall haue bene twyce conuicte of anye offence, concernynge anye of the laste recyted offences,
shall offende the thyrde tyme, and be thereof in forme abouesayde
lawefully conuicte : That then euery parson so offendynge and
conuicte, shall for his thyrde offence, forfeyte to oure Soueraygne
Lady the Quene, all his goodes and catelles, and shal suffer imprysonment duryng his lyfe. And yf anye person or persons that
for his fyrste offence, concernynge the premysses, shall be conuicte

[1 " Parson " often stands in this Act for *person*.]

in forme aforesayde, do not paye the somme to be payde by vertue of hys conuiction, in such maner and forme as the same oughte to be payde, within syxe wekes nexte after hys conuiction, that then euery person so conuicte, and so not payinge the same, shall for the same first offence, instede of the sayde somme, suffer imprisonmente by the space of syxe monethes, withoute bayl or maynepryse. And yf anye person or persons, that for his seconde offēce cōcerning the premisses, shalbe conuict in forme aforesayde, do not pay the sayed somme to be payed by vertue of his conuiction, and this estatute, in suche maner and forme as the same oughte to be payde, within .vi. wekes nexte after hys said seconde conuiction : that then euery person so conuicted and not so[1] paiyng the same, shall for the same seconde offence, in the stede of the sayde somme, suffer imprisonment during .xii. monethes, withoute bayle or maynepryse.   And that from and after the sayde feaste of the Natiuitie of S. John Baptyst next commynge, all and euery person and personnes, inhabiting within this Realme or anye other the Quenes Maiesties dominions, shall diligentlye and faythfully, hauynge no lawefull or reasonable excuse to be absente, endeuoure themselues to resorte to their paryshe Churche or Chappel accustomed, or vpon reasonable let thereof, to some vsual place where common Prayer, and suche Seruice of GOD shalbe vsed in suche tyme of let vpon euerye Sondaye, and other dayes ordayned and vsed to be kepte as holye dayes.   And then and there to abyde orderly, and soberly durynge the tyme of the common prayer, prechinges, or other seruice of GOD, there to be vsed and ministred, vpon payne of punyshmēt by the censures of the church.   And also vpon payne that euerye persone so offendynge shall forfete for euery suche offence .xii. d. to be leuyed by the Churchewardens of the paryshe, where suche offence shalbe done, to thuse of the poore of the same paryshe, of the goodes, landes, and tenementes of suche offendour, by waye of distresse. And for due execution hereof, the Quenes moste excellente Maiesty, the lordes Temporall, and all the commons in this present Parlyament assembled, dothe in Goddes name earnestly requyre and charge all the Archebyshoppes, Bishopes, and other ordinaries, that they shal endeuour themselues to the vttermost of their knowledges, that the due and true execution hereof may be had througe houte their diocesse, and charges, as they wyll answere before God, for suche euylles and plages, wherewith almyghty God maye iustlye punyshe his people for neglecting this good and holsome lawe.   And for theyr aucthoritie in this behalfe, be it further enacted by thaucthoritie aforesayde, that all and singular the same Archebyshopes, byshopes, and all other their officers, exercising ecclesiasticall iurisdiction as wel in place exempt as not exempt, within their diocesse, shall haue full power and aucthoritie by this acte, to reforme, correcte, and ponyshe by censures of the churche, all and singuler persons, which shall offende wythin any

[1 Misprints in both editions of 1559 for, so not.]

theyr iurisdictions or diocesse, after the sayde feaste of the Natiuitye of Sainct John Baptyst nexte commynge, againste this acte and statute. Any other lawe, statute, priuiledge, lybertie, or prouision heretofore made, had, or suffred to the contrarye notwithstandinge.

AND it is ordeyned and enacted by the aucthoritie aforesayde, that all and euerye iustices of Oyer and determiner, or Justices of Assyse, shall haue ful power and aucthoritye in euery of their open and general Sessions, to enquire here and determine al, and all maner of offences that shalbe committed or done contrary to any article conteyned in this present act, within the lymites of the Commission to them dyrected, and to make processe for thexecutiō of the same, as they may do againste any personne beinge indited before them of trespasse, or lawfully conuicted thereof.

PROUIDED alwayes and be it enacted by thaucthoritye afore-sayd, that all and euery Archbishoppe and Bishoppe, shall or may at al time and times at his libertie and pleasure, ioyne and associate himselfe, by vertue of this acte, to the said iustices of Oyer and determiner, or to the said iustices of assise, at euery of the sayd open and general Sessions, to be holden in any place within his diocesse, for and to the enquiry, hearing and determining of the offences aforesayde.

PROUIDED also and be it enacted by thaucthority aforesaid, that the bokes cōcernyng the sayd Seruices, shall at the costes and charges of the paryshioners of euerye paryshe, and Cathedrall Church, be attained and gotten before the sayd feast of the Natiuitye of Saint Jhon Baptist next folowing, and that all suche paryshes and Cathedral Churches or other places, wher the said bokes shalbe attained and gotten before the said feaste of the Natiuitye of Sainct Jhon Baptist, shal within three wekes next after the said bokes so attained and gotten, vse the said seruice and put the same in vre [1] accordyng to this acte.

AND be it further enacted by thaucthoritie aforesaid, that no parson or parsons shalbe at any time hereafter empeched or otherwyse molested of, or for any of the offences aboue mencioned, hereafter to be committed or done contrary to this act, onles he or they so offendynge, be therof indited at the next generall Sessions, to be holden before any such Justices of Oyer and determiner, or Justices of assise, next after any offence committed or done con-trarye to the tenor of this act.

PROUIDED alwayes, and be it ordeined, and enacted by the aucthoritie aforesaid, that al and singuler Lordes of the Parliament for the third offence aboue mencioned, shall be tried by their peres.

PROUIDED also, and be it ordeined, and enacted by thauctho-ritie aforesaid, that the Maior of London, and all other Maiors, Bayliffes, and other head officers of al, and singular Cities, Boroughes, and Townes Corporate within this Realme, Wales and

[1 Ure; use, practice.]

the marches of the same, to the which Justices of Assise do not commonly repayre, shall have ful power and aucthority by vertue of this acte, to enquire, here, and determine the offences abouesaid, and euery of them yerely, within .xv. daies after the feast of Easter, and S. Mighel tharchaungell, in like maner and fourme as Justices of Assise and Oyer and determiner may doo.

PROUIDED alwayes and be it ordeined and enacted by thaucthoritie aforesayd, that al and singuler Archbishops and Byshops, and euery of their Chauncellours, Commissaries, Archdeacons, and other ordinaries, hauynge any peculier ecclesiasticall iurisdiction, shal haue ful power and aucthority by vertue of this act, as wel to enquire in their visitation, Synodes, and elsewhere within their iurisdiction at any other time and place, to take occasions [1] and informations of al and euery the thinges aboue mencioned, done, cōmitted, or perpetrated within the limits of their iurisdictions and aucthoritie, and to punish the same by admonicion, excōmunication, sequestration, or depriuation and other censures and processe in like fourme as heretofore hath ben vsed in like cases by yͤ Queenes ecclesiastical lawes.

PROUIDED alwayes and be it enacted, that whatsoeuer person offending in the premisses, shall for the offence firste receyue ponishment of the ordinary, hauing a testimonial therof vnder the said ordinaries seale, shal not for the same offence eftsones be cōuicted before the Justices.   And lykewise receiuynge for the sayd fyrst offence ponishment by the Justices, he shal not for the same offence eftsoones receyue ponishment of the ordinary.   Any thinge conteyned in this act to the contrary notwithstandyng.

PROUIDED alwayes and be it enacted, that suche ornamēts of the Churche, and of the ministers therof, shalbe reteined and be in vse as was in this Churche of England, by aucthority of Parliament, in the second yere of the raygne of Kyng Edward the vi. vntil other order shalbe therin takē by thaucthority of the Quenes Maiestie, with the aduise of her Cōmissioners appointed and auctorized vnder the great Seale of England, for causes ecclesiastical, or of the Metropolitan of this Realme.   And also that if there shal happen any contempte or irreuerence to be vsed in the ceremonies or rites of the Church, by the misusinge of the orders appointed in this boke : The Quenes Maiestie may by the like aduise of the sayd commissioners, or Metropolytan, ordeine and publish such further ceremonies or rites as may be most for the aduauncemēt of Gods glory, the edifiyng of his Church, and the due reuerence of Christes holy mysteries and Sacramentes.

AND be it further enacted by the aucthoritie aforesaid, that al lawes, statutes and ordinaunces, wherin or whereby any other Seruice administration or Sacramentes or Common prayer, is limited, established, or set forth to be vsed within this Realme, or any other the Quenes dominions or Countryes, shall from hensforth be vtterly voyde and of none effect.

[1 Misprint in both editions of 1559 for accusations.]

THE PREFACE.

THERE was neuer anye thynge by the witte of man so well deuised, or so sure established, whiche (in continuaunce of tyme) hath not been corrupted : as (emong other thynges) it may plainly appeare by the Common prayers in the churche, commonly called diuine seruice : the firste originall and ground wherof, if a man woulde serche out by auncient fathers, he shall fynde that the same was not ordeyned but of a good purpose, and for a greate aduauncemente of godlines. For they so ordred the matter, that all the whole Byble (or the gretest part therof) should be red ouer ones in the yere entending therby, that the clergie and specially suche as wer Ministers of the congregacion, should (by often reading and meditacion of Gods word), be styrred vp to godlines themselues, and be more able also to exhorte other by holesome doctrine, and to confute them that wer aduersaries to the truth. And further that the people (by daily hearynge of holy scripture read in the Churche) should continually profite more and more in the knowelege of God, and be the more enflamed with the loue of his true religion. But these many yeres passed, thys godly and decent ordre of the auncient fathers, hath been so altered, broken, and neglected, by planting in vncertain Stories, Legendes, Respondes, Verses, vain Repeticions, Commemoracions, and Sinodalles, that commonly when any booke of the Bible was begon, before thre or foure Chapiters wer red out, al the rest wer vnredde. And in this sort the booke of Esay was begon in Aduent, and the boke of Genesis in Septuagesima : but they were onely begonne, and neuer red through. After lyke sorte wer other bokes of holy scripture vsed. And moreouer, wheras Sainct Paule woulde haue such language spoken to the people in the Churche, as they might onderstande, and haue profite by hearing thesame, the seruice in this churche of Englande (these many yeres) hath been redde in Latine to the people, whiche they understoode not, so that they haue heard with their eares only, and their hartes, spirite, and mynd, haue not been edified therby. And furthermore, notwithstandyng that thauncient fathers haue devyded the Psalmes into seuen porcions, wherof euery one was called a Nocturne, now of late tyme, a fewe of them haue been daily sayd (and oft repeated) and the rest vtterly omitted. Moreouer, the nombre and hardnesse of the rules, called the Pye, and the manifolde changeinges of the seruice, was the cause, that to turne the boke onely, was so harde and intricate a matter, that many tymes there was more businesse to find out what should be read, then to reade it when it was found out.

These inconueniences therefore considered, here is set furthe suche an ordre, whereby thesame shalbe redressed. And for a readinesse in this matter, here is drawen out a kalendre for that purpose, which is plain and easy to be vnderstanden, wherin (so muche as may be) the reading of holy scriptures is so set furth, that all thinges shalbe doen in ordre, without breaking one piece therof from another. For this cause be cut of Anthemes, Respondes, Inuitatories, and such lyke thinges, as dyd breake the continual course of the reading of the scripture. Yet because ther is no remedy, but that of necessitie there must be some rules, therefore certayn rules are here set furth, which as they be fewe in nombre, so they be plain and easy to be onderstanden. So that here you haue an ordre for prayer (as touching the reading of holy scripture) much agreable to the mynd and purpose of thold fathers, and a great deale more profitable and commodious, then that which of late was vsed. It is more profitable, because here are left out many thinges, whereof some be vntrue, some vncertayn, some vain and supersticious, and is ordeyned nothing to be readde but the very pure woord of God, the holye scriptures, or that which is euidently grounded vpon the same, and that in such a language and ordre, as is most easy and playne for the vnderstandyng bothe of he readers and hearers. It is also more commodious, bothe for the shortnesse therof, and for the playnesse of the ordre, and for that the rules be fewe and easye. Furthermore, by thys ordre, the Curates shall nede none other bookes for their publique seruice, but this booke, and the Bible, by the meanes wherof, the people shal not be at so great charge for bookes, as in tyme paste they haue been.

And where hertofore there hath been great diuersitie, in saying, and singyng in churches within thys realme, some folowing Salisburye vse, some Herford vse, some the vse of Bangor, some of Yorke, and some of Lincolne : now from hence furth, all the whole realme, shall haue but one vse. And if any would iudge this way more paynfull, because that all thynges must be readde vpon the booke, wheras before by the reason of so often repeticion, they could say many thinges by heart ; if those men will weigh their labour, with the profite and knowledge, which daily they shall obteyne by readyng vpon the booke, they will not refuse the pein, in cõsideracion of the great profite that shal ensue therof.

And forasmuche as nothyng can almost be so playnly set furth, but doubtes may ryse in the vse and practising of the same : To appease all such diuersitie (if any aryse), and for the resolucion of all doubtes concerning the maner howe to vnderstand, do, and execute the thinges conteined in this boke : the parties that so dout, or diuersly take any thing, shal alway resort to the Bishoppe of the dyocesse, who by hys discrecion shall take ordre for the quyeting and appeasing of the same : so that the same ordre be not contrary to any thyng conteyned in this booke. And yf the the Byshoppe of the Dyocesse be in any doubte, then may he sende for the resolucion therof vnto the Archebishoppe.

Though it be appoyncted in the afore written Preface, that all thynges shalbe readde and song in the Church, in the Englishe tongue, to the ende that the congregacion may bee thereby edifyed ; yet it is not meant, but when men say Mornyng and Euening prayer priuately, they may say thesame in any language that they themselues do vnderstande.

And all Priestes and Deacons, shalbe bounde to say dayly, the Morning and Euenyng prayer, eyther priuately or openly, except they be letted by preaching, studying of diuinitie, or by some other urgent cause.

And the Curate that ministreth in euery paryshe Churche or Chapell, beyng at home, and not beyng otherwyse reasonably letted, shall say thesame in the Parishe Church or Chapell where he ministreth, and shall toll a belle therto, a convenient tyme before he begyn, that such as be disposed may come to heare Goddes woorde, and to praye with him.

OF CEREMONIES,

WHY SOME BE ABOLISHED, AND SOME RETAYNED.

OF suche Ceremonies as be vsed in the churche, and haue hadde their beginning by the institucion of man : Some at the firste were of Godlye entent and purpose deuysed, and yet at length, turned to vanitie and supersticion : some entered into the Churche, by vndiscrete deuocion and suche a zeale as was withoute knowledge : and for because they were winked at in the beginning, they grue daily to more and more abuses, which not only for their vnprofit-ablenes, but also because they haue muche blynded the people, and obscured the glorye of God, are woorthy to be cut away, and cleane reiected. Other there be, which although they haue been deuysed by manne, yet it is thought good, to reserue them still, aswel for a decent ordre in the churche (for the which they wer first deuised) as because they pertaine to edificacion : wherunto all thinges doen in the Churche (as the Apostle teacheth) ought to be referred. And although the kepyng or omitting of a Ceremonye (in it selfe considered) is but a small thyng : yet the wilfull and contempteous transgression, and breakyng of a common ordre, and discipline : is no small offence before God.

Let all thynges be doen emong you (saith S. Paule) in a semelye and dewe ordre. The appoynctment of the which ordre, per-teyneth not to priuate men ; therefore no man ought to take in hande, nor presume to appoincte or alter any publique or com-mon ordre in Christes Church, excepte he be lawfully called and aucthorised therunto.

And wheras as in this our tyme, the mindes of menne are so diuerse, that some thinke it a great matter of conscience, to de-parte from a piece of the least of their Ceremonies (they be so addicted to their old customes) and again on the other side, some be so newe fangled, that they would innouate all thing, and so do despise the olde, that nothing can like them, but that is newe : it was thought expediēt, not so muche to haue respect how to please and satisfie either of these parties, as how to please God, and profite them bothe. And yet lest anye man shoulde be offended (whom good reasō might satisfie) here be certain causes rendered why some of the accustomed Ceremonies be put away, and some retained and kept still.

Some are put away, because the great excess and multitude of them, hath so encreased in these latter days, that the burthen of them was intollerable ; whereof S. Augustine in his tyme complained, that they were growē to suche a nombre, that the state of christian people was in worse case (cōcerning that matter) then wer the Jewes. And he counsailed that such yoke and burthen shoulde be taken away, as tyme woulde serue quietly to doe it.

But what woulde sainct Augustine haue sayde, if he had seen the Ceremonies of late dayes vsed emong vs ? wherunto the multitude vsed in his time was not to bee compared.   This our excessiue multitude of Ceremonies was so greate, and many of them so darke, that they did more confounde and darken, then declare and set furthe Christes benefites vnto vs.

And besides this, Christes Ghospell is not a Ceremoniall lawe (as muche of Moses lawe was) but it is a religion to serue God, not in bondage of the figure, or shadowe, but in the fredome of spirite, beyng content onelye with those Ceremonies, which doe serue to a decent ordre, and godlye discipline, and suche as be apte to styrre vp the dull minde of manne, to the remembraunce of his duetie to God, by some notable and speciall significacion, whereby he might be edified.

Furthermore, the moste weightie cause of the abolishement of certain Ceremonies was, that thei wer so farre abused, partly by the supersticious blindnesse of the rude and vnlearned, and partly by the vnsaciable auarice of such as sought more their owne lucre, then the glorye of God : that the abuses could not well be taken awaye, the thing remaining still.   But now as cōcerning those persones, whiche peraduenture will bee offended, for that some of the old Ceremonies are retained stil : if thei consider, that without some Ceremonies it is not possible to kepe anye ordre, or quyet discipline in the Churche, they shall easely perceiue iust cause to refourme their iudgementes. And if they thinke muche that anye of the olde dooe remain, and would rather haue all deuysed newe : Then such men graunting some Ceremonies conuenient to be had, surelye where the olde maye be well vsed, there they cannot reasonably reproue thold onely for their age without bewraying of their awn foly.   For in such a case, they ought rather to haue reuerence vnto them, for their antiquitie, if they will declare themselfes to be more studious of vnitie and concord, then of innouaciōs and new fanglenesse, whiche (asmuch as maye bee with the true settyng furth of Chrystes Religion) is always to be eschewed.   Furthermore, such shall haue no iust cause with the Ceremonies reserued, to be offended : For as those bee taken away, whiche wer moste abused, and dyd burthen mennes consciēces without any cause : so the other that remain are retained for a Dysciplyne and ordre, whiche (vpon iust causes) maye bee altered and chaunged, and therfore are not to be estemed equall with Goddes lawe.   And moreouer thei be neither darke nor dombe Ceremonies, but are

so set furthe, that euerye manne may vnderstand what they dooe
meane, and to what vse they dooe serue.   So that it is not lyke,
that they in tyme to come, shoulde bee abused, as the other haue
been.   And in these oure doynges, we condempne no other
nacions, nor prescribe any thing, but to our awne people onelye.
For wee thinke it conuenient that euery countrey should vse such
Ceremonies, as they shall thinke best, to the setting furth of
Goddes honour, or glorye, and to the reducyng of the people to a
moste perfect and Godly liuyng, without errour or Supersticion.
And that they should put away other thynges, whiche from
tyme to tyme, they perceyue to bee moste abused, as in mennes
ordinaunces, it often chaunceth diuersely in diuers countreys.

THE TABLE AND KALENDAR

EXPRESSYNG THE ORDRE OF THE PSALMES AND LESSONS,
TO BEE SAID AT THE MORNING AND EUENING PRAYER
THROUGHOUT THE YERE, EXCEPTE CERTEIN PROPRE
FEASTES, AS THE RULES FOLOWYNG
MORE PLAYNELY DECLARE.

THE ORDER HOW THE PSALTER IS APPOYNTED TO BE READDE.

THE Psalter shalbe readde through, ones euery moneth, and because that some Monethes bee longer then some other be; It is thought good, to make them euen by this meanes.

To euery moneth shalbe appointed (as concerning this purpose) iust xxx dayes.

And because January and Marche hathe one daye aboue the sayed nomber, and February, which is placed betwene them bothe, hath onely xxviii dayes, February shall borow of either of the monethes (of January and Marche) one day, and so the Psalter, which shalbe redde in February, must begin the last daie of January, and ende the first daie of Marche.

And where as May, July, August, October and December, hath xxxi dayes a pece, it is ordred that the same Psalmes shalbe redde the laste day of the sayed Monethes, which were redde the daye before, so that the Psalter may beginne againe the first daie of the next Monethe ensuyng.

Now to knowe what Psalmes shalbe redde euery daie, looke in the Kalender, the nomber that is appointed for the Psalmes, and then fynde thesame nomber in this Table, and vpon that nomber shall you see, what Psalmes shalbe sayde at Morning and Euening prayer.

And where the cxix Psalme, is deuided into xxii porcions, and is ouerlong to be redde at one time : it is so ordred, that, at one time, shal not be readde aboue foure or fyve of the sayd porcions, as you shall perceiue to be noted in this Table folowyng.

And here is also to be noted, that in this Table, and in all other partes of the seruice, where any Psalmes are appoyncted, the nombre is expressed after the greate Englyshe Bible, whiche from the ix Psalme, vnto the cxlviii Psalme (folowing the deuision of the Hebrues) doth vary in nombres from the common Latine translacion.

THE TABLE

THE ORDER

THOLD Testament is appointed for the fyrst lessons, at Morning
and Euening prayer, and shal be read through, euerye yere once,
excepte certaine bokes and Chapiters, whiche be leaste edifying,
and mighte beste bee spared, and therefore bee lefte vnread.

The newe Testament is appointed for the seconde Lessons, at
Mornyng and Euenyng prayer, and shalbe read ouer orderly euery
yere thryse, besyde the Epistles and Gospels : except the Apocalips, out of the which there bee onely certayne Lessons appointed,
vpon diuerse proper feastes.

And to knowe what Lessons shalbe readde euery daye : fynde
the day of the moneth in the Kalender folowing ; and there ye
shal perceyue the bokes and Chapiters that shalbe read for the
Lessons, both at Mornynge and Eueninge prayer.

And here is to bee noted, that whensoeuer there bee any proper
Psalmes or Lessons appointed for the Sondayes or for anye feaste
moueable or vnmoueable : then the Psalmes and Lessons, appointed
in the kalender shalbe omitted for that tyme.

Ye must note also that the Collect Epistle and Gospell, appointed for the Sondaie shal serue al the weke after, except there
fall some feast that hath his proper.

This is also to bee noted, concernyng the Leape yeares, that
the xxv daye of February, which in Leape yeare is coumpted for
two dayes, shal in those two dayes, alter nether Psalme nor Lesson :
but the same Psalmes and Lessons, whiche be sayde the first daye,
shall also serue for the second daye.

Also, wheresoeuer the beginnyng of any Lesson, Epistle or
Gospel is not expressed : there ye muste beginne at the beginning
of the Chapiter.

And wheresoeuer is not expressed howe farre shalbe read, there
shall you reade to the ende of the Chapiter.

¶ Proper lessons to be read for the first lessons, both at mornyng prayer and Euenyng prayer, on the Sondayes throughout the yeare, and for som also the seconde Lessons.

	Mattens.	Euēsong.
Sondayes of Advent.		
The first	Esa. i.	Esa. ii.
ii.	v.	xxiiii.
iii.	xxv.	xxvi.
iiii.	xxx.	xxxii.
Sondayes after Christmas.		
The first	xxxvii.	xxxviii.
ii.	xli.	xliii.
Sondayes after the Epiphany.		
The first	xliiii.	xlvi.
ii.	li.	liii.
iii.	lv.	lvi.
iiii.	lvii.	lviii.
v.	lix.	lxiiii.
Septuage.	Gen. i.	Gen. ii.
Sexagesi.	iii.	vi.
Quinqua.	ix.	xii.
Lent.		
i Sonday	xix.	xxii.
ii.	xxvii.	xxxiiii.
iii.	xxxix.	xlii.
iiii.	xliii.	xlv.
v.	Exod. iii.	Exod. v.
v	ix.	x.
Ester daye.		
i Lesson	xii.	xiii.
ii Lesson	Rom. vi.	Act ii.
Sondayes after Easter.		
The first	Nu. xvi.	Nu. xxii.
ii.	xxiii.	xxv.
iii.	Deut. iv.	Deut. v.
iiii.	vi.	vii.
v.	viii.	ix.

	Mattens.	Euēsong.
Sondaye after Ascēsion daie.	Deut. xii.	xiii.
Whitsondaye.		
i Lesson	Deut. xvii.	Deut. xxiii.
ii Lesson	Act x. Then Peter opened his. &c.	Actes xix. It fortuned whē Appollo went to Corinth. &c. *vnto* after these thynges.
Trinitie Sondaye.		
i Lesson	Gen. xviii.	Josue i.
ii Lesson	Math. iii.	
Sōdaies after the Trinitye.		
The first	Josue x.	Jos. xxiii.
ii.	Jud. iiii.	Jud. v.
iii.	i Kyng ii.	i Kyng iii.
iiii.	xii.	xiii.
v.	xv.	xv.
vi.	ii Kyng xii.	ii Kyng xxi.
vii.	xxii.	xxiiii.
viii.	iii King xiii.	iii King xvii.
ix.	xviii.	xix.
x.	xxi.	xxii.
xi.	iiii King v.	iiii King ix .
xii.	x.	xviii.
xiii.	xix.	xxiii.
xiiii.	Jere. v.	Jere. xxii.
xv.	xxxv.	xxxvi.
xvi.	Ezech. ii.	Eze. xiv.
xvii.	xvi.	xviii.
xviii.	xx.	xxiiii.
xix.	Dan. iii.	Dan. vi.
xx.	Joel ii.	Mich. vi.
xxi.	Abacuk ii.	Prouer. i.
xxii.	Prouer. ii.	ii.
xxiii.	xi.	xii.
xxiiii.	xiii.	xiiii.
xxv.	xv.	xvi.
xxvi.	xvii.	xix.

Lessons proper for holy dayes.

	Mattens.	Euensong.		Mattens.	Euensong.
S. Andrew.	Prouer. xx.	Prou. xxi.	Annunciation of our Ladye.	Eccle. ii.	Eccle. iii.
S. Thomas the apostle.	xxiii.	xxiiii.	Wensday afore Easter.	Osee xiii.	Ose xiiii.
Natiuitie of Christ.			Thursday before Easter.	Dan. ix.	Jere xxxi.
i Lesson	Esaie ix.	Esaie. vii. God spake onsagain to Achas. &c.	Good Frydaye.	Gene. xxii.	Esaie liii.
ii Lesson	Luk ii, *vnto* and vnto men good wyll.	Tit. iii. The kyndnes and loue. &c.	Easter Euē.	Zach. ix.	Exod. xiii.
S. Steuē.			Mōday in easter weke.		
i Lesson	Pro. xxviii.	Eccle. iiii.	i Lesson	Exod. xvi.	xvii.
ii Lesson	Act vi.& vii. Stephen ful of faith and powre, &c., *vnto* And when .xl. yeres, &c.	Act.vii. And when .xl. yeres were expired, there appered unto Mouses.&c. *vnto* Steph full of the holy. &c.	ii Lesson	Matthew xxviii.	Act. iii.
			Tuesday in Easter.[2]		
			i Lesson	Exod. xx.	Exo. xxxii.
			ii Lesson	Luke xxiiii. *vnto* And beholde.ii.of them.	i Corinth.xv.
Sainct Jhon.			S. Marke.	Eccle. iiii.	Eccle. v.
i Lesson	Eccle. v.	Eccle. vi.			
ii Lesson	Apoc. i.	Apoc. xxii.	Philippe & Jacob.	vii.	ix.
Innocēts.	Jere. xxxi. *vnto* More-ouerIhearde Ephraim.	Wysdō i.	Ascension daye.	Deut. x.	Deut. xi.
			Mondaye in Whytson weake.	xxx.	xxxi.
Circumcision daye.			Tuesday in Whytson weake.	xxxii.	xxxiiii.
i Lesson	Gen. xvii.	Deut. x. and nowe Israel. &c.	Sainct Barnabe.		
			i Lesson	Eccle. x.	Eccle. xii.
ii Lesson	Rom. ii.	Colloss ii.	ii Lesson	Act. xiiii.	Ac. xv. *vnto,* After certein dayes
Epiphanie Daye.					
i Lesson	Esa. lx.	Esa. xlix.	S. John Baptiste.		
ii Lesson	Luk iii.,and it fortuned. &c.	John ii.after this he went to Capernaū.	i Lesson	Mala. iii.	Mala. iiii.
			ii Lesson	Math. iii.	Mathew xiiii. *vnto,* When Jesus heard.
Conuersiō of S. Paule.			Sainct Peter.		
i Lesson	Wisedō.v.	Wisdō. vi.[1]	i Lesson	Eccle. xv.	Eccle. xix.
ii Lesson	Act. xxii., *vnto* they hearde him.	Act. ii.	ii Lesson	Actes iii.	Actes iiii.
			Sainct James.	Eccl. xxi.	xxiii.
Purification of ye virgin Mary.	Wisdō. ix.	Wysed. xii.	Sainct Bartholomewe.	xxv.	xxix.
Sainct Mathie.	Wisdō. xix.	Eccle. i.	Sainct Mathew.	xxxv.	xxxviii.

[1 Misprint for xxvi.]   [2 Week omitted.]

Lessons proper for holy days.

	Mattens.	Euensong.			Mattens.	Euensong.
Sainct Michael.	Eccl.xxxix.	Eccl. xliiii.	All Saintes.			
Sainct Luke.	li.	Job i.		i Lesson	Wised. iii. *vnto* blessed is rather the baren.	Wisdõ. v. *vnto* hys ielousy also.
Sainct Simon & Jude.						
i Lesson	xxiiii.[1]	xlii.		ii Lesson	He. xi., xii., Sainctes by fayth *vnto* If you endure chastening.	Apo. xix. *vnto* And I sawe an angell stande.
ii Lesson	xxv.					

Proper Psalmes on certain dayes.

	Mattens.	Euensong.		Mattins.	Evensong.
Christmas day.	Psal. xix. xlv. lxxxv.	Psal. lxxxix. cx. cxxxii.	Ascension daye.	Psal. viii. xv. xxi.	Psal. xxiiii. lxviii. cviii.
Easter daie.	ii. lvli. cxi.	cxiii. cxiiii. cxviii.	Witsondaye.	xlviii. lxvii.	ciiii. cxlv.

[1 Both chapters should have been assigned for the first lesson. See New Calendar.]

❡ A BRIEFE DECLARATION

WHEN EUERY TERME BEGINNETH AND ENDETH.

BE it knowen that Easter Terme beginneth alwaies, ye .xviii. daie after Easter, rekening Easter daie for one. And endeth the Mondaie next after the Ascension daie.

Trinitie Terme beginneth alwaie the Fridaie next after Trinitie Sondaie, and endeth the .xxviii. daie of June.

Michaelmas Terme beginneth the nynth or tenth daie of October, and endeth the .xxviii. or .xxix. daie of Nouember.

Hillarie Terme beginneth the .xxiii. or .xxiiii. daie of Januarie, and endeth the .xii. or .xiii. daie of Februarie.

In Easter Terme on the Ascension daie. In Trinitie Terme, on the Natiuitie of Sainct John Baptist. In Michaelmas Terme, on the feast of All Sainctes. In Hillarie Terme on the feast of the Purification of our Lady. The Quenes Judges of Westminster dooe not vse to sit in Judgemente nor vpon any Sondaies.

¶ AN ALMANACK FOR .XXX. YERES.

¶ The yeres of our Lorde.	¶ The Golden Nomber.	The Epacta.	¶ The Sicle of the Sunne.	Domini-call letter.	Easter daie.
M.D.LIX	ii	xxii	xxviiii	A.	xxvi Marche.
M.D.LX	iii	iii	i	G. F.	xiiii Aprill.
M.D.LXI	iiii	xiv	ii	E.	vi Aprill.
M.D.LXII	v	xxv	iii	D.	xxix Marche.
M.D.LXIII	vi	vi	iiii	C.	xi Aprill.
M.D.LXIIII	vii	xvii	v	B. A.	ii Aprill.
M.D.LXV	viii	xxviii	vi	G.	xxii Aprill.
M.D.LXVI	ix	ix	vii	F.	xiiii Aprill.
M.D.LXVII	x	xx	viii	E.	xxx March.
M.D.LXVIII	xi	i	ix	D. C.	xviii Aprill.
M.D.LXIX	xii	xii	x	B.	x April.
M.D.LXX	xiii	xxiii	xi	A.	xxvi Marche.
M.D.LXXI	xiiii	iv	xii	G.	xv Aprill.
M.D.LXXII	xv	xv	xiii	F. E.	vi Aprill.
M.D.LXXIII	xvi	xxvi	xiiii	D.	xxii Marche.
M.D.LXXIIII	xvii	vii	xv	C.	xi Aprill.
M.D.LXXV	xviii	xviii	xvi	B.	iii Aprill.
M.D.LXXVI	xix	o	xvii	A. G.	xxii Aprill.
M.D.LXXVII	i	xi	xviii	F.	vii Aprill.
M.D.LXXVIII	ii	xxii	xix	E.	xxx Marche.
M.D.LXXIX	iii	iii	xx	D.	xxix Aprill.
M.D.LXXX	iiii	xiv	xxi	C. B.	iii Aprill.
M.D.LXXXI	v	xxv	xxii	A.	xxvi Marche.
M.D.LXXXII	vi	vi	xxiii	G.	xv Aprill.
M.D.LXXXIII	vii	xvii	xxiiii	F.	xxxi Marche.
M.D.LXXXIIII	viii	xxviii	xxv	E. D.	xix Aprill.
M.D.LXXXV	ix	ix	xxvi	C.	xi Aprill.
M.D.LXXXVI	x	xx	xxvii	B.	iii Aprill.
M.D.LXXXVII	xi	i	xxviii	A.	xvi Aprill.
M.D.LXXXVIII	xii	xii	I	G. F.	vii April.

❧ JANUARY HATH .XXXI. DAIES.

			Psalmes.	MORNYNG PRAIER.		EUENYNG PRAIER.	
				i Lesson.	*ii Lesson.*	*i Lesson.*	*ii Lesson.*
iii	A	Kalend. *Circum-*	i	Gen. xvii	Roma ii	Deut. x	Collos ii
	b	iiii No. [*cision*	ii	Genesis i	Math. i	Gene ii	Roman i
xi	c	iii No.	iii	iii	ii	iiii	ii
	d	Prid. No.	iiii	v	iii	vi	iii
xix	e	Nonas.	v	vii	iiii	viii	iiii
viii	f	viii Id.*Epiphanie.*	vi	Esay lx	Luke iii	Esa. xlix	Jhon ii
	g	vii Id.	vii	Genesi ix	Math. v	Gene xi	Roma v
xvi	A	vi Id.	viii	xii	vi	xiii	vi
v	b	v Id.	ix	xiiii	vii	xv	vii
	c	iiii Id.	x	xvi	viii	xvii	viii
xiii	d	iii Id.Sol in Aqua.	xi	xviii	ix	xix	ix
ii	e	Prid. Id.	xii	xx	x	xxi	x
	f	Idus.	xiii	xxii	xi	xxiii	xi
x	g	xix kl. Februarii.	xiiii	xxiiii	xii	xxv	xii
	A	xviii kl.	xv	xxvi	xiii	xxvii	xiii
xvii	b	xvii kl. Terme be-	xvi	xxviii	xiiii	xxix	xiiii
vii	c	xvi kl. [gin.	xvii	xxx	xv	xxxi	xv
	d	xv kl.	xviii	xxxii	xvi	xxxiii	xvi
xv	e	xiiii kl.	xix	xxxiiii	xvii	xxxv	1 Corin. i
iiii	f	xiii kl.	xx	xxxvi	xviii	xxxvii	ii
	g	xii kl.	xxi	xxxix	xix	xxxix	iii
xii	A	xi kl.	xxii	xl	xx	xli	iiii
i	b	x kl.	xxiii	xlii	xxi	xliii	v
	c	ix kl.	xxiiii	xliiii	xxii	xlv	vi
ix	d	viii kl. *Con.Paule.*	xxv	xlvi	Actes xxii	xlvii	Acte xxvi
	e	vii kl.	xxvi	xlviii	Mat. xxiii	xlix	1 Cor. vii
xvii	f	vi kl.	xxvii	l	xxiiii	Exodi i	viii
vi	g	v kl.	xxviii	Exodi ii	xxv	iii	ix
	A	iiii kl.	xxix	iiii	xxvi	v	x
xiiii	b	iii kl.	xxx	vi	xxvii	vii	xi
iii	c	Prid kl.	i	viii	xxviii	ix	xii

¶ FEBRUARY HATH .XXVIII. DAIES.

			Psalmes.	MORNYNG PRAIER.		EUENYNG PRAIER.	
				i Lesson.	*ii Lessō.*	*i Lesson.*	*ii Lesson.*
	d	Kalend.	ii	Exod. x	Marke i	Exodi. xi	i Cor. xiii
xi	e	iiii *Puri. Mary.*	iii	xii	ii	xiii	xiiii
xix	f	iii No.	iiii	xiiii	iii	xv	xv
viii	g	Prid. No.	v	xvi	iiii	xvii	xvi
	A	Nonas.	vi	xviii	v	xix	ii Cori. i
xvi	b	viii Id.	vii	xx	vi	xxi	ii
v	c	vii Id.	viii	xxii	vii	xxiii	iii
	d	vi Id.	ix	xxiiii	viii	xxxii	iiii
xiii	e	v Id.	x	xxxiii	ix	xxxiiii	v
ii	f	iiii Id. Sol. in	xi	xxxv	x	xl	vi
	g	iii Id. [Pisces	xii	Leu. xviii	xi	Leui. xix	vii
x	A	Prid. Id. Terme	xiii	xx	xii	Nume. x	viii
	b	Idus. [end.	xiiii	Nume. xi	xiii	xii	ix
xviii	c	xvi kl. Marche.	xv	xiii	xiiii	xiiii	x
vii	d	xv kl.	xvi	xv	xv	xvi	xi
	e	xiiii kl.	xvii	xvii	xvi	xviii	xii
xv	f	xiii kl.	xviii	xix	Luke, di. i	xx	xiii
iiii	g	xii kl.	xix	xxi	di. i	xxii	Galath. i
	A	xi kl.	xx	xxiii	ii	xxiiii	ii
xii	b	x kl.	xxi	xxv	iii	xxvi	iii
	c	ix kl.	xxii	xxvii	iiii	xxviii	iiii
	d	viii kl.	xxiii	xxix	v	xxx	v
ix	e	vii kl.	xxiiii	xxxi	vi	xxxii	vi
	f	vi kl. *S. Mathias.*	xxv	xxxiii	vii	xxxiiii	Ephesi. i
xvii	g	v kl.	xxvi	xxxv	viii	xxxvi	ii
vi	A	iiii kl.	xxvii	Deut. i	ix	Deut. ii	iii
	b	iii kl.	xxviii	iii	x	iiii	iiii
xiiii	c	Prid. kl.	xxix	v	xi	vi	v

MARCHE hath .XXXI. DAIES.

			Psalmes.	MORNYNG PRAIER.		EUENYNG PRAIER.	
				i Lesson.	*ii Lesson.*	*i Lesson.*	*ii Lesson.*
iii	d	Kalend.	xxx	Deut. vii	Luke xii	Deut. viii	Ephe. vi
	e	vi No.	i	ix	xiii	x	Philip. i
xi	f	v No.	ii	xi	xiiii	xii	ii
	g	iiii No.	iii	xiii	xv	xiiii	iii
xix	A	iii No.	iiii	xv	xvi	xvi	iiii
viii	b	Prid. No. Ho. 5.	v	xvii	xvii	xviii	Colloss. i
	c	Nonas. [Mi. 42.	vi	xviii	xviii	xx	ii
xvi	d	viii Id.	vii	xxi	xix	xxii	iii
v	e	vii Id.	viii	xxiii	xx	xxiiii	iiii
	f	vi Id.	ix	xxv	xxi	xxvi	i Thess. i
xiii	g	v Id. [tium.	x	xxvii	xxii	xxviii	ii
ii	A	iiii Id. Equinoc-	xi	xxix	xxiii	xxx	iii
	b	iii Id. Sol in Ari-	xii	xxxi	xxiiii	xxxii	iiii
x	c	Prid. Id. [ete.	xiii	xxxiii	Jhon i	xxxiiii	v
	d	Idus.	xiiii	Josue i	ii	Josue ii	ii Thes. i
xviii	e	xvii kl.	xv	iii	iii	iii	ii
vii	f	xvi kl. Aprilis.	xvi	iiii	iiii	iiii	iii
	g	xv kl.	xvii	v	v	v	i Timo. i
xv	A	xiiii kl.	xviii	vi	vi	vi	ii iii
iiii	b	xiii kl.	xix	vii	vii	vii	iiii
	c	xii kl.	xx	viii	viii	viii	v
xii	d	xi kl.	xxi	ix	ix	ix	vi
i	e	x kl.	xxii	x	x	xi	ii Tim. i
	f	ix kl.	xxiii	xii	xi	xx	ii
ix	g	viii kl.	xxiiii	xxi	xii	xxii	iii
	A	vii kl. *Annunci-*	xxv	xxiii	xiii	xxiiii	iiii
xvii	b	vi kl. [*atiō.*	xxvi	Judic. i	xiiii	Judic. ii	Titus i
vi	c	v kl.	xxvii	iii	xv	iiii	ii iii
	d	iiii kl.	xxviii	v	xvi	vi	Philem i
xiiii	e	iii kl.	xxix	vii	xvii	viii	Hebres i
iii	f	Prid. kl.	xxx	ix	xviii	x	ii

¶ APRILL HATH .XXX. DAIES.

			Psalmes	MORNYNG PRAIER.		EVENYNG PRAIER.	
				i Lesson.	*ii Lesso.*	*i Lesson.*	*ii Lesson.*
	g	Kalend.	i	Judic. xi	Jhon xix	Judi. xii	Hebre.iii
xi	A	iiii No.	ii	xiii	xx	xiiii	iiii
	b	iii No.	iii	xv	xxi	xvi	v
xix	c	Prid. No.	iiii	xvii	Actes i	xviii	vi
viii	d	Nonas.	v	xix	ii	xx	vii
xvi	e	viii Id.	vi	xxi	iii	Ruth i	viii
v	f	vii Id.	vii	Ruth ii	iiii	iii	ix
	g	vi Id.	viii	iiii	v	i Regū. i	x
xiii	A	v Id.	ix	i Regū. ii	vi	iii	xi
ii	b	iiii Id.	x	iiii	vii	v	xii
	c	iii Id.	xi	vi	viii	vii	xiii
x	d	Prid. Id. Sol. in	xii	viii	ix	ix	Jacob i
	e	Idus. [Tauro.	xiii	x	x	xi	ii
xviii	f	xviii kl. Maii.	xiiii	xii	xi	xiii	iii
vii	g	xvii kl.	xv	xiiii	xii	xv	iiii
	A	xvi kl.	xvi	xvi	xiii	xvii	v
xv	b	xv kl.	xvii	xviii	xiiii	xix	i Peter i
iiii	c	xiiii kl.	xviii	xx	xv	xxi	ii
	d	xiii kl.	xix	xxii	xvi	xxiii	iii
xii	e	xii kl.	xx	xxiiii	xvii	xxv	iiii
i	f	xi kl.	xxi	xxvi	xviii	xxvii	v
	g	x kl.	xxii	xxviii	xix	xxix	ii Peter i
ix	A	ix kl. *S. George.*	xxiii	xxx	xx	xxxi	ii
	b	viii kl.	xxiiii	ii Regū. i	xxi	ii Reg. ii	iii
xvii	c	viikl. *Marke Euā.*	xxv	iii	xxii	iiii	i Jhon i
vi	d	vi kl.	xxvi	v	xxiii	vi	ii
	e	v kl.	xxvii	vii	xxiiii	viii	iii
xiiii	f	iiii kl.	xxviii	ix	xxv	x	iiii
iii	g	iii kl.	xxix	xi	xxvi	xii	v
	A	Prid. kl.	xxx	xiii	xxvii	xiiii	ii iii Jhō

❡ MAIE HATH .XXXI. DAIES.

			Psalmes.	MORNYNG PRAIER.		EUENYNG PRAIER.	
				i Lesson.	*ii Lesson.*	*i Lesson.*	*ii Lesson.*
xi	b	Kalend. *Phil. et*	i	ii Reg. xv	Acte viii	ii Re. xvi	Judas. i
	c	vi No. *[Ja.]*	ii	xvii	xxviii	xviii	Roma. i
xix	d	v No.	iii	xix	Matth. i	xx	ii
viii	e	iiii No.	iiii	xxi	ii	xxii	iii
	f	iii No.	v	xxiii	iii	xxiiii	iiii
xvi	g	Prid. No.	vi	iii Regū. i	iiii	iii Reg. i	v
v	A	Nonas.	vii	ii	v	ii	vi
	b	viii Id.	viii	iii	vi	iiii	vii
xiii	c	vii Id.	ix	v	vii	ix	viii
ii	d	vi Id.	x	ix	viii	x	ix
	e	v. Id. Sol. in Gemi.	xi	xi	ix	xii	x
x	f	iiii Id.	xii	xiii	x	xiiii	xi
	g	iii Id.	xiii	xv	xi	xvi	xii
xviii	A	Prid. Id.	xiiii	xvii	xii	xviii	xiii
vii	b	Id.	xv	xix	xiii	xx	xiiii
	c	xvii kl. Junii.	xvi	xxi	xiiii	xxii	xv
xv	d	xvi kl.	xvii	iiii Reg. i	xv	iiii Reg. ii	xvi
iiii	e	xv kl.	xviii	iii	xvi	iiii	i Corin. i
	f	xiiii kl.	xix	v	xvii	vi	ii
xii	g	xiii kl.	xx	vii	xviii	viii	iii
i	A	xii kl.	xxi	ix	xix	x	iiii
	b	xi kl.	xxii	xi	xx	xii	v
ix	c	x kl.	xxiii	xiii	xxi	xiiii	vi
	d	ix kl.	xxiiii	xv	xxii	xvi	vii
xvii	e	viii kl.	xxv	xvii	xxiii	xviii	viii
vi	f	vii kl.	xxvi	xix	xxiiii	xx	ix
	g	vi kl.	xxvii	xxi	xxv	xxii	x
xiiii	A	v kl.	xxviii	xxiii	xxvi	xxiiii	xi
iii	b	iiii kl.	xxix	xxv	xxvii	xxv	xii
	c	iii kl.	xxx	I Esdra i	xxviii	i Esd. ii	xiii
xi	d	Prid. kl.	xxx	iii	Marke i	iiii	xiiii

B

❡ JUNE HATH .XXX. DAIES.

			Psalmes.	MORNYNG PRAIER.		EUENYNG PRAIER.	
				i Lesson.	*ii Lesso.*	*i Lesson.*	*ii Lesson.*
	e	Kalend.	i	i Esdra iiii	Marke ii	i Esd. v	i Cor. xv
xix	f	iiii No.	ii	vi	iii	vi	xvi
viii	g	iii No.	iii	vii	iiii	vii	ii Corin. i
xvi	A	Prid.	iiii	viii	v	viii	ii
v	b	Nonas.	v	ix	vi	x	iii
	c	viii Id.	vi	ii Esdra i	vii	iii	iiii
xiii	d	vii Id.	vii	iiii	viii	v	v
ii	e	vi Id.	viii	vi	ix	viii	vi
	f	v Id.	ix	ix	x	xiii	vii
x	g	iiii Id.	x	Hester i	xi	Hester ii	viii
	A	iii Id. *Barnabe Ap.*	xi	iii	Acte xiiii	iiii	Actes xv
xviij	b	Prid. Id.	xii	v	Mark xii	vi	ii Cor. ix
vii	c	Idus. Julii. Sol. in	xiii	vii	xiii	viii	x
	d	xviii kl. [Can.	xiiii	ix	xiiii	Job i	xi
xv	e	xvii kl.	xv	Job ii	xv	iii	xii
iiii	f	xvi kl.	xvi	iiii	xvi	v	xiii
	g	xv kl. Terme	xvii	vi	Luke i	vii	Galath. i
xii	A	xiiii kl. [begin.	xviii	viii	ii	ix	ii
i	b	xiii kl.	xix	x	iii	xi	iii
	c	xii kl.	xx	xii	iiii	xiii	iiii
ix	d	xi kl.	xxi	xiiii	v	xv	v
	e	x kl.	xxii	xvi	vi	xvii, xviii	vi
xvii	f	ix kl.	xxiii	xix	vii	xx	Ephesi. i
vi	g	viii kl. *Jhon*	xxiiii	Mala. iii	Math. iii	Mal. iiii	Math. xiiii
	A	vii kl. [*Baptist.*	xxv	Job xxi	Luke viii	Job xxii	Ephesi. ii
xiii	b	vi kl.	xxvi	xxiii	ix	xxiiii, xxv	iii
iii	c	v kl.	xxvii	xxvi, xxvii	x	xxviii	iiii
	d	iiii kl.	xxviii	xxix	xi	xxx	v
xi	e	iii kl. *S. Peter Ap.*	xxix	xxxi	Actes iii	xxxii	Actes iiii
	f	Prid. kl.	xxx	xxxiii	Luke xii	xxxiiii	Ephes. vi

¶ JULY HATH .XXXI. DAIES.

			Psalmes.	MORNYNG PRAIER.		EUENYNG PRAIER.	
				i Lesson.	ii Lesson.	i Lesson.	ii Lesson.
xix	g	Kalend.	i	Job xxxv	Luke xiii	Iob xxxvi	Philip. i
viii	A	vi No.	ii	xxxvii	xiiii	xxxviii	ii
	b	v No.	iii	xxxix	xv	xl	iii
xvi	c	iiii No.	iiii	xli	xvi	xlii	iiii
v	d	iii No. [ende.	v	Prouer i	xvii	Prou. ii	Coloss. i
	e	Prid. No. Terme	vi	iii	xviii	iiii	ii
xiii	f	Nonæ. Dog daies	vii	v	xix	vi	iii
ii	g	viii Id.	viii	vii	xx	viii	iiii
	A	vii Id.	ix	ix	xxi	x	i Thessa. i
x	b	vi Id.	x	xi	xxii	xii	ii
	c	v. Id.	xi	xiii	xxiii	xiiii	iii
xviii	d	iiii Id.	xii	xv	xxiiii	xvi	iiii
vii	e	iii Id.	xiii	xvii	Jhon i	xviii	v
	f	Prid. Id. Sol. in	xiiii	xix	ii	xx	ii Thess. i
xv	g	Idus. [Leo.	xv	xxi	iii	xxii	ii
iiii	A	xvii kl. Augusti.	xvi	xxiii	iiii	xxiiii	iii
	b	xvi kl.	xvii	xxv	v	xxvi	i Timo. i
xii	c	xv kl.	xviii	xxvii	vi	xxviii	ii, iii
i	d	xiiii kl.	xix	xxix	vii	xxx	iiii
	e	xiii kl.	xx	xxxi	viii	Eccles. i	v
ix	f	xii kl.	xxi	Eccles ii	ix	iii	vi
	g	xi kl.	xxii	iiii	x	v	ii Tim. i
xvii	A	x kl.	xxiii	vi	xi	vii	ii
vi	b	ix kl.	xxiiii	viii	xii	ix	iii
	c	viii kl. JamesApo.	xxv	x	xiii	xi	iiii
xiiii	d	vii kl.	xxvi	xii	xiiii	Jerem. i	Titus i
iii	e	vi kl.	xxvii	Jere. ii	xv	iii	ii, iii
	f	v kl.	xxviii	iiii	xvi	v	Philem. i
xi	g	iiii kl.	xxix	vi	xvii	vii	Hebres i
	A	iii kl.	xxx	viii	xviii	ix	ii
xix	b	Prid. kl.	xxx	x	xix	xi	iii

B 2

¶ AUGUST HATH .XXXI. DAIES.

			Psalmes.	MORNYNG PRAIER.		EUENYNG PRAIER.	
				i Lesson.	_ii Lesso._	_i Lesson._	_ii Lesson._
viii	c	Kalend Lammas.	i	Jere. xii	Jhon xx	Jer. xiii	Hebr. iiii
xvi	d	iiii No.	ii	xiiii	xxi	xv	v
v	e	iii No.	iii	xvi	Actes i	xvii	vi
	f	Prid. No.	iiii	xviii	ii	xix	vii
viii	g	Nonas.	v	xx	iii	xxi	viii
ii	A	viii Id.	vi	xxii	iiii	xxiii	ix
	b	vii Id.	vii	xxiiii	v	xxv	x
x	c	vi Id.	viii	xxvi	vi	xxvii	xi
	d	v Id.	ix	xxviii	vii	xxix	xii
xviii	e	iiii Id.　S. Laur-	x	xxx	viii	xxxi	xiii
vii	f	iii id.　　[ence.	xi	xxxii	ix	xxxiii	Jacobi. i
	g	Prid. Id.	xii	xxxiiii	x	xxxv	ii
xv	A	Idus.　　[bris.	xiii	xxxvi	xi	xxxvii	iii
iiii	b	xix kl.　Septem-	xiiii	xxxviii	xii	xxxix	iiii
	c	xviii kl.　Sol in	xv	xl	xiii	xli	v
xii	d	xvii kl.　[Virgo.	xvi	xlii	xiiii	xliii	i Peter i
i	e	xvi kl.	xvii	xliiii	xv	xlv, xlvi	ii
	f	xv kl.	xviii	xlvii	xvi	xlviii	iii
ix	g	xiiii kl.	xix	xlix	xvii	l	iiii
	A	xiii kl.	xx	li	xviii	lii	v
xvii	b	xii kl.	xxi	Lameēt. i	xix	Lamē. ii	ii Pet. i
vi	c	xi kl.	xxii	iii	xx	iiii	ii
	d	x kl.	xxiii	v	xxi	Ezech. ii	iii
xiiii	e	ix kl. _Bartho Apo._	xxiiii	Ezech. iii	xxii	vi	i Jhon i
iii	f	viii kl.	xxv	vii	xxiii	xiii	ii
	g	vii kl.	xxvi	xiiii	xxiiii	xviii	iii
xi	A	vi kl.	xxvii	xxxiii	xxv	xxxiiii	iiii
	b	v kl.	xxviii	Daniel i	xxvi	Dani. ii	v
xix	c	iiii kl.	xxix	iii	xxvii	iiii	ii, iii Jhō.
viii	d	iii kl.	xxx	v	xxviii	vi	Jude i
	e	Prid. kl.	xxx	vii	Matth. i	viii	Roma

❡ SEPTEMBER HATH .XXX. DAIES.

			Psalmes.	MORNYNG PRAIER.		EUENYNG PRAIER.	
				i Lesson.	*ii Lesson.*	*i Lesson.*	*ii Lesson.*
xvi	f	Kalend.	i	Daniel ix	Math. ii	Danie. x	Roma. ii
v	g	iiii No.	ii	xi	iii	xii	iii
	A	iii No.	iii	xiii	iiii	xiiii	iiii
xiii	b	Prid. No.	iiii	Ozee i	v	Oze ii, iii	v
ii	c	Nonas. Dog daies	v	iiii	vi	v, vi	vi
	d	viii Id. [end.	vi	vii	vii	viii	vii
x	e	vii Id.	vii	ix	viii	x	viii
	f	vi Id.	viii	xi	ix	xii	ix
xviii	g	v Id.	ix	xiii	x	xiiii	x
vii	A	iiii Id.	x	Joel i	xi	Joel ii	xi
	b	iii Id.	xi	iii	xii	Amos i	xii
xv	c	Prid. Id.	xii	Amos ii	xiii	iii	xiii
iiii	d	Idus.	xiii	iiii	xiiii	v	xiiii
	e	xviii kl. Octobris.	xiiii	vi	xv	vii	xv
xii	f	xvii kl. Sol in	xv	viii	xvi	ix	xvi
i	g	xvi kl. [Libra.	xvi	Abdias i	xvii	Jonas i	i Corin. i
	A	xv kl.	xvii	Jonas ii, iii	xviii	iiii	ii
ix	b	xiiii kl.	xviii	Miche i	xix	Mich ii	iii
	c	xiii kl.	xix	iii	xx	iiii	iiii
xvi	d	xii kl.	xx	v	xxi	vi	v
vi	e	xi kl. *S.Matthew.*	xxi	vii	xxii	Naum i	vi
	f	x kl.	xxii	Naum ii	xxiii	iii	vii
xiii	g	ix kl.	xxiii	Abacuc i	xxiiii	Abacu. ii	viii
iii	A	viii kl.	xxiiii	iii	xxv	Soph. i	ix
	b	vii kl.	xxv	Sopho ii	xxvi	iii	x
xi	c	vi kl.	xxvi	Agge. i	xxvii	Agge. ii	xi
	d	v kl.	xxvii	Zachari. i	xxviii	Zach. ii, iii	xii
xix	e	iiii kl.	xxviii	iiii, v	Marke i	vi	xiii
viii	f	iii kl. *S.Michaell.*	xxix	vii	ii	viii	xiiii
	g	Prid. kl.	xxx	ix	iii	x	xv

❡ OCTOBER HATH .XXXI. DAIES.

			Psalmes.	MORNYNG PRAIER.		EUENYNG PRAIER.	
				i Lesson.	_ii Lesso._	_i Lesson._	_ii Lesson._
xvi	A	Kalend.	i	Zachari xi	Mark iiii	Zacha xii	i Cor. xvi
v	b	vi No.	ii	xiii	v	xiiii	ii Cor. i
xiii	c	v No.	iii	Malach i	vi	Mala ii	ii
ii	d	iiii No.	iiii	iii	vii	iiii	iii
	e	iii No.	v	Toby i	viii	Toby ii	iiii
x	f	Prid. No.	vi	iii	ix	iiii	v
	g	Nonas.	vii	v	x	vi	vi
xviii	A	viii Id.	viii	vii	xi	viii	vii
vii	b	vii Id. Terme be-	ix	ix	xii	x	viii
	c	vi Id. [gin.	x	xi	xiii	xii	ix
xv	d	v Id.	xi	xiii	xiiii	xiiii	x
iiii	e	iiii Id.	xii	Judith i	xv	Judit ii	xi
	f	iii Id.	xiii	iii	xvi	iiii	xii
xii	g	Prid. Id. Sol. in	xiiii	v	Luke di. i	vi	xiii
i	A	Idus. [Scorpi.	xv	vii	di. i	viii	Gala. i
	b	xvii kl. Novem-	xvi	ix	ii	x	ii
ix	c	xvi kl. [bris.	xvii	xi	iii	xii	iii
	d	xv kl. _Luke Euan._	xviii	xiii	iiii	xiiii	iiii
xvii	e	xiiii kl.	xix	xv	v	xvi	v
vii	f	xiii kl.	xx	Sapien i	vi	Sapi ii	vi
	g	xii kl.	xxi	iii	vii	iiii	Ephesi i
xiiii	A	xi kl.	xxii	v	viii	vi	ii
iii	b	x kl.	xxiii	vii	ix	viii	iii
	c	ix kl.	xxiiii	ix	x	x	iiii
xi	d	viii kl.	xxv	xi	xi	xii	v
	e	vii kl.	xxvi	xiii	xii	xiiii	vi
xix	f	vi kl.	xxvii	xv	xiii	xvi	Philip. i
viii	g	v kl. _Simon and_	xxviii	xvii	xiiii	xviii	ii
	A	iiii kl. [_Ju._	xxix	xix	xv	Eccls. i	iii
xvi	b	iii kl.	xxx	Eccle. ii	xvi	iii	iiii
v	c	Prid. kl.	xxx	iiii	xvii	v	Colloss.

❡ NOUEMBER HATH .XXX. DAIES.

					Psalmes.	MORNYNG PRAIER.		EUENYNG PRAIER.	
						i Lesson.	*ii Lesson.*	*i Lesson.*	*ii Lesson.*
xiiii	d	Kalend.	*All*		i	Sapie. iii	Heb.xi, xii	Sapi. v	Apoc. xix
ii	e	¹ No.	[*Sainctes.*		ii	Eccls. vi	Luk. xviii	Eccl. vii	Collo. ii
	f	¹ No.			iii	viii	xix	ix	iii
	g	Prid. No.			iiii	x	xx	xi	iiii
x	A	Nonas.			v	xii	xxi	xiii	i Thes. i
	b	viii Id.			vi	xiiii	xxii	xv	ii
xviii	c	vii Id.			vii	xvi	xxiii	xvii	iii
vii	d	vi Id.			viii	xviii	xxiiii	xix	iiii
	e	v Id.			ix	xx	Jhon i	xxi	v
xv	f	iiii Id.			x	xxii	ii	xxiii	ii Thes. i
iiii	g	iii Id.			xi	xxiiii	iii	xxv	ii
	A	Prid. Id.			xii	xxvi	iiii	xxvii	iii
xii	b	Idus. Sol. in Sag.			xiii	xxviii	v	xxix	i Timo. i
i	c	xviii kl.	Decem-		xiiii	xxx	vi	xxxi	ii, iii
	d	xvii kl.	[ber.		xv	xxxii	vii	xxxiii	iiii
ix	e	xvi kl.			xvi	xxxiiii	viii	xxxv	v
	f	xv kl.			xvii	xxxvi	ix	xxxvii	vi
xvii	g	xiiii kl.			xviii	xxxviii	x	xxxix	ii Timo. i
vi	A	xiii kl.			xix	xl	xi	xli	ii
	b	xii kl.			xx	xlii	xii	xliii	iii
xiiii	c	xi kl.			xxi	xliiii	xiii	xlv	iiii
iii	d	x kl.			xxii	xlvi	xiiii	xlvii	Titus i
	e	ix kl. *S. Clement.*			xxiii	xlviii	xv	xlix	ii, iii
	f	viii kl.			xxiiii	l	xvi	li	Phile. i
xix	g	vii kl.			xxv	Baruch i	xvii	Baru. ii	Hebre. i
	A	vi kl.			xxvi	iii	xviii	iiii	ii
viii	b	v kl.	[ende.		xxvii	v	xix	vi	iii
	c	iiii kl.	Terme		xxviii	Esay i	xx	Esay ii	iiii
xvi	d	iii kl.	[*Apo.*		xxix	iii	xxi	iiii	v
v	e	Prid. kl. *Andrew*			xxx	v	Actes i	vi	vi

[¹ iiii. iii. omitted.]

❡ DECEMBER hath .XXXI. DAIES.

			Psalmes.	MORNYNG PRAIER.		EUENYNG PRAIER.	
				i Lesson.	*ii Lesso.*	*i Lesson.*	*ii Lesson.*
	f	Kalend.	i	Esay vii	Actes ii	Esa viii	Hebr. vii
xiii	g	¹ No.	ii	ix	iii	x	viii
ii	A	iii No.	iii	xi	iiii	xii	ix
x	b	Prid. No.	iiii	xiii	v	xiiii	x
	c	Nonas.	v	xv	vi	xvi	xi
xviii	d	viii Id.	vi	xvii	di. vii	xviii	xii
vii	e	vii Id.	vii	xix	di. vii	xx, xxi	xiii
	f	vi Id.	viii	xxii	viii	xxiii	James i
xv	g	v Id.	ix	xxiiii	ix	xxv	ii
iiii	A	iiii Id.	x	xxvi	x	xxvii	iii
	b	iii Id.	xi	xxviii	xi	xxix	iiii
xii	c	Prid. Id. Sol in	xii	xxx	xii	xxxi	v
i	d	Idus. [Capri.	xiii	xxxii	xiii	xxxiii	i Peter i
	e	xix kl. Januarii.	xiiii	xxxiiii	xiiii	xxxv	ii
ix	f	xviii. kl.	xv	xxxvi	xv	xxxvii	iii
	g	xvii kl.	xvi	xxxviii	xvi	xxxix	iiii
xvii	A	xvi kl.	xvii	xl	xvii	xli	v
vi	b	xv kl.	xviii	xlii	xviii	xliii	ii Peter i
	c	xiiii xl.	xix	xliiii	xix	xlv	ii
xiiii	d	xiii kl.	xx	xvi	xx	xlvii	iii
	e	xii kl. *Thomas Ap.*	xxi	xlviii	xxi	xlix	i Jhon i
	f	xi kl.	xxii	l	xxii	li	ii
xi	g	x kl.	xxiii	lii	xxiii	liii	iii
	A	ix kl.	xxiiii	liiii	xxiiii	lv	iiii
xix	b	viii kl. *Christmas.*	xxv	Esay ix	Luke xxii	Esay vii	Titus iii
viii	c	vii kl. *S. Stephen.*	xxvi	lvi	Act vi, vii	lvii	Actes vii
	d	vi kl. *S. Jhon Euā*	xxvii	lviii	Apocali. i	lix	Apoc. xxii
xvi	e	v kl. *Innocentes.*	xxviii	Jere xxxi	Acte xxv	lx	i Jhon 5
v	f	iiii kl.	xxix	Esaie lxi	xxvi	lxii	ii Jhon i
	g	iii kl.	xxx	lxiii	xxvii	lxiiii	iii Jhō i
xiii	A	Prid. kl.	xxx	lxv	xxviii	lxvi.	Jude i

[¹ iiii. omitted.]

THE ORDRE WHERE MORNING AND EUENING PRAYER

SHALBE VSED AND SAYDE.

The Morning and Euening praier shalbe vsed in the accustomed place of the churche, chapel, or Chauncell, except it shalbe otherwise determined by the ordinary of the place: and the chauncels shall remain, as they haue done in tymes past.

And here is to be noted, that the Minister at the time of the cōmunion, and at all other tymes in hys ministracion, shall vse suche ornamentes in the church, as wer in vse by aucthoritie of parliamēt in the second yere of the reygne of king Edward the .VI. according to the acte of parliament set in the beginning of thys booke.

AN ORDRE FOR MORNING

PRAYER DAYLY THROUGHOUT THE YERE.

At the beginning both of Morning Prayer, and lykewyse of Euening Prayer, the Minister shall reade with a lowde voyce, some one of these sentences of the Scriptures that folowe. And then he shall say that, which is written after the said sentences.

AT what tyme soeuer a synner doth repent him of his sin from the bottome of hys harte ; I wil put al his wickednes out of my remembraunce sayeth the Lord. *Eze. xviii.*

I do know mine awne wickednes, and my syne is alwaies against me. *Psalm li.*

Turne thy face awaye from our sinnes (O lorde) and blotte out all our offences. *Psalm li.*

A sorowful spirite is a sacrifice to God : despise not (O Lorde) humble and contrite hartes. *Psalm li.*

Rende your hartes, and not your garmentes, and turne to the Lorde your God, because he is gentle and mercyful, he is pacient and of muche mercie, and such a one that is sory for your afflictions. *Ioel ii.*

To the, O Lorde God belongeth mercies and forgeuenes : for we haue gone away from the, and haue not harkened to thy voice, whereby we myght walcke in thy lawes, whiche thou hast appoincted for vs. *Daniel ix.*

Correct vs, O Lorde, and yet in thy iudgement, not in thy furie, least we shoulde be consumed and brought to nothyng. *Iere. ii.*

Amende your liues, for the kyngdome of God is at hande. *Math. iii.*

I will go to my father, and say to him, father, I haue sinned against heauen, and againste the, I am no more worthy to be called thy sonne.

Luke xv.

Entre not in to iudgement wyth thy seruaunts, O Lorde, for no fleshe is rightous in thy sight.

Psal. cxlii.

If we saye that we haue no synne, we deceyue ourselues, and there is no truthe in vs.

1 Iohn i.

DERELY beloued Brethren, the Scripture moueth vs in sondry places, to acknowledge and confesse our manifolde sinnes and wickednes, and that we should not dissemble nor cloke them before the face of almighty God our heauenly father, but confesse them with an humble, lowly, penitent and obedient harte to the ende that we may obtaine forgeuenes of the same by his infinite goodnesse and mercie. And although we ought at all tymes humbly to knowledge our synnes before God, yet ought we moste chiefly so to doe, when we assemble and mete toguether, to rendre thankes for the greate benefites that we haue receiued at his handes, to sette furth his moste worthie praise, to heare his moste holye worde, and to aske those thynges whiche be requisite and necessarie, aswel for the bodye as the soule. wherfore I praye and beseche you, as many as be here presente, to accompany me wyth a pure harte and humble voice, vnto the throne of the heauenly grace, sayeng after me.

A generall confession, to be saide of the whole congregacion after the minister, knelyng.

ALMIGHTIE and most merciful father, we haue erred and straied from thy waies, lyke lost shepee we haue folowed to much the deuises and desires of our owne hartes. We haue offended against thy holy lawes : We haue left vndone those thinges whiche we ought to haue done, and we haue done those thinges which we ought not to haue done, and there is no health in vs, but thou, O Lorde, haue mercy vpon vs miserable offendours. Spare thou them O God, whiche confesse their faultes. Restore thou them that be penitent, accordyng to thy promises declared vnto mankynde, in Christe Jesu our Lorde. And graunt, O most merciful father, for his sake, that we may hereafter lyue a godly, ryghtuous, and sobre life, to the glory of thy holy name. Amen.

The absolution to be pronounced by the Minister alone.

ALMIGHTY God, the father of our Lord Jesus Christ, which desireth not the deathe of a sinner, but rather that he maye turne from his wickednesse and lyue : and hath geuen power and commaundement to hys Ministers, to declare and pronounce to his people beyng penitent, the absolution and remission of their synnes : he pardoneth and absolueth all them which truly repent, and vnfeinedly beleue his holy gospel. Wherefore we beseche

him to graunt vs true repentaunce and hys holy spirite, that those
thynges may please hym, whych we doe at thys present, and that
the rest of our life hereafter may be pure and holy : so that at the
last we may come to his eternall ioye, through Jesus Christe our
lorde.

The people shal aunswere.

Amen.

Then shall the Minister beginne the Lordes Prayer wyth a loude voice.

OUR Father, whiche arte in heauē, hallowed be thy name.   Thy
kyngdō come.   Thy will be done in earth as it is in heauē.   Geue
vs this day our dayly breade.   And forgeue vs our trespasses, as
we forgeue them that trespasse against vs.   And lead vs not into
temptacion.   But deliuer vs from euil.   Amene.

Then likewise he shall saye.

O Lord, open thou our lippes.

Aunswere.

And our mouthe shall shewe furth thy prayse.

Prieste.

O God, make spede to saue vs.

Aunswere.

O Lord, make haste to helpe vs.

Prieste.

Glory be to the father, and to the sonne : and to the holye Ghoste.
As it was in the beginning, is nowe and euer shalbe : worlde
without ende.   Amen.
Praise ye the Lorde.

Then shalbe sayde or song, this Psalme folowyng.

O COME let vs syng vnto the lord : let vs hartely reioyce in the
strength of our saluacion.
Let vs come before his presence wyth thankesgeuinge : and
shewe oureselfe gladde in hym wyth Psalmes.
For the Lorde is a great god : and a greate Kynge, aboue all
goddes :
In his hand are al the corners of the earth : and the strength of
the hilles is his also.
The Sea is his, and he made it and his handes prepared the
drie lande.
O come, let vs worshippe and fal doune : and knele before the
lorde our maker.
For he is the Lord our god : and we are the people of his pasture, and the shepe of his handes.

To day if ye wyl heare his voyce, harden not your hartes : as in the prouocaciō, and as in the daie of temptaciō in the wildernesse.

When your fathers tempted me : proued me, and sawe my workes.

Fortie yere long was I greued with this generacion, and saide : it is a people that doe erre in their hartes : for they haue not knowen my wayes.

Vnto whom I sware in my wrath that the shoulde not enter into my rest.

Glory be to the father, and to the sonne : &c.

As it was in the beginning, is now, &c.

Then shal folowe certeyn Psalmes in order, as they bene appoincted in a table made for that pourpose, excepte there be proper Psalmes appointed for that day, and at thend of euerye Psalme throughout the yere, and likewise in thende of Benedictus, Benedicite, Magnificat, *and* Nunc Dimittis, *shal be repeated.*

Glory be to the father, and to the sonne, &c.

Then shalbe redde two lessons distinctly with a loude voyce, that the people may heare. The first of the olde Testament, the seconde of the newe, Lyke as they be appointed by the Kalender, except there be proper Lessons, assigned for that daye : the Minister that readeth the Lesson, standyng and turning him so as he may best be heard of all such as be present, And before euery lesson, the Minister shal saye thus. The fyrst, second, thyrd, or fourth chapiter of Genesis *or* Exodus, Mathewe, Marke, *or other like, as is appoincted in the Kalender, And in thend of euerye chapiter, he shall saye,*

¶ Here endeth such a Chapiter of suche a Booke.

And (to the ende the people maye the better heare) in suche places where they do synge, there shall the lessons be songe in a plaine tune after the maner of distinct readinge : and likewise the Epystle and gospell.

After the firste lesson shall folowe, Te deum laudamus *in Englyshe dayly throughe the whole yere.*

Te Deum.

We prayse the, O God, we knoweledge the to be the Lorde

All the earth doth worship the, the Father euerlastynge.

To the al Aungels crye aloude, the heauens and all the powers therein.

To thee Cherubin, and Seraphin, continually do crye.

Holy, holy, holy, Lorde God of Sabaoth.

Heauē and earth are ful of the maiestye of thy glory.

The glorious company of the Apostles prayse the.

The goodly felowship of the Prophetes prayse the.

The noble armye of Martyrs, prayse the.

The holye Churche through out al the worlde dothe knowledge the.

The father of an infinite Maiestye.

Thy honourable true, and onely sonne.

Also the holy ghost the comforter.

Thou art the kyng of glory, O Christe.

Thou arte the euerlastynge sonne of the father.

When thou tokest vpon the to deliuer man, thou diddest not abhore the virgins wombe.

Whē thou haddeste ouercome the sharpnes of death thou diddest open the kyngdome of heauen to al beleuers.

Thou syttest on the ryght hand of God, in the glorye of the father.

We beleue that thou shalt come to be our iudge.

We therefore pray the, helpe thy seruāts whom thou hast redemed wyth thy precious bloude.

Make them to be numbred with thy saintes, in glorye euerlasting.

O Lord saue thy people : and blesse thine heritage.

Gouern theme and lifte them vp for euer.

Day by day we magnifye the.

And we worshyp thy name euer world without ende.

Vouchsafe, O Lorde, to kepe vs thys daye withoute synne.

O Lorde, haue mercy vpon vs, haue mercie vpon vs.

O Lorde, let thy mercy lyghten vpon vs : as our trust is in the.

O Lorde, in the haue I trusted : let me neuer be confounded.

Or this canticle, Benedicite omnia opera Domini domino.

O ALL ye worckes of the Lorde, blesse ye the Lorde : praise him, and magnify him for euer.

O ye Aungels of the Lord, blesse ye the Lorde : praise ye him, and magnifye him for euer.

O ye heauens, blesse ye the Lorde : prayse him, and magnifye him for euer.

O ye waters that be aboue the firmamente, blesse ye the Lorde : prayse him, and magnifye him for euer.

O all ye powers of the lord, blesse ye the Lorde : prayse hym, and magnifie him for euer.

O ye Sonne, and Mone, blesse ye the Lorde : prayse hym, and magnifie him for euer.

O ye starres of heauen, blesse ye the Lorde : praise him, and magnifie him for euer.

O ye showers, and dewe, blesse ye the Lorde : prayse him, and magnifie him for euer.

O ye windes of God, blesse ye the Lorde : prayse him, and magnifye him for euer.

O ye fyre and heate, blesse ye the Lord : praise him, and magnifie him for euer.

O ye Winter and Sommer, blesse ye the Lorde : praise him, and magnifye him for euer.

O ye dewes and frostes, blesse ye the Lorde : praise him, and magnifie him for euer.

O ye froste and cold, blesse ye the Lorde : praise him, and magnifie him for euer.

O ye Ice and Snowe, blesse ye the Lorde : praise him, and magnifie him for euer.

O ye nightes and daies, blesse ye the Lord : praise him, and magnifie him for euer.

O ye light and darknes, blesse ye the Lorde : prayse him, and magnifie him for euer.

O ye lyghtenynges and cloudes, blesse ye the Lorde : prayse him, and magnifie him for euer.

O let the earth blesse the Lorde : yea, let it praise hym, and magnifie hym for euer.

O ye mountaynes and hills : blesse ye the Lorde, prayse hym, and magnifie hym for euer.

O al ye grene thynges vpon the earthe, blesse ye the Lord : praise him, and magnifie hym for euer.

O ye welles, blesse ye the Lorde : praise him, and magnyfie hym for euer.

O ye Seas, and fluddes, blesse ye the Lorde : praise hym, and magnifie hym for euer.

O ye whales, and all that moue in the waters, blesse ye the Lorde : prayse him, and magnifie him for euer.

O all ye foules of the aire, blesse ye the lord, praise him, and magnifie him for euer.

O all ye beastes, and cattell, blesse ye the Lorde : praise him, and maignifye him for euer.

O ye children of men blesse ye the Lord : praise him, and magnifye him for euer.

O let Israel blesse the Lorde : praise him, and magnify him for euer.

O ye prestes of the lord, blesse ye the Lord : prayse hym, and magnifye him for euer.

O ye seruauntes of the Lord, blesse ye the Lord : prayse him, and magnifye him for euer.

O ye sprites and soules of the righteous, blesse ye the Lord : prayse him, and magnify him for euer.

O ye holy and humble men of herte blesse ye the Lord : praise him, and magnifye him for euer.

O Ananias, Azarias, and Misael, blesse ye the lord : prayse him, and magnifye him for euer.

Glory be to the father, and to the Sonne : and to the holye Ghoste.

As it was in the begynninge, is nowe, and euer, etc.

And after the second lesson shalbe vsed and sayde Benedictus, *in Englyshe, as foloweth,*

BLESSED be the Lord God of Israell : for he hath visited and redemed his people ; Benedictus.

And hath raised vp a mighty saluacion for vs : in the house of hys seruaunt Dauid ;

As he spake bi the mouth of his holy prophetes : which haue benne sence the worlde began ;

That we should be saued from our enemyes : and from the handes of al that hate vs ;

To performe the mercy promised to our forfathers : and to remember his holy couenant ;

To perfourme the othe whiche he sware to our forefather Abraham : that he would geue vs ;

That we beyng deliured out of the handes of oure enemies : might serue him withoute feare ;

In holynesse and ryghtuousnesse before hym all the dayes of our lyfe.

And thou Chylde, shalt be called the Prophete of the hyghest : for thou shalt go before the face of the Lorde to prepare hys wayes ;

To geue knowledge of saluacion vnto hys people : for the remission of theyr synnes,

Through the tender mercie of our God : whereby the day spring from on hyghe, hath visited vs ;

To geue light to them that sitte in darckenes, and in the shadowe of death : and to guyde our feete into the waye of peace.

Glory be to the father, and to the sonne, and to the holy Gost.

As it was in the beginning, is now, and euer shalbe : worlde wythout ende. Amen.

Or the .C. Psalme. Jubilate.

O be joyfull in the Lorde (al ye landes :) serue the Lorde wyth gladnes, and come before hys presence wyth a song.

Be ye sure that the Lord he is God : it is he that hath made vs, and not we ourselues ; we are hys people, and the shepe of his pasture.

O go your way into his gates wyth thankesgeuing, and into his courtes wyth prayse : be thanckefull vnto hym, and speake good of hys name.

For the Lorde is gracious, his mercy is euerlastyng : and his truth endureth from generacion to generacyon.

Glory be to the Father, &c. As it was in the, &c. Amen.

Then shal be sayd the Crede, *by the Minister and the people, standyng.*

I BELEUE in God the father almightie maker of heauen and earth.   And in Jesus Christ hys onely sonne our Lorde, which was conceiued by the holy ghoste, borne of the Virgen Mary.   Suffred vnder Ponce Pylate, was crucified dead and buried, he descended into Helle.   The thirde daye he rose agayn from the deade.   He ascended into heauen, and sitteth on the ryghte hande of God the Father almightie.   From thence he shall come to iudge the quicke and the deade.   I beleue in the holy Ghoste.   The holy Catholique Churche.   The cōmunion of sainctes.   The forgeuenesse of sinnes. The resurrectiō of the body.   And the life euerlasting.   Amen.

And after that, these prayers folowyng, aswell at Euenyng praier as at Mornyng prayer: al devoutlye knelyng.   The Minister firste pronouncinge with a loude voyce.

The Lorde be with you.
Answer. And with thy spirite.
The Minister. Let vs praie.
Lorde haue mercy vpon vs.
  Christ haue mercy vpon vs.
Lorde haue mercy vpon vs.

Then the Minister, Clarkes, and people ; shall saye the Lordes praier in Englyshe, with a loud voice.

Oure father Which, &c.

Then the Minister ; standing vp shal say.

O lorde, shewe thy mercy vpon vs.
Aunswere. And graunte vs thy saluacion.
Prieste. O Lorde saue the Queene.
Aunswere. And mercifully here vs when we call vpon the.
Priest. Endue thy ministers with rightuousnes.
Aunswere. And make thy chosen people ioyful.
Priest. O Lorde saue thy people.
Aunswere. And blesse thyne enheritaunce.
Priest. Geue peace in our tyme, O Lorde.
Aunswere. Because there is none other that fyghteth for vs, but onely thou, O God.
Priest. O God make clene our hartes with in vs.
Aunswere. And take not thy holy spirite from vs.

Then shal folowe three Collectes.   The firste of the daye, whiche shall be the same that is appoincted at the Communion, The seconde for peace, The thirde for Grace to liue wel.   And the two leaste Collectes shal neuer altre, but dayly be sayde at Mornyng praier, throughoute al the yere, as foloweth.

¶ *The seconde Collecte for Peace.*

O GOD, whiche art authour of peace, and louer of cōcord, in know-ledge of whom standeth our eternal lyfe, whose seruice is perfect fredom; defend vs thy humble seruaūts in al assaultes of our enemies

that we surely trusting in thy defence, may not feare the power
of any aduersaries : through the might of Jesu Christ our lord.
Amen.

The thirde Collecte for Grace.

O LORDE our heauenly father, almightie and euerlastyng God,
whiche hast safely broughte vs to the begynnyng of thys day : defende vs in the same wyth thy myghtye power, and graunte that
this daie we fall into no synne, nether rūne into any kinde of
daunger : but that al our doinges may be ordred by thy gouernaunce, to doe alwayes that is rightuous in thy sighte : through
Jesus Christe our Lorde. Amen.

AN ORDER

FOR EUENING PRAIER

THROUGHOUT THE YERE.

The Priest shal saie.

OUR Father, which, &c.

Then likewise he shal saye.

O Lord open thou our lippes.
Aunswere. And our mouth shall shewe furth thy prayse.
Priest. O God make spede to saue vs.
Aunswere. Lord, make haste to helpe vs.

Priest.

Glory be to the father, and to the sonne : and to the holy ghoste.
As it was in the beginninge, is nowe, and euer shal be : worlde
wythout ende. Amen.
Praise ye the Lorde.

*Then Psalmes in ordre, as they be appoincted in the Table for Psalmes,
except there be proper Psalmes appointed for that day. Then a Lesson
of the olde Testament, as is appointed likewise in the kalender, except
there be propre lessons appointed for that day. After that,* Magnificat *in
Englishe, as foloweth.*

My soule doeth magnifie the Lorde.
And my sprit hath reioysed in god my sauiour.
For he hath regarded the lowelines of his handmaiden.
For beholde from hencefurth al generacions shall call me
blessed.
For he that is mightie hath magnified me : and holy is his
name.

And his mercy is on them that feare him : throughout all generacions.

He hath shewed strength with his arme ; he hath scatered the proude in the imagination of their hertes.

He hath put downe the mightye from theyr seate : and hath exalted the humble and meke.

He hath filled the hungry with good thinges : and the ryche he hath sent empty away.

He remembring his mercy, hath holpen his seruaunte Israel : as he promysed to our forefathers, Abraham and his sede for euer.

Glory be to the Father, and to the sonne, and to the holy Ghoste.

As it was in the beginninge, is nowe, and euer shalbe, world without ende. Amen.

Or the xcviii. Psalme Cantate domino canticum nouum.

O SINGE vnto the Lorde a newe songe : for he hath done marueilous thinges.

With his owne right hande, and with his holy arme : hath he gotten him selfe the victorye.

The Lord declared his saluacion : his righteousnes hath he openly shewed in the syght of the Heathen.

He hath remembred his mercy and truthe towarde the house of Israel : and all the endes of the worlde haue sene the saluacion of our God.

Shewe your selfes ioyfull vnto the Lorde, all ye landes : synge, reioyce and geue thankes.

Prayse the Lorde vpon the harpe : synge to the harp with a Psalme of thankesgeuing.

With trumpettes also and shawmes : O shewe your selfes ioyfull before the Lord the kynge.

Let the Sea make a noyse, and all that therein is : the rounde worlde and they that dwell therin.

Let the floudes clappe their handes, and let the hylles be ioyful togyther before the Lord : for he is come to judge the earth.

With righteousnes shal he judge the worlde : and the people with equitie.

Glory be to the Father, and to the Sonne, and to the holy Ghoste.

As it was in the beginninge, is nowe, and euer shalbe, worlde without ende. Amen.

Then a lesson of the new testament.   And after that (Nunc dimittis) *in Englyshe, as foloweth.*

LORDE, nowe lettest thou thy seruaunt departe in peace : according to thy worde.

For myne eyes haue sene thy saluacion.

Whiche thou haste prepared before the face of all people ;
To be a lyght to lyghtē the Gentiles : and to be the glorye of thy
people Israell.
Glorye be to the father, and to the sonne, and to the holy
ghoste.
As it was in the beginning, is nowe, and euer shall be, worlde
withoute ende. Amen.

Or els thys Psalme, Deus misereatur nostri *in Englyshe.*

GOD be merciful vnto vs, and blesse vs : and shew vs the light
of his countenaunce, and bee mercifull vnto vs.
That thy way maie be knowen vpon earth : thy sauinge healthe
amonge all nacions.
Let the people praise thee O God : yea, let all the people praise
thee.
O let the nacions reioyce and be glad : for thou shalte iudge the
folke righteouslye, and gouerne the nacions vpon earth.
Let the people praise thee, O God : let all the people praise
thee.
Then shall the earth bringe foorth her increse : and God, euen
our owne God, shall geue vs his blessinge.
God shall blesse vs : and all the endes of the worlde shall feare
him.
Glory be to the Father, &c.
As it was in the beginning, &c.

*Then shal folow the Crede, with other prayers, as is before appoynted at
Morning prayer, after* Benedictus. *And with the Collectes : Fyrste of
the day, the seconde of peace, the thyrde for ayde agaynste all peryls, as
hereafter foloweth, whiche two last Collectes shalbe daylye sayde at
Euenyng Prayer wythout alteracion.*

The seconde Collecte at Euenynge Prayer.

O GOD, from whome all holy desires, all good counsailes, and
all iust woorkes do procede : geue vnto thy seruauntes that peace,
whiche the worlde cannot geue : that bothe our hertes may be set
to obey thy commaundemētes, and also that by thee, we beynge
defended from the feare of our enemies, may passe our time in
rest and quietnes. Through the merites of Jesus Chryste our
sauiour. Amen.

The thyrde Collecte for ayde, against all peryls.

LYGHTEN oure darckenesse, wee beseche thee (O Lorde,) and
by thy greate mercye defende vs from all perils and daungers of
this nyghte, for the loue of thy onely sonne oure Sauioure Jesus
Christe. Amen.

*In the feastes of Christmas, the Epiphany, S. Mathye, Easter, the Assen-
cion, Pentecost, S. John Baptyst, S. James, S. Bartholomew, S. Mathew,
S. Simon, and Jude, S. Andrew, and Trinitie Sonday : Shalbe songe
or sayde immediatly after* Benedictus, *thys confession of our Christen
faythe.*

WHOSOEUER wyll be saued : before all thynges it is necessarye
that he holde the catholyke faythe.

Whiche Faithe, excepte euerye one dooe kepe holy, and vndefyled :
withoute doubt he shall perysh euerlastingly.

And the Catholyke Faythe is this : that we worshyp one God in
Trinitie, and trinitie in vnitie.

Neyther confounding the persons : nor deuidinge the substaunce.

For there is one persone of the Father, an other of the Sonne :
and another of the holy ghost.

But the Godhed of the Father, of the Sonne, and of the holy
Ghost, is al one : the glory equall, the maiesty coeternall.

Suche as the Father is, such is the sonne : and suche is the holy
ghost.

The father vncreate, the sonne vncreate : and the holy ghoste
vncreate.

The Father incomprehensible, the sonne incomprehensible : and
the holy Ghoste incomprehensible.

The father eternall, the sonne eternall : and the holye Ghoste
eternall.

And yet they are not thre eternalles : but one eternall.

As also there be not thre incomprehensibles, nor thre vncreated :
but one vncreated, and one incomprehensible.

So likewyse the Father is almighty, the sonne almighty : and
the holy ghoste almighty.

And yet are not there thre Almighties, but one almighty.

So the father is God, the sonne is God : and the holye Ghoste is
God.

And yet are they not thre Gods : but one God.

So lykewyse the father is Lord, the sonne Lorde : and the holy
ghoste Lorde.

And yet not thre Lordes : but one Lord.

For like as we be compelled by the Christian verity : to
acknowledge euery person by hym selfe to be God, and Lorde.

So are we forbiddē by the Catholique Religion : to say there be
thre Gods, or thre Lordes. .

The father is made of none : neyther created, nor begotten.

The sonne is of the Father alone : not made, nor created, but
begotten.

The holye Ghoste is of the Father, and of the Sonne : neither
made, nor created, nor begotten, but proceding.

So there is one father, not thre fathers, one sonne, not thre
sonnes : one holy Ghost, not thre holy Ghostes.

And in this trinitie, none is afore, or after other : none is greater, nor lesse than other.

But the whole thre persons : be coeternall toguether and co-equall.

So that in all thinges as is aforesayde : the Unitye in Trinitie, and the Trinitie in vnitie is to be worshypped.

He therefore that wil be saued : must thus thincke of the Trinitie.

Furthermore, it is necessarye to euerlasting saluation : that he also beleue rightlye in the Incarnation of oure Lorde Jesu Christ.

For the right Faythe is, that we beleue and Confesse : that oure Lorde Jesus Christe the sonne of God, is God and Man ;

God of the Substaunce of the father, begotten before the worldes : and man of the substaūce of his mother, borne in the worlde.

Perfect god, and perfect man of a reasonable Soule, and humaine flesh subsistynge.

Equal to the father as touchyng his godhead : and inferior to the father, touchyng his manhode.

Who although he be God and man : yet he is not two, but one Christ.

One, not by conuersion of the Godhead into fleshe : but by taking of the manhode into God ;

One altogether, not by confusion of Substaunce : but by vnitie of person.

For as the reasonable soule and flesh is but one man : so God and man is but one Christ.

Who suffred for our saluation : descended into hell, rose againe the thirde day from the deade.

He ascended into heauen : he sitteth on the ryghte hand of the father, God Almighty, from whence he shall come to iudge the quicke and the dead.

At whose comming all men shal rise againe with their bodies : and shall geue accompt for their owne worckes.

And they that have done good, shall go into life euerlasting : and they that have done euel, into euerlastyng fyre.

This is the Catholike faith, whiche except a man beleue faith-fully, he can not be saued.

Glory be to the father, and to the sonne : and to the holy Ghoste.

As it was in the beginninge, is nowe, and euer shalbe : worlde without ende.   Amen.

Thus endeth the order of Morning and Eueninge Prayer through the whole yere.

LETANI

VPON SŌDAIES, WEDNESDAIES, AND FRIDAYES,

AND AT OTHER TYMES, WHEN IT SHALBE COMMAUNDED BY THE ORDINARYE.

O GOD the father of heauen : haue mercy vpon vs miserable synners.

O God the Father of heauen : etc.

O God the sonne redemer of the worlde : haue mercye vpon vs miserable synners.

O God the sonne redemer of, etc.

O God the holye Ghoste, proceding from the father and the Sonne : haue mercye vpon vs miserable synners.

O God the holy ghoste, proceding from, etc.

O holy, blessed, and glorious Trinitie, three persons and one god : haue mercy vpon vs miserable synners.

O holy, blessed, and glorious trinitye thre persons, etc.

Remember not, Lorde our offences, nor the offences of our forefathers, neyther take thou vengeaunce of oure synnes : spare vs good Lorde, spare thy people whome thou haste redemed with thy moste precious bloude, and be not angry with vs for euer.

Spare vs good Lorde.

From all euil and mischief, from synne, from the craftes and assaultes of the Deuil, from thy wrath, and from euerlasting dampnation.

Good Lorde delyuer vs.

From all blyndnes of herte, from pride, vayne glorye, and hypocrisy, from enuy, hatred and malice, and all vncharitablenes.

Good Lorde delyuer us.

From fornicacion and all other deadly synne: and frome all the deceiptes of the worlde, the Fleshe and the Deuill.

Good Lorde delyuer vs.

From lightninges and tempestes, from plague, pestilence and famine, from battayle and murther, and from soudeine death.

Good Lorde delyuer vs.

From all sedicion and priuey conspiracye, from all false doctrine and heresy, from hardnes of harte, and cõtempte of thy worde and commaundement.

Good Lorde delyuer vs.

By the misterye of thy holye Incarnacion, by thy holy Natiuitie and circumcision, by thy Baptysme, fastynge and temptacion.

Good Lorde delyuer vs.

By thyne agonye and bloudy sweate, by thy crosse and passion, by thy precious deathe and buriall, by thy glorious resurrection, and ascencion, and by the commynge of the holy Ghoste.

Good Lorde delyuer vs.

In al tyme of our tribulacion, in al tyme of our welth, in the houre of death, and in the daye of iudgement.

Good Lorde delyuer vs.

We synners do beseche the to heare vs (O Lord God,) and that it may please the to rule and gouerne thy holy Churche vniuersally, in the right way.

We beseche the to heare vs good Lorde.

That it may please the, to kepe and strengthen in the true worshipping of the in righteousnes and holynes of lyfe, thy seruaunt Elizabeth our most gracious Quene and gouernour.

We beseche the to heare vs good Lorde.

That it may please the, to rule her harte in thy faith, feare, and loue, that she may euermore haue affiaunce in the, and euer seke thy honoure and glory.

We beseche the to heare vs good Lorde.

That it may please the, to be her defender and keper, geuing her the victory ouer al her enemyes.

We beseche the to heare vs good Lorde.

That it may please the to illuminate all Byshoppes, Pastours, and ministers of the Church, with true knowledge, and vnderstanding of thy words, and that both by their preaching and liuinge, they may sette it furth and shewe it accordingly.

We beseche the to heare vs good Lorde.

That it maye please thee to endue the Lordes of the Counsayle, and all the nobilitie, with grace, wisedom, and vnderstanding.

We beseche the to heare vs good Lorde.

That it may please thee to blesse and kepe the Magistrates, geuing them grace to execute iustice, and to maynteyne truthe.

We beseche the to heare vs good Lorde.

That it may please the to blesse, and kepe al thy people.
We beseche the to heare vs good Lorde.

That it may please thee to geue to all nacions, vnitie, peace and concorde.
We beseche the to heare vs good Lorde.

That it maye please the to geue vs an harte to loue and dread the, and diligētly to lyue after thy cōmaūdemētes.
We beseche the to heare vs good Lorde.

That it maye please the to gyue all thy people encrease of grace, to heare mekely thy worde, and to receyue it wyth pure affeccion, and to bring furthe the fruites of the spirit.
We beseche the to heare vs good Lorde.

That it may please the to bring into the way of truth all suche as haue erred, and are deceyued.
We besech the to heare vs good Lorde.

That it maye please thee to strengthen suche as dooe stande, and to comforte, and helpe the weake-harted, and to rayse theym vp that falle, and finally to beate downe Sathan vnder our feete.
We beseche the to heare vs good Lorde.

That it may please the to succour, helpe and comforte all that be in daunger, necessitie, and tribulation.
We beseche the to heare vs good Lorde.

That it maye please thee to preserue all that trauayle, by lande or by water, al women labouringe of chylde, all sycke persons and yonge chyldren, and to shew thy pitye vpon all prisoners and captiues.
We beseche the to heare vs good Lorde.

That it may please the to defende, and prouide for the fatherles children and widowes, and all that be desolate and oppressed.
We beseche the to heare vs good Lorde.

That it may please the to haue mercy vpon all men.
We beseche the to heare vs good Lorde.

That it may please the to forgeue our enemyes, persecutours and slaunderers, and to turne theyr hertes.
We beseche the to heare vs good Lorde.

That it may please the to geue and preserue to our vse the kindly fruites of the earth, so as in due tyme we maye enioye them.
We beseche the to heare vs good Lorde.

That it may please the to geue us true repentaunce, to forgeue vs all our sinnes, negligences, and ignoraunces ; and to endue vs with the grace of thy holy spirite, to amende our lyues according to thy holy worde.
We beseche the to heare vs good Lorde.

Sonne of God : we beseche thee to heare vs.
Sonne of God : we beseche thee to heare vs.

O Lambe of God, that takest away the synnes of the worlde.
Graunt vs thy peace.

O Lambe of God that takest awaye the synnes of the worlde.
Haue mercy vpon vs.

O Christ heare vs.
O Christe heare vs.

Lorde haue mercy vpon vs.
Lorde haue mercy vpon vs.

Christe haue mercy vpon vs.
Christe haue mercy vpon vs.

Lorde haue mercy vpon vs.
Lorde haue mercy vpon vs.

Our [1] father whiche art in heauen. &c.
And leade vs not into temptacion.
But delyuer vs from euyll.

Amen.

The Versycle. O Lorde deale not with vs after our synnes.
The Aunswere. Neither rewarde vs after our iniquities.

Let vs praye.

O GOD merciful father, that dispisest not the syghing of a contrite hart, nor the desyre of suche as be sorowfull, mercyfully assiste our praiers that we make before the, in all our troubles and aduersities, whensoeuer they oppresse vs. And graciouslye hear vs, that those euilles, whiche the crafte and subtiltie of the deuel, or man worketh against vs, be broughte to noughte, and by the prouidence of thy goodnesse they may be dispersed, that we thy Seruauntes, beyng hurt by no persecucions, may euermore geue thanckes to the, in thy holy Church, through Jesus Christ our Lorde.
O Lord aryse, helpe vs, and deliuer vs for thy names sake.

O GOD we haue hearde with our eares, and our fathers have declared vnto vs the noble worckes that thou diddeste in their dayes, and in the olde tyme before them.
O Lord aryse, helpe vs, and deliuer vs, for thyne honoure.

Glory be to the father, and to the sonne, and to the holye Goste :

[1 This mode of arranging the Lord's Prayer occurs six times, and may be explained from a rubric in the Salisbury Breviary :—*Notandum est, quod nunquam in ecclesia Sarisburiensi incipitnr* Pater noster *a sacerdote in audientia ad aliqu̇od servitium, nisi ad missam tantum. Et postea dicat sacerdos in audientia.* Et ne nos. *Chorus.* Sed libera. Dominica Prima Adventus, Ad Matutinas, Noct., 1.]

As it was in the beginninge, is nowe, and euer shalbe : worlde without ende.   Amen.

From our enemyes defende vs, O Christ.
Graciously loke vpon our afflictions.

Pitifully beholde the sorowes of our harte.
Mercifully forgeue the synnes of thy people.

Fauourably with mercy heare our prayers.
O sonne of Dauid haue mercy vpon vs.

Bothe now and euer, vouchesafe, to heare vs, O Christe.
Graciously hear vs, O Christ,
Graciously heare vs, O Lorde Christ.

The Versycle. O Lorde let thy mercy be shewed vpon vs.
The Aunswere. As we do put our trust in the.

Let vs praye.

WE humbly beseche the, O father, mercifullye to loke vpon oure infirmities, and for the glory of thy names sake, turne from vs all those euilles that we moste righteously haue deserued : and graunte that in all oure troubles we maye put our whole truste and confydence in thy mercye, and euermore serue the in holynes and purenes of liuing, to thy honour and glory : throughe our onely mediatoure and aduocate Jesus Christe our Lorde.   Amen.

[A Prayer for the Queenes Majesty.

O LORD our heuenly father, high and mighty king of kynges, Lorde of lordes, the onely ruler of princes, which doest from thy throne beholde all the dwellers vpō earth, most hartely we beseche the with thy fauoure to beholde our mooste gracious soueraigne Lady Quene Elizabeth, and so replenyshe her with the grace of thy holy spirit, that she may alway incline to thy wil, and walcke in thy waye : Indue her plentifully wyth heauenly gifts : Graunt her in health and wealthe longe to liue : strēgth her that she may vanquish and ouercome al her enemies : And finally after this life she may attaine euerlasting joye and felicitie, thorowe Jesus Christ our Lorde.   Amen.

ALMIGHTY and euerlastinge God, whiche onely workest great mervailes, sende downe vpon our Bishoppes and Curates, and al congregacions committed to their charge, the healthful spirit of thy grace, and that they may truely please thee, Powre vpon them the continuall deawe of thy blessinge : Graunte this, O Lorde, for the honour of our aduocate and mediatoure, Jesus Christ.   Amen.

¶ *A Prayer of Chrisostome.*

ALMIGHTY God, which hast geuen vs grace at this tyme with one accorde, to make our common supplications vnto thee, and doest promyse that whē two or three be gathered together in thy name thou wilt graunt their requestes : fulfyl nowe, O Lorde, the desyres and peticions of thy seruauntes, as may be most expediēt for them, graunting vs in this world knowledge of thy truthe, and in the world to come lyfe euerlasting. Amen.

¶ ii. Corin. xiii.

THE grace of oure Lorde Jesus Christe, and the loue of God, and the felowship of the holye ghoste, bee wyth vs all euermore. Amen.

¶ *For rayne, yf the tyme requyre.*

O GOD heauenly father, whiche by thy Sonne Jesus Christe, haste promysed to all theim that seke thy kingdome and the righteousnes therof, all thinges necessary to their bodelye sustenaunce : Sende vs, we besech the, in this oure necessitie, such moderate raine and showers, that we may receyue the fruytes of the earthe to our comforte and to thy honoure, throughe Jesus Christ our Lorde. Amen.

¶ *For fayre weather.*

O LORDE God, which for the synne of man diddest ones drowne al the world, excepte eyght persons, and afterward of thy great mercy diddest promise neuer to destroy it so againe : we humblye besech the, that althoughe we for our iniquities haue worthely deserued this Plague of raigne and waters ; yet vpon oure true repentaunce, thou wilt sende vs suche wether, wherby we may receyue the fruites of the yearth in due season, and learne bothe by thy punishment to amende our liues, and for thy clemency to geue thee prayse and glorye, throughe Jesus Christ our Lorde. Amen.

¶ *In the tyme of dearth and famyne.*

O GOD heauenly Father, whose gyft it is that the rayne dothe fall, the earth is frutefull, beastes encrease, and fyshes do multiply : Behold, we besech thee, the afflictions of thy people, and graunte that the scarcitye and dearthe (which we do now moste iustly suffer for our iniquitye) maye through thy goodnes be mercifully tourned into cheapnesse and plenty, for the loue of Jesu Christ our Lorde, to whome with thee and the holye Ghoste be Prayse for euer. Amen.

¶ *In the tyme of Warre.*

O ALMIGHTY God, king of al kinges, and gouernoure of al thinges, whose power no creature is hable to resiste, to whome it belongeth iustly to punyshe synners, and to be mercyfull vnto them that truely repente, Saue, and deliuer vs (we humbly beseche thee)

from the handes of our enemyes, abate their pryde, aswage theyr
malyce, and confounde theyr deuyses, that we beynge armed with
thy defence, maye be preserued euermore from all peryls to glorifye
thee, whiche art the onely geuer of all victory, throughe the merites
of thy onely sonne Jesus Christ our Lorde.   Amen.

¶ *In the tyme of any common plague or syckenesse.*

O ALMIGHTYE God, whiche in thy wrathe, in the tyme of king
Dauid didst slea with the plague of pestilence, thre score and ten
thousande, and yet remēbringe thy mercy, diddest saue the rest :
haue pitie vpon vs miserable synners, that nowe are vysited with
great sicknesse, and mortalitie, that like as thou diddest then
commaunde thyne angel to cease from punishing ; So it may now
please thee to withdrawe frō vs this plague, and greuous syckenesse, throughe Jesus Christe oure Lorde.   Amen.

O GOD, whose nature and propertie is euer to haue mercy, and to
forgeue, receyue our humble peticions : and thoughe we be
tyed and bounde with the chayne of our synnes,
yet let the pitifulnes of thy great mercy
lose vs, for the honoure of Jesus
Christes sake, our mediatoure
and aduocate.
Amen.]

THE COLLECTES, EPISTLES, AND GOSPELLES, TO BE VSED AT THE
CELEBRACION OF THE LORDES SUPPER, AND HOLY
COMMUNION, THROUGHE THE YERE.

¶ *The i Sondaie of Aduent.*

The Collect.

ALMIGHTY God, geue vs grace that we maye caste awaie the
woorkes of darkenesse and put vpon vs the armour of lyght, nowe
in the tyme of this mortall lyfe, (in the whiche thy sonne Jesus
Christe, came to visite vs in great humilitie) that in the laste daye,
when he shall come agayne in his glorious Maiestie, to iudge bothe
the quicke and the dead, we may ryse to the lyfe immortall : through
hym, who lyueth and reigneth wyth thee and the holy ghoste nowe
and ever.   Amen.

The Epistle.   Rom. xiii. 8-end.
OWE nothing . . . fulfyl the lustes of it.

The Gospell.   Matt. xxi. 1-14.
AND when they drew nigh . . . denne of theues.

The seconde Sondaie.

The Collecte.

BLESSED Lorde, whiche haste caused all holye Scriptures, to
bee written for our learninge : Graunte vs that wee maye in suche
wyse heare them, reade, marke, learne, and in wardly digest theim,
that by paciēce and comforte of thy holye worde we maye embrace,
and euer holde faste the blessed hope of euerlasting lyfe, which
thou hast geuen vs in oure sauiour Jesus Christe.   Amen.

The Epistle.   Rom. xv. 4-13.
WHATSOEUER thinges . . . through the power of the holy gost.

The Gospell.   LUC. xxi., 25-33.
THERE shalbe signes . . . but my worde shall not passe.

The iii Sondaie.

The Collect.

LORDE we beseche thee geue eare to oure praiers, and by thy
gracious visitacion, lighten the darkenesse of oure harte, by our
Lorde Jesus Christ.   Amen.

The Epistle. 1 Cor. iv., 1-2.

LET a man this wise esteme vs, . . . haue prayse of God.

The Gospel. Matt. xi., 2-10.

WHEN John beyng in prison . . . prepare thy waye before thee.

¶ *The iiii Sondaie.*

The Collecte.

LORDE, raise vp, we praie the, thy power, and come emōg vs, and with great might succour vs, that whereas through oure sinnes and wickednesse we be sore let, and hyndred, thy bountifull grace and mercy, throughe the satisfaccion of thy sonne our Lorde may spedely deliuer vs, to whō with thee and the holye ghost, be honour and glory, worlde without ende.   Amen.

The Epistle. Philipp. iv., 4-7.

REIOYCE in the LORD alway, . . . through Christ Jesu.

The Gospell. John i., 19-28.

THIS is recorde of John, . . . where John dyd baptyse.

On Christmas daie.

The Collect.

ALMIGHTIE God, which haste geuen vs thy onely begotten sonne, to take oure nature vpon hym, and this daie to be borne of a pure virgine, graunte that we being regenerate, and made thy children by adoptiō and grace, may daiely be renued by thy holy spirit, through the same our Lorde Jesus Christ who liueth and reigneth with thee and the holy ghost, now and euer.   Amen.

The Epistle. Heb. i., 1-12.

GOD in tymes past . . . and thy yeares shal not fayle.

The Gospel. John i., 1-14.

IN the beginnynge was the word, . . . ful of grace and trueth.

¶ *S. Stephenes Daye.*

The Collect.

GRAUNT vs, O Lorde to learne to loue our enemies, by thexample of thy Martir sainct Stephen who praied for his persecutours : To thee, whiche lyuest, and reignest, etc.

¶ Then shal folow a Collect of the Natiuitie, which shalbe sayd continually vnto newe yeares daye.

The Epistle. Acts vii., 55-end.

AND Stephin, beyng ful of the holy ghost . . . he fell aslepe.

The Gospell. Matt. xxiii., 34-end.

BEHOLD, I send vnto you prophetes, . . . in the name of the Lorde.

¶ *Sainct Jhon Euangelistes daye.*

The Collecte.

MERCIFUL Lorde, we beseech thee, to cast thy bryght beames of lyght vpon thy Churche, that it beyng lightened by the doctrine of thy blessed Apostle and Euangelist John may attaine to thy euerlasting gyftes through Jesus Christ our lorde. Amen.

The Epistle. 1 John i.-end.

THAT which was from the beginnyng . . . and his word is not in vs.

The Gospel. John xxi., 15-end.

JESUS sayde vnto Peter, Folow thou me . . . bookes that should be wrytten.

The innocentes daye.

The Collect.

ALMIGHTIE god, whose praise this daie the yonge Innocentes, thy witnesses haue confessed and shewed furthe, not in speakynge, but in diyng · mortifie and kill all vices in vs, that in our conuersacion, our life maie expresse thy faith, which with oure tongues, we doe confesse, through Jesus Christ our Lorde.

The Epistle. Apoc. xiv., 1-5.

I LOOKED, and lo, a lambe . . . the throne of God.

The Gospel. Matt. ii., 13-18.

THE Angel of the Lord appeared . . . because they were not.

¶ *The Sondaye after Christmas daye.*

The Collect.

ALMIGHTIE God, whiche hast geuen vs, thy onely begotten sonne to take our nature vpō hym, and thys daye to be borne of a pure Virgine : graunt that we beyng regenerate, and made thy chyldren by adopcion and grace, may daily be renued by thy holy spirite throwe the same our Lorde Jesus Christ, who liueth and reygneth, etc. Amen.

The Epistle. Gal. iv., 1-7.

AND I saye, that the heyre . . . hevre of God through Christ.

The Gospel.   Matt. i., 1-end.

THYS is the booke of the generacion of Jesus Christ . . . and
called his name JESUS.

¶ *The Circumcision of Christe.*

The Collect.

ALMIGHTIE God, whiche madest thy blessed sonne to bee Circumcised, and obedient to the lawe for man, graunt vs the true
Circumcision of the spirit, that our hartes, and al members, beyng
mortified frō al worldly and carnall lustes, may in al thynges obey
thy blessed wil, through the same thy sonne Jesus Christ our
lorde.

The Epistle.   Rom. iv., 8-14.

BLESSED is that man . . . and the promyse of none effect.

The Gospel.   Luc. ii., 15-21.

AND it fortuned . . . before he was conceyued in the wombe.

¶ If there be a Sondaie, betwene the Epiphanie and the Circumcision,
then shalbe vsed the same Collect, Epistle and Gospell at the Cōmunion,
whiche was vsed vpon the daie of Circumcision.

¶ *The Epiphanie.*

The Collect.

O GOD, which by the leadynge of a starre, diddest manifest thy
onely begotten sonne to the Gentiles, mercifully graunt that wee,
whiche knowe thee now by faithe, maie after thys lyfe haue the
fruicyon of thy gloryous Godhed, through Christe our Lorde.
Amen.

The Epistle.   Ephes. iii., 1-12.

FOR this cause I Paul am a priesoner of Jesus Christ . . . which
is by faith of hym.

The Gospel.   Matt. ii., 1-12.

WHEN Jesus was borne in Bethleē . . . returned into their own
countrey another waye.

The i Sondaie after the Epiphanie.

The Collect.

LORDE we beseche thee, mercifully to receiue the prayers of thy
people, whiche call vpon thee, and graunt that thei maie both perceiue and knowe what thynges they ought to doe, and also haue
grace and power, faithfully to fulfill the same, through Jesus
Christe our Lorde.   Amen.

The Epistle. Rom. xii. 1-5.

I BESECHE you therfore brethrē, . . . one anothers membres.

The Gospel. Luke ii. 42-52.

THE father and mother of Jesus wente to Jerusalem . . . fauoure with God and men.

¶ *The ii Sondaye after the Epiphanie.*

The Collect.

ALMIGHTIE and euerlastynge God, whiche doest gouerne all thynges in heauen and yearth, mercifully here the supplicacions of thy people and graunte vs thy peace all the dayes of our lyfe.

The Epistle. Rom. xii. 6-16.

SEING that we haue dyuers gyftes, . . . but make youreselues equall to them of the lower sorte.

The Gospel. John ii. 1-11.

AND the third daye was there a mariage in Cana, . . . and his dysciples beleued on him.

¶ *The iii Sondaye.*

The Collect.

ALMYGHTIE and euerlastyng God, mercyfully loke vpon our infirmities, and in all our daungers and necessities, stretche furth thy right hande, to helpe and defende vs ; through Christ our Lorde.

The Epistle. Rom. xii. 16-21.

BE not wyse in youre own opinions. . . . ouercome thou euill with goodnes.

The Gospell. Matt. viii. 1-13.

WHEN he was come downe from the mountaine, . . . And his seruaunt was healed in the selfesame houre.

¶ *The iiii Sondaye.*

The Collect.

GOD whiche knowest vs to be set in the middest of so many and greate daungiers, that for mannes frailnesse, wee can not alwaies stande uprightely : Graunt to vs the health of body and soule, that all those thinges, whiche wee suffer for synne, by thy helpe we may well passe and ouercome, through Christ our Lorde.

C

The Epistle.   Rom. xiii. 1-7.

LET euery soule submytte hymselfe . . . honoure, to whom honoure pertayneth.

The Gospel.   Matt. viii. 23-34.

AND when he entred into a ship, . . . that he would departe out of their coastes.

¶ *The v Sondaye.*

The Collect.

LORDE we beseche the to kepe thy Churche and housholde cōtinually in thy true religiō, that thei which doe leane onely vpon hope of thy heauēly grace, may euermore be defended by thy myghtie power, throughe Christe our Lorde.

The Epistle.   Coloss. iii. 12-17.

PUT on as the electe of God, . . . geuing thankes vnto God the father by hym.

The Gospel.   Matt. xiii. 24-30.

THE kyngdome of heauen is lyke . . . but gather the wheate into my barne.

The vi Sunday (if there be so many) shal haue the same Collect, Epistle, and Gospel, that was vpon the v Sondaie.

¶ *The Sondaie called Septuagesima.*

The Collect.

O LORD, wee beseche thee fauourably to heare the prayers of thy people, that wee whyche are iustly punyshed for our offences, maie be mercyfully delyuered by thy godnes, for the glory of thy name, throughe Jesu Christe our Sauiour, who liueth and reygneth, etc.

The Epistle.   1 Cor. ix. 24-27.

PERCEIUE ye not, how that they which runne . . . I myselfe shoulde be a cast-awaye.

The Gospel.   Matt. xx. 1-16.

THE kyngdome of heauen is like vnto . . . For many be called, but few be chosen.

¶ *The Sondaie called Sexagesima.*

The Collect.

LORDE GOD, whiche seest that we put not our truste in any thyng that we doo : mercifully graūt that by thy power, we maie be defended agaynst all aduersitie : through Jesus Christ our Lorde.

The Epistle. 2 Cor. xi. 19-31.

YE suffre fooles gladly, . . . knoweth that I lie not.

The Gospel. Luke viii. 4-15.

WHEN much people were gathered together, . . . and brynge orth fruite through pacience.

¶ *The Sondaie called Quinquagesima.*

The Collect.

O LORD whiche doest teache vs that all our doynges without charitie, are nothyng worthe, sende thy holy ghoste, and powre in our hartes that moste excellent gift of charitie, the verie bonde of peace and all vertues, without the whyche whosoeuer liueth is compted dead before thee : Graunte thys for thy onely sonne Jesus Christes sake.

The Epistle. 1 Cor. xiii.

THOUGHE I speake with the tongues of men and of aungels . . . but the chiefe of these is loue.

The Gospell. Luke xviii. 31-43.

JESUS toke vnto him the xii, and sayde vnto them : . . . gaue prayse vnto God.

¶ *The i daie of Lent.*

The Collect.

ALMIGHTIE and euerlastyng god, whiche hatest nothyng that thou haste made, and doest forgyue the synnes of all thē that be penitent ; create and made in vs newe and contrite hartes, that we worthely lamētyng our synnes : and knowledgyng our wretched-nesse, maie obtain of thee, the God of all mercye, perfect remissyon and forgiuenesse, throughe Jesus Christ.

The Epistle. Joel ii. 12-17.

TURNE you vnto me with all youre hertes, . . . Where is now their God ?

The Gospell. Matt. vi. 16-21.

WHEN ye fast, be not sad as the Hipocrytes are, . . . there wyl youre hertes be also.

The i Sondaie in Lent.

The Collect.

O LORDE, which for our sake diddest fast fourtye dayes and fourty nightes : geue vs grace to vse suche abstinence, that, our fleshe beyng subdued to the spirite, we maye euer obeye thy godly mocions in ryghteousnesse and true holynesse, to thy honoure and glorye, whiche liuest and reignest, &c.

The Epistle.   2 Cor. vi. 1-10.

WE, as helpers exhorte you, . . . and yet possessinge all thinges.

The Gospell.   Matt. iv. 1-11.

THEN was Jesus ledd awaye of the spyrite into wildernes, . . . the aungels came and ministred vnto hym.

¶ *The ii Sondaie.*

The Collect.

ALMIGHTIE God, whiche doest se that we haue no power of oureselues, to helpe oureselues ; kepe thou vs bothe outwardly in oure bodies, and inwardely in our soules, that we may be defēded frō all aduersities whiche maye happen too the bodye, and frome all euell thoughtes, whyche maye assaulte and hurte the soule : through Jesus Christe, &c.

The Epistle.   1 Thess. iv. 1-8.

WE beseche you brethren, and exhorte you . . . which hath sent his holy spyrite amonge you.

The Gospell.   Matt. xv. 21-28.

JESUS wente thence, and departed . . . And her daughter was made whole euen the same time.

¶ *The iii Sondaye.*

The Collect.

WE beseche thee almightie God, loke vppon the hartie desires of thy humble seruauntes : and stretche furthe the right hande of thy maiestie, to be oure defence agaynst all our enemies : through Jesus Christ our Lorde.

The Epistle.   Ephes. v. 1-14.

BE you the folowers of God as dere children, . . . and Christe shal geue thee lyghte.

The Gospell.   Luke xi. 14-28.

JESUS was casting out a deuell that was dumme . . . yea, happy are they that here the worde of God and kepe it.

¶ *The iiii Sondaye in Lent.*

The Collect.

GRAUNTE we beseche the Almighty God, that wee which for our euil dedes are worthely punished by the comforte of thy grace, may mercifully be releued.   Through our Lorde Jesus Christ.

The Epistle.   Gal. iv. 21-31.

TELL me, ye that desire to be vnder the lawe, . . . we are not children of the bonde-woman, but of the free-woman.

The Gospell.   John vi. 1-14.

JESUS departed ouer the see of Galilee, . . . This is of a trueth the same Prophet that shulde come into the worlde.

¶ *The v Sondaye in Lent.*

The Collect.

WE besech the almighty God, mercifully to loke vpō thy people, that by thy great goodnes thei mai be gouerned and preserued euermore, both in bodie and soule, through Jesus Christ our Lord.

The Epistle.   Heb. ix. 11-15.

CHRIST beynge an hie Priest of good thinges to come, . . . mighte receaue the promes of eternall inheritaunce.

The Gospell.   John viii. 46-59.

WHICH of you can rebuke me of synne? . . . but Jesus hyd himself, and wente out of the temple.

¶ *The Sondaye next before Easter.*

The Collecte.

ALMIGHTY and euerlasting God, whiche of thy tēder loue towardes man, haste sente oure sauioure Jesus Christ to take vpon him our flesh, and to suffer death vpon the crosse, that al man-kynde should folowe the example of hys greate humilitie, merci-fullye graunte that we both folowe the example of his pacience, and be made partakers of hys resurreccion, throughe the same Jesus Christ our Lorde.   Amen.

The Epistle.   Philipp. ii. 5-11.

LET the same mynd be in you, that was in Christe Jesu : . . . vnto the prayse of God the father.

The Gospell.   Matt. xxvi. xxvii. to ver. 56.

AND it came to passe, whē Jesus had fynished . . . and Mary the mother of James and Joses, and the mother of Zebedes children.

¶ *Monday before Easter.*

The Epistle.   Isaiah lxiii.

WHAT is he this, that cometh from Edom, with stayned reade kolored clothes of Bosra? . . . for they haue not called vpon thy name.

The Gospell.   Mark xiv.

AFTER two dayes was Easter, and the dayes of swete bred. . . .
Before the cocke crow twyce, thou shalt deny me thre tymes.
And he began to wepe.

¶ *Tuesdaye before Easter.*

The Epistle.   Esai. l.

THE Lorde God hath opened myne eare, . . . namely that ye
shall slepe in sorowe.

The Gospell.   Mark xv.

AND anone in the dawning, the hye prestes . . . And Mary
Magdalene, and Mary Joses behelde, where he was layed.

¶ *Wednesday before Easter.*

The Epistle.   Heb. ix. 16-28.

WHEREAS is a Testament, there must also . . . shall he
appeare agayne without synne vnto saluacion.

The Gospell.   Luke xxii.

THE feast of swete bread drew nye, . . . For we ourselues haue
heard of his owne mouth.

¶ *At Euensong.*

The First Lesson, Lamenta. i. vnto the ende.

¶ *Thursday before Easter.*

The Epistle.   1 Cor xi. 17-34.

THIS I warne you of, and commende not, . . . Other thynges
will I set in order when I come.

The Gospell.   Luke xxiii.

THE whole multitude of them arose, . . . But rested on the
Sabboth daye, accordyng to the commaundement.

On good Friday.

The Collects.

ALMIGHTY god, we beseche the graciouslye to beholde this thy
familye, for the whyche oure Lord Jesus Christ, was contented to
be betraied, and geuen vp into the handes of wicked mē, and to
suffer death vpon the crosse, who lyueth and reygneth, with thee
and the holy ghoste now and euer, etc.

ALMYGHTY and euerlastynge God, by whose Spirite the whole body of the churche is gouerned and sanctifyed : receyue oure supplications and praiers, whiche we offer before thee, for all estates of menne in thy holye congregation, that euerye membre of the same, in hys vocation, and ministerye, maye truely, and godlye serue thee : thoroughe our Lorde Jesus Christe.

MERCIFUL God, who haste made all men, and hatest nothinge that thou haste made, nor wouldest the deathe of a synner, but rather that hee should be conuerted, and liue : haue mercy vpon all Jewes, turkes, infidels, and heritikes, and take from them all ignoraunce, hardnes of herte, and contempte of thy worde : and so fetche them home blessed Lorde, to thy flocke, that they may be saued emonge the remnaunte of the true Israelites, and be made one folde vnder one shepeherde, Jesus Christ our Lord ; who lyueth and reigneth, &c.

The Epistle. Heb. x. 1-25.

THE lawe (whiche hathe but a shadowe . . . because ye see the daye draweth nye.

The Gospel. John xviii. xix.

WHEN Jesus had spoken these wordes, . . . for the sepulcre was nye at hande.

Easter Euen.

The Epistle. 1 Peter iii. 17-22.

IT is better (if the wyll of God be so) . . . and myght subdued vnto hym.

The Gospel. Matt. xxvii. 57-66.

WHEN euen was come, there came a riche man of Arimathia . . . and sealed the stone.

¶ *Easter Daie.*

¶ At mornyng praier in stede of the Psalme, O come let vs, &c., these Anthemes shalbe song or saide.

CHRIST risyng againe from the ded, now dieth not. death from hencefurth hath no power vpon him. for in that he died, hee died but once to put awaie sinne, but in that he liueth, he liueth vnto God. And so likewyse accompt yourselues deade vnto sinne, but liuing vnto God in Christ Jesus our Lorde. Amen.

CHRIST is risen again, the first fruites of them that slepe, for seing that by man came death, by man also commeth the Resurreccion of the ded, for as by Adam al men do die, so by Christe al men shalbe restored to lyfe.

The Collect.

ALMIGHTY God, whiche through thy only begotten sonne Jesus Christe, haste ouercome deathe, and opened vnto vs, the gate of euerlasting lyfe wee humbly beseche thee, that, as by thy speciall grace preuentyng vs, thou doest put in our mindes good desires, so by thy continuall helpe we maye bryng thesame to good effect : through Jesus christ our lord who, &c.

The Epistle. Coloss. iii. 1-7.

IF ye be rysen agayne with Christ, . . . some tyme when ye lyued in them. .

The Gospell. John xx. 1-10.

THE first daye of the Sabbathes . . . Then the disciples went awaye agayne to theyr owne home.

¶ *Mondaie in Easter weke.*

The Collect.

ALMIGHTY God, whiche through thy only begotten sonne Jesus Christe, haste ouercome deathe, and opened vnto vs, the gate of euerlastyng lyfe : wee humbly beseche thee, that as by thy speciall grace, preuentyng vs, thou doest put in our mindes good desires, so by thy continuall helpe we may bryng the same to good effect ; through Jesus christ our lord, who, &c.

The Epistle. Acts x. 34-43.

PETER opened hys mouth and sayde ; . . . shall receyue remissiō of synnes.

The Gospell. Luke xxiv. 13-35.

BEHOLDE two of the disciples wente that same daye . . . and howe they knewe him in breakyng of bread.

¶ *Tuisday in Easter wieke.*

The Collect.

ALMIGHTY father, whiche hast geuen thy onelye sonne to die for our sinnes, and to rise again for our iustificacion : graunt vs so to put away the leauen of malice, and wickednes, that we may alwaye serue thee in purenesse of lyuynge and trueth, through Jesus Christ our Lorde.

The Epistle. Acts xiii. 26-41.

Ye men and brethren, Children of the generacion of Abraham, . . . thoughe a man declare it vnto you.

The Gospell. Luke xxiv. 36-48.

JESUS stode in the myddes of his disciples . . . And ye are wytnesses of these thynges.

¶ *The fyrst Sondaye after Easter.*

The Collect.

ALMIGHTYE God, &c., *as at the Communion on Easter daye.*

The Epistle. 1 John v. 1-12.

AL that is borne of GOD ouercommeth the world. . . . and he that hath not the sonne of God, hath not lyfe.

The Gospell. John xx. 19-23.

THE same daye at nyghte . . . And whosoeuers synnes ye retayne, they are retayned.

¶ *The ii Sondaye.*

The Collecte.

ALMIGHTY God, whiche hast geuen thy holie sonne to be vnto vs bothe a sacrifice for synne and also an ensample of Godlye lyfe : geue vs the Grace that wee maie alwaies mooste thanckefully receiue that his inestimable benefite, and also dayly endeuour our selues to folowe the blessed steppes of his most holy lyfe.

The Epistle. 1 Peter ii. 19-25.

THIS is thanckworthy, yf a man . . . vnto the shepeherde and Bisshoppe of youre soules.

The Gospel. John x. 11-16.

CHRISTE sayed to his disciples, I am the good shepeheard, . . and there shalbe one folde, and one shepeherde.

The iii Sondaie.

The Collect.

ALMIGHTY God, whiche shewest to al men that be in errour the light of thy truth, to thentent that thei may returne into the waie of rightuousnes Graunt vnto al them that be admitted into the felowship of christes religiō, that thei may eschew those thinges that be contrarye to their profession, and folowe al such thinges as bee agreable to the same, through our Lorde Jesus Chryst.

The Epistle. 1 Peter ii. 11-17.

DEARLY beloued, I beseche you . . . Honoure the kynge.

The Gospel.   John xvi. 16-22.

JESUS sayed to his disciples ; After a litle whyle . . . and your ioye shall no man take from you.

The iiii Sonda ie.

The Collect.

ALMIGHTY God, whiche dost make the mindes of all faithful menne to be of one wil, graunt vnto thy people, that they may loue the thyng which thou commaundest, and desire that which thou dost promise, that emong the sondry, and manifolde chaunges, of the worlde, oure hartes may surely ther be fixed wheras true ioyes are to be found, through christ, &c.

The Epistle.   James i. 17-21.

EUERY good gift, and euery perfect gift, . . . whiche is able to saue youre soules.

The Gospell.   John xvi. 5-14.

JESUS sayed vnto his disciples ; Nowe I goe my waye . . . he shall take of myne, and shewe vnto you.

¶ The v Sondaie.

The Collect.

LORD, from whom all good thinges do come, graūte vs thy humble seruaūtes, that by thy holy inspiraciō we may thinke those thinges that be good, and by thy mercifull guiding, may performe the same, through oure Lorde Jesus Christe.   Amen.

The Epistle.   James i. 22-27.

SEE that ye be doers of the worde, . . . and to kepe hym selfe vnspotted of the worlde.

The Gospell.   John xvi. 23-33.

VERELY, verely, I saye vnto you, Whatsoeuer ye shall aske . . . but be of good cheere, I haue ouercome the worlde.

¶ Assencion daye.

The Collecte.

GRAUNTE we beseche the, almighty God, that lyke as we do beleue thy onelye begotten sonne our Lord to haue ascended into the heauens : so we maye also in harte and mynde thether ascende, and wyth hym contynually dwell.

The Epistle.   Acts i. 1-11.

In the former treatise (deare Theophilus) . . . euen as ye haue sene him goe into heauen.

The Gospel. Mark xvi. 14-20.

JESUS appeared vnto the eleuen as they sate at meat . . . and confirming the worde with miracles folowynge.

¶ *The Sonday after the Ascencion daye.*
The Collect.

O GOD the Kynge of glorye, whyche haste exalted thyne onely sonne Jesus Christe, wyth greate triumphe, vnto thy kyngedome in heauen, we beseche thee leue vs not comfortlesse, but sende to vs thyne holye ghost, to comfort vs, and exalt vs to the same place, whether oure Sauioure Christe is gone before, who lyueth and reigneth, &c.

The Epistle. 1 Peter iv. 7-11.

THE ende of all thinges is at hande . . . to whome be prayse and dominion for euer and euer. Amen.

The Gospell. John xv. ver. 26, 27 ; xvi. 1-4.

WHEN the comforter is come . . . ye may remembre then that I tolde you.

¶ *Whitsundaye.*
The Collecte.

GOD whiche as vpon this day, hast taught the hartes of thy faithful people, by the sendynge to thē the lyghte of thy holye spirite : graunte vs by the same spirite, to haue a righte iudgemente in all thinges, and euermore to reioyce in his holy comforte, throughe the merites of Christ Jesu oure sauiour, who lyueth and reigneth with the, in the vnitie of the same spirit, one God, world without ende. Amen.

The Epistle. Acts ii. 1-11.

WHEN the fiftie dayes were come to an end, . . . we heare them speake with our owne tongues the great workes of God.

The Gospell. John xiv. 15-27.

JESUS sayde vnto his disciples ; Yf ye loue me . . . And as the father gaue me commaundement, euen so do I.

¶ *Mondaye in Whitsonweeke.*
The Collect.

¶ God, which, hast geuen, &c. *As vpon Wytsonday.*

The Epistle. Acts x. 34-48.

PETER opened his mouth and sayde. Of a trueth . . . Then prayed they him to tary a fewe dayes.

The Gospel.   John iii. 16-21.

GOD so loued the worlde, that he gaue . . . how that they are wrought in God.

¶ *The Tuesday after Wytsondaye.*

The Collect.

GOD whiche hast geuen, &c.   As vpon Wytsonday.

The Epistle.   Acts viii. 14-17.

WHEN the Apostles whiche were at Jerusalem . . . and they receaued the holy ghoste.

The Gospell.   John x. 1-10.

VERELY, verely I say vnto you ; He that entreth not . . . and that they mighte haue it more abundauntly.

¶ *Trinite Sondaie.*

The Collect.

ALMIGHTY and euerlastynge God, which haste geuen vnto vs thy seruauntes, grace (by the confession of a true faith) to acknowledge the glory of the eternall Trinitie, and in the power of the deuyne Maiesty, to worshyppe the vnitie : we beseche thee, that through the stedfastnes of this faith, we maye euermore be defended from al aduersitie, which liuest and reignest one God, worlde without ende.   Amen.

The Epistle.   Apoc. iv.

AFTER this I looked, and behold, a dore . . . and for thy wylles sake they are, and were created.

The Gospel.   John iii. 1-15.

THERE was a manne of the Pharises, . . . perishe not, but haue euerlastyng lyfe.

¶ *The first Sonday after Trinitie Sonday.*

The Collect.

GOD, the strength of al them that trust in thee, mercyfully accept oure praiers.   And because the weakenes of our mortal nature can do no good thing wythout thee, graunt vs the helpe of thy grace, that in kepyng of thy commaundementes, we may please thee, both in wil and dede ; through Jesus Christ our Lord.

The Epistle.   1 John iv. 7-21.

DEARLY beloued, let vs loue one another : . . . that he whiche loueth God, shulde loue his brother also.

The Gospell. Luke xvi. 19-31.

THERE was a certayne riche man, . . . though one rose from death againe.

¶ *The ii Sonday.*

The Collect.

LORD make vs to haue a perpetual feare and loue of thy holy name, for thou neuer failest to help and gouerne them whom thou doest bryng vp in thy stedfast loue : graunt this, &c.

The Epistle. 1 John iii. 13-24.

MARUAYLE not my brethren though the worlde hate you. . . . euen by the spirite whiche he hath geuen vs.

The Gospel. Luke xiv. 16-24.

A CERTAINE man ordeyned a great supper, . . . shal taste of my supper.

¶ *The iii Sonday.*

The Collect.

LORD, we beseche the mercifully to heare vs, and vnto whome thou haste geuen hartye desyre to praye : graūt that by thy mighty ayde we may be defēded throughe Jesus Christe oure Lorde.

The Epistle. 1 Peter v. 5-11.

SUBMYTTE yourselues euery man one to another . . . To hym be glory and dominion for euer and euer. Amen.

The Gospell. Luke xv. 1-10.

THEN resorted vnto him all the Publicans . . . ouer one synner that repenteth.

¶ *The iiii Sondaye.*

The Collect.

GOD the Protectour of al that trust in thee, without whō nothing is stronge, nothing is holye : encrease and multiplye vpon vs thy mercy ; that thou being our ruler and guyde, we may so passe throughe thinges tēporal, that we finallye lose not the thinges eternall : Graunte this heauenly father, for Jesu Christes sake oure Lorde.

The Epistle. Rom. viii. 18-23.

I SUPPOSE that the affliccions off this lyfe, . . . euen the delyuer-aunce of our bodies.

The Gospel.   Luke vi. 36-42.

BE ye mercifull as youre father also is mercyful. . . . the mote that is in thy brothers eye.

¶ *The v Sonday.*
The Collect.

GRAUNT Lord, we beseche the, that the course of this worlde maye bee so peasebly ordered by thy gouernaūce ; that thy congregaciō may ioyfully serue the in al godly quietnes, through Jesus Christe oure Lorde.

The Epistle.   1 Peter iii., 8-15.

BE you all of one mynde and of one hearte, . . . but sanctifie the Lorde God in your hertes.

The Gospel.   Luke v. 1-11.

IT came to passe that (when the people . . . and forsoke all, and folowed him.

¶ *The vi Sondaye.*
The Collecte.

GOD which hast prepared to thē that loue the such good thinges as passe al mās vnderstādīg : powre into our hartes such loue towarde thee, that we louyng the in al thinges may obteyne thy promises whiche excede al that we can desire, through Jesus Christ our Lorde.

The Epistle.   Romans vi. 3-11.

KNOWE ye not, that all we whiche are baptysed . . . but are alyue vnto God, through Jesus Christe our Lorde.

The Gospell.   Matt. v. 20-26.

JESUS sayed vnto his disciples ; excepte youre ryghteousnesse . . . till thou haue payed the vttermoste farthyng.

¶ *The vii Sonday.*
The Collect.

LORD of al power and might, which art the auctoure and geuer of al good thīges : graffe in our hartes the loue of thy name, encrease in vs true religiō, nourishe vs with al goodnesse, and of thy great mercy kepe vs in the same, throughe Jesus Christ oure Lorde.

The Epistle.   Rom. vi. 19-23.

I SPEAKE grosly, because of the weaknes of your fleshe. . . . but eternall lyfe is the gifte of God ; through Jesus Christ our Lord.

The Gospel. Mark viii. 1-9.

IN those dayes, when there was a verye great companie, . .
And he sent them awaye.

¶ *The viii Sonday.*

The Collect.

GOD, whose prouidence is neuer deceiued, we hūblye beseche
the, that thou wilt put away frō vs al hurtfulthinges, and geue to
vs those thinges, which be profitable for vs, through Jesus Christ
our Lorde.

The Epistle. Rom. viii. 12-17.

BRETHREN, we are detters, not to the fleshe, . . . that we may
be also gloryfied together with hym.

The Gospell. Matt. vii. 15-21.

BEWARE of false Prophetes, . . . he shall entre into the kyngdome of heauen.

¶ *The ix Sonday.*

The Collect.

GRAUNT to vs Lord we beseche the, the spirit to thīke and do
alwaies suche thinges as be rightful, that we which cannot be without the, may by the be able to liue accordyng to thy wil, through
Jesus Christ oure Lorde.

The Epistle. 1 Cor. x. 1-13.

BRETHREN, I would not that ye should be ignoraūt, . . . that ye
may be hable to beare it.

The Gospel. Luke xvi. 1-9.

JESUS sayd vnto his disciples ; There was a certaine riche man,
. . . they may receaue you into euerlasting Habitacions.

The x Sondaie.

The Collect.

LET thy mercifull eares, O Lorde, be open to the prayers of thy
humble seruauntes, and that they may obtain their peticions, make
thē to aske suche thinges as shal plase thee, throughe Jesus Christe
our Lorde.

The Epistle. 1 Cor. xii. 1-11.

CONCERNYNG spirituall giftes (brethren) I would . . . deuydyng
to euery manne a seuerall gifte, euen as he will.

The Gospell.   Lake xix. 41-47.

AND when he was come nere to Hierusalem, . . . And he taught daylie in the Temple.

The xi Sondaie.

The Collect.

GOD, which declarest thy almighty power, moste chiefly in shew-yng mercie and pitie : geue vnto vs abūdauntly thy grace, that wee running to thy promises, maie be made partakers of thy heauenly treasure ; throughe Jesus Christe our Lorde.

The Epistle.   1 Cor. xv. 1-11.

BRETHREN, as perteyning to the Gospell, . . . so we preached, and so haue ye beleued.

The Gospell.   Luke xviii. 9-14.

CHRISTE told thys parable vnto certayne . . . And he that humbleth himselfe shalbe exalted.

The xii Sondaie.

The Collect.

ALMIGHTYE and euerlàstynge God, whiche arte always more ready to heare, then we to praye, and arte wont to geue more, than eyther we desyre, or deserue : Powre doune vpon vs the aboūdaunce of thy mercy, forgeuyng vs those thinges wherof our conscience is afrayed, and geuyng vnto vs that that our praier dare not presume to aske, through Jesus Christ oure Lorde.

The Epistle.   2 Cor. iii. 4-9.

SUCHE trust haue we through Christ to God-ward . . . the ministracion of righteousnes excede in glory.

The Gospell.   Mark vii. 31-37.

JESUS departed from the coastes of Tyre and Sydon, . . . and the dumme to speake.

The xiii Sondaye.

The Collect.

ALMYGHTY and merciful God, of whose onely gift it commeth that thy faythful people do vnto the true and laudable seruice : Graunte we beseche the, that we may so runne to thy heauenly promises, that we fayle not finally too attayne thesame, thorowe Jesus Christ our Lorde.

The Epistle.   Gal. iii. 16-22.

TO Abraham and his sede were the promyses made. . . . should be geuen vnto them that beleue.

The Gospell.   Luke x. 23-37.

HAPPY are the eyes whiche see the thinges that ye see. . . . Goe, and doe thou lykewyse.

The xiiii Sundaye.

The Collect.

ALMIGHTY and euerlastynge God, geue vnto vs the encrease of faythe, hope, and charitie, and that we maye obtayne that whiche thou doest promyse : Make vs to loue that, whiche thou doest commaunde, through Jesus Christ our Lord.

The Epistle.   Gal. v. 16-24.

I SAYE ; Walke in the spirite, . . . haue crucified the fleshe with the affeccions and lustes.

The Gospell.   Luke xvii. 11-19.

AND it chaunced as Jesus went to Jerusalem, . . . thy fayth hath made the whole.

The xv Sondaye.

The Collect.

KEPE, we beseche the, O Lorde, thy church with thy perpetuall mercy, and because the frailtye of man withoute the, can not but fall : Kepe vs euer by thy helpe, and leade vs to all thynges profitable to our saluation, throughe Jesus Christe oure Lorde.   Amen.

The Epistle.   Gal. vi. 11-18.

YE see howe large a letter I haue writtē vnto you . . . Brethren, the grace of our Lorde Jesu Christ be with your spirite.   Amen.

The Gospel.   Matt vi. 24-34.

NO manne can serue two Masters, . . . Sufficient vnto the daye is the trauayl thereof.

The xvi Sondaye.

The Collect.

LORDE wee beseche the, lette thy continuall pitie clense and defende thy congregacion, and, because it can not continue in saufetie without thy succour, preserue it euermore by thy helpe and goodnese, through Jesus Christe our Lorde.

The Epistle.   Ephes. iii. 13-21.

I DESIRE that you faint not because of my tribulacions . . . throughoute al generacions from tyme to tyme.   Amen.

The Gospel.   Luke vii. 11-17.

AND it fortuned, that Jesus went into a Citie called Naim, . . . and throughout all the regions which lye round about.

The xvii Sondaye.

The Collect.

LORDE we pray the, that thy grace maye alwaies preuente and folowe vs, and make vs continuallye too be geuen to all good workes, thorough Jesus Christe our Lorde.

The Epistle.   Ephes. iv. 1-6.

I (WHICH am prisoner of the Lordes) exhorte you, . . . whiche is aboue all, and through all, and in you all.

The Gospel.   Luke xiv. 1-11.

AND it chaunced that Jesus went into the house . . . and he that humbleth hymselfe, shalbe exalted.

¶ The xviii Sondaie.

The Collect.

LORDE we beseche the, graunte thy people grace to auoyde the infectyons of the deuyll, and wyth pure harte and mynde to folowe thee, the onely God, throughe Jesus Christe our Lorde.

The Epistle.   1 Cor. i. 4-8.

I THANKE my God alwaies on your behalfe, . . . in the daye of the comyng of oure Lorde Jesus Christ.

The Gospell.   Matt. xxii. 34-46.

WHEN the Phariseis had herde, that Jesus . . . aske hym any more questions.

The xix Sonday.

The Collect.

O GOD, forasmuche as without the, we are not able to please the : graute that the worckinge of thy mercie, maye in all thynges directe and rule our hertes ; throughe Jesus Christe our Lorde.

The Epistle.   Ephes. iv. 17-32.

THIS I saye, and testifie through the Lord, . . . euen as God for Christes sake hathe forgeuen you.

The Gospell. Matt. ix. 1-8.

JESUS entred into a shippe and passed ouer, . . . whiche had geuen suche power vnto men.

The xx Sondaie.

The Collect.

ALMIGHTYE and merciful God, of thy bountifull goodnes, kepe vs, frō all thinges that may hurt vs, that we being ready, bothe in bodye and soule : may with fre heartes, accomplishe those thinges, that thou woldest haue doen : through Jesus Christ our lord.

The Epistle. Ephes. v. 15-21.

TAKE hede therfore, howe ye walke circumspectlye : . . . submittyng yourselues one to another, in the feare of God.

The Gospell. Matt. xxii. 1-14.

JESUS sayde to his disciples ; The kyngdome of heauen . . . For many be called, but fewe are chosen.

¶ The xxi Sondaye.

The Collect.

GRAUNTE we beseche the merciful Lorde to thy faythful people, pardon and peace, that they may be clensed from al their synnes, and serue the with a quyet mynde, throughe Jesus Christ our Lorde.

The Epistle. Ephes. vi. 10-20.

MY brethren, be strong through the Lord, . . . that therein I maye speake frely, as I oughte to speake.

The Gospel. John iv. 46-54.

THERE was a certaine ruler, whose sonne was sicke at Capernaum. . . . when he came out of Jewry into Galilee.

¶ The xxii Sondaye.

The Collect.

LORDE we beseche the to kepe thy housholde, the churche in cōtinual godlines, that through thy protection, it may be free from all aduersities, and deuoutlie geuen to serue thee in good workes, to the glory of thy name : Through Jesus Christ our Lord. Amen.

The Epistle. Philipp. i. 3-11.

I THANKE my God with all remembraunce of you . . . vnto the glory and prayse of God.

The Gospell.   Matt. xviii. 21-35.

PETER sayde vnto Jesus ; Lorde how oft shall I forgeue my brother, . . . yf ye from your hartes forgeue not euery one his brother their trespasses.

¶ *The xxiii Sondaie.*

The Collecte.

GOD our refuge and strength, whych art the aucthour of all godlynes, be redy to heare the deuout prayers of the churche, and graũt that those thynges, whyche we aske faithfullie, we may obteine effectually.   Throughe Jesu Christ our Lorde.   Amen.

The Epistle.   Philipp. iii. 17-21.

BRETHREN, be folowers together of me, . . . is hable also to subdue al thynges vnto hym selfe.

The Gospell.   Matt. xxii. 15-22.

THEN the Pharises went out and toke counsayle, . . . they meruayled, and left hym, and wente their waye.

The xxiiii Sondaie.

The Collect.

LORDE wee beseche thee assoyle thy people from their offences, that thoroughe thy bountyfull goodnesse we may be delyuered frõ the bandes of al those sinnes which by our frailtie we haue committed : graunte this, &c.   Amen.

The Epistle.   Coloss. i. 3-12.

WE geue thankes to God, the father of our Lorde Jesus Christe, . . . which hath made vs meete of the inheritaunce of sainctes in lyght.

The Gospel.   Matt. ix. 18-31.

WHYLE Jesus spake vnto the people, beholde, there came a certaine ruler, . . . And thys noyse was abrode in all that lande.

¶ *The xxv Sondaye.*

The Collect.

STYRE vp we beseche the, O Lorde, the wylles of thy faithfull people, that they, plenteously bringyng furthe the fruicte of good workes, may of the be plenteously rewarded.   Through Jesus Christe our Lorde.   Amen.

The Epistle.   Jer. xxiii. 5-8.

BEHOLD, the tyme commeth, . . . and they shal dwel in theyr owne lande agayne.

The Gospell.   John vi. 5-14.

WHEN Jesus lift vp his eies, and sawe a great companye . . . This is of a trueth thesame Prophete that shoulde come into the worlde.

¶ If there be any mo Sondayes before Aduent Sondaie, to supply the same shalbe taken the seruice of some of those Sondayes, that were omitted betwene Thepiphany and Septuagesima.

S. Andrewes daie.
The Collect.

ALMIGHTY God whiche diddest geue suche grace vnto thy holy Apostle saincte Andrewe, that hee redily obeied the callyng of thy Sonne Jesus Christe, and folowed him without delaie, graunt vnto vs all that we beyng called by thy holie worde, may furthwith geue ouer our selves obediently to folowe thy holy commaundemētes, through thesame Jesus Christ our lord.   Amen.

The Epistle.   Rom. x. 9-21.

IF thou knowledge with thy mouthe, that Jesus is the Lord, . . . a people that beleueth not, but speaketh agaynst me.

The Gospel.   Matt. iv. 18-22.

As Jesus walked by the sea of Galilee, . . . And they immediately left the ship and their father, and folowed hym.

Sainct Thomas the Apostle.
The Collect.

ALMIGHTY euerlyuyng God, which for the more confirmacion of the fayth, diddest suffer thy holy apostle Thomas, to be doubtful in thy sonnes resurreccion, graunt vs so perfectly, and withoute all doubte to beleue in thy sonne Jesus Christe, that oure faith in thy sight neuere be reproued.   Heare vs, O Lorde, throughe thesame Jesus Christ, to whome with thee, and the holy ghoste, &c.

The Epistle.   Ephes. ii. 19-22.

NOW are ye not straungers nor foreiners, . . . an habitacion of God through the holy goste.

The Gospell.   John xx. 24-31.

THOMAS one of the twelue, which is called Didimus, . . . and that throughe beleuing ye myght haue lyfe through hys name.

¶ *The Conuersion of Sainct Paule.*
The Collect.

GOD, whyche haste taught all the worlde, through the preachinge of thy blessed Apostle sainct Paule : Graunte, we beseche

thee, that we whiche haue hys wonderfull Conuersion in remembraunce, maye folowe and fulfyll thy holy doctrine that he taughte;
Throughe Jesu Christ our Lorde.   Amen.

The Epistle.   Acts ix. 1-22.

AND Saul yet breathyng out threatnynges, . . . affirming that
thys was very Christe.

The Gospell.   Matt. xix. 27-36.

PETER aunswered and said vnto Jesus ; . . . But many that are
first shalbe last, and the last shalbe first.

¶ *The purification of saincte Marie the virgine.*

The Collecte.

ALMYGHTIE and euerlasting God, we humbly besiche thy
maiestie, that as thy onely begotten sonne, was this daye presented in the Temple, in the substaunce of our fleshe, so graunte
that we maye be presented vnto the with pure and cleare myndes ;
by Jesus Christ our Lord.

The Epistle.

¶ *The same that is appointed for the Sondaye.*

The Gospel.   Luke ii. 22-27.

WHEN the tyme of their purificacion . . . And he came by
inspiracion into the temple.

¶ *Saint Mathies daye.*

The Collect.

ALMYGHTIE god, whiche in the place of the traitoure Judas,
diddest chose thy faythfull seruaunt Mathie to be of the number
of thy twelue Apostles : graunte that thy Churche beyng alwaye
preserued from false Apostles may be ordered and guided, by
faithful and true Pastours ; through Jesus Christ our Lorde.

The Epistle.   Acts i. 15-26.

IN those dayes, Peter stode vp in the middes . . . and he was
coumpted with the eleuen Apostles.

The Gospel.   Matt. xi. 25-30.

AT that tyme Jesus aunswered, and sayde : I thanke thee, . . .
for my yoke is easie, and my burden is light.

The Annunciacion of the Virgine Marie.

The Collect.

WE besiche thee Lorde, powre thy grace into our hartes, that, as
we haue knowen Christe thy sonnes incarnacion, by the message

of an Angell : so by his crosse and passion, we maye be brought vnto the glory of his resurreccion : through thesame Christ our Lord.

The Epistle.   Isaiah vii. 10-15.

GOD spake once agayne vnto Ahaz, saying ; . . . that he maye knowe to refuse the euill, and choose the good.

The Gospel.   Luke i. 26-38.

AND in the sixth moneth the Angell Gabriell was sente . . . And the Angell departed from her.

¶ *S. Markes daie.*

The Collecte.

ALMYGHTIE God, which haste instructed thy holy Churche with the heauenly doctrine of thy Euangelist sainct Marke : geue vs grace so to be established by thy holy Gospell, that we be not like chyldren, caried awaie with euery blast of vain doctrine : Through Jesus Christ our Lorde.

The Epistle.   Ephes. iv. 7-16.

VNTO euery one of vs is geuen grace, . . . vnto the edifying of itselfe through loue.

The Gospel.   John xv. 1-11.

I AM the true Vine, and my father is an husbandman. . . . and that your ioy might be full.

¶ *S. Philip and James.*

The Collecte.

ALMIGHTYE God, whom truely to knowe is euerlasting life : graunt vs perfectly to knowe thy sōne Jesus Christ to be the waie, the truthe, and the life, as thou hast taught sainct Philippe, and other the Apostles, through Jesus Christ our Lorde.

The Epistle.   James i. 1-12.

JAMES the seruaunt of God, and of the Lorde Jesus Christe, . . . which the Lorde hath promised to them that loue hym.

The Gospel.   John xiv. 1-14.

AND Jesus sayde vnto hys disciples, Let not your hertes be troubled . . . If ye shall aske any thyng in my name, I will doe it.

St Barnabie Apostle.

The Collect.

LORDE almightie, whiche hast endued thy holy Apostle Barnabas, with synguler gyftes of thy holye Ghoste : let vs not be desti-

tute of thy manifolde gyftes, nor yet of grace to vse them alwaye
to thy honor and glory, through Jesus Christ our Lorde.

The Epistle.   Acts xi. 22-30.

TYDINGES of these thinges came vnto the eares of the congregacion . . . and sent it to the elders by the handes of Barnabas and
Saul.

The Gospel.   John xv. 12-16.

THIS is my commaundemente, that ye loue together, . . . of the
father in my name, he may geue it you.

¶ *S. Jhon Baptist.*

The Collect.

ALMIGHTIE god, by whose prouidence thy seruaunte Jhon
Baptist, was wonderfully borne, and sente to prepare the waye of
thy sonne our sauiour, by preachynge of penaunce : make vs so to
folowe hys doctrine, and holy lyfe, that we maie truly repent,
accordyng to his preachyng, and after his example, constantlye to
speake the truthe, boldly rebuke vice, and paciently suffer for the
truthes sake : through Jesus Christ our Lorde.

The Epistle.   Esai. xi. 1-11.

BE of good chere my people, O ye Prophetes, . . . and shall
kyndely entreat those that beare yong.

The Gospel.   Luke i. 57-80.

ELIZABETHES tyme came that she should be deliuered, . . . when
he shoulde shewe himselfe vnto the Israelites.

¶ *Sainct Peters daye.*

The Collecte.

ALMIGHTIE God, which by thy sonne Jesus Christ, haste geuen
to thy Apostle S. Peter many excellente gyftes, and commaundeste
him earnestly to fede thy flocke. Make we beseche thee, all
Byshoppes and Pastours diligently to preache thy holy worde, and
the people obediently to folowe thesame, that they may receyue
the Crowne of euerlasting glory, throughe Jesus Christ our Lorde.

The Epistle.   Acts xii. 1-11.

AT the same tyme Herode the kynge stretched furthe his handes
. . . and from all the waityng for of the people of the Jewes.

The Gospell.   Matt. xvi. 13-19.

WHEN Jesus came into the coastes of the citie . . . and whatsoeuer thou losest in earth, shalbe losed in heauen.

¶ *Saincte James the Apostle.*

The Collect.

GRAUNTE, O merciful God, that as thy holy Apostle sainct James, leauynge his father, and al that he had, without delay, was obedient vnto the calling of thy sonne Jesus Christe, and folowed him : so we, forsakyng al worldly and carnal affeccions, may euermore be ready to folowe thy commaundemētes, throughe Jesu Christ oure Lorde. Amen.

The Epistle. Acts xi. 27-30; xii. 1-3.

IN those dayes came prophetes frō the citie of Jerusalem vnto Antioche. . . . he proceded further and toke Peter also.

The Gospel. Matt. xx. 20-28.

THEN came to him the mother of Zebedes children, . . . to geue his life a redempcion for many.

S. *Bartholomewe.*

The Collect.

O ALMIGHTY and euerlasting God ; whiche haste geuen grace to thine Apostle Bartholomew, truely to beleue, and to preache thy woorde : Graūt, wee beseche the, vnto thy church, both to loue that he beleued, and to preache that he taughte, throughe Christe oure Lorde.

The Epistle. Acts v. 12-16.

BY the handes of the Apostles were many signes . . . and they were healed euery one.

The Gospell. Luke xxii. 24-30.

AND there was a strife among them, . . . and sytte on seates iudging the twelue tribes of Israel.

¶ *Saincte Mathewe.*

The Collect.

ALMIGHTY God whiche by thy blessed sonne dyddest call Mathewe from the receipte of Custome to be an Apostle, and Euangelist : Graunt vs grace to forsake all couetous desyres, and inordinate loue of ryches, and to folowe thy sayde sonne Jesus Christe, who liueth and reigneth, &c.

The Epistle. 2 Cor. iv. 1-6.

SEYNG that we haue suche an office, . . . knowlege of the glory of God, in the face of Jesus Christe.

The Gospell. Matt. ix. 9-13.

AND as Jesus passed forth frō thence, . . . for I am not come to cal the righteous, but synners to repentaunce.

¶ *S. Michael and all Aungelles.*

The Collecte.

EUERLASTYNGE God, whiche haste ordeined, and constituted the seruices of all Aungelles, and men, in a wondreful order : mercifully graunte that they whiche alway do the seruice in heauen, may by thy appoinctmente succour and defende vs in earth, through Jesus Christe oure Lorde, &c.

The Epistle. Apoc. xii. 7-12.

THERE was a great battayl in heauen : . . . because he knoweth that he hath but a short tyme.

The Gospell. Matt. xviii. 1-10.

AT the same tyme came the disciples vnto Jesus, . . . beholde the face of my father, whiche is in heauen.

Sainct Luke the Euangelist.

The Collect.

ALMIGHTIE God, which calledst Luke the phisicion, (whose praise is in the Gospel) to be a Physicion of the soule, it maye please the by the wholesome medicines of his doctrine, to heale all the diseases of our soules, through thy sonne Jesu Christ our Lorde.

The Epistle. 2 Tim. iv. 5-15.

WATCHE thou in all thinges, . . . For he hath greatly withstande our wordes.

The Gospel. Luke x. 1-7.

THE Lorde appointed other seuenty . . . For the labourer is worthy of his reward.

¶ *Simon and Jude Apostles.*

The Collecte.

ALMIGHTY God, which haste builded thy congregacion vpon the foundaciō of the Apostles, and Prophetes, Jesu Christ him selfe being the head corner-stone : graunt vs so to be ioyned together in vnitie of spirite by their doctrine, that we may be made an holye tēple acceptable to the, through Jesu Christe our Lorde. Amen.

The Epistle.   Jude i. 1-8.

JUDAS, the seruaunte of Jesus Christe, . . . and speake euell of them that are in auctoritie.

The Gospel.   John xv. 12-27.

THIS commaunde I you, that ye loue together. . . . because ye haue bene with me from the begynnynge.

¶ *All Sainctes.*

The Collect.

ALMIGHTY God, which hast knit together thy elect in one communion and felowship, in the misticall body of thy son Christ our Lord : graunt vs grace so to folowe thy holy sainctes in all vertues and Godly liuing, that we may come to those inspeakeable ioyes whiche thou haste prepared for them that vnfainedly loue the, through Jesus Christ oure Lorde.   Amen.

The Epistle.   Apoc. vii. 2-12.

BEHOLDE, I John sawe another Angell ascende . . . and might, be vnto our God for euermore.   Amen.

The Gospell.   Matt. v. 1-12.

JESUS seeing the people, went vp into the mountaine : . . . For so persecuted they the Prophetes whiche were before you.

THE ORDRE

FOR THE

ADMINISTRACION OF THE LORDES SUPPER,

OR

HOLY COMMUNION.

So many as entend to be partakers of the holy Cōmunion, shall signifie their names to the Curate ouer night ; or els in the mornyng, afore the beginning of morning prayer or immediately after.

And if any of those be an opē and notorious euil liuer, so that ye congregaciō by him is offended, or haue done any wrong to hys neighbours by word or dede : ye Curate hauyng knowledge therof, shal cal hym, and aduertyse hym, in any wise not to presume to the Lordes table, vntil he haue opēly declared him self to haue truely repented, and amended his former naughty lyfe, that the Cōgregacion may therby be satisfyed, which afore were offēded, and that he haue recōpensed the parties, whō he hath done wrong vnto, or at the least declare him selfe to be in full purpose so to doe, as sone as he cōueniently may.

Thesame order shall the Curate vse with those, betwixt whome he perceyueth malice and hatred to raigne, not suffering them to be partakers of the Lordes table, vntyll he know them to be reconciled. And if one of the parties so at variance, be content to forgeue from the bottome of hys hart, all that the other hath trespassed agaynste him, and to make amends for that he hym self hath offended : and the other partye wyll not be perswaded to a godly vnitye, but remain stil in his frowardnes and malice : The Minister in that case, ought to admit the penitent person to the holy Communyon, and not hym that is obstinate.

The table, hauyng at the Communion tyme a fayre whyte linnen cloth vpon it, shall stand in the body of the churche, or in the chauncell where mornyng prayer and euenyng prayour be appointed to be sayd. And the priest, standyng at the Northe syde of the table, shal say the Lordes prayour wyth this collecte followyng.

ALMIGHTY God, vnto whom al hartes be open, al desires knowe, and from whom no secretes are hyd : clēse the thoughtes of our hartes by the inspiracion of thy holy spirite, that we may perfectly loue the, and worthily magnify thy holy name, through Christe our Lorde. Amen.

Then shal the Priest rehearse distinctly al the .x. Commaundementes, and
the people knelyng, shal after euery Commaundemēte aske Goddes mercye
for theyr transgressyon of the same, after thys sorte.

Minister. God spake these wordes, and saide, I am the Lord
thy God, Thou shalt haue none other Goddes but me.

People. Lorde haue mercye vpon vs, and encline our hartes to
kepe this lawe.

Minister. Thou shalt not make to thy self any grauen ymage,
nor the likenes of any thyng that is in heauen aboue, or in the
earth beneth, or in the water vnder the earth. Thou shalt not
bow doune to them, nor worshyppe thē, for I the Lord thy
God am a gelous God, and visite the synne of the fathers vppon
the children, vnto the thyrde and iiii. generacyon of them that hate
me, and shew mercie vnto thousandes in theim that loue me, and
keepe my commaundementes.

People. Lorde haue mercye vpon vs, and encline our hartes to
kepe this lawe.

Minister. Thou shalt not take the name of the Lorde thy God
in vaine, for the Lorde wil not holde hym giltlesse that taketh his
name in vaine.

People. Lorde haue mercie vpon vs, and encline our, &c.

Minister. Remembre that thou kepe holy the Sabboth daie : .vi.
dayes shalt thou laboure, and doe all that thou haste to do, but
the .vii. day is the Sabboth of the lorde thy god. In it thou shalt
do no maner of worke, thou ād thy sonne and thy daughter, thy
man seruaunt, and thy mayd seruaunt, thy Catel, and the straunger
that is within thy gates : For in .vi. daies the Lord made heauen
and earth, the Sea and all that in them is, and reasted the seuenth
daye, Wherefore the Lorde blessed the seuenth daye and halowed
it.

People. Lorde haue mercy vpon vs, and encline our. &c.

Minister. Honour thy father and thy mother, that thy daies
may be long in the lāde which the Lord thy God geueth the.

People. Lorde haue mercy vpon vs, and encline. &c.

The Minister. Thou shalt not do murther.

People. Lorde haue mercy vpon vs, and encline. &c.

Minister. Thou shalt not committe adultery :

People. Lorde haue mercy vpon vs, and encline. &c.

Minister. Thou shalt not steale.

People. Lorde haue mercy vpon vs, &c.

Minister. Thou shalte not beare false wytnesse agaynste thy
neyghboure.

People. Lorde haue mercy vpon vs, and encline our hartes to
kepe this lawe.

Minister. Thou shalt not couet thy neighbours house, Thou
shalt not couet thy neighbours wife, nor his seruaunt, nor his
maide, nor his oxe, nor his asse, nor any thing that is his.

People. Lord haue mercy vpon vs, and write al these thy lawes in our hartes we beseche the.

¶ *Then shall folowe the Collect of the day with one of these two Collectes folowyng for the Quene, the Priest standyng vp and saying.*

Let vs praye   Priest.

ALMIGHTY God, whose kyngdom is euerlasting, and power infinite, haue mercy vpō the whole congregacion, and so rule the heart of thy chosē seruant Elizabeth our Quene and gouernoure that she (knowing whose minister she is) may aboue all thinges, seke thy honoure and glorye : and that we her subiectes, (duly considering whose aucthority she hath) may faithfully serue, honour, and humblye obey her in the and for the, according to thy blessed worde, and ordinance, Through Jesus Christ our Lord, who with the and the holye ghost, lyueth and reygneth euer one God, worlde without ende.   Amen.

ALMIGHTY and euerlastinge God, we be taughte by thy holy word, that the hartes of Princes are in thy rule and gouernaūce, and that thou doest dispose, and turne them as it semeth best to thy Godly wysedome : we humbly beseche thee, so to dispose and gouerne the harte of Elizabeth, thy seruaunte, our Quene and gouernour, that in all her thoughtes, wordes, and workes she may euer seke thy honoure and glorye, and studye to preserue thy people committed to her charge, in welth, peace and godlynes. Graunt this O merciful father, for thy deare sonnes sake Jesus Christ our Lorde.   Amen.

Immediately after the Collectes, the Priest shall reade the Epystle beginning thus.

The Epystle written in the.   Chapter of.

And the Epystle ended, he shal say the Gospel, beginninge thus.

The Gospell wrytten in the.   Chapter of.

And the Epistle and Gospel being ended, shalbe said the Crede.

I BELEUE in one God, the father almighty maker of heauen and earthe, and of all thynges visible and inuisible : And in one Lorde Jesu Christe, the onely begotten sonne of GOD, begotten of his father before al worldes, god of God, lyghte of lyghte, verye God of verye God, gotten, not made, beynge of one substance wyth the father, by whome all thinges were made, who for vs men, and for our salvacion came doune from heauen, and was incarnate by the holy Ghoste, of the Virgine Mary, and was made man, and was crucified also for vs, vnder poncius Pilate.   He suffered and was buried, and the thyrde day he rose againe accordinge to the Scriptures, and ascended into heauen, and sitteth at the right hāde of the father. And he shal come againe with glory, to judge both the quicke and the deade, whose Kyngdome shall haue none ende. And I beleue in the holye Ghoste, The Lorde and geuer of life, who procedeth from the father and the sonne, who with the father and the sonne together is worshipped and glorified, who spake by the Prophetes. And I beleue one catholicke and Apostolicke Churche. I acknowledge one Baptisme, for the remission of synnes. And I loke for the resurreccion of the dead : and the lyfe of the worlde to come. Amen.

After tho Crede yf there be no sermon, shall folowe one of the Homelies alredy set furth, or hereafter to be set furth by commune aucthoritie.

After suche Sermon, homely, or exhortacion, the Curate shall declare vnto the people, whether there be anye holy dayes or fastynge dayes the weke folowyng, and earnestly exhorte theim to remembre the poore, saying one, or moe of these sentences following, as he thinketh most conuenient by his discretion.

LET your light so shyne before men, that they maye see your good workes, and glorifye youre father whyche is in heauen. Math. v.

Laye not vp youreselues treasure vpon the earthe, where the ruste and mothe doeth corrupte, and where theeues breake through and steale : But lay vp for youreselues treasures in heauen, where neyther rust, nor motthe doeth corrupt, and where theeues do not breake thorowe and steale. Math. vi.

Whatsoeuer you woulde that menne shoulde do vnto you, euen so doe vnto them, for this is the lawe and the Prophetes. Math. vii.

Not euery one that sayeth vnto me Lord, Lord, shall entre into the Kingdome of heauen ; but he that doeth ye wyl of my father whiche is in heauen. Math. vii.

Zache stode furth, and sayde vnto the Lord, beholde Lord, the halfe of my goodes I gyue to the poore, and yf I haue done any wronge to any man, I restore foure folde. Luk. xix.

Who goeth a warefare at any tyme of his owne coste ? Who planteth a vyneyarde, and eateth not of the fruicte thereof ? Or who feedeth a flocke, and eateth not of the mylke of the flocke ? i. Cor. ix.

If we haue sowen vnto you spiritual thinges, is it a great matter, yf we shal reape your worldly thinges ? i. Cor. ix.

Do ye not knowe, that they whiche minister aboute holy thinges, lyue of the sacrifyce ? whyche wayte of the aultare, are partakers with the aultare. Euen so hath the Lorde also ordeyned : that they whiche preache the Gospell, shoulde lyue of the gospel. i. Cor. ix.

He which soweth lytle shal reape lytle ; and he that soweth plenteously, shal reape plenteously. Let euery man doe accordynge as he is dysposed in his harte, not grudgynglye or of necessitie : for God loueth a cherefull gyuer. ii. Cor. ix.

Let hym that is taughte in the woorde, minister vnto him that teacheth, in all good thinges. Be not deceiued, God is not mocked : for whatsoeuer a man soweth, that shall he reape. Gala. vi.

Gala vi.   Whyle we haue tyme, let vs do good vnto al men, and specially vnto them, whiche are of the householde of faythe.

i. Tim. vi.   Godlynes is great ryches, yf a man be contente with that he hath : for we brought nothynge into the worlde, neyther may we cary any thing out.

i. Tim. vi.   Charge them whyche are ryche in thys worlde, that they be ready to giue, and glade to distribute, laying vp in store for them selues a good foundacion, against the time to come, that they may attayne eternal lyfe.

Hebr. vi.   God is not vnrighteous, that he wil forget your workes and laboure that procedeth of loue, whiche loue ye haue shewed for his names sake, whiche haue ministered vnto sainctes, and yet do minister.

Heb. xiii.   To do good, and to distribute, forget not, for with such sacrifices God is pleased.

i. Iohn iii.   Whoso hath thys worldes good, and seeth his brother haue nede and shutteth vp his cōpassyon from hym, how dwelleth the loue of God in hym ?

Tob. iiii.   Geue almose of thy goodes, and turne neuer thy face from any poore man, and then the face of the Lorde shall not be turned away from the.

Tob. iiii.   Be mercifull after thy power. If thou hast muche gyue plenteously, if thou hast litle, doe thy diligence gladly to geue of that litle, for so gatherest thou thy selfe a good rewarde in the day of necessitye.

Pro. xix.   He that hath pitye vpon the poore, lendeth vnto the Lorde : and looke what he layeth out : it shalbe paied him agayne.

Psal. lxi.   Blessed be the man that prouydeth for the sycke, and nedy, the Lorde shall deliuer him, in the time of trouble.

Then shal the Churchewardens, or some other by them appoyncted, gather the deuocion of the people, and put the same into the poore mens boxe, and vpon the offeryng[1] daies appoincted, euery man and woman shal pay to the Curate the due and accustomed offerings, after whiche done, the Priest shal saie.

Let vs pray for the whole estate of Christes Churche militant here in earth.

If ther be no almes geuē vnto the poore, then shall the words of accepting our almes bee lefte out vnsayd.   ALMIGHTYE and euerliuing God, whych by thy holye Apostle hast taughte vs to make prayers and supplicacyons, and to geue thanckes for all men : We humbly besche thee moste mercifully (to accepte our almose) and to receyue these our prayers whyche we offer vnto thy diuine maiestie, beseechyng the to inspire continually, the vniuersal Churche wyth the spiryte of truthe, vnitye, and concorde : And graunt that all they that do confesse thy holy

[1 These had originally been Christmas, Easter, Whitsuntide, and the feast of the dedication of the parish church : but in 1536 Henry VIII. commanded the feast of the nativity of Saint John the Baptist, and that of Saint Michael, to be substituted for the last two.]

name, may agree in the truthe of thy holy woorde, and lyue in vnytye and godlye loue. We beseche thee also to saue and defend alle Christyane Kynges, Prynces, and Gouernours, and specially thy seruaunt, Elyzabeth our Quene that vnder her we may be godly and quietly gouerned: and graunt vnto her whole Counsaill, and to all that be put in aucthoritye vnder her, that they may truely and indifferently minister iustice, to the punishement of wyckednes and vice, and to the maintenaunce of goddes true religion and vertue. Giue grace (O heauenly Father) to al Bishopes, Pastours and Curates, that they may bothe by theyr life and doctrine set furth thy true and liuely worde and rightely and duely administer thy holy Sacramentes: and to all thy people gyue thy heauenlye grace, and especially to thys congregacion heare present, that with meke harte and due reuerence, they may heare ād receiue thy holy worde, truely seruyng the in holines and ryghtuousnes all the dayes of theyr lyfe. And we moost humbly beseche the of thy goodnes (O Lord) to comfort and succoure all theym whyche in thys transi-tory lyfe bee in trouble, Sorowe, nede, sicknes, or any other aduersity. Graunt this, O father, for Jesus Christes sake our onely Mediatour and aduocate. Amen.

Then shal folowe this exhortacion, at certayne tymes when the Curate shal see the people negligent to come to the holy Communyon.

WE be come together at thys tyme, derely beloued brethren to fede at the Lordes supper, vnto the whyche in Goddes behalf I bydde you all that be heare present, and beseche you for the lorde Jesus Christes sake, that ye wyll not refuse to come thereto, beyng so louingly called, and bidden of God him selfe. Ye know howe greuous and vnkynde a thing it is, when a manne hath prepared a riche feaste: decked his table with al kynde of prouisyō, so that there lacketh nothinge but the gestes to sitte downe: and yet they whych be called wythout anye cause, mooste vnthankfully refuse to come. Whyche of you in suche a case woulde not be moued? Who woulde not thyncke a greate iniurie and wrong done vnto hym? Wherefore moste derely beloued in Christe take ye good heade, lest ye, wythdrawyng your selues frō this holy supper, and prouoke Goddes indignation against you, it is an easy matter for a man to say, I will not communicate, because I am otherwise letted with worldly busynes, but suche excuses be not so easily accepted and allowed before god. If any man say, I am a greuous sinner, and therefore am afrayed to come. Wherefore thē do ye not re-pēt and amēde? Whē god calleth you, be you not ashamed to say ye wil not come? when you should returne to god, wil you ex-cuse your self and say that you be not redy? Cōsidre ernestly with your selues howe litle such feined excuses shall auaile before God. They that refused the feaste in the Gospell, because they had bought a farme, or would trie their yokes of oxen, or because they were maried, were not so excused, but cōpted vnworthy of the

D

heuēly feast. I for my part am here present and according to myne office, I bid you in the name of god, I cal you in Christes behalf, I exhort you, as you loue your owne Saluation, that ye wil be partakers of this holy Communion.   And as the sonne of God, did vouchesafe to yelde vp his soule by death vpō the crosse for your healthe, euen so it is youre duety to receyue the Cōmunion together in the remembraunce of his death as he hymselfe commaunded.   Nowe, yf ye wyll in no wise thus do, consider with your selues, how great iniury ye doe vnto God, and howe sore punishment hangeth ouer your heades for thesame.   And whereas ye offende God so sore in refusing this holy banquet, I admonishe, exhorte, and beseche you, that vnto this vnkyndenes ye wyll not adde any more.   Whiche thing ye shall doe yf ye stand by as gasers and lokers of them that do Communicate, and be no partakers of the same your selues.   For what thing can this be accompted els, thē a further contempt and vnkindenes vnto God ?   Truly it is a greate vnthankefulnes to saye naye when ye be called, but the faulte is muche greater, when men stande by, and yet wyll neyther eate, nor drincke this holye Communion with other.   I praie you what can this be ells but euen to haue the misteries of Christ in derision : it is sayde vnto al : Take ye and eate, take and drincke ye al of this, do this in remēbraunce of me.   With what face then, or with what countenaūce shal ye here these wordes ?   what wyl this be els, but a neglecting, a despisyng, and mockynge of the Testament of Christ ?   wherfore rather thē you shold so do, departe you hence, and geue place to them that be Godly dysposed.   But when you departe, I beseche you pondre with yourselves, from whome ye departe : ye departe from the Lordes Table : ye depart from your brethren, and from the banket of most heauēly foode.   These thynges (yf ye earnestly consydre) ye shall by Goddes grace, returne to a better mynde, for the obteining wherof, we shall make our humble peticions while we shal receiue the holy Communion.

And some tyme shalbe said this also, at the discretion of the Curat.

DERELY beloued, for asmuche as our dutye is to rendre to almighty God our heauenly father most harty thanckes for that he hathe geuen his sonne our Sauiour Jesus Christ not onely to die for vs, but also to be oure Spirituall fode, and sustenaunce, as it is declared vnto vs, aswel by Goddes worde, as by the holy sacramētes of his blessed body and bloud, the which being so comfortable a thing to them whiche receiue it worthelye and so daungerous to them, that wil presume to receyue it, vnworthely.   My duty is to exhorte you to considre the dignitie of the holy mistery, and the great peril of the vnworthy receiuīg therof, and so to searche and examine youre owne consciēces, as you shold come holy and cleane to a moste godly and heuenly feast, so that in no w se you come but in the mariage garment, required of God in holy scripture, and so come and be receyued as worthye partakers of suche a heauenly Table, the waye and meanes therto is.

First to examine your liues and conuersation by the rule of Goddes commaundementes and wherinsoeuer ye shall perceyue your selues to haue offended eyther by wil, worde, or deede, there bewayle your owne synfull liues, confesse your selues to almighty God, with ful purpose of amendement of life. And yf ye shal perceiue your offences to be such, as be not only against God, but also against your neighbours. Then ye shal reconcyle youre selues vnto them, ready to make restituciō and satisfactiō according to the vttermost of your powers for all iniuries and wrōges done by you to any other, and likewise being ready to forgeue other that haue offended you as you would haue forgeuenes of your offēces at Goddes hande. For otherwyse the receiuing of the holy Cōmunion doth nothing els, but encrease your dampnation.

And because it is requisite that no manne shoulde come to the holye Communion, but with a ful trust in goddes mercy, and with a quiet conscience : therfore yf there be any of you, which by the meanes aforesaid cānot quiet his owne conscience, but requireth further comforte or counsail, then let him come to me, or some other discrete and learned minister of gods word, and open his griefe, that he may receiue suche ghostly counseil, aduise, and comfort, as his conscience may be releued, and that by the minis-tery of Gods word, he may receyue comfort, and the benefyte of absolution, to the quieting of his conscience, and aduoiding of all scruple and doubtfulnes.

¶ *Then shall the Priest say this exhortation.*

DERELY beloued in the Lorde : Ye that mynde to come to the holye Communion of the bodye and bloude of oure sauioure Christe, must consyder what saincte Paule writeth vnto the Cōr-inthiens, howe he exhorteth all persones diligentlye to trye and examyne them selues, before they presume to eate of that breade, and drincke of that cuppe. For as the benefyte is greate, yf wyth a trulye penitente herte and lyuely faith we receiue that holy sacra-ment (for then we spiritually eate the fleshe of Christ, and drincke his bloude, then we dwell in Christe and Christe in vs, we be one wyth Christ, and Christe with vs) so is the daunger great, if we receyue the same vnworthely. For then we be gilty of the body and bloud of Christ our sauiour. We eate and drincke our owne dampnation, not cōsidering the lordes bodye. we kindle Gods wrath against vs, we prouoke him to plague vs with diuers diseases, and sundrye kyndes of death. Therfore if any of you be a blas-phemer of god, an hinderer or slaunderer of his worde, an adul-terer, or be in malyce or enuye, or in anye other greuous crime, bewaile your Sinnes, and come not to this holy table, lest after the taking of that holy sacrament, the deuil enter into you, as he entred into Judas, and fil you full of al iniquities, and bring you to destruction both of bodye and soule. Judge therefore your selues (brethren) that ye be not iudged of the Lord. Repēt you truly for your sinnes past, haue a liuely and stedfast faithe in Christ our sauiour. Amende your liues, and be in perfect charitie wyth all men, so shal ye be mete partakers of those holy misteries. And aboue al thinges ye must geue most humble and herty thankes to God the father, the sone, and the holye ghost, for the redemption of the world by the deathe and passion of our sauiour Christ, bothe God and man, who did humble him selfe, euen to the deathe, upon the crosse, for vs miserable sinners which lay in darckenes, and shadowe of death, that he mighte make vs the children of God, and exalte vs to euerlasting life.   And to thende that we should alwaie remembre the exceadinge greate loue of our master and onelie sauiour Jesu Christ, thus diyng for vs, and the innumerable benefites (which by his precious bloudsheading) he hath obteined to vs, he hath instituted and ordeined holy misteries, as pledges of his loue, and continuall remembraunce of his death, to our great and endles comfort. To him therfore with the father and the holye Ghost, let vs geue (as we are moste bounden) continuall thankes, submitting our selues wholy to his holie will and pleasure, and studiyng to serue him in true holines and righteousnes, al the daies of our life. Amen.

Then shall the Priest saye to them that come to receyue the holy Communion.

YOU that do truly and ernestly repente you of youre sinnes, and be in loue, and charite with your neighbors and entende to lede a newe lyfe, folowing the commaundementes of God, and walkynge from hence furthe in his holy waies : Draw nere and take this holy Sacrament to your comforte make your humble confession to almighty God, before this congregation here gathered together in his holye name, mekely knelynge vpon your knees.

¶ *Then shall this generall confession be made, in the name of all those, that are mynded to receyue this holy Communiõ, either by one of thē, or els by one of the ministers, or by the priest him selfe, all kneling humbly vpon their knees.*

ALMIGHTY God, father of oure Lorde Jesus Christe, maker of all thynges, Judge of all menne, we acknowledge and bewayle oure manifolde synnes and wyckednesse, whiche we from tyme to tyme moste greuously haue committed, by thoughte woorde and deede, against thy diuine Maiestie, prouokynge mooste iustlye thy wrathe and indignation againste vs : we do earnestly repente, and bee hartely sorye for these oure misdoinges, the remembraunce of them is greuous vnto vs : the burthen of theim is intollerable : haue mercy vpon vs, haue mercye vpon vs, mooste mercyfull father, for thy sonne oure Lorde Jesus Christes sake, forgeue vs all that is paste, and graunte that we may euer hereafter serue and please the, in newenes of lyfe, to the honour and glorye of thy name throughe Jesus Christ our Lorde. Amen.

¶ *Then shall the priest or the Bishop (beyng present) stande vp, and turning himself to the people shall say thus.*

ALMIGHTYE God, oure heauenly father, who of his great mercy hathe promised forgeuenes of sinnes, to al them, whiche with hartye repentaunce and true faithe turne to hym : haue mercye vpon you, pardon and deliuer you from all your sinnes, confirme and strengthen you in all goodnes, and bring you to euerlastyng lyfe ; through Jesus Christ our Lorde. Amen.

Then shall the Priest also saye.

Here what comfortable wordes our sauiour Christ saithe to all them that truly turne to him.

¶ COME vnto me all that trauaile and be heauy laden, and I shal refreshe you. So God loued the world that he gaue his onely begotten sonne, to thende that al that beleue in him, should not perishe but haue life euerlastyng.

Heare also what S. Paule saithe.

¶ This is a true saieng, and worthy of all men to be receyued, that Jesus Christ came into the worlde to saue synners.

Heare also what S. John saieth.

¶ If any manne sinne, we haue an aduocate with the father, Jesus Christ the righteous, and he is the propiciation for our sinnes.

¶ *After the whiche the priest shall procede saying.*

Lift vp your hartes.

Aunswere. We lyfte them vp vnto the Lorde.

Priest. Let vs geue thanckes vnto our Lorde God.

Aunswere. It is mete and right so to do.

¶ *Priest.* It is very mete, right, and our bounden duety that we should at al times, and in all places, geue thanckes to the, O Lord holy father, almighty euerlasting God.

Here shall folow the proper prefaces, according to the tyme, yf there be any specially appointed, or els immediatly shal folow :

Therfore with aungelles &c.

¶ PROPER PREFACES.

Upon Christmas day and seuen dayes after.

BECAUSE thou dyddest geue Jesus Christ, thyne onely Sonne, to be borne as this daye for vs, who by the operation of the holy ghoste was made very man of the substaunce of the virgin Mary his mother, and that without spot of synne, to make vs clene from al sinne. Therefore with aungels &c.

Upon Easter daye, and vii dayes after.

BUT chiefly are we boūde to praise the for the glorious resurrectiō of thy sonne Jesus Christ our lord, for he is the very paschal
lambe, whiche was offred for vs, and hath takē awaye the sinne of
the world, who by his death hath destroyed death, and by his
rising to life againe, hath restored to vs euerlasting life. Therefore with aungels

Upon the Ascencion day, and vii dayes after.

THROUGH thy most deare beloued sōne, Jesus Christ our Lorde,
who after his moste glorious resurrection, manifestly appered to al
his Apostles, and in their sight ascended vp into heauē, to prepare
a place for vs, that where he is, thether might we also ascende,
and reigne with him in glory. Therfore with aungels &c.

Upon Wytsonday, and vi daies after.

THROUGH Jesu Christ our Lord, according to whose mooste
true promyse, the holye ghoste came downe this daye from heauen,
with a soddine great sounde, as it had bene a mighty wynde,
in the lykenes of fiery tonges lyghtinge vpon the Apostles, to
teache them, and to leade them to all truth, geuing them bothe
the gyfte of diuers languages, and also boldnes with feruent zeale,
constantly to preache the gospel vnto all nacions, whereby we are
broughte out of darcknes and errour into the cleare light and true
knowledge of the, and of thy sonne Jesus Christ. Therefore with
Aungels &c.

Upon the feaste of Trinitie onely.

IT is very mete right, and our boundē dutie, that we should at
all times, and in all places, geue thankes to the, O Lorde, almightie and euerlastinge God, which art one god, one lord, not one
only person, but thre persōs in one substaūce, for that whiche we
beleue of the glorye of the father, the same we beleue of the sonne,
and of the holy ghost, without any difference or inequalitie.
Therefore &c.

¶ *After which preface, shall folow immediatly.*

THERFORE with Aungelles and Archangelles, and wyth all the
company of heauen, we laude and magnify thy glorious name,
euermore praising thee, and saying : Holy, holy, holy, lord god of
hostes, heuē and earth are ful of thy glory, glory be to the, O
Lord most hyghe.

¶ *Then shall the priest knelynge downe at Gods borde, say in the name of
all them that shall receyue the communion, this prayer folowing.*

WE do not presume to come to this thy table (O merciful Lorde)
trustinge in oure owne rightuousnesse, but in thy manifolde and
great mercies, we be not worthy so muche as to gather vp the

crōmes vnder thy Table, but thou arte the same Lord, whose property is alwaies to haue mercy. Graūt vs therefore gracious Lorde, so to eate the fleshe of thy deare sonne Jesus Christ, and to drinke his bloude, that oure synful bodies may be made cleane by his body, and our soules washed through his most precious bloud, and that we may euermore dwell in him, and he in vs.

Then the priest standing vp, shal say as foloweth :

ALMIGHTY God our heauenly father whiche of thy tender mercye, diddest giue thine onely Sonne Jesus Christ, to suffer death vpon the Crosse for our redēption, who made ther (by his one oblation of himself once offered) a ful, perfect and sufficient sacrifice, oblation, and satisfaction for the synnes of the whole worlde, and didde institute, and in his holy gospel commaunde vs to continue a perpetual memory of that his precious deathe, vntyll his comminge againe : Heare vs O merciful father, we besech the, and graunt that we receiuyng these thy creatures of breade and wine, accordinge to thy sonne our sauiour Jesu Christes holy institution, in remembraūce of his death and passion, may be partakers of his moste blessed body and bloude, who in the same night that he was betraied, toke bread, and when he had geuen thankes, he brake it, and gaue it to his disciples, saying : Take, eate, this is my bodie, which is geuen for you. Doe this in remembraunce of me. Likewise after supper he toke the cuppe, and when he had geuen thankes, he gaue it to them, saying : Drinke ye all of this, for this is my bloude of the new Testament, whiche is shedde for you and for many, for remission of sinnes : doe this as oft as ye shall drinke it in remembraunce of me.

¶ *Then shall the minister fyrste receyue the Communion in bothe kyndes him selfe, and next deliuer it to other Ministers (yf any be there present, that they may helpe the chief minister) and after to the people in their handes·knelīg. And when he deliuereth the breade, he shall saye.*

THE bodie of our lord Jesu Christ, which was geuen for the, preserue thy body and soule into euerlastinge life : and take and eate this in remembraunce that Christ died for thee, feede on him in thine heart by faith, with thankesgeuynge.

And the minister that deliuereth the cuppe shall saye.

THE bloude of our lorde Jesu Christ, which was shedd for the, preserue thy body and soule into euerlasting life: and drinke this in remembraunce that Christes bloude was shedde for thee, and be thankeful.

Then shall the priest say the Lordes prayer, the people repetynge after him euery peticion.

¶ *After shalbe sayde as foloweth.*

O LORDE and heauenly father, we thy hūble seruaunts, entierly desire thy fatherly goodnes mercifully to accept this our Sacrifice of praise and thankesgeuing moste humblye besechynge thee to graunte, that by the merites and death of thy sonne Jesus Christ, and throughe faith in his bloude, we (and all thy whole church,) may obteine remissiō of our sinnes, and al other benefites of his passion. And here we offer and presente vnto the, O Lord, our selues, our soules, and bodies, to be a reasonable, holy, and liuely sacrifice vnto the, humblye beseching the, that al we which be partakers of this holye comunion, may be fulfilled with thy grace, and heauēly benediction. And although we be vnworthye throughe our manifolde sinnes, to offer vnto the any sacrifice, yet we beseche the to accept this our bounden duty and seruice, not weighing our merites, but pardoning our offences, throughe Jesus Christ our Lord, by whō and with whom, in the vnitie of the holy ghoste, all honour and glorye be vnto the, O father almighty, world without ende. Amē.

Or this,

ALMIGHTY and euerlastinge God, we moste hartely thācke the, for that thou doest vouchsafe to fede vs, whiche haue duly receiued these holy misteries, with the spiritual fode of the moste precious body and bloude of thy sonne, our sauiour Jesus Christ, and doest assure vs therby of thy fauour and goodnes towarde vs, and that we be very mēbres incorporate in thy mistical body, whiche is the blessed cōpany of al faithful people, and be also heyres through hope of thy euerlastīg kingdō, by the merites of the most precious death and passiō of thy deare sone. We now most humbly beseche the, O heuenly father, so to assist vs with thy grace, that we may cōtinue in that holy felowship, and do all suche good workes as thou hast prepared for vs to walke in, throughe Jesus Christe our Lord ; to whō with the and the holy ghost be all honour and glory, world without ende. Amen.

Then shalbe sayde or songe.

GLORYE be to God on hyghe. And in earthe peace, good wyll towardes men. We prayse thee, we blesse thee, we worshyppe thee, we glorifye thee, wee geue thanckes to thee, for thy greate glorye. O Lorde God, heauenlye Kynge, God the father Almightie. O Lorde the onely begotten Sonne Jesu Christ. O Lord God, Lambe of God, Sonne of the father, that takest awaye the sinnes of the worlde, haue mercye vpon vs : Thou that takest awaye the Sinnes of the worlde, haue mercy vpon vs. Thou that takest away the synnes of the worlde, receiue our praier. Thou that syttest at the right hande of God the Father, haue mercy vpon vs. For thou onely art holy : Thou only art the Lorde, thou only O Christe with the holy Ghost, art most highe in the Glory of God the father. Amen.

Then the Priest or the Byshop, if he be present, shal let them depart with this blessing.

THE peace of God, which passeth all vnderstanding, kepe youre hartes, and mindes in the knowlege and loue of God, and of his Sonne Jesu Christe, oure Lorde. And the blessing of God almyghty, the Father, the Sonne, and the holy Ghost, be among you, and remayne with you alwaies. Amen.

¶ Collectes to be sayd after thoffertory when there is no Communiō ; euery suche daye one. And thesame maye be sayde also as often as occasion shall serue, after the Collectes, either of Morning and Evening Praier, Communion, or Letany, by the discretion of the minister.

ASSIST vs mercifully, O Lorde, in these our Supplications and Praiers, and dispose the way of thy seruauntes towarde the attaine-ment of euerlasting saluation, that emong al the chaunges, and chaunces of this mortal lyfe, thei may euer be defēded by thy moste gratious, and redy helpe. Through Christ our Lorde. Amen.

O ALMIGHTY Lorde and euerliuyng God, vouchesafe we beseche the, to direct, sanctifie, and gouerne bothe oure heartes, and bodies, in the wayes of thy lawes, and in the worckes of thy commaunde-mentes, that through thy most mighty protection, both here and euer, we maye bee preserued in bodye and Soule : throughe oure lorde and Sauioure Jesus Christe. Amen.

GRAUNT we beseche the almighty God, that the wordes which we haue herd this daye with our outward eares, may through thi grace be so graffed inwardly in our hartes, that they may bring furth in vs the fruite of good liuing, to the honour and praise of thy name : throughe Jesus Christ our Lorde. Amen.

PREUENTE vs O Lorde in all our doynges, with thy most gratious fauoure, and further vs with thy continuall helpe, that in al our workes begonne, continued, and ended in the : we may glorify thy holy name, and finally by thy mercy, obteine euerlasting lyfe, Through Jesus Christ our Lorde. Amen.

ALMGHTY God, the founteine of all wisedom, which knowest oure necessities before we aske, and our ignoraunce in asking, we beseche the to haue cōpassiō vpon our infirmities, and those thinges which for our vnworthiness we dare not, and for oure blindenes we cannot aske, vouchesafe to geue vs for the worthines of thy sonne Jesus Christe our Lorde. Amen.

ALMIGHTY God, whiche haste promysed to here the peticions of them that aske in thy sonnes name, we beseche the mercifully to encline thine Eares to vs that haue made nowe nowe our praiers and supplications vnto the, and graunt that those thinges which we haue faithfully asked, according to thy wil, may effectually be obteined to the relief of our necessitie, and to the setting furth of thy glory through Jesus Christ our Lorde. Amen.

¶ Upon the holy daies (yf there be no Communion,) shalbe said al that is appointed at the Communion, vntyll the ende of the homely, concluding

with the generall praier, for the whole estate of Christes Churche militant here in earth, and one, or moe of these Collectes before rehersed, as occasion shall serue.

¶ *And there shalbe no celebration of the lordes supper except there be a good number to Communicate wyth the Priest, according to his dyscretion.*

¶ *And yf there be not aboue xx persons in the Parish of discretion to receyue the Communiõ, yet there shalbe no communion except foure or thre at the least cõmunicate with the priest.   And in Cathedral and collegiate churches, where be many Priestes and Deacons, they shall all receyue the communion with the minister euery Sonday at the leaste, except they haue a reasonable cause to the contrary.*

¶ *And to take awaye the superstition, whiche any person hath, or myghte haue in the breade and wyne, it shall suffice that the breade be suche as is vsual to be eaten at the table, with other meates, but the beste and purest wheate breade, that conueniently may be gotten.   And yf anye of the breade or wyne remaine, the Curate shall haue it to hys owne vse.*

¶ *The bread and wyne for the Communion shalbe prouided by the Curate, and the church wardeines, at the charges of the Paryshe, and the paryshe shalbe discharged of suche summes of money, or other duties, which hitherto they haue payed for the same by order of their houses euery Sondaye.*

¶ *And note that euery Parishioner shall communicate, at the leaste thre tymes in the yere, of whiche Easter to be one : and shall also receyue the sacramentes, and other rytes, according to the order in this boke appoincted. And yerely at Easter, euery Parishioner shall recon with his Person, Vicar or Curate, or his, or their deputie or deputies, and paye to them or hym, all ecclesiastical duties, accustomably due then and at that tyme to be payed.*

❡ THE MINISTRACION OF BAPTISME

TO BE VSED IN THE CHURCHE.

It appeareth by aūciēt writers, that the Sacrament of Baptisme in the old old tyme, was not cōmonly Ministred, but at two times in the yeare, at Easter aud Whytsontide, at which tymes it was opēly ministred in the presence of al the congregacion : which custome (now being growen out of vse,) although it can not for many consideracions bee well restored agayne, yet it is thought good to folow the same as nere as cōueniently may be. Wherfore the people are to be admonished, that it is most conuenient that Baptisme should not be ministred but vpon Sondayes, and other holy dayes, when the most nombre of people may come together, aswel for that the congregacion there present maye testifie the receyuing of them that be newly Baptized into the nomber of Christes Church, as also because in the Baptisme of Infants euerye man present may be put in remembraunce of his awne profession made to God in hys Baptisme. For which cause also, it is expedient that Baptisme be ministred in the English tongue. Neuertheles (if necessitie so require) children may at al tymes be Baptized at hame.

❡ *When there are children to be baptized vpon the Sonday, or holy day, the parentes shal geue knowledge ouer nighte, or in the morning, afore the beginning of Mornyng prayour, to the curate. And then the Godfathers, Godmothers, and people with the children, must be ready at the Fonte, eyther immediatly after the last Lesson at Morning Prayour, or els immediatly after the last Lesson at Euening Praiour, as the Curat by his discretion shall appoincte. And then standinge there, the Priest shall aske whether the children be Baptized or no. If they aunswer, No. Then the priest say thus.*

DERELY beloued, forasmuche as al mē be conceiued and borne in synne, and that our sauiour Christ saith, none cā entre into the kingdom of God (except he be regenerate, and borne a new of water and the holy gost) I beseche you to cal vpō God the father, throughe our lord Jesus Christ, that of his boūteous mercy, he wil graūt to these childrē, that thing which by nature thei can not haue, that they may be baptized with water and the holy Ghost, and receiued into Christes holy churche, and be made liuely membres of the same.

Then the Priest shall say.

Let vs praye.

ALMIGHTI and euerlasting God, whiche of thy great mercy diddest saue Noe and his familie in the Arcke, frō perishing by water, and also diddest saufly lead the children of Israel, thy people, through the redde Sea, figuring therby thy holy Baptisme : and by the Baptisme of thy welbeloued sonne Jesus Christe, diddest sanctifye the floude Jordane, and al other waters, to the mistical washinge away of synne : We beseche the (for thine infinite mercies) that thou wilte mercifully loke vpon these children, sanctify them and washe thē with thy holy gost, that they beyng deliuered from thy wrath, may be receiued into the Arcke of Christes churche, and beyng stedfast in faithe, ioyfull throughe hope, and roted in charitie, may so passe the waues of this troublesome world, that finally they may come to the lāde of euerlasting life, there to reigne with the, worlde without ende, through Jesus Christ our Lorde. Amen.

ALMIGHTY and immortal God, the aide of al that nede, the helper of al that fly to the for succour, the life of thē that beleue, and the resurrectiō of the deade, we cal upō the for these infātes, that they, coming to thy holy Baptisme, may receyue remission of their sinnes by spiritual regeneracion, receiue them (O Lorde) as thou haste promised by thy welbeloued sonne, saynge : Aske and you shall haue ; seke, and you shall fynde : knocke and it shalbe opened vnto you : So geue now vnto vs that aske. Let vs that seeke, fynde open thy gate vnto vs that knocke, that these infantes enioy the euerlastīg benediction of thy heauēly wasshing, and may come to the eternal kingdome whiche thou haste promised by Christ our Lorde. Amen.

¶ *Then shall the Priest saye*

Heare the words of the Gospel, written by Sainct Marke in the tenth Chapiter.

Marke x. AT a certayne tyme they brought children to Christ that he should touche theim, and his Disciples rebuked those that brought thē. But when Jesus sawe it, he was displeased, and sayde vnto them. Suffre lytle children to come vnto me, and forbydde them not ; For to suche belongeth the Kyngdome of God. Verely, I saye vnto you ; whosoeuer doeth not receiue the kingdome of God, as a lytle chylde : he shall not entre therin. And when he had taken thē vp in his armes : he put his handes vpon them, and blessed them.

¶ *After the Gospel is redde, the minister shal make this briefe exhortacion vpon the wordes of the Gospell.*

FRENDES, ye heare in this Gospell the woordes of our sauiour Christe, that he commaunded the chyldren to bee broughte vnto him : howe he blamed those that woulde haue kepte theym from hym, how he exhorted all men to folowe their innocencye. Ye perceiue how by his outward gesture and dede he declared his good wil towarde thē. For he embraced thē in his armes, he laied his hands vpon them, and blessed them, doubt not you therfore, but ernestly beleue that he wil likewise fauourably receiue these present infãts, that he wil embrace thē with the armes of his mercy, that he wil geue vnto them the blessing of eternal life : and make them partakers of his euerlasting kingdome. Wherfore we being thus perswaded of the good wyl of our heauēly father, towardes these enfants declared by his son Jesus Christ, and nothing doubting, but that he fauourably alloweth this charitable woorke of ours, in bringing these children to his holye Baptisme : let vs faithfully and deuoutly geue thākes vnto him, and saye

ALMIGHTY and euerlasting God, heauenly Father, we geue thee humble thākes, that thou haste vouchedsaufe to call vs to the knowledge of thy grace and fayth in the, encrease this knowledge, and confirme this faith in vs euermore : Geue thy holy spirit to these enfantes, that they may be borne againe, and be made heyres of euerlasting saluacion, throughe our Lorde Jesus Christ. who liueth and reigneth with the, and the holy spirite, nowe and for euer. Amen.

Then the Priest shal speake vnto the Godfathers and Godmothers, on this wyse :

WELBELOUED frendes, ye haue broughte these children here to be baptised, ye haue praied that our lord Jesus christ, would vouchesaufe to receiue them, to lay his hādes vpon them, to blesse them, to release them of their sinnes, to geue theim the kingdom of heauen, and euerlasting lyfe. Ye haue heard also that our Lord Jesus Christ hath promised in his Gospel, to graūt all these thīges that ye haue praied for : which promise he for his part wil most surely kepe and performe. Wherfore after this promise made by Christ, these infants muste also faythfully for their part promise by you that be their sureties, that they wil forsake the divil and al his woorkes, and constantly beleue Gods holy word, and obediently kepe his commaundements.

Then shal the Priest demaunde of the Godfathers and Godmothers thes questions.

DOEST thou forsake the deuil and all his workes, the vaine pompe and glorye of the world, with al couetous desires of the same, and the carnal desires of the flesh, so that thou wilt not folow, nor be led by them ?

Aunswere. I forsake them al.

The Minister. Doest thou beleue in god the father almighty, maker of heauē and earth ? And in Jesus christ his only begotten sonne our Lord, and that he was cōceiued by the holy Ghost, borne of the virgin Mary : that he suffred vnder Poncius Pilate, was crucifyed, dead and buried, that he went doune into hel, and also did rise againe the thirde day : that he ascended into heauen, and sitteth at the right hād of god the father almighty ; and frō thēce shall come againe at the ende of the worlde, to iudge the quicke and the dead ?   And doest thou beleue in the holy Ghoste the holy Catholicque Churche, the comunion of sainctes, the remission of synnes, the resurreccion of the fleshe, and euerlasting lyfe after death ?

Aunswere. All this I stedfastly beleue.

Ministre. Wylt thou be baptised in this fayth ?

Aunswere. That is my desyre.

¶ *Then shal the Priest say.*

O MERCIFUL God, graunte that the olde Adam in these children maye be so buried, that the newe man may be raysed vp in them. Amen.

Graunte that all carnal affeccions maye dye in them, and that all thinges belonginge to the spirite may liue and growe in them. Amen.

Graunte that they may haue power and strēgth to haue victory, and to triumphe against the Divil, the worlde, and the flesh. Amen.

Graunt that whosoeuer is here dedicated to thee, by our office and ministerie, may also be endued with heauēly vertues, and euerlastingly rewarded through thy mercy, O blessed Lord God, who doest liue and gouern al thinges worlde without ende.   Amen.

ALMIGHTY euerliuing God, whose most derely beloued son Jesus Christe, for the forgeuenes of our sinnes, did shed out his moste precious syde bothe water and bloude, and gaue cōmaundement to his disciples that they should go teache al nacions, and baptise them in the name of the father, the sonne, and of the holy Ghost : Regard, we beseche the, the supplicacions of thy congregacion, and graunt that al thy seruantes whiche shalbe baptised in this water, may receue the fulnes of thy grace, and euer remaine in the nombre of thy faithful and elect chyldren, through Jesus Christ our Lord.   Amen.

Then the Priest shal take the Childe in his handes, and aske the name ; and naming the Childe, shal dippe it in the water, so it be discretely and warely done, saying,

N. I Baptise the in the name of the Father, and of the Sonne, and of the holy Ghost.   Amen.

¶ *And yf the Childe be weake, it shall suffice to powre water vpon it, saying the foresaid wordes.*

N. I Baptize the in the name of the Father, and of the sonne, and of the holy Ghost.   Amen.

Then the Priest shall make a Crosse vpon the Childes forehead, saying :

WE receiue this Childe into the cōgregacion of Christes flocke, and do sygne him with the signe of the crosse, in token that hereafter he shal not be ashamed to confesse the faith of Christ crucified, and manfully to fight under his bāner against sinne, the worlde, and the deuyll, and to continue Christes faithful souldiour and servaunt vnto his liues ende.   Amen.

Then shal the Priest say,

SEYING now, derely beloued brethren that these children be regenerate and graffed into the bodye of Christes cōgregacion, let vs geue thankes vnto God for these benefites, and with one accorde make our praiours vnto almighty God, that thei may lead the reste of their lyfe according to this beginning.

Then shal be sayd.

Our Father which art &c.

Then shal the Priest say,

We yelde the harty thankes most merciful father, that it hathe pleased thee to regenerate this enfant with thy holy spirite, to receyue him for thine owne childe by adoption, and to incorporate him into thy holy congregacion. And humbly we beseche thee to graunt that he being dead vnto sinne and lyuing vnto righteous-nes, and being buried with Christ in his death, maye crucify the old man, and vtterly abolyshe the whole bodye of synne, that as he is made partaker of the deathe of thy sonne, so he maye be partaker of hys resurreccion, so that finally with the residue of thy holy congregaciō, he may be inheritour of thine euerlasting king-dome.   Through Christ our Lord.   Amen.

¶ *At the laste ende, the Priest calling the Godfathers and Godmothers together, shal say this shorte exhortation folowing.*

FORASMUCHE as these children haue promysed by you to forsake the Deuil and his woorkes, to beleue in God, and to serue hym, you must remember that it is your parts and duties to see that these enfants be taughte, so sone as they shalbe able to learne, what a solempne vowe, promyse, and professiō they haue made by you.   And that they may know these thinges the better ; ye shal cal vpon theim to heare Sermōs, And chiefly you shal prouide that they may learne the Crede, the Lordes praier, and the Ten Commaundementes in the English tōgue ; and al other thinges which a Christian mā ought to know and beleue to his soules health.   And that these childrē may be vertuously brought vp, to leade a Godly and a christiā life, remembrīg alwaies that Baptisme doeth represent vnto vs our profession, which is to folow the exāple of our sauiour Christ, and to be made like vnto hym, that as he died and rose again for vs : so should we (whiche are Baptised) dye from sinne, and ryse again vnto rightuousnes, continually mortifiyng al our euyll and corrupt affections, and dailye procedynge in all vertue and godlynes of liuing.

¶ *The Minister shal commaunde that the chyldren be bronght to the Byshop to be confyrmed of him, so sone as they can saye in theyr vulgare tongue the articles of the faythe, the Lordes praier, and the x. Commaundementes, and be further instructed in the Catechisme set furth for that purpose, accordyngly as it is there expressed.*

OF THEM THAT BE

BAPTISED IN PRIUATE HOUSES,

IN TYME OF NECESSITIE.

¶ *The Pastours and Curates shal oft admonish the people, that they deferre not the Baptisme of enfantes any longer then the Sonday, or other holy day, next after the childe be borne vnlesse vpon a great and reasonable cause declared to the Curate, and by him approued.*

And also they shal warne theim that without great cause, and necessity, they baptize not children at home in their houses. And when great nede shall compelle theim so to doe, that then they minister on this fassion.

Fyrste let theim that be present cal vpon God for hys grace, and say the Lordes prayour, yf the time wil suffre. And then one of them shall name the childe, and dippe him in the water, or powre water vpon him, saying these wordes.

N. I Baptise the in the name of the Father, and of the Sonne, and of the holy Ghoste. Amen.

And let them not doubte, but that the childe so Baptised, is lawfully and sufficiently Baptised, and ought not to be Baptised agayne in the Church. But yet neuerthles, if the child whyche is after this sorte Baptised, do afterwarde liue, it is expediente that he be broughte into the Churche, to the entent the Priest may examyne and trie, whether the child be lawfully Baptised or no. And yf those that bryng any childe to the Churche do answere that he is already Baptised: then shal the Priest examine them further.

¶ By whome the childe was Baptised?

¶ Who was present when the childe was Baptised?

¶ Whether they called vpon God for grace and succour in that necessitie?

¶ Wyth what thing, or what matter they did Baptyse the Chylde?

¶ Wyth what wordes the childe was Baptised?

¶ Whether they thinke the childe to be lawfully and perfectly Baptised?

¶ *And yf the Minister shall proue by the aunswers of suche, as brought the childe, that all thinges were done as they oughte to be: Then shal not he Christen the childe againe, but shall receyue him, as one of the flocke of the true Christian people, saiynge thus.*

I CERTIFY you, that in this case ye haue done wel, and according vnto due ordre concerning the Baptising of this childe, whiche beyng borne in Originall sinne and in the wrathe of God, is nowe by the lauer of regeneracion in Baptisme, receiued into the nōber of the childrē of God, and heires of euerlasting life, for our Lorde Jesus Christ doeth not deny his grace and mercy vnto such infātes, but most louīgly doth cal thē vnto him : as the holy gospel doth witnes to our cōfort on this wise.

Marke x.

AT a certaine time they brought childrē vnto Christ that he should touche them, and his dysciples rebuked those that brought thē. But when Jesus saw it, he was displeased, and said vnto thē : Suffre litle children to come vnto me, and forbid theim not, for to such belongeth the kingdome of God.   Verely I say vnto you, whosoeuer doth not receiue the kingdom of God as a litle child, he shal not entre therin.   And when he had takē thē vp in his armes, he put his handes vpō them, and blessed them.

¶ *After the Gospel is redde, the minister shal make this exhortacion vpon the wordes of the Gospel.*

FRENDES, ye heare in this Gospell the wordes of oure saviour Christe, that he commaunded the chyldren to bee brought vnto hym : howe he blamed those that woulde haue kepte theym from him, howe he exhorted all men to folowe their innocencye : Ye perceiue how by his outward gesture in dede he declared his good wil toward thē.   For he embraced thē in his armes, he laied his hands vpon thē, and blessed thē, doubt not you therefore, but earnestly beleue, that he hath likewise fauourably receiued this presēt infant, that he hathe embraced hym wyth the armes of hys mercy, that he hath geuē vnto him the blessīg of eternal life, and made him partaker of his euerlastīg kingdō.   Wherfore we beyng thus perswaded of the good wil of our heeuēly father declared by his sonne Jesus Christ towards this infāt, Let vs faithfully and deuoutly geue thākes vnto him, and say the praier, which the lord him self taught, and in declaraciō of our faith, let vs recite the articles conteined in our Crede.

¶ *Here the Minister with the Godfathers, and Godmothers shall say.*

OUR Father which &c.

¶ *Then the Priest shal demaūd the name of the child, which beyng by the Godfathers, and Godmothers pronounced, the Minister shall say,*

¶ DOEST thou in the name of this child orsfake the deuil, and al his workes, the vaine pompe, and glory of the world, with al the couetous desires of the same, the carnal desires of the fleshe, and not to folowe and be ledde by them ?
Aunswere. I forsake them al.
¶ *The Minister.* Doest thou in the name of this childe professe this faith, to beleue in God the father almighty, maker of heauē and earth   And in Jesus Christ his only begotten son our Lord, and that he was conceiued by the holy ghost, borne of the virgin

Mary : that he suffered vnder pōce Pilate, was crucified, dead, and buried, that he wēt doune into hel, and also did rise again the iii daye : that he ascended into heauē, and sytteth at the ryght hande of God the father almightye : and from thence he shal come again at the ende of the world, to iudge the quicke and the dead ? And do you in his name beleue in the holy gost the holy Catholicque church, the cōmuniō of sainctes, the remission of sinnes, resurreccion of the fleshe, and euerlasting life after death

Aunswere. All this I steadfastly beleue.

Let vs pray.

ALMIGHTY and euerlasting God, heauēly father, we geue thee humble thanckes, for that thou hast vouchedsafed to call vs to the knowledge of thy grace and faythe in thee : increase this know-ledge, and confyrme this faythe in vs euermore : Geue thy holye spirite to this infante,that he beynge borne agayne and beynge made heyre of euerlastynge saluaciō, through our Lord Jesus Christ, may continue thy seruāt, and atteine thy promise, thɪough the same our Lorde Jesus Christ thy sonne, who liueth and reigneth with the in the vnitie of the same holy spirit euerlasting. Amen.

Then shal the Minister make this exhortacion, to the Godfathers and Godmothers.

FORASMUCHE as this childe hath promised by you to forsake the deuil and al his workes, to beleue in God, and to serue him : you must remēbre that it is your part and dutie, to see that this enfante be taught (so sone as he shalbe able to learne) what a solēpne vowe promise, and professiō he hath made by you. And that he may know these thīges the better, ye shal call vpon him to hear sermōs. And chiefly ye shal prouide that he may learne the Crede, the Lordes praier and the x Commaundemētes in the English tongue, and al other thinges which a Christian mā ought to know, and beleue to his soules health, and that this chyld may be vertuously brought vp, to leade a godly, and a christian lyfe. Remēbring alway that Baptisme doeth represēt vnto vs our pro-fession, which is to folow the example of our Sauiour Christ, and be made like vnto him, that as he died and rose againe for vs, so shoulde we which are Baptized, dye from sinne, and rise againe vnto righteousnes, continually mortifying all our euil and corrupt affec-tions, and daily proceding in al vertue, and godlines of liuing, etc :

¶ As in Publique Baptisme.

¶ *But if they which bring the enfantes to the Church, do make an vn-certeine aunswere to the Priestes questions, and say that they cannot tel what they thought, didde, or said, in yᵗ great feare, and trouble of minde : (as ofte times it chaunseth) thē let the Priest Baptise him in forme aboue written, cōcernīg publique Baptisme, sauing that at the dipping of the chylde in the Fonte, he shal vse this forme of wordes.*

If thou be not Baptized al ready. *N.* I baptise the in the name of the father, and of the Sonne, and of the holy Ghoste. Amen.

❡ CONFIRMACION,

WHEREIN IS CONTEINED A CATECHISME FOR CHILDREN.

To thende that confirmaciō may be ministred to the more edifying of suche, as shal receiue it (according unto S. Paules doctrine, who teacheth that al things should be doen in ye Church, to the edification of the same) it is thought good that none hereafter shalbe cōfyrmed but suche as cā saie in their mother tongue the articles of the faith, the Lordes praier, and the x Commaundementes: And can also answere to suche questiōs of this short Catechisme, as the Bishop (or suche as he shal appoinct) shal by hys discretion appose theim in. And this order is most conuenient to be obserued for diuers consideracions.

First, because that when children come to the yeres of discrecion, and haue learned what their godfathers and godmothers promised for thē in Baptisme, they may then themselues wyth their owne mouthe, and wyth their awne consent, openly before the Churche, ratifie and confyrme the same, and also promise that by the grace of God, they shall euermore endeuour themselfes faithfully to obserue and kepe suche thynges, as they by theyr owne mouth and confession haue assented vnto.

Secondly, forasmuche as Confirmacion is ministred to theym that be Baptised, that by imposition of handes and prayer, they may receiue strenghte[1] and defence agaynst all temptacions to synne, and the assaultes of the worlde and the Deuill: it is most mete to be ministred when children come to that age, that partely by the frailtye of their awne fleshe, partely by the assaultes of the worlde and the Deuil, thei begyn to be in daunger to fal into sondry kyndes of synne.

Thirdly, for that it is agreable wyth the vsage of the Churche, in times paste, wherby it was ordeined that Confirmacion shoulde be ministred to them that were of perfecte age, that they, beyng instructed in Christes religion, should openly professe their awne faithe, and promise to be obedient vnto the wyl of God.

And that no man shal thyncke that any detryment shall come to children by diferring of their Confirmacion; he shal knowe for truth, that it is certeine by Goddes worde, that children beyng baptised, haue all thynges necessarie for their saluacion, and be vndoubtedly saued.

[1 Evidently a misprint for strengthe.]

෨ A CATECHISME,

THAT IS TO SAY,

AN INSTRUCTION TO BE LEARNED OF EUERY CHILDE
BEFORE HE BE BROUGHT TO BE CONFIRMED OF THE BISHOPPE.

Question. WHAT is your name?

Aunswere. N. or *M.*

Question. Who gaue you this name?

Aunswere. My Godfathers and Godmothers in my Baptisme, wherein I was made a membre of Christe, the childe of God, and an inheritour of the kingdome of heauen.

Question. What did your godfathers and godmothers thē for you?

Aunswere. They did promise, and vowe iii thinges in my name. First, that I should forsake the deuil, and all his workes and pompes, the vanities of the wicked worlde, and al the sinful lustes of the fleshe. Secondly, that I should beleue al the articles of the Christian faith. And thirdely, that I should kepe Goddes holy wil and Commaundemētes, and walke in the same al the daies of my lyfe.

Question. Doest thou not thynke that thou art bounde to beleve and to do, as they haue promised for the?

Answer. Yes verely, and by Goddes helpe so I wil. And I hartely thanke our heauenly Father, that he hath called me to this state of saluatiō, through Jesus Christe our sauiour. And I pray God to geue me his grace, that I may continue in the same vnto my lyues ende.

Question. Reherse the Articles of thy belefe.

Aunswere. I beleue in God the Father almighty, maker of heauen and of earth. And in Jesus Christe his onely Sōne our Lorde. Whiche was conceiued of the holy Ghost. Borne of the Virgine Mary. Suffered vnder Ponce Pylate, was crucifyed, deade and buried, he descended into hell. The thyrd day he rose agayne from the dead. He ascended into heuen, and sitteth at the right hand of God the Father almighty. From thence he shal come to iudge the quicke and the dead. I beleue in the Holy ghost. The holy catholike Churche. The Communion of saynctes. The forgiuenes of synnes. The resurrection of the body. And the lyfe euerlastinge. Amen.

Question. What doest thou chiefly learne in these artycles of thy beliefe?

Aunswere. Firste, I learne to beleue in God the father, who hath made me and al the worlde.

Secondlye, in God the sonne, who hath redemed me and all mankinde.

Thirdly, in God the holy Ghost, who sanctifieth me and all the elect people of God.

Question. You said, that your godfathers and godmothers, dyd promise for you, that you shoulde kepe Gods commaundementes. Tell me how many there be ?

Aunswere. Tenne.

Question. Whiche be they ?

Aunswere. The same which God spake in the .xx. cha of Exodus, saying : I am the Lord thy God whyche haue brought the out of the lād of Egypt, oute of the house of bondage.   Thou shalt haue none other goddes but me.

II. Thou shalt not make to thy selfe any grauen Image nor the lykenes of any thyng that is in heauen aboue, or in the earthe beneth, nor in the water vnder the earthe : thou shalt not bow doune to them nor worship them.   For I the Lorde thy God, am a gelous God, and visyte the sinnes of the fathers vpon the chyldren, vnto the iii and fourth generacion of them that hate me, and shewe mercye vnto thousandes of them that loue me, and kepe my commaundementes.

III. Thou shalt not take the name of the Lord thy God in vaine, for the Lorde will not holde hym guiltles that taketh his name in vaine.

IIII.   Remember thou kepe holy the Sabboth day.   Syxe daies shalt thou laboure, and do all that thou hast to do : but the vii day is the Sabboth of the Lord thy God.   In it thou shalt do no maner of worcke, thou, and thy sonne, and thy daughter, thy man seruaunt, and thy maydseruaunt, thy cattel, and the strounger that is wythin thy gates : for in sixe daies the Lord made heauen and earth, the sea, and al that in them is, and rested the vii day, wherfore the Lorde blessed the vii day, and halowed it.

V. Honour thy father and thy mother, that thy daies may be long in the lande, whiche the Lorde thy God geueth the.

VI. Thou shalt do no murther.

VII. Thou shalt not committe adultery.

VIII. Thou shalt not steale.

IX. Thou shalt not beare false wytnes agaynste thy neighbour.

X. Thou shalt not couet thy neyghbours house, thou shalt not couet thy neyghboures wyfe, nor hys seruaunt, nor hys mayde, nor hys oxe nor hys asse, nor any thyng that is hys.

Question. What doest thou chiefly learne by these commandementes ?

Aunswere. I learne two thynges.   My duty towardes God, and my dutye towardes my neighbour.

Question. What is my duety towardes God ?

Aunswere. My dutye towardes God is, to beleue in him, to feare him, and to loue hym with all my harte, with al my mynde, with al my soule, and with all my strengthe.   To worship hym.   To geue hym thanckes.   To putte my whole truste in hym.   To call

vpon hym.   To honour hys holy name and hys woorde, and to
serue hym truely all the dayes of my lyfe.

Question. What is thy dutye toward thy neighbour?

Aunswere. My dutye towardes my neyghbour is to loue hym as
my selfe : And to do to all men as I would they should do vnto
me. To loue, honour, ād succour my father and mother. To
honour and obey the Kyng,[1] and his minysters. To submitte my
selfe to al my gouernours, teachers, spiritual Pastours and Maisters.
To order my selfe lowly and reuerently to all my betters. To hurte
no body by worde, nor dede. To be true and iuste in all my deal-
yng. To beare no malice nor hatred in my harte. To kepe my
handes from pickyng and stealyng, and my tongue from euil speak-
yng, liyng and slaunderyng. To kepe my body in temperaunce,
sobernes, and chastitie. Not to couet nor desire other mennes
goodes. But learne and labour truely to get myne awne liuyng,
and to do my dutye in that state of life, vnto whiche it shal please
God to cal me.

Question. My good child know this, that thou art not able to do
these thinges of thy self, nor to walke in the commaundementes
of God, and to serue hym, wythout hys specyall grace, whyche
thou must learne at al tymes to cal for by diligent prayer. Let me
heare therfore, if thou canst saye the Lordes praier.

Aunswere. Our Father whiche art in heauen ; Hallowed be thy
name. Thy kyngdom come. Thy wil be done in earth, as it is
in heauē. Geue vs this day our daily bread. And forgeue vs our
trespasses, as we forgeue them that trespasse against vs. And
leade vs not into temptacion. But deliuer vs from euil. Amen.

Question. What desirest thou of God in this praier?

Aunswere. I desire my Lord God our heauēly Father, who is
the geuer of al goodness, to send his grace vnto me, and to all
people, that we may worship hym, serue hym, and obeye hym as
we ought to doe. And I pray vnto God, that he will sende vs all
thynges that be nedefull, bothe for our soules and bodies. And that
he will be merciful vnto vs, and forgeue vs our sinnes : and that it
wil please him to saue and defende vs in al daungers ghostly and
bodily : and that he will kepe vs from all synne and wikednes, ād
from our ghostly enemy, and from euerlastyng death. And this I
trust he wil do of his mercye and goodnes, throughe our lord Jesu
Christ. And therefore I say. Amen. So be it.

¶ *So sone as the children can saye in theyr mother tongue, the articles of
the faith, the Lordes prayer, the .x. commaundementes, and also can
aunswere to such questyone of thys shorte Catechisme, as the Bishoppe
(or suche as he shall appoinct) shal by hys discretyon appose them in,
then shal they be brought to the Byshop (by one that shalbe his god-
father or godmother, that euery childe may haue a witnes of his Con-
firmacyon.*

[1 Both editions of 1559 have this manifest misprint for queen and her.]

¶ And the Bishoppe shal confirme them on this wise.

﹩﹦ CONFIRMATION.[1]

OUR helpe is in the name of the Lorde.
Aunswere. Whiche hath made bothe heauen and earth.
Minister. Blessed is the name of the Lorde.
Aunswere. Hencefurthe worlde without ende.
Minister. Lorde heare our prayer.
Aunswere. And let our crie come to the.

¶ Let us pray.

ALMIGHTYE and euerliuyng God, whyche hast vouchedsaufe to regenerate these thy seruauntes by water and the holy Ghost; and hast geuen vnto them forgeuenes of al theyr synnes : strengthen them we besche the (O Lorde) with the holy Ghoste the comforter, and daiely encrease in them thy manifolde giftes of grace, the spirite of wisedome and vnderstanding : the spirite of counsail and ghostly strength, the spirite of knowledge and true godlinesse, and fulfyll them (O Lord) with the spirite of thy holy feare. Amen.

¶ Then the Bishop shal laye hys hande vpon euery childe seuerally, saying,

DEFENDE, O Lorde, this childe with thy heauenly grace that he may continue thine for euer, and daiely encrease in thy holy spirite more and more, vntill he come vnto thy euerlastyng kingdome Amen.

¶ Then shal the Bishop saye,

Let vs praie.

ALMIGHTIE euerlyuyng God, whiche makest vs bothe to will, and to do those thynges that be good, and acceptable vnto thy Maiestie, vpon whome our humble supplications vnto the for these children, vpon whome (after the example of thy holy Apostles) we haue laied our handes, to certifie theim (by thys signe) of thy fauour, and gracious goodnes toward them, let thy fatherly hande we besche the euer be ouer them, let thy holy spirite euer be with them, and so leade them in the knowledge ād obedience of thy worde that in the ende they may obtaine the euerlasting lyfe : through our Lorde Jesus Christe, who with the and the holy Ghost liueth and reigneth one God, worlde without ende.   Amen.

¶ Then the Bishop shal blesse the children, thus saying.

THE blessing of God almightye, the Father, the Sonne, and the Holy ghoste, be vpon you, and remayne with you for euer.   Amen.

¶ The Curate of euery paryshe, or some other at his appoinctmēt, shal diligently vpon Sondayes and holy dayes, haulfe an houre before Evēyng

prayer, opēly in the Churche instruct and examyne so many children of his parish sent vnto him, as the time wil serue and as he shal thinke conuenient, in some part of this Catechisme.

¶ *And al fathers, and mothers, maisters, and dames, shal cause theyr children, seruaunts, and prentises (whyche haue not learned theyr Catechisme to come to the Churche at the tyme appoyncted, and obediently to heare, and be ordred by the Curate, vntyll suche time as they haue learned all that is here appoincted for theim to learne. And whensoeuer the Byshop shall geue knowledge for chyldren to be brought afore him to any conuenyent place, for their confirmation: then shal the Curate of euery Paryshe eyther bryng or sende in wrytyng the names of all those children of hys Paryshe, whiche can say the Articles of their fayth, the Lordes prayer, and the x Commaundementes, and also how many of them can answere to thother questions conteined in this Catechisme.*

¶ *And there shall none be admitted to the holy communion; vntil suche tyme as he can saye the Catechisme and be confirmed,*

THE FOURME OF
SOLEMPNIZACION OF MATRIMONYE.

First, the banes must be asked thre seuerall Sondaies or holy daies, in the tyme of seruice, the people beyng present, after the accustomed maner.

And yf the persons that would be maryed dwell in diuerse Paryshes, the banes must be asked in both Parishes and the Curate of the one Paryshe shall not solempnize matrimonye betwyxt thē, wythout a certifycate of the banes beyng thryse asked, from the Curate of the other Parysh.   At the daie appoincted for solempnizacyon of Matrimonye, the persones to be maryed shal come into the body of the Churche, wyth theyr frendes and neighbours. And there the Pryest shall thus saye.

DEARELY beloued frendes, we are gathered together here in the sight of God, and in the face of his congregacion, to ioyne together this mā and this womā in holy matrimony, which is an honorable state, instytuted of GOD in Paradise, in the time of mānes innocencie, signifiyng vnto vs the mistical vnion that is betwixt Christ and his Churche : which holy state Christe adourned and beautified with his presence and firste myracle that he wrought in Cana of Galile, and is commended of sainct Paul to be honourable emong all men, and therfore is not to be enterprised, nor taken in hande vnaduisedly, lightly or wantonly, to satisfye mennes carnall lustes and appetytes, lyke brute beastes that haue no vnderstandyng ; but reuerently, discretely, aduisedly, soberly, and in the feare of God, duely consideryng the causes for the which matrimony was ordeined. One was the procreation of children, to be brought vp in the feare and nurtoure of the Lorde, ād praise of God.   Secondly, it was ordeined for a remedy agaynste sinne and to auoide fornication, that suche persones as haue not the gifte of continencie might mary, and kepe themselues vndefiled membres of Christes body. Thirdly, for the mutual societie, helpe, and comfort, that the one ought to haue of the other, bothe in prosperity and aduersitye, into the whiche holy state these two persones present, come nowe to be ioyned.   Therefore if any man can shewe any iust cause, why thei may not lawfully be ioyned together let hym now speake, or els hereafter for euer holde his peace.

And also speakynge to the persons that shalbe maryed, he shall saie.

I REQUIRE and charge you (as you wil aunswere at the dreadful day of iudgement, when the secretes of all hartes shalbe disclosed) that if either of you doe knowe any impedyment, why ye may not be lawfully ioyned together in Matrimony, that ye confesse it. For be ye well assured, that so many as be coupled together, otherwyse than Goddes worde doeth allowe, are not ioyned together by God, neither is their Matrimonye lawfull.

At whyche day of Maryage, if any man do allege and declare any impediment, why they may not be coupled together in matrymony by Gods law, or the lawes of thys realme, and wyll be bound, and sufficient sureties with him to the parties, or els put in a cautȳo to the ful value of suche charges, as the persons to be maryed do susteine to proue hys allegation : thē the solempnization must be deferred vnto suche tyme as the truthe be tried. If no impediment be alledged, then shall the curate saye vnto the man,

N. WILT thou haue thys woman to thy wedded wyfe, to lyue together after Goddes ordynaunce in the holye estate of Matrimony? Wylt thou loue her, comforte her, honour, and kepe her, in sickenes, and in healthe ? And forsakyng al other, kepe the onely to her, so long as you both shall liue ?

The man shall aunswere,

I will.

Then shall the Priest saye to the woman,

N. WILT thou haue this man to thy wedded housband, to lyue together after Goddes ordynaunce in the holy estate of matrimony ? wilt thou obey hym and serue him, loue, honour, and kepe him, in syckness and in health ? And forsakynge al other, kepe the onely to him so lōg as ye bothe shal liue

The woman shall aunswere,

I will.

Then shall the Minister saie,

Who geueth this woman to be maried vnto this man ?

¶ *And the Minister receiuyng the womā at her father or frendes handes, shall cause the man to take the woman by the right hand, and so either to geue their trouth to other. the man first saying.*

I. *N.* take the. *N.* to my wedded wyfe, to haue and to hold from thys day forward, for better, for worse, for richer, for porer, in sickenes, and in healthe, to loue and to cheryshe, tyll death vs departe ; according to Gods holy ordinaunce, and therto I plight the my trouth.

Then shall they louse their handes, and the woman takyng againe the man by the right hande, shall saie.

I. *N.* take the. *N.* to my wedded husbande, to haue and to holde, from this day for ward, for better, for worse, for richer, for poorer, in sickenes, ād in health, to loue, cherish, and to obey, till death vs departe, accordynge to godes holy ordinaunce : and therto I geue the my trouth.

Then shall they again louse theyr handes, and the man shal geue vnto the womā a ring, laying thesame vpō the booke, with the accustomed dutie to the Priest and Clerke. And the Priest taking the ryng, shal delyuer it vnto the mā, to put it vpon the fourth finger of the womās left hād. And the mā taught by the Priest, shal say.

WITH this ring I the wed : with my body I the worship : and with all my worldly goodes, I the endow. In the name of the Father, and of the Sōne, and of the holy Ghost.   Amen.

Then the man leauyng the ryng vpon the fourth finger of the womans left hande, the Minister shall saye.

O ETERNALL God, creatoure and preseruer of all mankynd, giuer of all spirytuall grace, the aucthour of euerlastyng life : send thy blessyng vpon these thy seruauntes, thys man and this woman, whom we blesse in thy name, that as Isaac and Rebecca lyued faithfully together : So these persons may surely performe and kepe the vow and couenaunt betwixte them made, wherof this ring geuen, and receiued, is a token and pledge, and may euer remain in perfect loue and peace together, and liue according vnto thy lawes, thorough Jesus Christ our Lorde.   Amen.

¶ *Then shal the Priest ioyne their right handes together and say.*

Those whome God hath ioyned together, let no man put a sonder.

Then shall the Minister speak unto the people.

FOR asmuche as .N. and .N. haue cōsented together in holy wedlocke, and haue witnessed the same before God, and thys company, and therto haue giuen and pledged, their trouth eyther to other, and haue declared the same by geuyyng and receiuyng of a ryng, and by ioynyng of handes I pronounce that thei be man and wife together.   In the name of the father, of the sōne and of the holy Ghost.   Amē.

And the Minister shal adde this blessyng.

GOD the Father, God the Sonne, God the holy Ghost, blesse, preserue, and kepe you, the Lorde mercifully wyth his fauour loke vpon you, and so fil you with al spiritual benediction, and grace, that you may so lyue together in thys life, that in the world to come, you may haue life euerlastyng.   Amen.

¶ *Thē the Ministers or Clerckes goyng to lhe Lordes table, shall saie, or syng this Psalme folowyng* Beati omnes.

Psal. cxxviii.   BLESSED are all they that feare the Lorde, and walke in his waies.

For thou shalt eate the labour of thy handes, O wel is the, and happy shalt thou be.

Thy wife shalbe as the fruitfull vine vpon the walles of thy house.

Thy children like the Oliue braunches rounde about thy table.

Lo thus shall the man be blessed : that feareth the lorde.

The Lorde from out of Sion shal blesse the : that thou shalt see Hierusalem in prosperitie, al thy life long :

Yea, that thou shalt see thy childres children, and peace vpon Israel.

Glory be to the. &c.

As it was. &c.

Or elles this Psalme folowyng Deus misereatur.

GOD be mercifull vnto vs and blesse vs : and shewe vs the lyght Psal. lxvii. of his countenaunce, and be merciful vnto vs.

That thy waie maie be knowen vpon the earth : thy sauyng healthe among al nacions.

Let the people prayse the (O God) yea, let all the people praise the.

O let the nacions reioyce and be glad, for thou shalt iudge the folke ryghteously, and gouerne the nacions vpon the earth.

Let the people praise the (O God) lette all the people praise the.

Then shall the earthe bryng furthe her encrease, and God, euen our God, shal geue vs his blessyng.

God shall blesse vs, and al the endes of the worlde shall feare him.

Glory be to the Father. &c.

As it was in the be. &c.

The Psalme ended, and the man and the woman knelyng afore the Lordes table : The Priest standyng at the Table, and turnyng hys face towarde them, shal saie,

Lorde haue mercie vpon vs.

Aunswere. Christe haue mercie vpon vs.

Minister. Lorde haue mercie vpon vs.

OUR FATHER WHICHE ART. &c.

And leade vs not into temptation.

Aunswere. But deliuer vs from euil. Amen.

Minister. O Lorde, saue thy seruaunt, and thy handmaide.

Aunswere. Whyche put their trust in the.

Minister. O Lorde sende them helpe from thy holy place.

Aunswere. And euermore defende them.

Minister. Be vnto them a towre of strength.

Aunswere. From the face of their enemie.

Minister. O Lorde heare our praier.

Aunswere. And let our crie come vnto the.

¶ The Minister.

O GOD of Abraham, God of Isaac, God of Jacob, blesse these thy seruauntes, and sowe the sede of eternal life in their mindes, that whatsoeuer in thy holy worde they shal profitably learne, they may in dede fulfil the same. Loke, O Lorde mercifully vpon theim from heauen, and blesse them. And as thou diddest send thy blessing vpon Abraham and Sara to their greate comforte : so vouchesaufe to sende thy blessing vpō these thy seruauntes, that they obeiyng thy will, and alway beyng in saufetie vnder thy protection, may abide in thy loue vnto their liues ende, throughe Jesu Christe our Lorde. Amen.

¶ This prayer next folowyng shal be omitted where the woman is past childe birth.

O MERCIFULL Lorde, and heauenly Father, by whose gracious gifte mankynde is encreased, we beseche the assiste with thy blessyng these two persones, that they may bothe be fruitefull in procreation of children, also liue together so long in godly loue and honestie, that they may see their childers children, vnto the thirde and fourthe generacion vnto thy praise and honour : through Jesus Christe our Lorde. Amen.

O GOD whiche by thy mightie power hast made all thinges of naught, which also after other thinges set in ordre, diddest appoinct that out of mā (created after thyne owne ymage and similitude) womā should take her beginning, and knitting thē together, diddest teache that it shoulde neuer be lawfull to put a sōder those, whome thou by matrimonie haddest made one : O God which haste cōsecrated the state of matrimonie to suche an excellent misterie, that in it is signified and represented the spiritual mariage and vnitie betwixte Christe and his Churche : Loke mercifully vpon these thy seruauntes, that both this man may loue his wife, accordyng to thy worde (as Christe did loue his spouse the Churche, who gaue himselfe for it, louyng and cherishing it, euen as his owne fleshe). And also that this woman may be louyng and amiable to her housband as Rachel, wise as Rebecca, faithfull and obedient as Sara, and in all quietnes, sobrietie, and peace, be a folower of holy and Godly matrones, O Lorde blesse them bothe, and graūt them to enherite thy euerlastyng kyngdome : throughe Jesus Christe our Lorde. Amen.

¶ Then shall the Priest save,

ALMIGHTIE God, which, at the beginnyng did create our firste parentes Adam and Eue, and did sanctifie and ioyne them together in mariage, powre vpō you the richesse of his grace, sanctifie, and blesse you, that ye may please hym both in body and soule, and liue together in holy loue, vnto your liues ende. Amen.

Then shal begyn the Communion, and after the Gospel shalbe saied a Sermon, wherin ordinarily (so oft as there is any mariage) thoffice of a man and wife shalbe declared, accordyng to holy Scripture, or if there be no sermon, the Minister shal reade this that foloweth.

AL ye which be maried, or whiche entend to take the holy estate of Matrimonie vpon you : heare what holy scripture doth say, as touching the dutie of housbandes towarde their wiues, and wiues toward their housbādes.

Saincte Paul (in his Epistle to the Ephesians, the v Chapiter) doeth geue this commaundement to all maried men.

Ye housbandes loue your wiues, euen as Christ loued the Churche, and hath geuen hymselfe for it, to sanctifie it, purgyng it in the fountaine of water, throughe the worde, that he might make it vnto hym selfe a glorious congregacion, not hauyng spot or wrincle, or any suche thyng, but that it shoulde be holy and blameles. So men are bounde to loue their owne wyues, as their owne bodies. He that loueth his owne wife loueth hym selfe. For neuer did any man hate his owne fleshe, but nourisheth and cherisheth it, euen as the Lorde doeth the congregacion, for we are mēbres of his body : of his flesh and of hys bones.

For this cause shall a man leaue father and mother, and shalbe ioined vnto his wife, and thei two shalbe one flesh. This mistery is great, but I speake of Christe and of the congregacion. Neuerthelesse, let euery one of you so loue his owne wyfe, euen as hym selfe.

Likewise the same sainct Paule (wrytyng to the Collossians) Collos iii. 1. speaketh thus to all mē that be maried. Ye men, loue your wyues, and be not bitter vnto them.

Heare also what saincte Peter Thapostle of Christe, whiche i. Pet. iii. was him selfe a maried man (saith vnto al men) that are maried. Ye housbandes, dwel with your wyues according to knowledge. Geuynge honour vnto the wyfe as vnto the weaker vessell, and as heires together of the grace of lyfe, so that your praiers be not hyndred.

Hetherto ye haue hearde the dutie of the housbande toward the wyfe.

Now likewise ye wyues heare and learne your dutie towarde your housbandes, euen as it is plainely sette furth in holy scripture.

Saincte Paule (in the forenamed Epistle to the Ephesians) Ephe. v. teacheth you thus : Ye women, submit youre selfes vnto youre owne housbandes as vnto the Lorde : for the housbande is the wyues headde, euen as Christe is the headde of the Churche. And he is also the sauioure of the whole bodye. Therefore as the Churche or congregacion, is subiecte vnto Christe. So likewyse lette the wyues also be in subiection vnto their owne housbandes in al thinges. And againe he sayeth : Let the wife reuerence her housbande. And (in his Epistle to the Collossians) Sayncte Paule Col. iii.

geueth you thys shorte lesson. Ye wyues, submitte youre selues vnto youre owne housbandes, as it is conuenient in the Lorde.

i. Pet. iii.

Saincte Peter also doeth instructe you verye godly thus, saiynge. Let wyues be subiecte to their owne housbandes, so that if anye obey not the woorde, they may be wonne withoute the woorde by the conuersacion of the wyues, whyle they beholde your chaste cōuersacion coupled with feare, whose apparell let it not be outward, with broided haire and trymmyng aboute with golde, eyther in puttinge on of gorgeous apparell, but let the hidde manne, whiche is in the harte, be without all corruption, so that the spirite be milde and quiete, whiche is a precious thynge in the sighte of God. For after thys maner (in the olde tyme) did the holy women whiche trusted in God apparell them selues, beynge subiect to their owne housbādes : as Sara obeyed Abraham, callynge hym Lorde, whose daughters ye are made, doynge well, and beyinge not dismayde with any feare.

The newe maried persones (the same day of their mariage) must receyue the holy Communion.

¶ THE ORDER FOR THE

VISITACION OF THE SICKE.

The Priest entryng into the sicke persones house, shall saye.

Peace be in this house, and to all that dwel in it.

When he commeth into the sicke mannes presence, he shall saye knelynge doune.

REMEMBRE not Lorde oure iniquities, nor the iniquities of our forefathers. Spare vs good Lorde, spare thy people, whome thou hast redemed with thy most precious bloude and bee not angry with vs for euer.

Lorde haue mercy vpon vs.
Christe haue mercy vpon vs.
Lorde haue mercy vpon vs.
¶ Our father whiche art in heauen. &c.
And leade vs not into temptacion.
Aunswere. But deliuer vs from euel. Amen.
¶ *Minister.* O Lorde saue thy seruaunt.
¶ *Aunswere.* Whiche putteth his trust in the.
¶ *Minister.* Sende him helpe from thy holy place.
¶ *Aunswere.* And euermore myghtely defende him.
¶ *Minister.* Let the enemy haue none aduauntage of him.
¶ *Aunswere.* Nor the wicked approche to hurte him.
¶ *Minister.* Be vnto him O Lorde a strong Towre.
¶ *Aunswere.* From the face of his enemy.
¶ *Minister.* Lorde heare our praiers.
¶ *Aunswere.* And let our crie come vnto the.

¶ *Minister,*

O Lorde loke doune from Heauen, beholde, visite, and releue this thy seruaunt. Loke vppon him with the eies of thy mercye, geue him comforte and sure confidence in the, defende him from the daunger of the enemy, and kepe him in perpetual peace, and saufety : Through Jesus Christe our Lorde. Amen.

HEARE vs almighty, and most mercifull God, and sauiour, extend thy accustomed goodnes, to this thy seruaunt whiche is greued with syckenesse, visit him O Lorde, as thou diddest visit,

E

Peters wifes mother, and the capiteines seruaunt.   So visit and restore vnto this sicke person his former health (if it bee thy wil) or els geue him grace so to take thy visitation, that after this painful life ended, he may dwell with the in life euerlastyng.   Amen.

¶ Then shal the Minister exhorte the sicke person after this forme or other lyke.

DERELY beloued know this, that almighty god is the lorde of life and death, and ouer al thinges to theym perteinyng, as youthe, strength, helthe, age weaknesse, and sicknes, wherfore, whatsoeuer your syckenesse is, knowe you certainlye, that it is Goddes visitacion.   And for what cause soeuer this sicknes is sent vnto you : whether it bee to trie youre patience for the example of other, and that your faith may be founde in the dai of the lord laudable, glorious, and honorable, to the encrease of Glory, and endles felicitie : Or els it be sent vnto you, to correct, and amende in you whatsoeuer dothe offende the eies of our heauenly father : knowe you certeinly, that yf you truly repent you of your sinnes, and beare your sickenes patiently, trustyng in Gods mercy for his dere sonne Jesus Christes sake, and rendre vnto him humble thankes for his fatherly visitacion, submittyng your selfe wholly to his will, it shall turne to your profite, and helpe you forwarde in the right waye that leadeth vnto euerlastyng life.   Take therfore in good worthe, the chastemente of the lord, for whom the lord loueth he chastiseth.   yea, as S. Paul saith, he scourgeth euery sonne which he receiueth : If you endure chastisement, he offereth himself vnto you as vnto his own children.   What sonne is he that the father chastiseth not ?   If ye be not vnder correction (whereof all true children are partakers) then are ye bastardes, and not children.   Therfore seying, that when our carnal fathers do correct vs, we reuerently obey the, shal we not now muche rather be obedient to our spirituall father, and so liue ?   And they for a few daies do chastise vs after their owne pleasure, but he doth chastise vs for our profit to thentent he maye make vs partakers of his holines.   These wordes good brother, are Gods wordes, and written in holy Scripture for our comforte and instruction, that we sholde paciently and with thankesgeuing, beare our heaueuly fathers Correction, whensoeuer by any maner of aduersitie it shal please his gratious goodnes to visite vs.   And there shoulde be no greater comforte to christien persons, than to be made like vnto christ, by sufferyng patiently aduersities, troubles, and Sickenesses.   For he him selfe went not vp to ioye, but firste he suffered paine : hee entred not into his glorye, before he was crucified : So truly our way to eternall ioye, is to suffer here with Christe, and our doore to entre into eternall life : is gladly to die with Christ, that we may ryse againe from death and dwell with him in euerlastynge life.   Nowe therfore, taking your sickenesse, whiche is thus profitable for you paciently : I exhorte you in the

If the persō visited be very sicke then the Curate may ende his exhortacion in thys place.

name of God, to remember the profession whiche you made vnto
GOD, in your Baptisme. And forasmuche as after this lyfe there
is accompte to be geuen vnto the rightuous iudge, of whome all
must be iudged without respect of persons : I require you to examine
your selfe and your state, bothe towarde God and man, so that ac-
cusynge and condempning your self for your owne faultes, you
may fynde mercy at our heauenly fathers hande, for Christes sake,
and not be accused and condempned in that fearful iudgement.
Therfore I shal shortly rehearse the Articles of our faith, that ye
may know whether you do beleue as a Christien man shoulde, or no.

¶ Here the minister shall reherse the articles of the faith saieng thus

DOEST thou beleue in God the father almighty.

And so furth, as it is in Baptisme.

¶ Then shal the minister examine whether he be in charitie, with all the
worlde : exhortyng hym to forgiue from the botome of his hart, al persons
that haue offended hym, and if he haue offended other, to aske them for-
geuenesse ; And wher he hathe done iniury or wrong to any man, that
he make amendes to the vttermost of his power.   And if he haue not afore
disposed his goodes, let him thē make his wil.   (But mē must be oft ad- This may be
monished that they set an order for their temporall goodes and landes, done before
when they be in health.)   And also declare his debtes, what hee oweth, and the minister
what is owyng vnto him, for discharging of his conscience, and quietnes of begin his
his executours.   The minister may not forget, nor omitte to moue the praiers as he
sicke person (and that most earnestly) to liberalitie towarde the poore. shal se cause

¶ Here shall the sicke persone make a speciall confession, if he feele hys con-
science troubled with any weighty matter.   After whiche confession the
priest shall absolue him after this sorte.

OUR Lorde Jesus Christ who hath left power to hys Churche to
absolue all sinners, whiche truly repente, and beleue in him : of
hys greate mercie forgeue thyne offences, and by his aucthoritie
committed to me, I absolue the from al thy synnes.   In the name
of the father and of the sonne &c.   Amē.

¶ And then the priest shal say the Collect folowyng.

¶ Let vs praie.

O MOST merciful God, whiche according to the multitude of thy
mercies, dost so put awai the sinnes of those whiche truly repent,
that thou remēbrest them no more, open thy eie of mercy vpon
this thy seruaunt, who most earnestly desireth pardon, and forgeuenes.   Renue in him most louyng father, whatsoeuer hath
been decaied, by the fraud, and malice of the deuel, or by his
owne carnall will, and frailnes, preserue, and continue this sicke
membre in the vnitie of thy churche, consider his contricion, accept hys teares, asswage his paine, as shalbe sene to thee most
expedient for him.   And forasmuche as he putteth his full trust

E 2

only in thy mercy, impute not vnto him his former sinnes, but take him to thy fauour, through the merites of thy moste derely beloued sonne Jesus Chriest.   Amen.

¶ *Then the Minister shal saie this Psalm.*

*In te, domi-
ne, spe.*
Psal. xxi.[1]

IN the, O Lorde haue I put my trust, let me neuer bee put to confusion, but ridde me, and deliuer me into thy ryghtuousnesse, encline thine eare vnto me and saue me.

Be thou my strong holde wherunto I may alway resorte : thou hast promysed to helpe me, for thou art my house of defence, and my Castel.

Deliuer me o my God out of the hande of the vngodly : out of the hande of the vnrightuous and cruell man.

For thou O lorde God art the thyng that I long for : thou art my hope euen from my youth.

Through the haue I ben holden vp euer sence I was borne : thou art he that toke me out of my mothers wōbe, my prayse shall alway be of the.

I am become as it were a monster vnto many : but my sure truste is in the.

O let my mouth be filled with thy praise : (that I may sing of thy glory) and honor all the daie longe.

Cast me not away in the tyme of age : forsake me not when my strength faileth me.

For myne enemies speake againste me, and they that laye wayte for my soule, take their counsail together, saiynge : God hath forsaken hym, persecute hym, and take hym, for there is none to deliuer hym.

Go not farre from me, O God : my God, haste the to helpe me.

Let them be confounded and perishe, that are against my soule : let them be couered with shame and dishonoure that seke to do me euill.

As for me, I will paciētly abide alwaie : and wil praise the, more and more.

My mouthe shall dayely speake of thy righteousnes, and saluacion : for I knowe no ende therof.

I will go furth in the strength of the Lorde God : and will make mencion of thy righteousnesse onely.

Thou (O God) haste taughte me from my youthe vp vntill nowe : therefore I will tell of thy wonderous workes.

Forsake me not (O God) in myne olde age, when I am gray headed : vntil I haue shewed thy strength vnto this generacion, and thy power to all them that are yet for to come.

Thy righteousnesse (O God) is very hygh, and great thinges are they that thou haste done : O God, who is lyke vnto the?

O what great troubles and aduersities hast thou shewed me?

[1 A misprint for lxxi.]

and yet diddest thou turne and refreshe me, yea, and broughtest me from the depe of the earth agayne.

Thou hast broughte me to great honour : and comforted me on euery side.

Therfore will I prayse the and thy faythefulnes (O God) plaiynge vpon an instrument of Musicke : vnto the will I synge vppon the Harpe, O thou holy one of Israell.

My lippes will be faine, when I sing vnto the : and so will my soule whome thou hast deliuered.

My tongue also shal talke of thy righteousnesse al the day long : for thei are confounded and brought vnto shame, that seke to do me euill.

Glory be to the Father, and to the Sonne, and to the holy Ghoste.

As it was in the begynnynge, is nowe and euer shalbe worlde without ende. Amen.

Addyng thys.

O Sauiour of the worlde, saue vs, whyche by thy crosse and precious bloude hast redemed vs, helpe vs we beseche the, O God.

¶ Then shal the Minister saye.

THE almightie Lorde, whiche is a moste strong tower to all them that put their trust in him, to whom all thinges in heauen, in earthe, and vnder the earthe doe bowe and obey, be nowe, and euermore thy defence, and make the knowe and fele, that there is no other name vnder heauen geuen to man, in whome, and throughe whome thou mayest receyue healthe and saluacion, but onely the name of oure Lorde Jesus Christe. Amen.

❡ THE

COMMUNION OF THE SICKE.

Forasmuche as al mortal men be subiecte to many soubdein perilles, diseases, and sicknesses, and euer vncertaine what time they shal departe out of this lyf. Therfore to thentent they may be alwaies in a readines to die, whensoeuer it shal please Almightie God to cal them: The Curates shal diligently from tyme to tyme, but specially in the plague time, exhort their Parishioners to the oft receiuyng in the Churche, of the holy Communion of the body and bloude of our saviour Christ. Whiche (if thei do) thei shal haue no cause in their soubdeine visitation to be vnquieted for lacke of the same. But if the sicke persone be not able to come to the Churche, and yet is desirous to receiue the Communion in his house, then yee must giue knowledge ouer night, or elles early in the Mornīg to the Curate, signifying also how many be appoincted to communicate with him. And hauyng a cōuenient place in the sicke mans house, where the Curate may reuerently minister, and a good nomber to receiue the Communion with the sicke persone, with all thynges necessary for the same, he shal there minister the holy Communion.

The Collect.

ALMIGHTIE euerliuyng God, maker of mankynde, whiche doest correcte those whom thou doest loue, and chastisest euery one whome thou doest receiue, we beseche the to haue mercie vpon this thy seruaunt visited with thy hande, and to graunt that he may take his sickenesse paciently, and recouer his bodily helth (yf it be thy gracious wil), and whensoeuer his soule shal depart from the body, it may bee without spot presented vnto the: Throughe Jesus Christe our Lorde. Amen.

The Epistle.

Hebr. xii.   MY sōne, despise not the correction of the Lorde, neither faint when thou art rebuked of hym. For whome the Lorde loueth, him he correcteth : yea, and he scourgeth euery sonne whom he receiueth.

The Gospel.

Iohn v.   VERELY, verely I say vnto you, he that heareth my worde, and beleueth on hym that sent me, hath euerlastyng life, and shall not come vnto dampnacion, but he passeth from death vnto lyfe.

¶ *At the time of the distribucion of the holy Sacrament, the Priest shal first receiue the Communion hymselfe, and after minister vnto them that be appoincted to communicate with the sicke.*

¶ *But if any man, either by reason of extremitie of sickenes, or for lacke of warnyng in due time to the Curate, or for lacke of company to receiue with hym, or by any other iust impediment, do not receiue the Sacramēt of Christes body and bloud, then the Curate shall* instruct *hym, that if he do truely repent hym of his synnes, and stedfastly beleue that Jesus Christe hath suffred death vpon the crosse for him, and shed his bloud for his redempcion, earnestly remembryng the benefites he hath therby, and geuing him hartie thākes therfore, he doth eate and dryncke the body and bloude of our sauiour Christe, profitably to his soules health, although he doe not receiue the Sacrament with his mouthe.*

¶ *When the sicke person is visited, and receiueth the holy Communion al at one time, then the Priest, for more expediciō, shal cut of the fourme of the visitacion at the Psalme,* In the, O Lorde haue I put my trust, *and go streight to the Communion.*

¶ *In the time of* plague, Swette, *or such other like contagious tymes of sickenesses or diseases, whē none of the Paroshe or neighbours can be gotten to communicate with the sicke in their houses, for feare of the infection, vpon speciall request of the diseased, the minister may alonly communicate with hym.*

THE ORDER FOR THE
BURIALL OF THE DEAD.

¶ *The prieste metyng the corpse at the Church style, shal saye, Or els the priestes and clerkes shall syng, and so go eyther vnto the churche, or towardes the graue.*

Ihon xi.

I AM the resurrection and the life (saith the Lord) he that beleueth in me: yea, thoughe he were dead, yet shall he liue. And whosoeuer liueth, and belieueth in me, shall not dye for euer.

Job xix.

I KNOWE that my redemer lyueth, and that I shal rise out of the earth in the last daye, and shal be couered agayne with my skinne, and shall se God in my flesh : yea, and I my selfe shall beholde hym, not with other, but with thesame eyes.

i Tim. vi.

WE brought nothinge into this worlde, neither may we cary any thyng out of this worlde.

Job i.

The Lord geueth, and the Lorde taketh awaye. Euen as it hath pleased the Lorde so commeth thynges to passe: Blessed be the name of the Lorde.

¶ *When they come to the graue, whyles the corps is made redy to be layd into the earth, ye priest shal say, or the priestes, and clerkes shal sing.*

Job xi.[1]

MAN that is borne of a woman hathe but a shorte tyme to lyue, and is full of miserye : he commeth vp, and is cut doune lyke a floure, he flyeth as it were a shadow, and neuer continueth in one staye. In the middest of life we be in death, of whom mai we seke for succour but of the, O Lorde, whiche for our sinnes iustly arte displeased : yet O Lorde God most holy, O Lorde moste mightye, O holy, and moste mercifull Sauiour, deliuer vs not into the bitter paynes of eternall death. Thou knowest Lord the secretes of our hertes, shut not vp thy mercifull eyes to our prayers. But spare vs Lorde moste holy, O God moste mighty, O holy and mercifull Sauiour, thou most worthy iudge eternall, suffer vs not at our last houre for any paines of death to fall from the.

¶ *Then whyle the earth shal be cast vpon the body by some standing by, the priest shall saye.*

FOR asmuche as it hath pleased almightie God of his great mercy to take vnto hym selfe the Soule of oure deare brother, here

[1 Misprint for Job xiv.]

departed, we therfore committe hys bodye to the grounde, earthe, to earthe: ashes, to ashes, dust, to dust, in sure, and certein hope of resurrection to eternall lyfe, throughe oure Lorde Jesus Christe, who shall change oure vyle body that it may be lyke to his glorious body, according to the mighty workynge whereby he is able to subdue al thynges to hym selfe.

Then shalbe sayde, or songe.

I HEARDE a voyce from heauen saiyng vnto me, wryte from hencefurth, blessed are the dead whiche dye in the Lorde. Euen so sayeth the spirite that they reste from their labours.

Then shall folowe this lesson, taken out of the .xv. Chap. to the Corin. the first Epistle.

CHRIST is rysen from the dead, and become the fyrst frutes of them that slept. For by a man came deth, and by a man came the resurrecciō of the dead. For as by Adam al die, euen so by Christ shal al be made aliue, but euery manne in his owne order. The fyrste is Christe, then they that are Christes at his comming. Then commeth the ende when he hathe deliuered vp the kynge-dome to God the father, when he hath put doune all rule, and all aucthoritie and power. For he must reygne till he haue put hys enemies vnder hys fete. The laste enemye that shalbe destroyed is deathe. For he hath putte all thynges vnder his feete. But when he sayeth, all thynges are putte vnder hym, it is manifeste that hee is excepted, whyche dyd putte all thynges vnder hym. When al thinges are subdued vnto him, then shall the sonne also hym self be subiecte vnto him that put all thynges vnder hym, that God maye be al in all, elles what do they whyche are baptised ouer the deade, if the dead rise not at all? Why are they then baptised ouer them · yea, and why stande we alway then in ieopardye? By our reioysinge which I haue in Christ Jesu our Lorde, I dye daily. That I haue foughte wyth beastes at Ephesus after the maner of men, what auaūtageth it me, if the dead ryse not agayne? Lette vs eate and drincke, for to morow we shall dye. Be not ye deceyued ; euil wordes corrupt good maners. Awake truly out of slepe, and sinne not. For sōme haue not the know-ledge of God I speake this to your shame. But some manne wyl say how aryse the dead? with what body shal they come? thou foole, that whiche thou sowest is not quickened except it dye. And what sowest thou? thou sowest not that body that shalbe ; but bare corne, as of wheate, or some other: but God geueth it a bodye at hys plesure, to euerye sede his owne bodye. All fleshe is not one maner of flesh: but there is one maner of flesh of menne, an other maner of flesh of beasts, an other of fishes, an other of byrdes. There are also celestial bodyes, and there are bodies terrestriall. But the glory of the celestiall is one, and the

glory of the terrestrial is another.   There is one maner glory of
the Sonne, and another glory of the Mone, and another glory
of the starres.   For one starre differeth from another in glory: so
is the resurrection of the deade.   It is sowen in corrupciō, it riseth
againe in incorrupciō.   It is sowen in dishonoure, it riseth againe
in honoure.   It is sowen in weaknes, it ryseth againe in power.   It
is sowen a natural body, it ryseth againe a spirituall bodye.   There
is a natural body, and there is a spirituall body: as it is also
wryten, the fyrst man Adam was made a lyuynge soule, and the
laste Adam was made a quickeninge spirite.   How be it that is
not fyrst whyche is spirituall : but that whiche is naturall and then
that whiche is spirytual.   The first man is of the earth, earthye :
The seconde manne is the Lord from Heauen (heauenlye).   As is
the earthy, suche are they that be earthy.   And as is the heauenly,
such are they that are heauenly.   And as we haue borne the
ymage of the earthye, so shall we beare the ymage of the heauenly.
Thys saye I brethren, that fleshe and bloude cannot enherite the
kyngdome of God, neyther doth corruption enherite incorruption.
Beholde, I shewe you a mystery. we shall not all slepe : but we
shall al be chaunged, and that in a momente, in the twynkelynge
of an eye by the last trumpe.   For the trumpe shall blowe, and
the deade shall rise incorruptible, and we shall be chaunged.   For
this corruptible must put on incorruption, and this mortall must
put on immortalitye.   when this corruptible hath put on incor-
ruptiō, and this mortall hath put on immortalitye : then shall be
broughte to passe the sayinge that is wrytten, Deathe is swallowed
vp in victory : Deathe, where is thy stinge?   Hell where is thy
victory?   The stynge of deathe is sinne, and the strēgthe of sinne
is the lawe.   But thankes be vnto God, whyche hathe geuen vs
victory, through our Lord Jesus Christ.   Therfore my deare
brethren, be ye stedfast and vnmouable, alwaies rich in the worke
of the lorde, forasmuch as ye knowe, howe that your laboure is not
in vayne in the Lorde.

¶ *The Lesson ended, the Priest shall saye.*

Lorde haue mercye vpon vs.
Christe haue mercye vpon vs.
Lorde haue mercye vpon vs.
Our Father whiche arte in heauen. &c.
And leade vs not into temptacion.
Aunswere. But deliuer vs from euil.   Amen.

¶ *The Priest.*

ALMIGHTIE God, with whome do liue the spirites of thē that
depart hēce in the lorde and in whome the soules of thē that be
elected, after they be deliuered from the burthē of the flesh, be
in ioye and felicitie.   We geue the hearty thankes for that it hath

pleased the to deliuer this .N. oure brother, out of the miseries of
thys synneful worlde beseching the that it may please the of thy
gracious goodnes, shortelye to accomplishe the numbre of thyne
electe, and to haste thy kyngedome, that we with thys oure brother,
and all other departed in the true fayth of thy holy name, may
haue our perfect consummacion and blisse, both in bodye and
soule in thy eternall and euerlastynge glorie. Amen.

¶ *The Collect.*

O MERCIFULL God, the father of our Lord Jesus Christe, who
is the Resurrection and the lyfe, in whom whosoeuer beleueth
shall liue, thoughe he dye, and whosoeuer liueth, and beleueth in
hym, shall not dye eternally, who also taughte vs (by hys holy
apostle Paule), not to be sory as men without hope, for them that
slepe in hym : We mekely beseche the (O Father) to rayse vs
from the deathe of sinne vnto the lyfe of righteousnes, that when
we shall depart thys lyfe, we may rest in hym, as our hope is
thys oure brother doeth, and that at the generall resurrection in
the laste daye, we maye be founde acceptable in thy syghte, and
receiue that blessing which thy welbeloued sonne shall then pronounce to all that loue and fear the, saiynge : Come ye blessed
children of my father, receyue the Kyngedome prepared for you
frome the begynnynge of the worlde. Graunte thys, we beseche
the, O mercifull father, throughe Jesus Christe our mediatoure and
redemer. Amen.

¶ THE THANKESGEUINGE OF WOMEN AFTER CHILDE BYRTHE,

COMMUNELYE CALLED

THE CHURCHYNGE OF WOMEN.

The woman shall come into the Churche, and there shall knele downe in some conuenient place, nyghe vnto the place where the table standeth, and the priest standing by her, shal saie these wordes, or suche lyke, as the case shal require.

FORASMUCHE as it hath pleased almyghtye God of hys goodnes to geue you safe delyueraūce, and hath preserued you in the great daūger of childbyrth : ye shal therfore geue heartye thankes vnto God and praye.

¶ *Then shall the priest saye this Psalme.*

I HAUE lyfte vp myne eyes vnto the hylles, from whence commeth my helpe.

My helpe cōmeth euen from the Lord : whych hath made heauen and earth.

He wyll not suffre thy foote to be moued : and he that kepeth the, wil not slepe.

Beholde, he that kepeth Israell : shall neyther slomber nor slepe.

The Lorde hym selfe is thy keper : the Lorde is thy defence vpon thy ryght hande.

So that the sonne shall not burne the by daye, neither the moone by night.

The Lorde shal preserue the from al euil : yea, it is euen he that shal kepe thy soule.

The Lorde shal preserue thy goinge out, and thy commynge in : from thys tyme forth for euermore.

Glory be to the Father, and to the Sonne &c.

As it was in the beginynge, is now &c.

Lorde haue mercye vpon vs.

Christe haue mercye vpon vs.

Lorde haue mercye vpon us.

OUR FATHER WHICHE ARTE &c.

And leade vs not into temptacion.

Aunswere. But deliuer vs from euil. Amen.
Priest. O Lorde saue this woman thy seruaunt.
Aunswere. Whiche putteth her trust in the.
Priest. Be thou to her a strong Towre.
Aunswere. From the face of her enemy.
Priest. Lorde heare our praier.
Aunswere. And let our crie come vnto the.

Priest.

Let vs praie.

O ALMIGHTY God, which hast deliuered this woman thy seruaunte from the great paine and peril of childe birthe : Graunt we beseche the most mercifull Father, that she through thy help may bothe faithfully liue, and walke in her vocation, accordyng to thy wil, in this lyfe present, and also may be partaker of euerlastyng glory in the lyfe to come, throughe Jesus Christ our Lorde. Amen.

The woman that commeth to giue her thanckes, muste offer accustomed offerynges, aud if there be a Communion, it is conuenient that she receiue the holy Communion.

A COMMINATION AGAINST SINNERS,

*After Mornyng prayer, the people beyng called together by the ringyng of
a Bel, and assembled in the Churche, thēglish Letany shalbe saide after
thaccustomed maner, whyche ended the priest shal go into the pulpit and
saie thus.*

BRETHREN, in the Prymatyue churche there was a godly discipline, that at the beginyng of Lent, suche personnes as were notoryus
Synners, were putte to open penaunce and punyshed in thys world,
that their soules might be saued in the daie of the lord. And that
others admonyshed by theyr exāple myght be more afrayde to
offende. In the stede wherof (vntill the sayde Discypline maye be
restored agayne, whyche thynge is muche to be wyshed) it is
thought good that at this time (in your presence) shoulde be redde
the general sentences of goddes cursyng agaynst impenitent Synners, gathered out of the .xxvii. Chapiter of Deuteronomye, and
other places of Scripture. And that ye shoulde aunswere to euery
sentence. Amen. To thyntent that you being admonished of the
great indignation of God against Synners : may the rather be
called to earnest and true repentaunce, and maye walke more
warely in these daungerous daies, flieing from suche vices, for the
whyche ye affirme wyth your owne mouthes, the Curse of God to
be due.

CURSED is the man that maketh any carued, or molten Image,
an abhomination to the Lorde, the worke of the handes of the
craftes man, and putteth it in a secrete place to worship it.

¶ *And the people shal aunswere and saie*

Amen.

Minister. Cursed is he that cursethe his father, or mother.
Aunswere. Amen.
Minister. Cursed is hee that remoueth away the marcke of hys
neyghbours lande.
Aunswere. Amen.
Minister. Cursed is he that maketh the blynde to go oute of hys
way.
Aunswere. Amen.

Minister. Cursed is he that, letteth in iudgmēt, the right of the straunger, of them that be fatherles, and of widdowes.

Aunswere. Amen.

Minister. Cursed is he that smiteth his neighbour secretlye.

Aunswere. Amen.

Minister. Cursed is he that lieth with his neighbours wife.

Aunswere. Amen.

Minister. Cursed is he that taketh rewarde to slea the Soule of innocent bloude.

Aunswere. Amen.

Minister. Curseth is he that putteth hys trust in manne, and taketh manne for hys defence, and in hys harte goeth from the Lorde.

Aunswere. Amen.

Minister. Cursed are the vnmerciful, the fornicatours, and adulterers, and the couetous persones, the worshippers of ymages, slaunderers, dronkardes, and extorcioners.

Aunswere. Amen.

The Minister.

Nowe seyng that all they be accursed (as the Prophete Dauid Psa. cxviii. beareth wytnesse) whyche do erre, and go astraye from the commaundementes of God, let vs remembring the dreadful iudgemente hanginge ouer our heddes, and beyng always at hande returne vnto oure Lorde God, with all contricion and mekenes of hearte, bewailynge and lamenting our synful lyfe, knowledging and cōfessing our offences, and sekynge to brynge furth worthie fruictes of penaunce. For nowe is the Axe put vnto the roote of the trees, Math. iii. so that euery tree which bringeth not furth good fruict, is hewen downe and cast into the fire. It is a fearfull thing to falle into the Heb. x. handes of the lyuinge God: he shal poure doune raine vpon the Psal. x. synners, Snares, fyre, and brimstone, storme and tempeste, thys shalbe their portion to drincke. For lo, the Lorde is comen out Esai. xxvi. of his place, to visite the wickednesse of suche as dwel vpon the earth. But who may abyde the daye of his comming? Who Mal. iii. shalbe able to endure, when he apereth? His fanne is in his Math. iii. hande, and he wyll pourge hys floore, and gather his wheate into the barne, but he wyl burne the chaffe with vnquenchable fyre. The daye of the Lord commeth as a thefe vpon the night, and i. Thes. v. when men shall saye peace, and all thinges are saufe, then shal Rom. ii. soubdenly destruction come vpon them, as sorowe commeth vppon a woman trauailyng with childe, and they shall not escape. Then shall appeare the wrathe of God in the day of vēgeāce, which obstinate sinners, throughe the stubburnnes of theyr hearte, haue heaped vnto them selfe, whyche despysed the goodnes, pacyence, and longe sufferaunce of God, when he called them continually to repentaunce. Then shall they call vpon me, sayeth the Lorde, Prouer i. but I wyll not heare: they shall seke me early, but they shall not

Mat. xxv.

ii. Cor. vi.

Ihon ix.

Mat. xxv.

fynde me: and that because they hated knowledge, and receyued not the feare of the Lorde, but abhorred my counsail, and dispised my correcyon, then shall it be to late to knocke, when the dore shalbe shutte, and to late to crye for mercye, when it is the tyme of Iustice. O terryble voyce of most iust indgement, whiche shalbe pronounced vpon them, when it shalbe sayde vnto them: Go, ye cursed, into the fyre euerlastynge, whyche is prepared for the deuill and hys Aungeles. Therfore brethren take we hede by tyme, whyle the daie of saluacion lasteth, for the nyght commeth when none can worke: but let vs whyle we haue the lyght, beleue in the lyghte, and walke as the children of the lyght, that we be not caste into the vtter darckenes, where is wepyinge and gnasshynge of teeth. Lette vs not abuse the goodnes of God, whyche calleth vs mercyfully to amendement, and of hys endelesse pytye promysed vs forgeuenesse of that whyche is paste: If (wyth a whole mynde and true hearte) we returne vnto hym. For though our synnes be red as scarlet, they shalbe as whyte as snowe, and thoughe they be lyke purple, yet shall they be as whyte as wolle. Turne you cleane (sayeth the Lorde) from all your wickednes, and your synne shal not be your destruction. Cast awaye from you all your vngodlynes that ye haue done: make you newe heartes, and a newe spiryte: wherfore wyll ye dye, O ye house of Israell? Seiyng that I haue no pleasure in the deathe of hym that dyeth (sayeth the Lorde God.) Turne you then, and you shall lyue. Although we haue synned, yet haue we an aduocate with the Father, Jesus Christe the ryghteous, and he it is that obteyneth grace for our synnes, for he was wounded for our offences, and smytten for our wyckednesse. Let vs therfore returne vnto hym, who is the mercifull receyuer of all true penitent sinners, assuring oure selfe that he is ready to receyue vs, and most willyng to pardone vs, yf we come to him, with faythfull repentaunce. Yf we will submit our selues vnto him, and from henceforthe walke in his wayes. Yf we will take hys easy yoke, and lighte burthen vpon vs, to folowe hym in lowlines, pacience, and charitie, and be ordered by the gouernaunce of hys holy spirite, seking alwayes his glorie, and seruyng hym duely in our vocation with thankes geuynge. This yf we do, Christ wil deliuer vs from the curse of the law, and from the extreme malediction, which light vpon theym, that shalbe set on the left hand, and he wyll set us on hys ryght hande, and geue vs the blessed benediction of hys father, commaundynge vs to take possession of his gloryous kyngdome, vnto the whiche he vouche-saufe to brynge vs al, for hys infinite mercye.

Esay. i.

Ezechiel xxviii.[1]

Esai. iii.

Math. xi.

Math. xxv.

¶ *Then shall they all knele vpon theyr knees: And the Priestes and Clerckes knelynge (were they are accustomed to saye the Letany) shall say thys Psalme. Miserere mei Deus.*

Psal.

HAUE mercy vpon me, O God after thy great goodnes, according to the multitud of thy mercyes, do away myne offences.

[1 Misprint for xviii.]

Washe me throughly frō my wyckednes and clense me from my synne.

For I acknowledge my faultes, and my synne is euer before me.

Against the onely haue I synned, and done this euyll in thy sight, that thou mightest be iustyfyed in thy sayeng, and cleare when thou art iudged.

Beholde, I was shapen in wickednesse, and in synne hath my mother conceiued me.

But lo, thou requirest trueth in inwarde parties, and shalt make me to vnderstande wisedome secretlye.

Thou shalte purge me with hysoppe, and I shall be cleane, thou shalt washe me, and I shall be whyter then Snowe.

Thou shalt make me here of ioy and gladnesse : that the bones whiche thou hast broken may reioyce.

Turne thy face from my sinnes : and put oute all my misdedes.

Make me a cleane hearte (O God :) and renue a right spirite within me.

Cast me not away from thy presence : and take not thy holy spirite from me.

O geue me the comforte of thy helpe agayne : and stablysh me with thy free spirite.

Then shall I teache thy wayes vnto the wicked : and sinners shalbe conuerted vnto the.

Deliuer me from bloude giltines (O God) thou that art the God of my healthe : and my tonge shall synge of thy ryghteousnes.

Thou shalte open my lyppes (O Lord) my mouth shal shewe thy prayse.

For thou desirest no sacrifice, els woulde I geue it the : but thou delightest not in burnt offerynge.

The sacrifice of God is a troubled spirite : a broken and a contrite hearte O God, shalte thou not despise.

O be fauourable and gracious vnto Siō : builde thou the walles of Jerusalem.

Then shalt thou be pleased with the sacrifice of rightuuousnesse, with the burnt offerynges and oblations : then shall they offer yong bullockes vpon thine aultare.

Glory bee to the Father, and to the Sonne, and to the holy Ghoste.

As it was in the beginning, is nowe, and euer shal be world without ende.   Amen.

Lorde haue mercy vpon vs.

Christ haue mercy vpon vs.

Lorde haue mercy vpon vs.

Our father which arte in heauen. &c.

And leade vs not into temptacion.

Aunswere. But deliuer vs from euil.   Amen.

Minister.   O Lorde saue thy seruauntes.

Aunswere. Whiche put their trust in the.

Minister. Sende vnto them helpe from aboue.
Aunswere. And euermore mightely defende them.
Minister. Help vs, O God our sauiour.
Aunswere. And for the glorye of thy names sake deliuer vs, bee mercyfull vnto vs synners, for thy names sake.
The Minister. Lorde heare my praiers.
Aunswere. And let our crie come vnto thee.

Let vs praye.

O LORD, we besech the, mercifully heare our prayers, and spare al those which confesse their sinnes to the, that they (whose consciences by sin are accused) by thy merciful pardon may be absolued, throughe Christ our Lorde.   Amen.

O MOSTE mighty God, and mercyfull father which haste compassion of al men, and hatest nothing that thou haste made : whiche wouldest not the deathe of a synner, but that he should rather turne from synne, and be saued : mercifully forgeue vs oure trespasses, and comforte vs, whiche be grieued and weryed with the burden of oure synne.   Thy propertye is to haue mercy, to the onlye it apperteineth to forgeue synnes : spare vs therefore good Lorde, spare thy people whom thou haste redemed.   Enter not into iudgement wyth thy seruauntes, whiche be vyle earthe, and miserable synners, but so turne thyne yre from vs whyche mekely knowledge oure vylenes, and trulye repente vs of our faultes : so make haste to helpe vs in this worlde, that we maye euer liue wyth thee in the worlde to come, throughe Jesus Christe oure Lorde. Amen.

Then shall the people saye this that foloweth after the Minister.

TURNE thou vs, O good Lorde, and so shall we be turned : be fauourable O Lorde bee fauourable too thy people, whyche turne to the, in wepynge, fastyng, and prayinge, for thou art a mercifull God, full of compassion, longe sufferynge, and of a great pitie. Thou sparest when we deserue punishment, and in thy wrathe thynkest vpon mercye, spare thy people good Lorde, spare theym, and let not thy heritage be brought to confusion : heare vs O Lorde for thy mercy is greate, and after the multitude of thy mercies, loke vpon vs.[1]

[1 Some impressions of the Prayer Book by Jugge and Cawode have on the reverse of the last leaf :

This boke of praiers is to be solde as foloweth, and not aboue.

In Queers vnbounde.	ii. s. iiii. d.
In parchement bounde,	iii. s.
In paste or Borde bounde,	iii. s. viii. d.]

GODLY PRAYERS.

A generall confession of sinnes, to be said euery morning.

O ALMIGHTIE God, our heauenly Father, I confesse and knowledge, that I am a miserable and a wretched sinner, and haue
manifold waies most grieuouslie transgressed thy most godly
commaundements, through wicked thoughts, vngodly lusts, sinfull
words and deeds, and in my whole life. In sinne am I borne and
conceiued, and there is no goodnesse in mee ; inasmuch as if thou
shouldest enter into thy narrowe iudgement with me, iudging me
according vnto the same, I were neuer able to suffer or abide it,
but must needes perish and be dampned for euer : So little help,
comfort, or succoure is there either in me, or in any other creature.
Onely this is my comfort (O heauenly Father), that thou diddest
not spare thy onely deare beloued sonne, but diddest giue him vp
vnto the most bitter, and most vile and slaunderous death of the
Crosse for me, that hee might so pay the ransome for my sinnes,
satisfie thy iudgement, still and pacifie thy wrath, reconcile me
againe vnto thee, and purchase me thy grace and thy fauour, and
euerlasting life. Wherfore, through the merite of his most bitter
death and passion, and through his innocent bloodshedding, I
beseech the, O heauenly Father, that thou wilt vouchsafe to bee
gracious and mercifull vnto me, to forgiue and pardon me al my
sinnes, to lighten my harte with thy holy Spirit, to renue, confirme, and strengthen me with a right and a perfecte faith, and to
inflame mee in loue toward thee and my neighbour, that I may
hencefurth with a willing and a glad harte, walke as becommeth
me, in thy most godly commaundements, and so glorifie and praise
the euerlastingly. And also that I may with a free conscience
and quiet hert, in all manner of temptations, afflictions, or
necessities, and euen in the verie pangs of death, crie boldly and
merily vnto thee, and say : I beleue in God the Father Almightie,
maker of heauen and earth, and in Iesus Christ, &c. But, O
Lord God heauenly father, to comfort myselfe in affliction and
temptation with these articles of the Christian faithe, it is not in
my power, for faith is thy gift : and forasmuch as thou wilt bee
prayed vnto, and called vpon for it, I come vnto thee, to pray and
beseech the, both for that and for all my other necessities, euen

as thy deare beloued Sonne our Sauiour Iesus Christ himselfe
hath taught vs.   And from the very bottome of my heart I cry,
and say : Our Father, which art in heauen. &c.

¶ *Prayers to be said in the Morning.*

O MERCIFULL Lord God, heauenly Father, I render most high
laudes, praise, and thankes vnto thee, that thou hast preserued
me both this night, and all the time and daies of my life hitherto,
vnder thy protection, and hast suffered mee to liue vntill this
present houre.   And I beseech thee hartily, that thou wilt
vouchsaufe to receiue me this day, and the residue of my whole
life, from hencefurth into thy tuition, ruling and gouerning me
with thy holie Spirit, that all maner of darknes, of misbeleefe,
infidelitie, and of carnall lusts and affections, may be vtterly
chased and driuen out of my harte, and that I may be iustified
and saued both bodie and soule through a right and a perfect
faith, and so walke in the light of thy most godly trueth, to thy
glorie and praise, and to the profite and furtherance of my neighbour, through Iesus Christ our Lord and Sauiour.   Amen.

ALL possible thankes that wee are able, wee render vnto thee,
O Lord Iesus Christ, for that thou hast willed this night past to
bee prosperous vnto vs ; and we beseech thee likewise to prosper
all this same day vnto vs for thy glorie, and for the helth of our
soule : and that thou which art the true light, not knowing any
going downe, and which art the Sunne eternall, giuing life, foode,
and gladnes vnto all things, vouchsaufe to shine into our minds,
that we may not any where stumble to fall into any sin, but may
thorow thy good guiding and conducting, come to the life euerlasting.   Amen.

O LORD Iesus Christ, which art the true Sun of the world,
euermore arising, and neuer going downe, which by thy most
holesome appearing and sight, doest bring foorth, preserue,
nourish, and refresh all things, as well that are in heauen, as also
that are on earth : we beseech thee mercifully and fauourably to
shine into our hearts, that the night and darknesse of sins, and
the mists of errors on euery side driuen away, thou brightly
shining within our harts, we may all our life space go without
any stumbling or offence, and may decently and seemely walk, (as
in the day time,) being pure and cleane from the works of darknes,
and abounding in all good works which God hath prepared for vs
to walk in : which with the Father and with the holie Ghost liuest
and reignest for euer and euer.   Amen.

O GOD and Lord Iesus Christ, thou knowest, yea, and hast also
taught vs, how great the infirmitie and weakenesse of man is, and
how certaine a thing it is that it can nothing doe without thy
godly helpe.   If man trust to himselfe, it cannot bee auoyded, but

that hee must headlong runne and fall into a thousand vndoings and mischiefs. O our Father, haue thou pitie and compassion vpon the weakenesse of vs thy children, bee thou prest and readie to helpe vs, alwaies shewing thy mercie vpon vs, and prospering whatsoeuer we godly go about : so that, thou giuing vs light, wee may see what things are truely good in deede ; thou encouraging vs, wee may haue an earnest desire to the same ; and thou being our guide, wee may come where to obtaine them : for wee hauing nothing but mistrust in our selues, doe yeeld and commit our selues full and whole vnto thee alone, which workest all things in al creatures, to thy honour and glorie. So be it.

A prayer against temptation.

O LORD Iesus Christ, the only stay and fence of our mortall state, our onely hope, our onely saluation, our glorie, and our triumph, who in the flesh (which thou hadst for our only cause taken vpon thee) diddest suffer thy selfe to be tempted of Sathan, and who onely and alone of all men diddest vtterly ouercome and vanquish sinne, death, the world, the diuell, and all the kingdome of hell : and whatsoeuer thou hast so ouercommed, for our behoofe it is that thou hast ouercommed it : neither hath it been thy will to haue any of thy seruants to keepe battel or fight with any of the foresaid euils, but of purpose to rewarde vs with a crowne of the more glorie for it. And to the intent that thou mightest likewise ouerthrow Sathan in thy members, as thou haddest afore done in thine owne person, giue thou (wee beseech thee) vnto vs thy souldiers (O Lion most victorious of the tribe of Iuda) strength against the roring Lion, which continually wandreth to and fro, seeking whom he may deuoure. Thou being that same Serpent, the true giuer of health and life, that were nailed on high vpon a tree, giue vnto vs, thy little seelie ones, wilinesse against the deceitfull awayting of the most subtile serpent. Thou being a Lambe as white as snow, the vanquisher of Satans tyrañie, giue vnto vs thy little sheep the strength and vertue of thy spirit, that being in our owne selues weake and feeble, and in thee strong and valiant, wee may withstand and ouercome all assaults of the diuell, so that our ghostly enemie may not glorie on vs, but being conquered through thee, we may giue thankes to thy mercie, which neuer leaueth them destitute that put their trust in thee : who liuest and reignest God for euer without end. Amen.

A prayer for the obtaining of wisedome.

O GOD of our fathers, and Lord of mercie, thou that hast made all things with thy word, and ordeined man through thy wisdome, that he should haue dominion ouer the creatures which thou hast made, that he should order the world according to equitie and righteousnesse, and execute iudgement with a true heart : giue me wisedome, which is euer about thy seate, and put me not out Sap'en. ix

from among thy children : for I thy seruant and sonne of thy
handmaid am a feeble person, of a short time, and too young to
the vnderstanding of thy iudgementes and lawes : yea, though a
man be neuer so perfect among the children of men, yet if thy
wisedome be not with him, he shall be nothing worth.   O send
thy wisedome out of thy holie heauens, and from the throne of thy
maiestie, that she may be with me and labour with me, that I may
know what is acceptable in thy sight ; for she knoweth and vnder-
standeth all things, and she shall conduct me right soberly in thy
workes, and preserue me in her power : so shall my workes be
acceptable.   Amen.

A prayer against worldly carefulnesse.

O MOST deare and tender father, our defender and nourisher,
endue vs with thy grace, that we may cast off the great blindnesse
of our mindes, and carefulnesse of worldlie things, and maye put
our whole studie and care in keeping of thy holie law ; and that
wee may labour and trauaile for our necessities in this life, like
the birds of the ayre, and the lillies of the field, without care.   For
thou hast promised to be carefull for vs, and hast commaunded
that vpon thee we should cast al our care : which liuest and
reignest, world without end.   Amen.

A prayer necessarie for all persons.

O MERCIFULL God, I wretched sinner reknowledge myselfe
bound to keepe thy holie commaundements, but yet vnable to performe them, and to bee accepted for iust without the righteousnesse
of Iesus Christ thy onely Sonne, who hath perfectly fulfilled thy
law, to iustifie all men that beleeue and trust in him.   Therefore
graunt me grace, I beseech thee, to be occupied in doing of good
workes, which thou commaundest in holie scripture, all the daies of
my life, to thy glorie, and yet to trust onely in thy mercie, and in
Christes merites, to bee pourged from my sinnes, and not in my
good workes, be they neuer so many.   Giue me grace to loue thy
holie word feruently, to search the Scriptures diligently, to reade
them humblie, to vnderstand them truly, to liue after them effectually.   Order my life so, O Lord, that it be alwaye acceptable
vnto thee.   Giue me grace not to reioyce in any thing that dis-
pleaseth thee, but euermore to delight in those things that please
thee, be they neuer so contrary to my desires.   Teach me so to
pray, that my petitions may be graciously heard of the.   Keepe
me vpright among diuersities of opinions and iudgements in the
worlde that I neuer swarue from thy trueth taught in holie Scripture.   In prosperitie, O Lord, saue me, that I waxe not proude.
In aduersitie helpe me, that I neuer despaire nor blaspheme thy
holie name, but taking it patiently, to giue thee thankes, and trust
to be deliuered after thy pleasure.   When I happen to falle into
sinne through frailtie, I beseech thee to worke true repentance in

my heart, that I may bee sorie without desperation, trust in thy
mercie without presumption, that I may amend my life, and become truely religious without hypocrisie, lowly in heart without
faining, faithfull and trustie without deceit, merie without lightnesse,
sad without mistrust, sober without slouthfulnesse, content with
mine owne without couetousnesse, to tell my neighbour his faults
charitably without dissimulation, to instruct my household in thy
lawes truely, to obey our Kyng[1] and all gouernours vnder him vnfainedly, to receiue all lawes and common ordinances (which dis-
agreeth not from thy holie word) obediently, to pay euery man
that which I owe vnto him truely, to backbite no man, nor slander
my neighbour secretly, and to abhorre all vice, louing all goodnesse
earnestly. O Lord, graunt me thus to doe, for the glorie of thy holy
name. Amen.

A prayer necessary to be said at all times.

O BOUNTIFUL Jesu, O swete sauiour, O Christ the sonne of
God, haue pitie vpon me, mercifully heare me, and despyse not
my prayers. Thou hast created me of nothing, thou hast redemed
me from the bondage of sinne, death, and hel, nether with golde
nor siluer, but with thy moste precious body once offred vpon the
crosse, and thine own bloud shed once for al for my raunsome :
therefore cast me not away, whom thou by thy great wisdom haste
made : despise me not, whom ye hast redemed with such a precious
treasure. Nor let my wickednes destroy that, which thy goodnes
hath builded. Nowe whiles I liue, O Jesu haue mercy on me, for
if I dye oute of thy fauour, it wil be to late afterward to cal for thy
mercy : whiles I haue time to repent, loke vpon me with thy merciful eyes, as thou diddest vouchsafe to loke vpon Peter thine
Apostle, that I may bewaile my sinfull lyfe, and obteyne thy fauour,
and die therin. I reknowledge, that if thou shouldest deale with
me according to very iustice, I haue deserued euerlasting death.
Therefore I appele to thy high throne of merci trusting to obtaine
Gods fauoure, not for my merites, but for thy merites, O Jesu,
who hast geuen thy self an acceptable sacrifice to thy father, to
appease his wrath, and to bring all sinners, (truly repenting and
amending their euyl lyfe) into his fauour again. Accept me, O
lord, among the numbre of them that shal be saued, forgeue my
sines, geue me grace to leade a godly and innocent life, graunt me
thy heauenly wisdom, inspyre my heart with fayth, hope, and
charitie ; geue me grace to bee humble in prosperitie, pacient in
aduersitie, obedient to my rulers, faithful vnto them that trust me,
dealing truely with al men, to liue chastely in wedlocke, to abhorre
adultery, fornicacion, and al unclennes, to doe good after my power
vnto al men, to hurt no man, that thi name may be glorified in me,
during this present life, and that I afterward may obteine euerlasting
life, thorow thy merci, and ye merites of thi passion. Amen.

[1 So it stands even in the edition of 1567.]

¶ *Certaine prayers, taken oute of the seruice dayly, vsed in the quenes house.*

Munday.

ALMIGHTIE God, the Father of mercie, and God of all comfort, the which onely forgiuest sinne, forgiue vnto vs our sinnes, good Lorde, forgiue vnto vs our sinnes ; that by the multitude of thy mercies they may be couered, and not imputed vnto vs, and by the operation of the holy Ghost, we may haue power and strength hereafter to resist sin by our Sauiour and Lord Iesus Christ. Amen.

Tuesday.

O LORD GOD, which despisest not a contrite hart, and forgettest the sins and wickednes of a sinner, in what houre soeuer hee doth mourne and lament his olde maner of liuing : graunt vnto vs (O Lord) true contrition of hart, that we may vehemently despise our sinfull life past, and wholy be conuerted vnto thee, by our Sauiour and Lord Iesus Christ.   Amen.

Wednesday.

O MERCIFULL FATHER, by whose power and strength wee may ouercome our enemies both bodily and ghostly : graunt vnto vs, O Lord, that, according to our promise made in our baptisme, we may ouercome the chief enemies of our soule, that is, the desires of the world, the pleasures of the flesh, and the suggestiõs of the wicked spirit ; and so after leade our liues in holines and righteousnes, that we may serue thee in spirit and trueth, and that by our Sauiour and Lord Iesus Christ.   Amen.

Thursday.

O ALMIGHTY and euerlasting God, which not onely giuest euery good and perfite gift, but also encreasest those gifts that thou hast giuen : we most humbly beseech thee, (mercifull God) to increase in vs the gift of faith, that we may truely beleeue in thee, and in thy promises made vnto vs ; and that neither by our negligence, nor infirmitie of the flesh, nor by grieuousnesse of temptation, neither by the subtill crafts and assaults of the diuell wee bee driuen from faith in the blood of our Sauiour and Lord Iesus Christ.   Amen.

Friday.

GRAUNT vnto vs, O mercifull God, (wee most heartily beseech thee), knowledge and true vnderstanding of thy word, that all ignorance expelled, we may know what thy will and pleasure is in all things, and how to doe our duties, and truely to walke in our vocation, and that also we may expresse in our liuing, those things that we doe knowe, that we be not only knowers of thy worde, good Lord, but also bee workers of the same : by our Sauiour and Lorde Iesus Christ.   Amen.

Saturday.

O ALMIGHTY God, which hast prepared euerlasting life to all those that be thy faithfull seruaunts : graunt vnto vs, Lord, sure hope of the life euerlasting, that we, being in this miserable world, may haue some taste and feeling of it in our hearts : and

that not by our deseruing, but by the merits and deseruing of our
Sauiour and Lord Iesus Christ. Amen.

O MERCIFULL God, our only aide, succour, and strength at all
times ; graunt vnto vs, O Lord, that in the time of prosperitie we
be not proude, and so forget thee, but that with our whole power
and strength wee may cleaue vnto thee ; and in the time of
aduersitie, that wee fall not to infidelitie and desperation, but that
alwaies with a constant faith we may call for helpe vnto thee :
graunt this, O Lord, for our aduocates sake, and Sauiour Iesus
Christ. Amen.

O ALMIGHTIE and mercifull Lord, which giuest vnto thy elect Sunday.
people the holy Ghost, as a sure pledge of thy heauenly kingdome :
Graunt vnto vs, O Lord, thy holie spirit, that he may beare
witnesse with our spirit, that wee be thy children, and heires of
thy kingdome, and that by the operation of this thy spirit we may
kill all carnall lusts, vnlawfull pleasures, concupiscences, euill
affections, contrarie vnto thy will, by our Sauiour and Lord Iesus
Christ. Amen.

A prayer for trust in God.

THE beginning of the fall of man was trust in himselfe. The
beginning of the restoring of man, was distrust in himselfe, and
trust in God. O most gracious and most wise guide, our Sauiour
Christ, which doest lead them the right way to immortall blessed-
nesse, which trulie and vnfainedlie trusting in thee, commit themselues to thee : Graunt vs, that like as we be blind and feeble in
deed, so we may take and repute our selues, that we presume not
of ourselues, to see to ourselues, but so farre to see, that alway
wee may haue thee before our eyes, to followe thee, being our
guide, to bee readie at thy call most obediently, and to commit
our selues wholy vnto thee ; that thou, which only knowest the
way, maist leade vs the same way vnto our heauenly desires ; to
thee with the Father and the holie Ghost be glorie for euer.
Amen.

A prayer for the concorde of Christes church.

ARYSE Lorde, let thine enemies be scattered, thy haters put to
flight, the righteous and Christes disciples make pleasaunt and
mery, let them sing prayses and pleasaunt songes vnto thee, let
them blowe abrode thy magnificence, let them moste highly
auaunce thy maiestie, let thy glorye grow, let the kingdom of
Christ from heauen among the chosen be enlarged : bee thou the
father of the fatherles, the iudge of the widowes, and the protectour of them, namely[1] whom the world forsaketh, whose consciences be troubled, whom the world pursueth for Christes sake,
whiche be nedy and wrapped full of misery. In thy house O lord,
let vs dwel in peace and concord, geue vs al one heart, one minde,

[1 Namely: especially.]

one true interpretacion vpon thy word.   Pluck of the bandes, aswell from the consciences as from the bodies of the miserable captiues, and of them also whiche as yet bee hedged in within the lystes of death, and vnaduisedly striue against grace.   How drye (lord) is the flocke of thyne heritage !   I praye thee, powre downe largely the showres of thy graces, lette a more plenteous fruitefulnes chaunce, let thy people be strengthened with thy spirite : Graunt vs lord thy word aboundantly, so that there may be many preachers of thy Gospel, which maye within them selues holily conspire and agree.   Lette the church, the spouse of Christ, deale large spoyles of the conquered Sathan.   All that beleeue in thee, by Christe (O lorde God of health), mought lyft thee vp with prayses, might renoume thee and extolle thee.   We bee entered into the voyage of saluacion.   Conducte vs luckelye vnto the porte, that beeynge delyuered by thee from the verye death, we maye escape and come to the verye lyfe.   Finishe the thinge that thou hast begon in vs, make vs to increase from faith to faith, leaue vs not to our own wil and choise, for it is slippery and redy to fal.   To the thunderboltes of thy word put violence, that we may geue the glory to thee alonely.   Geue to thy people courage and power to withstande synne, and to obeye thy worde in all thinges : O Lorde God most glorious and excellent ouer all.

A prayer agaynst the enemies of Christes trueth.

DELYUER me O Lorde, from the vngodly and stiffenecked persons, for thou seest how in theyr hartes they ymagine mischiefe, and haue great pleasure to picke quarelles, theyr tongues bee more sharpe than any adders sting, and vnder theyr lippes lurketh poison of adders.   But, O merciful Lord, let me not fal into theyr handes, that they handle not me after theyr owne lustes.   Thou onely art my God, thou must heare my pieteous plaint : Lord, that rulest al together, that art the strength and power of my defence, bee thou as a sallet [1] on my head whensoeuer the vngodlye shal assault me : neyther suffre thou not the wicked thus to prosper in their matters.   Suffre not their croked and malicious stomackes to encrease, and spitefully reuyle thee.   Loke vpon thy poore wretches cause, and ridde me oute of these dayly greuaunces, then shall I with a right vp heart and pleasaunt countenaunce extoll and magnifye thy holye name.   Amen.

A prayer for pacience in trouble.

HOW hast thou (O Lord) humbled and plucked me downe.   I dare now uneths [2] make my prayers vnto thee, for thou art angrie with me, but not without my deseruing.   Certainly I haue sinned, Lord, I confesse it ;   I will not deny it ;   but, oh my God, pardon my trespasses, release my debts, render now thy grace againe vnto me, stop my woūds, for I am all to plagued and beaten : yet Lord this

[1 Sallet : a kind of helmet.]   [2 Uneths : scarcely, hardly.]

notwithstanding I abide patiently, and giue mine attendance on thee, continually waiting for reliefe at thy hand, and that not without skill ; for I haue receiued a token of thy fauour and grace towards me, I meane thy word of promise concerning Christ, who for me was offered on the Crosse for a ransome, a sacrifice and price for my sins : wherefore, acccording to that thy promise, defend me Lord by thy right hand, and giue a gracious eare to my requests, for al mans staies are but vaine. Beate downe therefore mine enemies thine owne selfe with thy power, which art mine onely ayder and protector, O Lord God almightie. Amen.

A prayer to be said at night going to bed.

O MERCIFULL Lorde God, heauenly Father, whether we sleepe or wake, liue or die, we are alwaies thine. Wherefore I beseech thee hartily that thou wilt vouchsafe to take care and charge of me, and not to suffer me to perish in the workes of darknesse, but to kindle the light of thy countenaunce in my heart, that thy godly knowledge may daily increase in mee, through a right and pure faith, and that I may alwayes bee found to walke and liue after thy will and pleasure, through Iesus Christ our Lord and Sauiour. Amen.

¶ *A prayer to be said at the houre of death.*

O LORD Iesus, which art the onely health of all men liuing, and the euerlasting life of them which die in faith : I wretched sinner giue and commit my self wholy uvto thy most blessed will. And I being sure that the thinge cannot perish which is committed vnto thy mercie, willingly now I leaue this fraile and wicked flesh, in hope of the resurrection, which in better wise shal restore it to me againe. I beseech thee, most mercifull Lord Iesus Christ, that thou wilt by thy grace make strong my soule against all temptations, and that thou wilt couer and defend me with the buckler of thy mercie against al the assaults of the diuell. I see and knowledge, that there is in myselfe no helpe of saluation, but all my confidence, hope, and trust, is in thy most mercifull goodnesse. I haue no merites, nor good workes, which I may alleage before thee. Of sinnes and euill workes (alas) I see a great heape, but through thy mercie, I trust to bee in the number of them, to whom thou wilt not impute their sinnes, but take and accept me for righteous and iust, and to bee the inheritour of euerlasting life. Thou, mercifull Lord, was borne for my sake, thou diddest suffer both hunger and thirst for my sake, thou diddest preach and teach, thou diddest pray and fast for my sake, thou diddest all good workes and dedes for my sake, thou sufferedst most grieuous paines and tormentes for my sake : And finally thou gauest thy most precious bodie to die, and thy bloud to bee shed on the crosse for my sake. Now most mercifull Sauiour, let all these things profit me, which thou freely hast giuen me, that hast giuen thy

selfe for me.   Let thy blood cleanse and wash away the spots and
foulenes of my sinnes.   Let thy righteousnesse hide and couer my
unrighteousnesse. Let the merites of thy passion and blood, bee the
satisfaction for my sinnes.   Giue me Lord thy grace, that my faith
and saluation in thy blood wauer not in me, but be euer firme and
constant, that the hope of thy mercie and life euerlasting neuer
decay in me, that charitie waxe not cold in me.   Finally, that the
weakenesse of my flesh bee not ouercome with the feare of death.
Graunt me, mercifull Sauiour, that when death hath shut vp the
eyes of my bodie, yet that the eyes of my soule may still beholde
and looke vpon thee : that when death hath taken away the vse
of my tongue and speech, yet that my heart may crie and say vnto
thee, *In manus tuas, Domine, commendo spiritum meum* (that is
to say) O Lord, into thy hands I giue and commit my soule :
Domine Iesu, accipe spiritum meum : Lord Iesu, receiue my
soule vnto thee, Amen.   Amen.

The forme
and maner of makynge
and consecrating
Bishoppes
Priestes
and
Deacons.

(,?,)

Anno a salutifero Virginis partu.

1559.

❡ THE PREFACE.

It is euident vnto all men diligently readinge holy scripture, and auncient autours, that from Thapostles tyme there hathe ben these orders of ministers in Christes churche, Bishoppes, Priestes, and Deacons : Whyche Offices, were euermore had in suche reuerente estimacion, that no man by his owne pryuate Aucthorytye, mighte presume to execute any of theim, excepte he were fyrst called tried, examined, and knowen to haue suche qualities, as were requisite for the same : And also by Publique prayer, with imposition of handes, approued and admitted there-unto. And therefore, to thentent, these orders should be con-tinued, and reuerently vsed, and estemed in this Churche of Englande, it is requisite, that no man not beynge at this present, Bishop, Priest, nor Deacon shall execute any of them, excepte he be called, tried, examined, and admitted, accordynge to the forme, hereafter folowinge. And none shalbe admitted a Deacon, excepte he be .xxi. yeares of age at the leaste. And euery man whiche is to be admitted a Priest, shalbe full foure and twenty yeares olde. And euery man whiche is to be consecrated a Bishoppe, shalbe fullye thyrtye yeares of age. And the Bishoppe, knowynge (eyther by hym selfe or by sufficient testimony) any person to be a man of vertuous conuersation, and without crime, and after examina-cion, and tryall, findynge hym learned in the Latine tongue, and sufficyently instructed in holy scripture, maye vpon a Sondaye, or holye daye in the face of the Churche, admitte hym a Deacon, in suche maner, and forme, as hereafter foloweth.

¶ THE FORME AND MANER

OF

ORDERYNGE OF DEACONS.

Fyrste, when the day appointed by the byshoppe is come, there shalbe an exhortacion declarynge the dutie, and office, of such as come to be admitted ministers, how necessary such orders are in the Churche of Christ. And also, how the people ought to esteme them in their vocation.

After thexhortacion ended, the Archedeacon, or his deputy shal presente such as come to the Bishop to be admitted, saiynge these wordes.

REUERENDE father in God, I present vnto you these persones presente, to bee admitted Deacons.

The Bishoppe. Take hede that the personnes whom ye present vnto vs, be apt, and mete for their learninge and godly cōuersation, to exercise their ministry duely to the honour of God, and edifying of hys church.

The Archedeacon shall aunswere.

I haue enquired of them, and also examined them and thinke them so to be

And then the Bishop shall say vnto the people.

BRETHREN, if there be any of you, who knoweth any impedimēt, or notable cryme, in any of these persons presented to be ordered deacōs, for the which he ought not to bee admitted to the same let hym come forthe in the name of GOD, and shewe what the crime or impediment is.

And if any great crime or impediment be obiected, the Bishop shal surcease from Orderynge that person, vntill such tyme as the party accused shall trie hym selfe clere of that cryme.

Then the Bishop commendynge suche as shalbe founde mete to be ordered to the prayers of the congregacion, with the Clerkes and people presente, shall saye, or singe the Letany, as foloweth with the prayers.

¶ *The Letany and Suffrages.*

O GOD the father of heauen : haue mercye vpon vs myserable synners.

O God the father of heauen.

O God the Sonne, redemer of the worlde : haue mercye vpon vs miserable sinners.

God the Sonne redemer of the etc.

O God the holye Ghoste, procedynge from the Father and the Sonne : haue mercye vpon vs miserable sinners.

O God the holy Ghoste, procedynge from etc.

O holy, blessed, and glorious trinitie, three persons and one God : haue mercye vpon vs miserable sinners.

O holy blessed, and glorious Trinitie, thre persones etc.

Remembre not Lorde our offences nor the offences of our fore-fathers, neyther take thou vengeaunce of our synnes : spare vs good Lorde, spare thy people whome thou haste redemed with thy moste precious bloude, and be not angrye with vs for euer.

Spare vs good Lorde.

From all euill and mischief, from synne, from the craftes and assaultes of the deuill, from thy wrath, and from euerlastinge dampnacion.

Good Lorde deliuer vs :

From all blyndnes of harte, from pryde, vayneglorye, and hypocrisye, from enuye, hatred, and malice, and all vncharitable-nes.

Good Lorde deliuer vs.

From Fornication and all other deadly Synne, and frome all the deceiptes of the worlde, the fleshe, and the Deuyll.

Good Lorde deliuer vs.

From lightninges and tempestes, from plague, pestilence and famine, from battayle, and murther, and from sodayne deathe.

Good Lorde deliuer vs.

From all sedicion and priuey conspiracye, frome all false doctrine and heresy, from hardnes of herte, and cõtempte of thy worde and commaundement :

Good Lorde deliuer vs.

By the misterye of thy holy Incarnacion, by thy holy Natiuitye and circumcision, by the Baptisme, fastynge, and temptacion.

Good Lorde deliuer vs.

By thine agonye and bloudy sweate, by thy crosse and passion, by thy precious deathe, and buryall, by thy glorious resurrection and Ascension, and by the commying of the holy Ghoste.

Good Lorde deliuer vs.

In all time of our tribulacion, in all time of our welth, in the houre of death, and in the day of iudgement :

Good Lorde deliuer vs.

We synners do beseche the to heare vs (O Lorde God), and that it maye please the to rule and gouerne thy holy Churche vniuersally, in the right waye.

We beseche the to heare vs good Lorde.

That it maye please the, to kepe and strengthen in the true worshippinge of the in righteousnes, and holynes of lyfe, thy seruaunte Elizabeth our most gracious Quene and gouernour.

We beseche the to heare vs good Lorde.

That it maye please the, to rule her herte in thy faythe, feare, and loue, that she may euermore haue affiance in the, and euer seke thy honoure and glory.

We beseche the to heare vs good Lorde.

That it maye please the to be her defender and keper, geuyng her the victory ouer all her enemyes.

We beseche the to heare vs good Lorde.

That it maye please the to illuminate all Bishoppes, Pastours, and Ministers of the Churche, with true knowledge and vnderstanding of thy worde, and that both by their preachynge and liuynge, they may set it furthe, and shewe it accordingly.

We beseche the to heare vs good Lorde.

That it may please the to endue the Lordes of the Cousayll and all the nobilitie, with grace, wisedome, and vnderstandinge.

We beseche the to heare vs good Lorde.

That it maye please the to blesse and kepe the Magistrates, geuynge them grace to execute iustice, and to maynteyne truthe.

We beseche the to heare vs good Lorde.

That it may please the to blesse, and kepe all thy people.

We beseche the to heare vs good Lorde.

That it maye please the to geue to all nacions, vnitie, peace and concorde.

We beseche the to heare vs good Lorde.

That it maye please the to geue vs an herte to loue, and dreade the, and diligently to lyue after thy commaundements.

We beseche the to heare vs good Lorde.

That it may please the to geue all thy people encrease of grace, to heare mekely thy worde and to receyue it wyth pure affeccion, and to bringe furth the fruites of the spirite.

We beseche the to heare vs good Lorde.

That it may please the, to bring into the way of truth all suche as haue erred, and be deceyued:

We beseche the to heare vs good Lorde.

F

That it maye please the, to strengthen suche as dooe stande, and to comforte, and helpe, the weake herted, and to rayse theym vp that falle, and finallye to beate doune Sathan vnder our feete.
We beseche the to heare vs good Lorde.

That it may please the, to succour, helpe, and comforte all that be in daunger, necessitie, and tribulation.
We beseche the to heare vs good Lorde.

That it maye please the to preserue all that travayle, by lande, or by water, all women labouringe of chylde, all sicke persones and yoūge chyldren, and to shew thy pytie vpon all prysoners and captyues.
We beseche the to heare vs good Lorde.

That it maye please the to defende and prouide for the fatherlesse chyldren and widdowes, and all that be desolate and oppressed.
We beseche the to heare vs good Lorde.

That it maye please the, to haue mercy vpon all men.
We beseche the to heare vs good Lorde.

That it may please the, to forgeue our enemies, persecutours and slanderers, and to turne their hertes.
We beseche the to heare vs good Lorde.

That it maye please the to geue, and preserue to oure vse, the kindely frutes of the earthe, so as in due tyme we maye enioy them.
We beseche the to heare vs good Lorde.

That it maye please the to geue vs true repentaunce, to forgeue vs all our sinnes, negligences and ignoraunces, and to endue vs with the grace of thy holy spirite, to amende oure lyues accordinge to thy holy worde.
We beseche the to heare vs good Lorde.

Sonne of God, we beseche the to heare vs.
Sonne of God, we beseche the to heare vs.

O Lambe of GOD, that takest awaye the sinnes of the worlde.
Graunte vs thy peace.

O Lambe of GOD, that takest awaye the synnes of the worlde.
Haue mercy vpon vs.

O Christe heare vs.
O Christe heare vs.

Lorde haue mercye vpon vs.
Lorde haue mercye vpon vs.

Christe haue mercye vpon vs.
Christe haue mercye vpon vs.

Lorde haue mercye vpon vs.
Lorde haue mercye vpon vs.

Oure father whiche arte in heauen. &c.
And leade vs not into temptacion.
But deliuer vs from euell.

¶ *The Versicle.* O Lorde, deale not with vs after our sinnes.
¶ *The Aunswere.* Neyther rewarde vs after our iniquities.

¶ Let vs praie.

O GOD mercifull father, that despisest not the sighinge of a contrite hert, nor the desyre of suche as be sorowfull, mercifully assiste oure prayers, that we make before the, in all oure troubles and aduersities, whensoeuer they oppresse vs, and graciouslye heare vs, that those euelles, whiche the crafte and subtilty of the deuel or man worketh agaynst vs, be broughte to noughte, and by the prouidence of thy goodnesse, they mai be dispersed, that we thy seruauntes, beynge hurte by no persecutions, maye euermore geue thankes to the, in thy holy Church, through Jesu Christ our Lorde.
O Lorde aryse, helpe vs, and deliuer vs for thy names sake.

O GOD, we haue hearde with our eares, and oure fathers haue declared vnto vs the noble worckes that thou diddest in their dayes, and in the olde tyme before them.
O Lorde aryse, helpe vs, and deliuer vs, for thyne honoure.

Glorye be to the father, and to the Sonne, and to the holye Ghoste.
As it was in the beginnynge, is nowe, and euer shalbee, worlde without ende. Amen.
From our enemyes defende vs, O Christe.
Graciously loke vpon our affliccions.

Pitifully beholde the sorowes of our herte.
Mercifully forgeue the synnes of thy people.

Fauourably with mercy, heare our prayers.
O sonne of Dauid, haue mercye vpon vs.

Both now and euer, vouchsafe to heare vs, O Christe.
Graciously heare vs : O Christ.
Graciously heare vs : O Lorde Christ.

The Versicle. O Lorde let thy mercy be shewed vpon vs.
The Aunswere. As we do put our trust in the.

¶ Let vs praye.

WE humbly beseche the O Father, mercifully to loke vpon our infirmities, and for the glory of thy names sake, turne from vs all

those euilles, that we moste righteouslye haue diserued, And
graunt that in all our troubles, we maye put oure whole truste and
confidēce in thy mercy, and euermore serue the in holines and
purenes of lyuing, to thy honour and glory : through oure onely
mediatour, and aduocate, Jesus Christe oure Lorde.   Amen.

ALMIGHTY God, whiche hast geuen vs grace, at this tyme with
one accorde to make our cōmon supplications vnto thee, and doest
promise, that whē two or thre be gathered in thy name, thou wilt
graūt their requestes, fulfill nowe O Lorde, the desires, and
peticions of thy seruauntes as maye be most expedient for them,
graunting vs in this worlde knowledge of thy truthe, and in the
worlde to come, lyfe euerlastynge.   Amen.

Then shalbe sayde also this that foloweth.

ALMIGHTYE God, whiche by thy diuine prouidence haste
appointed diuers orders of ministers in the churche, and diddest
inspire thyne holy Apostles, to chose into this ordre of Deacons
the fyrst martir S. Stephen, with other, mercifullye beholde these
thy seruauntes, nowe called to the like office, and administraciō,
replenishe them so with the truthe of thy doctrine, and innocencie
of life, that both by worde and good example, thei mai faithfully
serue the in this office to the glorie of thy name, and profite of
the cōgregaciō, through the merites of our sauiour Jesu Christ, who
lyueth and reygneth with the, and the holy Ghoste, nowe, and
euer.   Amen.

Then shall be songe or sayde the Communion of the daie, sauing
Thepistle shalbe redde out of Timothe, as foloweth

LYKEWISE, muste the Ministers be honest, not doble tonged,
not geuen to muche wine, neither gredy of filthy lucre, but
holdynge the mistery of the fayth, with a pure conscience.   And
let them first be proued, and then let them minister, so that no man
bee able to reproue them.   Euē so must theyr wiues be honest, not
euel spekers, but sobre, and faythful in all thinges.   Let the
Deacōs be the housbādes of one wife, and such as rule their
childrē wel, and their owne housholdes.   For they that minister
well, get them selfes a good degre, and a great liberty in the fayth,
which is in Christ Jesu.
These thinges write I vnto the, trustyng to come shortly vnto
the, but and if I tary long, that then thou mayst yet haue knowlege, how thou oughtest to behaue thy self in the house of God,
which is the cōgregation of the liuing God, the piller and ground
of truth, And without doubt, great is that mistery of godlines,
God was shewed in the flesh, was justified in the spyrit, was sene
among the aūgels, was preched vnto the Gētiles, was belued on in
the worlde, and receiued vp in glory.

Or els this out of the vi of the Actes.

THEN the xii called the multitude of the disciples together, and sayd, it is not mete that we shulde leaue the word of God, and serue tables. Wherfore, brethrē, loke ye out amōge you vii men of honest report and ful of the holy Ghoste, and wysedome, to whome wee may cōmit this busines, but we will geue our selues continually to prayer, and to thadministration of the worde. And that saiyng pleased the whole multitude. And they chose Stephen (a man full of faythe and ful of the holy Ghost) and Philippe, and Procorus, and Nichanor, and Timon, and Parmenas, and Nicholas a conuert of Antioche. These they set before the Apostles, and when thei had prayed, they layde their handes on them. And the worde of God encreased and the nombre of the disciples multiplied in Hierusalem greatly, and a great companye of the priestes were obedient vnto the faythe.

¶ *And before the Gospell the Bisshop sittyinge in a chayre, shall cause the Othe of the Quenes Soueraintie, and against the power and authoritye of all foreyn pontētates, to be ministred vnto euery of them that are to be ordered.*

¶ *The Othe of the Quenes Souerainte.*

I *A. B.* do utterly testifie and declare in my conscience that the quenes highnesse is the onely supreame Gouernour of this Realme and of all other her hyghnesse dominions and countreyes, aswell in all spirituall or ecclesiasticall thinges or causes : as temporall, and that no forrayn prince, person, prelate, state, or potentate, hath or ought to haue any jurisdiction, power, superioritie, preheminence or aucthoritie ecclesiasticall or spiritual within this realme, and therefore I do utterly renounce and forsake all forayn jurisdictions, powers, superiorities, and aucthorities, and do promyse that from henceforth I shall beare fayth and trewe allegyaunce to the Quenes hyghnes, her heyres and lawfull successours, and to my power shall assiste and defende all jurisdictions, priuileges, preheminnces, and aucthorities graunted or belonginge to the Quenes hyghnesse, her heyres and successours, or vnited and annexed to thimperiall Croune of thys realme, so helpe me God, and the contentes of thys boke.

¶ *Then shall the Bishoppe examine euery one of them that are to bee ordered, in the presence of the people, after thys maner folowynge.*

¶ *Then shall the byshop examine euery one of them, that are to be ordered, in the presence of the people, after this maner folowinge.* [1]

DO you trust that you are inwardly moued by the holy ghost, to take vpon you this office and ministraciō, to serue God, for the promotynge of his glory, and the edifying o his people?
Aunswere. I trust so.

---

[1] [The repetition of this rubric is curious. It is evidently an oversight.]

The Byshop. Do ye thinke that ye truly be called according to the wyll of our Lord Jesus Christ, and the due order of this realme to the ministery of the Churche?

Aunswere. I thinke so.

The Byshop. Do ye vnfeynedly beleue al the canonical scriptures, of the olde and new testament?

Aunswere. I do beleue.

The Byshop. Wyl you diligently read the same vnto the people assembled in the Churche, where you shall be appoyncted to serue?

Aunswere. I wyll.

The Byshop. It perteineth tc the office of a Deacon in the Churche where he shalbe appoincted, to assiste the Priest in diuine seruice, and speciallye when he ministreth the holye communnion, and to helpe hym in distribution thereof, and to reade holy Scriptures and Homelies in the congregation, and to instructe the youthe in the Catechisme, to Baptyse and to preache, yf he be admytted thereto, by the Byshoppe. And furthermore, it is his office where prouision is so made, to serche for the sycke, pore, and impotent people of the Parysh, and to intimate their estates, names, and places where they dwel, to the Curate, that by his exhortation they may be releued by the Parishe, or other conuenient almose: will you do this gladly and wyllinglye?

Aunswere. I wyll so do by the helpe of God.

The Byshop. Wyll you apply al your diligence to frame and fashiō your owne liues, and the lyues of all your family accordinge to the doctrine of Christe, and to make bothe yourselues and them (as much as in you lyeth) wholsome examples of the flocke of Christe?

Aunswere. I wyll so do, the Lorde beynge my helper.

The Byshop. Wyll you reuerently obey your Ordinary and other chiefe ministers of the Churche, and theim to whome the gouernemēt and charge is committed ouer you, folowing with a glad minde and wyl their godlye admonicions?

Aunswere. I wil thus endeuour my selfe, the Lord being my helper.

¶ *Then the Bishop, laying his handes seuerally vpon the head of euery of them, shall saye.*

Take thou aucthoritie to execute thoffice of a Deacō in the churche of God committed vnto the: in the name of the father, the sonne, and the holy Ghoste.   Amen.

Then shall the Byshop deliuer to euery one of them the New Testament, saying.

Take thou aucthoritie to reade the Gospell in the churche of God, and to preache the same, if thou be therunto ordinarily commaunded.

Then one of them appoynted by the byshoppe shall reade the Gospell of that daye.

Then shall the Byshop procede to the communion, and all that be ordered, shall tary and receyue the holy communion the same daye with the byshop.

The Communion ended, after the last collect, and immediately before benediction, shalbe said this Collecte folowynge.

ALMIGHTIE God geuer of all good thynges, whiche of thy great goodnes hast vouchedsaufe to accepte, and take these thy seruauntes vnto the Office of Deacōs in thy church make them, we beseche the, O LORDE, to be modest, humble, and constant in their Ministracion, to haue a ready wil to obserue al Spiritual discipline, that they hauyng alwaies the testimonie of a good consciēce, and continuyng euer stable and strong in thy sonne Christ, may so wel vse them selues in this inferiour Office, that they may be founde worthy to be called vnto the higher ministeries in thy Churche: through the same thy sonne our Sauiour Christe, to whome be glory and honour, worlde without ende. Amen.

¶ *And here it must be shewed vnto the Deacon, that he must continue in that Office of a Deacon, the space of a whole yere at the leaste (excepte for reasonable causes, it be otherwise seen to his Ordinary) to thentēt he may be perfecte, and wel expert in the thynges apperteinyng to the Ecclesiastical administracion : in executyng whereof, if he be founde faithful and diligent, he may be admitted by his Diocesan to the order of Priesthode.*

THE FOURME OF

ORDERYNG PRIESTES.

When the exhortacion is ended, then shal folowe the Communion. And for the Epistle shalbe red out of the twentieth Chapiter of the Actes of the Apostles, as foloweth.

FROM Mileto Paule sent messengers to Ephesus, and called the elders of the cōgregacion. whiche when they were come to him, he said vnto them. ye know that frō the first daie that I came into Asia, after what maner I haue been with you at all seasons, seruyng the Lord with al humblenes of mind, and with many teares and temptacions, whiche happened vnto me by the layinges awayt of the Jewes, because I wold kepe back nothing that was profitable vnto you, but to shew you and teach you openly, throughoute euery house : wytnessinge both to the Jewes, and also to the Grekes, the repentaunce that is towarde God, and the faythe whiche is toward our Lorde Jesus. And nowe beholde, I go bound in the Spirite vnto Jerusalem, not knowinge the thinges that shall come on me there, but that the holy ghost witnesseth in euerye citye, sayinge : that bandes and trouble abide me. But none of these thinges moue me, neither is my life deare vnto my self, that I might fulfyll my course with joye, and the ministration of the word which I haue receyued of the lord Jesu, to testifye the gospell of the grace of God. And nowe behold, I am sure that henceforth ye all (through whom I haue gone preachinge the kingdome of God) shall see my face no more. Wherfore I take you to record this day, that I am pure from the bloud of all men. For I haue spared no laboure, but haue shewed you all the counsaill of God. Take hede therfore vnto your selues, and to all the flocke emong whom the holy Ghost hath made you ouerseers, to rule the congregation of God whiche he hath purchased wyth hys bloude. For I am sure of this, that after my departing, shal greuous wolues enter in emong you, not sparing the flocke. Moreouer of your owne selues shall men aryse, speakynge peruerse thynges, to drawe disciples after them. Therfore awake, and remembre that by the space of three yeres I ceassed not to warne euerye one of you nyght and daye with teares.

And now brethren, I cōmende you to God, and to the word of his grace, whyche is able to builde further, and to geue you an inheritaunce emong al them whych are sanctified. I haue desired no mans siluer, golde or vesture. yea, you know your selues, that these hādes haue ministered vnto my necessities, and to them that were wyth me. I haue shewed you all thynges, how that so labouring, ye ought to receiue ye weake, and to remēbyre the wordes of the Lorde Jesu, how that he said: It is more blessed to geue, than to receyue.

¶ *Or ellse this thirde Chapiter of the fyrste Epistle to Timothe.*

THIS is a true saiyng: If any man desyre the office of a Byshoppe, ii. Tim. iii.[1] he desireth an honest worcke. A Bishop therfore must be blamelesse, the housbande of one wife, diligēt, sober, discrete, a keper of hospitalitie, apte to teache, not geuen to ouermuche wyne, no fyghter, not gredy of filthy lucre : but gentle, abhorryng fightyng abhorring couetousnes, one that ruleth well his owne house, one that hath children in subjectiō with all reuerence. For yf a man can not rule his owne house, how shall he care for the congregacion of God? he may not be a younge skoler, least he swel, and fal into the judgement of the euil speaker. He must also haue a good reporte of them which are without, least he fal into rebuke, and snare of the euil speaker.

Likewise must the ministers be honest, not doubletōgued, not geuen vnto much wyne, neyther gredy of fylthy lucre, but holding the ministery of the faithe, wyth a pure conscience, and let theim firste be proued, and then let them minister, so that no man be able to reproue thē.

Euen so must their wiues be honest, not euilspeakers : but sobre and faithful in all thinges. Let the Deacons be the housbādes of one wife, and such as rule their children wel, and their owne housholdes. For they that minister wel, get them selues a good degre, and great libertie in Faith whiche is in Christe Jesu.

These thinges write I vnto the, trusting to come shortly vnto the : but and if I tary long, that then thou maiest haue yet knowledge, how thou oughtest to behaue thy selfe in the house of God, whiche is the congregacion of the liuing God, the piller and ground of truth. And wythout doubte, greate is that mistery of Godlynes : God was shewed in the fleshe, was justifyed in the Spirite : was seen among the Aungelles, was preached vnto the Gentiles, was beleued on in the world, and receyued vp in glory.

¶ *After this shalbe redde for the Gospell a piece of the laste Chapiter of Mathewe, as foloweth.*

JESUS came and spake vnto them, saying : All power is geuen Mat. xxviii. vnto me in heauen, and in the earthe. Go ye therfore and teache al natiōs, Baptisyng theim in the name of the father, and of the Sonne, and of the holy Ghoste. Teachinge theim to obserue all thynges, whatsoeuer I haue commaunded you. And loo, I am with you alway, euen vntyl the ende of the worlde.

[1 Misprint for i Tim. iii.]

¶ Or elles this that foloweth of the .x. chapiter of John.

VERELY, verely, I say vnto you : He that entereth not in by the doore into the Shepefolde, but climbeth vp some other way, the same is a thefe and a Murtherer. But he that entreth in by the doore is the Shepeherde of the Shepe, to him the porter openeth, and the Shepe heareth his voyce, and he calleth his owne Shepe by name, and leadeth them out. And when he hath sent furth his owne Shepe, he goeth before thē, and the Shepe folowe hym, for they knowe his voice. A straunger wil they not folowe, but wyll flye from hym, for they knowe not the voyce of straungers. This Prouerbe spake Jesus vnto theim, but they vnderstode not what thynges they were, whiche he spake vnto theim. Then sayde Jesus vnto theim againe, verely verely, I say vnto you, I am the doore of the Shepe. All (euen as many as come before me) are Theues and Murtherers : but the Shepe did not heare them. I am the doore, by me yf any man enter in, he shalbe saufe, and go in and oute, and finde pasture. A thefe commeth not but for to steale, kylle, and to destroy. I am come that they mighte haue lyfe, and that they might haue it more aboundantly. I am the good shepeherde : a good Shepeherde geueth his lyfe for the Shepe. An hired seruaunt, and he whiche is not the Shepeherde (neither the Shepe are his owne) seeth the woulfe comming, and leaueth the Shepe and fleeth, and the woulfe catcheth, and skattereth the shepe. The hired seruaunt flieth, because he is an hired seruaūt, and careth not for the Shepe. I am the good Shepeherde, and knowe my Shepe, and am knowen of myne. As my Father knoweth me, euen so knowe I also my father. And I giue my lyfe for the Shepe, and other Shepe I haue, whiche are not of this folde. Them also muste I bryng, and they shall heare my voyce, and there shalbe one folde and one Shepeherde.

Or elles this, of the .xx. Chapiter of John.

THE same day at night, which was the first day of the Sabbothes, when the dores were shut (where the disciples were assēbled together for feare of the Jewes) came Jesus, and stode in the myddes, and said vnto them : Peace be vnto you. And whē he had so said, he shewed vnto theim his handes and his syde. Then were the Disciples glad, when they sawe the Lorde. Then sayd Jesus vnto them againe : Peace be vnto you. As my Father sent me, euen so sende I you also. And when he had sayde those wordes, he breathed on them, and saied vnto them : Receyue ye the holy Ghoste, whosoeuers synnes ye remitte, they are remitted vnto theim, and whosoeuers synnes ye retayne, they are retayned.

When the Gospel is ended, then shalbe said, or song.

COME holy ghoste, eternal God, proceding frō aboue.
Bothe from the Father and the Sonne, the God of peace and loue.

Visite our myndes, and into vs, thy heauēly grace inspyre.

That in all truthe and Godlinesse, we may haue true desire.

Thou art the very comforter, in al wo and distresse.

The heauenly gyft of God moste highe, whiche no tongue can expresse.

The fountaine and the liuely spring, of ioye celestial.

The fyre so brighte, the Loue so clere, and Vnction spirituall.

Thou in thy gyftes art manyfolde, wherby Christes Churche doeth stande,

In faythfull hartes wryting thy lawe, the finger of Goddes hande

According to thy promes made, thou geuest speche of Grace,

That throughe thy helpe, the prayse of God, maye sounde in euery place.

O holye Ghoste, into oure wittes, sende doune thine heauenly lyght,

Kyndle our hartes with feruent loue, to serue God daye and night.

Strengthe and stablyshe al oure weaknes, so feble and so frayle

That neyther fleshe, the worlde, nor Deuyll, against vs do preuayle

Put backe our enemy farre from vs, and graunt vs to obtayne,

Peace in our hartes with God and man, wythoute grudge, or dysdaine

And grante, O Lorde, that thou beyng our leader and our guyde,

We maye eschewe the snares of synne, and from thee neuer slyde.

To us suche plentie of thy grace, good Lord graunt, we the praye,

That thou maiest bee oure comforter, at the last dreadfull daye.

Of all stryfe and dissencion, O Lord dissolue the bandes,

And make the knottes of peace and loue, througheout all Christen landes.

Graunt vs O Lorde, through the to knowe, the father moste of might,

That of his dere beloued sonne we maye attayne the syghte

And that wyth perfyghte Faythe also, we may acknowledge the.

The spirite of them bothe, alway one God in persons thre.

Laude and prayse be to the father, and to the sonne equall.

And to the holy spirite also, one God coeternall.

And praye we that the onely Sonne, vouchesaufe his spirite to sende,

To all that do professe his name, vnto the worldes ende   Amen.

¶ *And then the Archedeacon shall present vnto the Byshop, all them that shall receyue the order of Priesthode that day, the Archdeacon sayinge*

REUEREND father in God, I present vnto you these persons presente, to be admitted to the order of Priesthode   *Cum interrogatione et responsione, vt in Ordine Diaconatus.*

And then the Bishop shall saye to the people.

GOOD people, these be they whom we purpose God wyllyng, to receyue thys daye vnto the holy offyce of Priesthode.   For after due examination, we find not the contrary, but that, they be lawfully called to their function and ministerye, and that they be persons mete for the same : but yet if there be any of you which knoweth any impediment, or notable crime in any of thē, for the whych he oughte not to be receiued into this holi ministery, now in the name of God declare the same.

And if any greate cryme or impediment be objected. &c. Vt supra in ordine Diaconatus vsque ad finem Litanie cum hac Collecta.

ALMIGHTY God, geuer of al good thynges, whyche by thy holy spirite hast appoyncted diuers orders of Ministers in thy churche, mercifully behold these thy seruaūtes, now called to ye office of priesthode, and replenish them so wyth the truth of thy doctryne, and innocencye of lyfe, that both by worde and good example, they may faithfully serue the in this office, to the glory of thy name, and profite of the congregacion, through the merites of our Sauiour Jesu Christe, who liueth and reigneth with the and the holy Ghoste, worlde without ende   Amen.

¶ *Then the Bishoppe shal minister vnto euery one of them, the Othe concernyng the Kynges[1] Supremacie as it is set out in the order of Deacons. And that doen, he shal saye vnto them, whiche are appoincted to receiue the said office, as hereafter foloweth.*

YOU haue heard brethrē, aswel in your priuate examinacion, as in the exhortacion, and in the holy lessons taken out of the Gospel, and of the writynges of the Apostles, of what dignitie and of howe great importaunce this Office is, wherunto ye be called. And now we exhorte you, in the name of our Lorde Jesus Christe, to haue in remembraunce, into how high a dignitie, and to how chargeable an office ye be called, that is to say, to be the messengers, the watchmen, the Pastours, and the Stewardes of the Lorde, to teache, to premonishe, to fede, and prouide for the Lordes familie : to seke for Christes shepe that be dispersed abrode, and for his children whiche be in the middest of this naughtie worlde, to be saued throughe Christe for euer.   Haue alwaies therfore printed in your remembraūce, how great a treasure is committed to your charge, for they be the shepe of Christe, whiche he bought with his death, and for whome he shed his bloud.   The Churche and congregacion whō you must serue, is his spouse and his body.   And if it shal chaunce the same churche, or any membre therof to take any hurte, or hinderaunce, by reason of your negligence, ye knowe the greatnesse of the faulte, and also of the horrible punishment whiche wil ensue. Wherefore, consider with your selues the ende of your ministery, towardes the children of God, toward the spouse and body of Christe, and see that you neuer cease your labour, your care and diligence, vntil you haue doen al that lieth in you, according to your bounden duty, to bringe al suche as are, or shalbe com-

[1 Misprint for Queen's.]

mitted to your charge, vnto that agrement in faith and knowledge of god, and to that rypenes aud perfectnes of age in Christe, that there be no place left emonge them, either for erroure in religion, or for viciousnes in lyfe.

Then, forasmuche as youre office is bothe of so greate Excellencie, and of so greate difficultie, ye see wyth howe greate care and study ye ought to apply your selues as wel that you may shew your selues kinde to that LORDE, who hath placed you in so highe a dignitie, as also to beware that neither you your selues offende, neither be occasion that other offende. Howebeit, ye can not haue a mynde and a wil therto of your selues, for that power and abilitie is geuen of God alone. Therfore ye se howe ye ought and haue nede, earnestly to pray for his holy spyrite. And seeing that you can not by any other meanes cōpasse the doing of so weighty a worke perteining to the saluation of man, but with doctrine and exhortation takē out of holy scripture, and wyth a lyfe agreable vnto the same : ye perceyue how studious ye ought to be in reding and in learnīg the holy scriptures, and in framīg the maners, both of your selues, and of them that specially perteine vnto you, according to the rulé of the same scriptures. And for this self same cause, ye se how you ought to forsake and set aside (as much as you may) al worldly cares and studies.

We haue a good hope, that you haue wel weighed and pondred these thinges with your selfes, long before this tyme, and that you haue clearly determined by Goddes grace to giue your selues wholy to this vocation, wher vnto it hath pleased God to cal you, so that (as muche as lieth in you) you applye your selues wholye to this one thing, and drawe all your cares and studies this waye, and to this ende. And that you wil continually pray for the heauenly assistence of the holy Ghoste, from God the father, by the mediation of our only mediatoure, and sauiour Jesus Christe, that by dailye readinge and weighing of the scriptures, ye may waxe riper and stronger in your ministery. And that you may so endeuour your selues from time to tyme to sanctifie the lyues of you, and yours, and to fashion them after the rule and doctrine of Christ. And that ye may be wholsome and godly examples and paternes, for the rest of the congregacion to folowe. And that this present congregacion of Christ here assembled, may also vnderstande your myndes and willes in these thinges, and that this youre promes shall more moue you to do your duties : ye shall aunswere playnely to these thinges, whyche we in the name of the congregation, shal demaunde of you, touching the same.

Do you thincke in your hart, that you be trulye called according to the wil of oure Lorde Jesus Christ, and the order of this Churche of Englande, to the ministerye of Priesthode ?

Aunswere. I thynke it.

The Byshop. Be you perswaded that the holy Scriptures cōteine sufficiently all doctrine requyred of necessitie for eternall

saluacion, throughe faythe in Jesu Christ? And are you determined wyth the sayde scriptures to instructe the people commytted
to your charge, and to teache nothing (as requyred of necessity to
eternall saluation) but that you shall be perswaded maybe concluded and proued by the scripture?

Aunswere. I am so perswaded, and haue so determined by
Goddes grace.

The Byshop. Will you then giue your faythfull diligence
alwaies, so to minister the doctrine and sacramentes, and the
dyscipline of Christe, as the Lorde hathe commaunded, and as
this Realme hathe receyued the same, accordynge to the commaundementes of God, so that you maye teache the people commytted to youre cure and charge wyth all dilygence to kepe and
obserue the same?

Aunswere. I wyll so do, by the helpe of the Lorde.

The Byshop. Will you be ready with all faithful diligence, to
banishe and driue away al erronious, and strange doctrines, contrary to Goddes worde, and to vse bothe publique and priuate
monitiōs and exhortaciōs, as wel to the sicke, as to the whole
within your cures, as nede shall requyre, and occasion be geuen?

Aunswere. I wyl, the Lorde beying my helper.

The Byshop. Will you be diligent in prayers, and in readynge
of the holy Scriptures, and such studies as helpe to the knowledge of the same, laying aside the study of the worlde and the
fleshe?

Answer. I wyl endeuor my self so to do, the lord being my
helper.

The Byshop. Wil you be diligent to frame and fashiō your
awne selues and your families, according to the doctryne of
Christ, and to make both your selues and them (as muche as in
you lieth) wholsome examples, and spectacles to the flocke of
Christe?

Answer. I wil so apply myselfe, the Lorde beyng my helper.

The Byshop. Wil you maintaine and set forwardes (as muche
as lieth in you) quietnesse, peace, and loue emonges al Christian
people, and specially among them that are, or shalbe, committed
to your charge?

Aunswere. I wil so do, the Lorde beyng my helper.

The Byshop. Will you reuerently obey your ordinarie, and
other chief ministers, vnto whome the gouernemēt and charge
is commytted ouer you, folowing wyth a glade mynde and wil,
their Godly admonicion, and submitting your selues to their
Godly iudgementes?

Answer. I wyl so do, the Lorde beyng my helper.

Then shall the Byshop saye.

ALMIGHTY God who hath geuen you this wyl to do all these
thinges, graunte also vnto you strengthe and power to perfourme

the same, that he may accomplyshe his worke, which he hath begon in you, vntyll the tyme he shall come at the latter day, to judge the quicke and the deade.

¶ *After this, the congregacion shalbe desired, secretly in theyr praiers to make humble supplications to God for the foresaid thinges, for the which praiers there shalbe a certain space kept in silēce.*

That doen, the Byshop shall praye in this wyse.

¶ Let vs praye.

ALMIGHTY God and heauenly father, whyche of thy infinite loue and goodnesse towardes vs, hast geuen to vs thy onely and moste dere beloued sonne Jesus Christ, to be our redemer and aucthor of euerlasting lyfe : who after he had made perfect our redemption by his death, and was ascended into heauen, sent abrode into the worlde hys Apostles, Prophetes, Euangelistes, Doctours, and Pastours, by whose labour and ministery he gathered together a greate flocke in al the partes of the worlde, to set furth the eternal praise of thy holy name. For these so great benefites of thy eternal goodnes, and for that thou hast vouchedsaufe to cal these thy seruaūtes here present, to the same office and ministerye, of the saluacion of mankynde, wee render vnto thee most hartie thankes, we worshyp and praise the, and we humbly besech the by the same thy sonne, to graunt vnto al vs, whiche either here, or elles where, cal vpon thy name, that we may shewe our selues thākeful to thee, for these and al other thy benefites, and that we may daily encrease and go forwardes in the knowledge and faithe of the, and thy sonne, by the holy spirit, so that aswell by these thy ministers, as by theim to whō they shalbe appoincted minis- ters, thy holy name may be alwaies glorified, and thy blessed kingdome enlarged, throughe the same thy sonne oure Lorde Jesus Christ, whiche liueth and reigneth with the, in the vnitie of the same holy spirite, worlde without ende. Amen.

¶ *When this praier is doen, the Bishop with the Priestes present, shall laye their handes seuerally vpon the heade of euery one that receyueth orders. The receiuers humbly kneling vpon their knees, and the Byshop saying.*

RECEIUE the holy Ghoste, whose synnes thou doest forgeue, they are forgeuē : and whose synnes thou doest retaine, they are retained : and be thou a faithful dispensour of the worde of God, and of his holye Sacramentes. In the name of the father, and of the sonne, and of the holy Ghost. Amen.

¶ *The Bishop shal deliuer to euery one of them, the Byble in hys hande, saying.*

TAKE thou aucthoritie to preache the worde of God, and to minister the holye Sacramentes in the congregacion, where thou shalt be so appoincted.

When this is doen, the congregacion shall synge the Crede, and also they shall go to the Communion, which all they that receiue orders shall take together, and remayne in the same place where the handes were layed vpon them, vntyl suche tyme as they haue receyued the Communion.

The Communion beyng doen after the last Collecte, and immediately before the benediction, shalbe sayde this Collecte.

MOST merciful father, we beseche the so to sēde vpon these thy seruaūtes thy heauenly blessing, that they may be cladde aboute with all Iustice, and that thy worde spoken by theyr mouthes may haue suche success, that it may neuer be spokē in vaine, Graunte also that we may haue grace to heare and receiue the same as thy most holy word, and the meane of our saluation, that in all our wordes and dedes we may seke thy glory, and the increase of thy kyngdome, through Jesus Christe our Lorde. Amen.

¶ *And yf the orders of a Deacon and Priesthod, be geuen bothe vpon one daye, then shall all thynges at the holye Communion be vsed as they are appoyncted at the Orderynge of Priestes. Sauynge that for the Epystle, the whole thirde chapiter of the fyrste to Timothe shalbe red, as it is set out before the Order of priestes. And immediately after the Epistle, the Deacons shalbe ordered. And it shall suffice the Letany to be sayed ones.*

THE FORME OF CONSECRATYNG

OF AN

ARCHEBISHOPPE OR BYSHOPPE.

The Epistle at the Communion.

THIS is a true saying, if a man desire the office of a Byshoppe, i. Tim. iii.
he desyreth an honest worke.   A Bishop therfore must be
blamelesse, the housbande of one wife, diligente, sober, discrete, a keper of hospitalitie, apte to teache, not geuen to
ouer muche wyne, no fighter, not gredy of filthi lucre : but
gētle, abhorring fighting, abhorrīg couetousnes, one that ruleth
wel his awne house, one that hath childrē in subjectiō, with all
reuerence.   For yf a man cannot rule hys awne house, how shal
he care for the cōgregaciō of God?   He may not be a younge
scholer, lest he swel, and fal into the judgement of the euyl
speaker.   He muste also haue a good reporte of them which are
without, lest he fal into rebuke, and snare of the euil speaker.

The Gospell.

JESUS sayde to Simon Peter : Simon Johanna, louest thou me John xxi.
more than these?   He sayde vnto him : Lord thou knowest that I
loue the.   He sayde vnto him : Fede my lambes.   He sayde to
hyme again the seconde tyme : Simon Johanna, louest thou me?
He sayde vnto hym : yea, Lord thou knowest that I loue the.
He sayde vnto hym : fede my shepe.   He sayde vnto hym the
thirde tyme : Simō Johanna louest thou me?   Peter was sory,
because he sayde vnto him the thirde time, louest thou me, and
he said vnto him : Lorde, thou knowest all thinges, thou knowest that I loue the.   Jesus said vnto him : fede my shepe.

*Or els out of the x Chap. of John, as before in thorder of Priestes.
After the Gospel and Credo ended, first the elected Bishop shalbe presented
by two Bishoppes vnto the Archebishoppe of that Prouince, or to some
other byshoppe appoincted by his commission: the Byshoppes that present
him, saying :*

MOST reuerende father in God, we presente vnto you this Godly
and well learned man, to be consecrated Byshop.

*Then shal the Archebishop demand the Quenes Mandate for the Consecra-
tion, and cause it to be red.   And the othe touching the knowledging of
the Queenes Soueraintie shalbe ministred to the person elected, as it is set
out in the order of Deacons.   And then shalbe ministred also, the othe of
due obediēce vnto tharchbishop, as foloweth.*

¶ *The Othe of due obedience to the Archebyshoppe.*

IN the name of God, Amen.   I *N.* chosen Byshop of the churche and sie of *N.* doe professe and promes all due reuerence and obedience to the Archebishop and to the Metropoliticall Churche of .*N.* and to their successours, so helpe me GOD, through Jesus Christe.

¶ *This othe shall not be made, at the consecration of an Archebishop.*

Then the archebishop shal moue the congregacion present to praye : saying thus to them.

BRETHREN, it is written in the Gospel of Sainct Luke, that our sauiour Christ continued the whole night in praier, or euer that he did chose and sende furth his .xii. Apostles.   It is written also in the Actes of the Apostles, that the Disciples whiche were at Antioche did fast and praie, or euer they laied haudes vpon, or sent furth Paule and Barnabas.   Let vs therfore folowing the example of our sauiour Christ, and his Apostles, first fal to praier, or that we admyt and sende furth this persone, presented vnto vs to the worke wherunto we trust the holy Ghoste hath called him.

And then shalbe said the Letany, as afore in the Order of Deacons.   And after this place.—That it may please the to illuminate all Byshoppes, &c. he shall saye.

THAT it may please the to blesse this our brother elected, and to sende thy grace vpon him, that he may duely execute the office whereunto he is called, to thedifying of thy Church, and to the honor, praise, and glory of thy name.

Aunswere. We beseche the to heare vs good Lorde.

Concluding the Letany in the ende, with this prayer.

ALMIGHTY God, geuer of all good thynges, whyche by thy holy spirite hast appointed diuers orders of ministers in thy church, mercifully beholde this thy seruaunt, now called to the worke and ministerie of a Byshoppe, and replenish him so with the truth of thy doctrine and innocencie of life, that bothe by worde and dede he may faithfully serue the in this office, to the glorye of thy name, and profite of thy congregacion : through the merites of our sauior Jesu Christ, who lyueth and reigneth with the and the holy Ghost, worlde without ende.   Amen.

¶ *Then the Archebyshop sytting in a chaire, shall say this to him that is to be consecrated.*

BROTHER, forasmuche as holy Scripture and the old Canons commaũdeth, that we should not be hasty in laying on handes, and admittyng of any person to the gouernement of the congregaciō of Christ, which he hath purchased with no lesse price, then theffusion of his awne bloud, afore that I admit you to this administracion whereunto ye are called, I wyll examine you in certaine articles, to the ende the congregacion presente, may haue a trial, and beare witnesse, howe ye be mynded to behaue your selfe in the Churche of God.

Are you perswaded that you be truely called to this ministra-cion, according to the wyll of oure Lorde Jesus Christe, and to the order of this Realme ?

Aunswere. I am so perswaded.

The Archebyshoppe. Are you perswaded that the holy scriptures cōteine sufficiently al doctrine, required of necessite for eternal saluacion, throughe the Faithe in Jesu Christ ? And are you de-termined with the same holy scriptures, to instructe the people committed to your charge, and to teache, or mainteine nothing as required of necessitie to eternal saluacion, but that you shalbe perswaded may be concluded, and proued by tbe same ?

Aunswere. I am so perswaded and determined by Goddes grace.

The Archebyshoppe. Will you then faithfully exercise your self in the said holy Scriptures, and cal vpon God by praier, for the true vnderstandinge of the same, so as ye maye be able by them to teache and exhorte with wholsome doctrine, and to withstande and conuince the gainsaiers ?

Aunswere. I wyl so do, by the helpe of God.

The Archebyshoppe. Be you redy with all faithfull diligence, to banishe and driue away al erronious and straunge doctrine, cōtrary to Goddes worde, and bothe priuately and opēly to cal vpon and encourage other to the same ?

Aunswere. I am redy, the Lorde beyng my helper.

The Archebyshoppe. Will you deny all vngodlines and worldly lustes, and lyue soberly, righteouslye, and Godly in thys world, that you may shewe your self in all thinges an exāple of good workes vnto other, that the aduersarie may be ashamed, hauing nothing to lay against you ?

Aunswere. I wil so do, the Lorde beyng my helper.

The Archebyshoppe. Wil you mainteine and set forwarde (as muche as shal lie in you) quietnes, peace and loue, emōg al men ; Ande such as be vnquiete, disobedient, and criminous within your diocesse, correct and punish, according to suche aucthoritie as ye haue by Goddes word, and as to you shalbe cōmitted by the ordi-naunce of this Realme ?

Aunswere. I wyl so do, by the helpe of God.

The Archebyshoppe. Will you shewe your self gentle, and be merciful for Christes sake to poore and nedy people, and to all straungers destitute of helpe ?

Aunswere. I wil shewe so my selfe, by Goddes helpe.

The Archebyshoppe. Almighty God our heauenly father, who

hath geuen you a good wyll to do all these thinges, graunt also
vnto you, strength and power to performe the same that he
accomplishyng in you, the good worke which he hath begon, ye
may be foūde perfect, and irreprehensible at the latter daye through
Jesu Christ our Lorde.   Amen.

*Then shalbe song or saied: Come Holy Ghoste, &c. as it is set out in the
Order of Priestes.*

That ended the Archebyshop shall saye.

Lorde heare our praier.
Aunswere. And let our crye come vnto the.

¶ Let vs praye.

ALMIGHTIE God, and mooste mercifull father, whiche of thy
infinite goodness, haste geuen to vs thy onely and moste dere
beloued sonne Jesus Christ, to be our redemer and aucthor of
euerlasting lyfe, who after that he had made perfecte our redemption by his death, and was ascēded into heauen, powred doune his
giftes aboundantly vpon men, makynge some Apostles, some
Prophetes, some Euāgelistes, some Pastours and Doctours, to the
edifying and making perfect of his cōgregacion : graunte we
beseche the, to this thy seruante, suche grace that he may euermore be ready, to sprede abrode thy Gospel, and glad tidinges of
recōcilement to God, and to vse the aucthoritie geuen vnto him,
not to destroye, but to saue, not to hurt, but to helpe, so that he
as a wise and faithfull seruaunt, geuing to thy family meat in due
season, maye at the last day be receiued into joye, through Jesu
Christ our Lorde, who with the, and the holy Ghost liueth and
reigneth one God, worlde without ende.   Amen.

*Then the Archebyshop and Bysshoppes present shall laye theyr handes vpon
the heade of the elected Byshop, the Archebyshoppe saying.*

TAKE the holy ghost, and remember that thou stirre vp the grace
of God, whiche is in the, by imposiciō of handes : for God hath not
geuen vs the spirit of feare, but of power, and loue, and of sober-
nesse.

Then the Archebyshoppe shal deliuer him the Byble, saying:

GEUE hede vnto reading, exhortacion and doctrine.   Thinke
vpon these thinges conteyned in this booke, be diligent in them,
that the encreasing comming thereby, may be manifest vnto all
mē.   Take hede vnto thy selfe, and vnto teaching, and be diligent
in doing theim, for by doing this, thou shalt saue thy selfe, and
theim that hear the.   Be to the flocke of Christ a shepherd, not
a woulfe, fede theim, deuoure them not, holde vp the weake, heale
the sycke, binde together the broken, bring againe the outecastes,
seke the lost.   Be so merciful, that you be not to remisse, so
minister Discipline, that you forget not mercy, that whē the chief

shepeherde shal come, ye may receiue the immercessible croune of glory, through Jesus Christ our Lord. Amen.

Then the Archbyshop shall procede to the Communion, wyth whome the newe consecrated Byshoppe with other, shal also communicate. And after the last Collecte immediatly before the benediction, shalbe said this praier.

MOST mercifull father, we beseche thee to sende doune vpon this thy seruaunt, thy heauenly blessynge, and so endue him with thy holy spirite, that he preachinge thy worde, maye not onely be earnest to reproue, beseche and rebuke with all pacience and doctrine, but also maye be to suche as beleue, an wholsome example in worde, in conuersacion, in loue, in faithe, in chastitie, and puritie, that faythfully fulfyllyng his course, at the latter daye he may receyue the crowne of righteoutnesse layde vp by the Lorde the ryghteous judge : who lyueth and reigneth, one God with the father and the holy Ghoste, world without ende. Amen.

*Richardus Graf-
tonus, Typographus, Regius
excudebat.*

Anno Domini 1559.

Cum Priwelegio ad Imprimendum solum.

APPENDICES.

CONTENTS.

I.—THE NEW CALENDAR.

1561.

❡ THE ORDER

HOW THE REST OF HOLY SCRIPTURE (BESIDE THE PSALTER) IS APPOINTED TO BE READ.

THE Old Testament is appointed for the first Lessons at Morning and Euenyng prayer, and shalbe read through every yere once, except certayne Bookes and Chapters, whiche be least edifying, and myght best be spared, and therefore be lefte vnread.

The newe Testament is appoynted for the seconde Lessons at Morning and Euening prayer, and shalbe read ouer orderly euery yere thrise, besyde the Epistles and Gospels : excepte the Apocalips, out of the which there be onlye certayne Lessons appoynted vppon diuers proper feastes.

And to knowe what Lessons shalbe read euery day : Fynde the day of the moneth in the Kalendar folowyng, and there ye shal perceaue the Bookes and Chapters that shalbe read for the Lessons both at Mornyng and Euenyng prayer.

And here is to be noted, that whensoeuer there be any proper Psalmes, or Lessons appoynted for the Sundayes, or for any Feast, moueable or vnmoueable : Then the Psalmes and Lessons appoynted in the Kalendar, shal be omitted for that tyme.

Ye must note also, that the Collecte, Epistle, and Gospell, appoynted for the Sundaye, shall serue all the weke after, except there fall some Feast that hath his proper.

When the yeres of our Lorde may be deuyed into foure euen partes, which is euery fourth yere : then the Sunday letter leapeth, and that yere the Psalmes and Lessons whiche serue for the .xxiii. day of February shalbe read agayne the day folowyng, except it be Sunday, whiche hath proper Lessons of the olde Testament, appoynted in the Table seruyng to that purpose.

Also, wheresoeuer the begynnyng of any Lesson, Epistle, or Gospell, is not expressed, there ye must begyn at the begynnyng of the Chapiter.

And wheresoeuer is not expressed howe farre shal be read : there shall you reade to the ende of the Chapiter.

Item, so ofte as the first Chapiter of Saint Mathie is read eyther for Lesson or Gospell : ye shal begyn the same at : The byrth of Jesus Christ was on this wyse. &c. And the thirde Chapiter of Saint Lukes Gospell shal be read vnto : So that he was supposed to be the sonne of Joseph.

❡ Proper Lessons to be read for the first Lessons, both at Mornyng prayer and Euenyng prayer, on the Sundayes throughout the yere, and for some also the seconde Lessons.

Sundaies of Advent.	Mattens.	Euensong.			
The Fyrst	Esay i	Esay ii	Sunday after Assention day.	Deut. xii	Deut. xiii
ii	v	xxiiii			
iii	xxv	xxvi	Whitsunday.	Mattens.	Euensong.
iv	xxx	xxxii	i Lesson	Deuter. xvi	Wisdome. i
Sundaies after Christmas	Mattens.	Euensong.	ii Lesson	Actes x Then Peter opened his. &c.	Acts xix It fortuned whenApollo went to Corinth.&c.vnto After these thynges.
The First	xxxvii	xxxviii			
ii	xli	xliii			
Sundaies after the Epiphany.	Mattens.	Euensong.			
The First	xliiii	xlvi	Trinity Sunday.	Mattens.	Euensong.
ii	li	liii	i Lesson	Gene. xviii	Josue. i
iii	lv	lvi	ii Lesson	Math. iii	
iv	lvii	lviii	Sundayes after the Trinitie.		
v	lix	lxiv			
Septuages.	Genesis i	Genesis ii	The Fyrst	Josue. x	Josue. xxiii
Sexagesim.	iii	vi	ii	Judic. iiii	Judic. v
Quinquage.	ix	xii	iii	i Kyng. ii	i Kyng. iii
Lent.	Mattens.	Euensong.	iv	xii	xiii
			v	xv	xvi
First Sunday.	xix	xxii	vi	ii King. xii	ii King. xxi
ii	xxvii	xxxiv	vii	xxii	xxiv
iii	xxxix	xlii	viii	iii King. xiii	iii King.xvii
iv	xliii	xlv	ix	xviii	xix
v	Exod. iii	Exod. v	x	xxi	xxii
vi	ix	x	xi	iiii King. v	iiii King. ix
Easter day.	Mattens.	Euensong.	xii	x	xviii
			xiii	xix	xxiii
i Lesson	Exod. xii	Exod. xiiii	xiv	Jerem. v	Jerem. xxii
ii Lesson	Roma. vi	Actes ii	xv	xxxv	xxxvi
			xvi	Ezech. ii	Ezech. xiv
¶ Sundayes after Easter.			xvii	xvi	xviii
			xviii	xx	xxiiii
The Fyrst	Num. xvi	Num. xxii	xix	Daniel iii	Daniel vi
ii	xxiii	xxv	xx	Joel ii	Miche. vi
iii	Deuter. iiii	Deut. v	xxi	Abacuc ii	Prouerb. i
iv	vi	vii	xxii	Prouer. ii	iii
v	viii	ix	xxiii	xi	xii
			xxiv	xiii	xiiii
			xxv	xv	xvi
			xxvi	xvii	xix

Lessons proper for holy dayes.

	Mattens.	Euensong.		Mattens.	Euensong.
S. Andrew. S. Thomas thapostle.	Prouer. xxi xxiii	Prouer. xxi xxiiii	Purification of the virgin Mary.	Wisd. ix	Wisdom xii
Natiuitie of Christ.			Saint Mathie.	Wisdom xix	Eccle. i
			Annunciation of our Lady.	Eccle. ii	Eccle. iii
i Lesson	Esay ix	Esai. vii God spake once agayne to Achas, &c.	Wednesday afore Easter.	Osee. xiii	Osee. xiiii
ii Lesson	Luke ii vnto. And vnto men of good wyll.	Titus iii The kyndnesse and loue, &c.	Thursday afore Easter.	Daniel ix	Jere. xxxi
S. Steuen. i Lesson ii Lesson	Prou. xxviii Act vi & vii Steuen full of fayth and power, &c. vnto. And when fortye yeres, &c.	Eccle. iiii Actes vii And when xlIyeres were expired, there appeared vnto Moses, &c. vnto Steuen full of the holy, &c.	Good Fryday. Easter Euen. Mundaye in Easter. weke. i Lesson ii Lesson Tuesdaye in Easter weke. i Lesson ii Lesson	Gen. xxii Zachari. ix Exod. xvi Mat. xxviii Exod. xx Luk xxiiii vnto And behold two of them.	Esay liii Exod. xiii Exo d. xvii Actes iii Ex od. xxxii I Corin. xv
Saint John. i Lesson ii Lesson	Ecclesi. v Apocal. i	Eccles. vi Apoca. xxii	S. Marke.	Eccle. iiii	Eccle. v
Innocentes.	Jerem xxxi, vnto Moreouer I hard Ephraim.	Wisdom i	Philippe & Jacob.	Eccle. vii	Eccle. ix
Circumcision day. i Lesson	Gene. xvii	Deu. x And now Israel.	Assention Day. Mundaye in Whitson weke. i Lesson	Deut. x. Gene. xi vnto, These are the generation of Sem.	iiii King ii Num. xi Gather vnto me 70 men, &c. vnto Moses and the elders returned.
ii Lesson Epiphany. i Lesson ii Lesson	Rom. ii Esay lx. Luke iii vnto So that he was supposed to be the sonne of Joseph.	Coloss. ii Esay. xlix Joh. ii vnto After this he went to Capernaum.	ii Lesson	i Cor. xii	
Conuersion of S. Paul. i Lesson ii Lesson	Wisdom v Actes xxii vnto They harde hym.	Wisdom vi Actes xxvi	Tuesdaye in Whitson weke.	I Kyng xix David came to Saule in Ramatha, &c.	Deuter xxx

	Mattens.	Euensong.		Mattens.	Euensong.
			Saint Mathew	Eccle. xxxv	Eccle.xxxviii
S. Barnabe.			Saint Michael.	xxxix	xliiii
i Lesson	Eccle. x	Eccle. xii	S. Luke.	li	Job i
ii Lesson	Actes xiiii	Actes xv vnto After certayne dayes.	S. Simon & Jude.		
Saint John Baptist.			i Lesson	Job xxiiii, xxv	xlii
i Lesson	Mala. iii	Mala. iiii	Al Saintes.		
ii Lesson	Math. xiii	Math. xiiii vnto When Jesus harde.	i Lesson	Wisd. iii vnto Blessed is rather the baren.	Wisdom. v vnto His ielousy also.
Saint Peter.					
i Lesson	Eccle. xv	Eccle. xix	ii Lesson	Hebr. xi, xii Saintes by fayth, vnto If ye endure chastenyng.	Apoca. xix vnto And I sawe an Angell stande.
ii Lesson	Actes iii	Actes iiii			
S. James.	Eccle. xxi	Eccle. xxiii			
Saint Bartylmew.	xxv	xxix			

Proper Psalmes on certayne dayes.

	Mattens.	Euensong.		Mattens.	Euensong.
Chrystmas day.	Psalme xix xlv lxxxv	lxxxix cx cxxxii	Assention day.	viii xv xxi	xxiiii lxviii cviii
Easter day.	ii lvii cxi	cxiii cxiiii cxviii	Whit sonday.	xlv lxvii	ciiii cxlv

The Almanack.

The Yeres of our Lorde.	The Golden Number.	Dominical Letter.	Septua-gesima.	The fyrst daye of Lent.	Easter day.	Rogation Weke.	Ascen-tion.	Whyt-sonday.	Advent Sunday.
1561	iiii	E.	2 Februa.	19 Febru.	6 April	12 Maii	25 1 Maii	15 Maii 1	30 Nouem.
1562	v	D.	25 Janua.	11	29 March	4	7	17	29
1563	vi	C.	7 Febru.	24	11 April	17	20	30	28
1564	vii	B. A.	30 Janu.	16	2	8	11	21	3 Decem.
1565	viii	G.	18 Febru.	7 March	22	28	31	10 June	2
1566	ix	F.	10	27 Febru.	14	20	23	2	1
1567	x	E.	26 Janu.	12	30 March	5	8	18 Maii	30 Nouem.
1568	xi	D. C.	15 Febru.	3 March	18 April	24	27	6 June	28
1569	xii	B.	6	23 Febru.	10	16	19	29 Maii	27
1570	xiii	A.	22 Janu.	8	26 March	1	4	14	3 Decem.
1571	xiiii	G.	11 Febru.	28	15 April	21	24	3 June	2
1572	xv	F. E.	3	20	6	12	15	25 Maii	30 Nouem.
1573	xvi	D.	18 Janua.	4	22 March	27 April	30 April	10 Maii	29
1574	xvii	C.	7 Febru.	24	11 April	17 Maii	20 Maii	30	28
1575	xviii	B.	30 Janua.	16	3	9	12	22	27
1576	xix	A. G.	19 Febru.	7 March	22	28	31	10 June	2 Decem.
1577	i	F.	3	20 Febru.	7	13	16	26 Maii	1
1578	ii	E.	26 Janu.	12	30 March	5	8	18	30 Nouem.
1579	iii	D.	15 Febru.	4 March	19 April	25	28	7 Junii	29
1580	iiii	C. B.	31 Janua.	17 Febru.	3	9	12	22	27
1581	v	A.	22	8	26 March	1	4	14	3 Decem.
1582	vi	G.	11 Febru.	28	15 April	21	4	3 Junii	2
1583	vii	F.	27 Janu.	13	31 March	6	9	19 Maii	1
1584	viii	E. D.	16 Febru.	3 March	19 April	25	28	7 Junii	29 Nouem.
1585	ix	C.	7	24 Febru.	11	17	20	30 Maii	28
1586	x	B.	30 Janu.	16	3	9	12	22	27
1587	xi	A.	12 Febru.	1 March	16	22	25	4 Junii	3 Decemb.
1588	xii	G. F.	4 Febru.	21 Febru.	7	13	16	26 Maii	1
1589	xiii	E.	26 Janu.	12 Febru.	30 March	5	8	18	30 Nouem.
1590	xiiii	D.	15 Febru.	4 March	19 April	25	28	7 June	29

[1 These two have evidently been misplaced.]

Note, that the supputation of the yere of our Lorde in the Churche of Englande, beginneth the .xxv. day of Marche, the same day supposed to be the fyrst day vpon whiche the worlde was created, and the day when Christe was conceyued in the wombe of the virgin Mary.

1578. ¶ *Of the Golden number.* The Golden number is so called, because it was written in the Kalender with letters of golde, right at that daye whereon the Moone changed : and it is the space of 19. yeeres, in the which the Moone returneth to the selfe same daye of the yeere of the Sunne : and therefore it is also called the Cycle of the Moone, in the which the Solstices and Equinoctials doe returne to all one point in the Zodiaque.

To finde it euerie yeere, you must adde one yeere to the yeere of Christ (for Christ was borne one yeere of the 19. already past) then diuide the whole by 19, and that which resteth is the Golden number for that yeere ; if there be no surplusage, it is then 19.

¶ *The Epact.* *Epactæ hemeræ* in Greeke, doeth signifie in Englishe, dayes set betwene, and therefore the 11. dayes and 3 houres, that are added to the yeere of the Moone, are called *Epactæ*, and are added to make the yeere of the Moone, which is but 354. dayes, iust with the yeere of the Sunne, which hath 365. dayes and a quarter.

To finde out the Epact of eche yeere, doe thus. To the Epact [1] of the yeere that last went before that yeere for which you would finde the Epact, adde 11. and the summe of these two make the Epact. If it surmount 30. then take 30. out, and that which resteth aboue 30. is the Epact you desire.

¶ *The vse of the Epact.* To knowe howe olde the Moone is at any time for euer by the Epact, doe thus : Adde vnto the dayes of your moneth, wherein you woulde knowe this, the Epact, and as many dayes moe as are moneths from March to that moneth, including both moneths, out of the which Substract 30. as often as you may, the age remaineth : if nothing remaine, the Moone changeth that day.

¶ For the more ease of the Reader, we have placed hereouer an Almanacke, inclusively comprehending, not onely howe to finde the Epact for the space of xxxii. yeeres to come, but also the Golden number afore specified, together with the Dominicall letter, Leape yeere, and vii. other moueable feastes, or dayes in the yeere, during the same time, as may appeare.

Note, that the Golden number and Dominicall letter doeth change euery yeere the first day of Ianuarie, and the Epact the first day of March for euer. Note also, that the yeere of our Lorde beginneth the xxv. day of March, the same day supposed to be the first day vpon which the worlde was created, and the day when Christ was conceiued in the wombe of the virgin Marie.

[1 The Epact for 1878 was xxii.]

	To fynde Easter for euer.						
Golden Number.	A	B	C	D	E	F	G
I	Apryl ix	x	xi	xii	vi	vii	viii
II	March xxvi	xxvii	xxviii	xxix	xxx	xxxi	Apryl i
III	Apryl xvi	xvii	xviii	xix	xx	xiiii	xv
IIII	Apryl ix	iii	iiii	v	vi	vii	viii
V	March xxvi	xxvii	xxviii	xxix	xxiii	xxiiii	xxv
VI	Apryl xvi	xvii	xi	xii	xiii	iiii	xv
VII	Apryl ii	iii	iiii	v	vi	Mar. xxxi	Apryl i
VIII	April xxiii	xxiiii	xxv	xix	xx	xxi	xxii
X	Apryl ix	x	xi	xii	xiii	xiiii	viii
X	Apryl ii	iii	Marc xxviii	xxix	xxx	xxxi	Apryl
XI	Apryl xvi	xvii	xviii	xix	xx	xxi	xxii
XII	Apryl ix	x	xi	v	vi	vii	viii
XIII	March xxvi	xxvii	xxviii	xxix	xxx	xxxi	xxv
XIV	Apryl xvi	xvii	xviii	xix	xiii	xiiii	xv
XV	Apryl ii	iii	iiii	v	vi	vii	viii
XVI	March xxvi	xxvii	xxviii	xxii	xxiii	xxiiii	xxv
XVII	Apryl xvi.	x	xi	xii	xxiii	xiiii	xv
XVIII	Apryl ii	iii	iiii	v	Mar. xxx	xxxi	Apryl i
XIX	Apryl xxiii	xxiiii	xviii	xix	xx	xxi	xxii

When ye haue founde the Sunday Letter in the vppermost lyne, guyde your eye downewarde from the same, tyll ye come ryght ouer agaynst the pryme, and there is shewed both what moneth, and what day of the moneth, Easter falleth that yere.

Septuagesima			ix		
Sexagesima		before Easter	viii		wekes.
Quinquagesima			vii		
Quadragesima			vi		

Rogations			v		
Whytsunday		after Easter	vii		wekes.
Trinitie Sunday			viii		

¶ *These to be obserued for holy dayes, and none other.*

That is to say: All Sundayes in the year. The dayes of the Feastes of the Circumcision of our Lorde Jesus Christ. Of the Epiphanie. Of the Purification of the blessed virgin. Of S. Mathie thapostle. Of the Annunciation of the blessed virgin. Of Saint Marke the Euangelist. Of Saint Philip & Jacob the Apostles. Of the assencion of our Lorde Jesus Christe. Of the Natiuitie of S. John Baptist. Of Saint Peter the Apostle. Of Saint James the Apostle. Of Saint Bartholomew Apostle. Of Saint Mathew the Apostle. Of Saint Michaell the Archangell. Of Saint Luke the Euangelist. Of S. Simon and Jude the Apostles. Of All Saintes. Of Saint Andrewe the Apostle. Of Saint Thomas the Apostle. Of the Natiuitie of our Lorde. Of Saint Stephan the Martir. Of Saint John the Euangelist. Of the holy Innocentes. Monday and Tuesday in Easter weke, Monday and Tuesday in Whitson weke.

¶ *A brief declaration when euery Term begynneth and endeth.*

Be it knowen that Easter Terme begynneth alwayes the .xviii. daye after Easter, reckenyng Easter day for one: and endeth the Munday next after the Assencion day.

Trinitie Terme begynneth .xii. dayes after Whitsunday, and continueth .xix. dayes.

Michaelmas Terme begynneth the .ix. or .x. day of October, and endeth the .xxviii. or .xxix. day of Nouember.

Hyllary Terme begynneth the .xxiii. or .xxiiii. day of January, and endeth the .xii. or .xiii. day of February.

¶ In Easter Term, on the Assencion day. In Trinitie Terme, on the Natiuitie of Saint John Baptist. In Michaelmas Terme, on the feaste of All Saintes. In Hyllary Terme, on the Feast of the Purification of our Lady: the Quenes Judges of Westminster do not vse to syt in iudgemente, nor vppon any Sundayes.

G

JANUARY HATH XXXI. DAYS.

Sunne {ryseth}{falleth} houre {vii mi. 3}{iiii mi. 37}				Psalmes.	MORNYNG PRAYER.		EUENYNG PRAYER.	
					i Lesson.	*ii Lesson.*	*i Lesson.*	*ii Lesson.*
iii	A	Kalend.	*Circumcision.*	i	Gen. xvii	Rom. ii	Deut. x	Colo. ii
	b	iiii No.	....	ii	Gene. i	Math. i	Gene. ii	Rom. i
xi	c	iii No.	....	iii	iii	ii	iiii	ii
	d	Prid. No.	....	iiii	v	iii	vi	iii
xix	e	Nonas.	....	v	vii	iiii	viii	iiii
viii	f	viii Id.	*Epiphanye....*	vi	Esay lx	Luk. iii	Esa. xlix	Joh. ii
	g	vii Id.	....	vii	Gen. ix	Math. v	Gen. xii	Rom. v
xvi	A	vi Id.	Lucian.........	viii	xiii	vi	xiiii	vi
v	b	v Id.	....	ix	xv	vii	xvi	vii
	c	iiii Id.	Sol in Aquario	x	xvii	viii	xviii	viii
xiii	d	iii Id.	....	xi	xix	ix	xx	ix
ii	e	Prid. Id.	....	xii	xxi	x	xxii	x
	f	Idus.	Hyllarii.......	xiii	xxiii	xi	xxiiii	xi
x	g	xix Kl.	Februarii......	xiiii	xxv	xii	xxvi	xii
	A	xviii Kl.	....	xv	xxvii	xiii	xxviii	xiii
xviii	b	xvii Kl.	....	xvi	xxix	xiiii	xxx	xiiii
vii	c	xvi Kl.	....	xvii	xxxi	xv	xxxii	xv
	d	xv Kl.	Prisca.........	xviii	xxxiii	xvi	xxxiii	xvi
xv	e	xiiii Kl.	....	xix	xxxv	xvii	xxxvii	i Cor.
iiii	f	xiii Kl.	Fabian.........	xx	xxxviii	xviii	xxxix	ii
	g	xii Kl.	Agnes.........	xxi	xl	xix	xli	iii
xii	A	xi Kl.	Vincent........	xxii	xlii	xx	xliii	iiii
i	b	x Kl.	....	xxiii	xliv	xxi	xlv	v
	c	ix Kl.	....	xxiiii	xlvi	xxii	xlvii	vi
ix	d	viii Kl.	Conuer Pauli.	xxv	Wisd. v	Act. xxii	Wisd. vi	Act. xxvi
	e	vii Kl.	....	xxvi	Ge. xlviii	Ma. xxiii	Ge. xlix	i Cor. vii
xvii	f	vi Kl.	....	xxvii	l	xxiiii	Exod. i	viii
vi	g	v Kl.	....	xxviii	Exod. ii	xxv	iii	ix
	A	iiii Kl.	....	xxix	iiii	xxvi	v	x
xiiii	b	iii Kl.	....	xxx	vii	xxvii	viii	xi
iii	c	Prid. Kl.	....	i	ix	xxviii	x	xii

1578. JANUARIE.

1. The first day of this moneth, Noah, after he had bene in the Arke 150 dayes, began to see the toppes of the high mountaines. *Gene.* 7. 24. and 8. 3, 5.

Also as vpon this day, Christ was circumcised according to the Lawe. *Luke* 2. 21.

6. The Magians as vpon this day (hauing ben guided vnto Beth-lehem by the direction of a starre) worshipped Christ, and offered vnto him golde, mirrhe, and frankensence. *Matth.* 2. 1. *usque* 13.

Also as vpon this day, Christ was baptized by John in Jordan, being about xxx. yeeres of age. *Matth.* 3. 13. *Luke* 3. 21, 23.

Also Christ as vpon this day, wrought his first miracle, in turning water into wine, at a marriage in Cana of Galile. *John* 2. 2, 11.

10. Nebuchad-nezzar the king of Babel as vpon this day, besieged the Citie of Jerusalem. 2 *Kings* 25. 1. *Jere.* 52. 4.

17. The good Prince Scanderbeg king of Epyrus, a scourge to the Turke, as vpon this day, died. 1466.

22. The Duke of Somerset as vpon this day, was beheaded. 1552.

25. Caius Caligula, his wife and daughter, as vpon this day, were slaine. *Anno Do.* 42.

27. Saint Paul, as vpon this day, of a persecuter was conuerted, as he iourneyed vnto Damascus. *Actes* 9. 3.

❡ FEBRUARY HATH XXVIII. DAYS.

Sunne { ryseth / falleth } hour { vii mi. 14. / iiii mi. 46. }				Psalmes	MORNYNG PRAYER.		EUENYNG PRAYER.	
					i Lesson.	*ii Lesson.*	*i Lesson.*	*ii Lesson.*
	d	Kalend.	Fast	ii	Exod. xi	Mark i	Exod. xii	1 Cor. xiii
xi	e	iiii No.	*Purifi Mary..*	iii	Wisd. ix	ii	Wisd. xii	xiiii
xix	f	iii No.	Blasii	iiii	Exo. xiii	iii	Exo. xiiii	xv
viii	g	Prid. No.	....	v	xv	iiii	xvi	xvi
	A	Nonas.	Agathe.......	vi	xvii	v	xviii	2 Cor. i
xvi	b	viii Id.	....	vii	xix	vi	xx	ii
v	c	vii Id.	..........[bus.	viii	xxi	vii	xxii	iii
	d	vi Id.	Sol in Pisci-	ix	xxiii	viii	xxiiii	iiii
xiii	e	v Id.	....	x	xxxii	ix	xxxiii	v
ii	f	iiii Id.	....	xi	xxxiiii	x	Leuit.xviii	vi
	g	iii Id.	....	xii	Leui. xix	xi	xx	vii
x	A	Prid. Id.	....	xiii	xxvi	xii	Num. xi	viii
	b	Idus.	....	xiiii	Num. xii	xiii	xiii	ix
xvii	c	xvi Kl.	Valentine	xv	xiiii	xiiii	xvi	x
vii	d	xv Kl.	Martii..........	xvi	xvii	xv	xx	xi
	e	xiiii Kl.	....	xvii	xxi	xvi	xxii	xii
xv	f	xiii Kl.	....	xviii	xxiii	Luke di. i	xxiiii	xiii
iiii	g	xii Kl.	....	xix	xxv	di. i	xxvii	Galat. i
	A	xi Kl.	....	xx	xxx	ii	xxxi	ii
xii	b	x Kl.	....	xxi	xxxii	iii	xxxv	iii
i	c	ix Kl.	....	xxii	xxxvi	iiii	Deut. i	iiii
	d	viii Kl.	....	xxiii	Deut. ii	v	iii	v
ix	e	vii Kl.	Fast	xxiiii	iiii	vi	v	vi
	f	vi Kl.	*S. Mathias* ...	xxv	Wisd. xix	vii	Eccle. i	Ephes. i
xvii	g	v Kl.	....	xxvi	Deut. vi	viii	Deut. vii	ii
vi	A	iiii Kl.	....	xxvii	viii	ix	ix	iii
	b	iii Kl.	....	xxviii	x	x	xi	iiii
xiiii	c	Prid. Kl.	....	xxix	xii	xi	xv	v

1578. FEBRUARIE.

2. As vpon this day, Christ our Saviour was offered vnto the Lord in the Temple at Jerusalem, and his mother, the Virgin Marie, was purified according to the law. *Luke* 2. 22.

8. As vpon this day, the Romanes began their spring, after Plinie.

9. As vpon this day, Noah (fourtie daies after he had seene the toppes of the mountaines) sent out of the Arke the Rauen, and after the Doue, of the which only the Doue returned. *Gene.* 8. 7, 8.

14. The Jewes, as vpon this day, slewe three hundreth of their enemies, in Shushan, but yet on the spoyle they layd not their hand. *Ester* 9. 15.

15. The Jewes kept this day for a feast, because nowe the sappe riseth in the trees.

16. The learned Clerke, Philip Melanthon, as vpon this day, was borne. *Anno* 1497.

17. Noah, as vpon this day, sent out of the Arke againe the Doue, which returning vnto him brought an Oliue branche in her bill, whereby he knewe, that the waters were abated vpon the earth. *Gene.* 8. 10, 11.

18. Martin Luther, the seruant of God, died as vpon this day. *Anno* 1546.

22. Martin Luther his body, as vpon this day, was translated to Witemberg, and buried in the chappell of the Castell there.

25. Noah, as vpon this day, sent the Doue out of the Arke the third time, and she returned no more. *Gene.* 8. 12.

❡ MARCHE HATH XXXI. DAYES.

Sunne {ryseth / falleth} houre {vi mi. 18. / v mi. 42.}				Psalmes.	MORNYNG PRAYER.		EUENYNG PRAYER.	
					i Lesson.	*ii Lesson.*	*i Lesson.*	*ii Lesson.*
iii	d	Kalend.	Dauid..........	xxx	Deu. xvi	Luk. xii	Deu. xvii	Ephe. vi
	e	vi No.	Cedde	i	xviii	xiii	xix	Phil. i
	f	v No.	....	ii	xx	xiiii	xxi	ii
	g	iiii No.	....	iii	xxii	xv	xxiiii	iii
xix	A	iii No.	....	iiii	xxv	xvi	xxvi	iiii
viii	b	Prid. No.	....	v	xxvii	xvii	xxviii	Coloss. i
	c	Nonas.	Perpetue	vi	xxix	xviii	xxx	ii
xvi	d	viii Id.	....	vii	xxxi	xix	xxxii	iii
v	e	vii Id.	....	viii	xxxiii	xx	xxxiiii	iiii
	f	vi Id.	....	ix	Josue. i	xxi	Josue ii	i Thess. i
xiii	g	v Id.	....	x	iii	xxii	iiii	ii
ii	A	iiii Id.	Gregory	xi	v	xxiii	vi	iii
	b	iii Id.	Sol in Ariete.	xii	vii	xxiiii	viii	iiii
x	c	Prid. Id.	....	xiii	ix	John i	x	v
	d	Idus.	......	xiiii	xxiii	ii	xxiiii	ii Thes. i
xviii	e	xvii Kl.	....	xv	Judg. i	iii	Judg. ii	ii
vii	f	xvi Kl.	Aprilis........	xvi	iii	iiii	iiii	iii
	g	xv Kl.	Edwarde	xvii	v	v	vi	i Tim. i
xv	A	xiiii Kl.	....	xviii	vii	vi	viii	ii. iii
iiii	b	xiii Kl.	....	xix	ix	vii	x	iiii
	c	xii Kl.	Benedict	xx	xi	viii	xii	v
xii	d	xi Kl.	....	xxi	xiii	ix	xiii	vi
i	e	x Kl.	....	xxii	xv	x	xvi	ii Tim. i
	f	ix Kl.	Fast	xxiii	xvii	xi	xviii	ii
ix	g	viii Kl.	*Annun. of Ma*	xxiiii	Eccle. ii	xii	Eccle. iii	iii
	A	vii Kl.	....	xxv	Judg. xix	xiii	Judg. xx	iiii
xvii	b	vi Kl.	....	xxvi	xxi	xiiii	Ruth i	Titus i
vi	c	v Kl.	....	xxvii	Ruth ii	xv	iii	ii. iii
	d	iiii Kl.	....	xxviii	iiii	xvi	i Kyng. i	Phile. i
xiiii	e	iii Kl.	....	xxix	i Kyng. ii	xvii	iii	Hebr. i
iii	f	Prid. Kl.	....	xxx	iiii	xviii	v	ii

1578. MARCH.

3. As vpon this day, the Temple of Jerusalem was finished and holied, 597. yeeres before Christ his birth. *Ezra* 6. 15. and I *Esdr.* 7. 5.

10. As vpon this day, Christ being on the other side of Jordan, was aduertised of the sicknesse of Lazarus. *John* 11. 3.

13. As on this day, was the fast of Ester. *Ester* 3. 12. and 4. 16.

16. As vpon this day, Lazarus was raised from death. *John* 11. 44.

20. As vpon this day, Christ entred into Jerusalem. *John* 12. 14, 15.

22. Marie Magdalen, as on this day, annointed Christ with precious oyntment. *John* 12. 3. *Matth.* 26. 7, 12.

24. Christ held his last supper, as vpon this day, and was taken. *Matth.* 26. 20.

25. Christ was crucified, dead and buried, as vpon this day. *Luke* 23. 33. *Mark* 15. 25. *Mat.* 27. 35.

This day also, was the day of preparation. *John* 19. 31, 42.

26. Christ as on this day, lay in the Sepulchre. *Matth.* 27. 62.

27. As vpon this day, was the resurrection of Christ. *Matth.* 28. 1, 2. *Luke* 24. 1.

Also as vpon this day, Jehoachin, king of Judah, was deliuered out of prison, by Euil Merodach King of Babylon, who after had his allowance at the Kinges table, all the dayes of his life. ii *King* 25. 27; 29, 30.

❡ APRYLL HATH XXX. DAYES.

Sunne {ryseth}{falleth} houre {vi mi. 17}{vi mi. 43}				Psalmes.	MORNYNG PRAYER.		EUENYNG PRAYER.	
					i Lesson.	ii Lesson.	i Lesson.	ii Lesson.
	g	Kalend.	....	i	i king. vi	John xix	i king. vii	Hebr. iii
xi	A	iiii No.	....	ii	viii	xx	ix	iiii
	b	iii No.	Richard	iii	x	xxi	xi	v
xix	c	Prid. No.	Ambrose	iiii	xii	Actes i	xiii	vi
viii	d	Nonas.	....	v	xiiii	ii	xv	vii
xvi	e	viii Id.	....	vi	xvi	iii	xvii	viii
v	f	vii Id.	....	vii	xviii	iiii	xix	ix
	g	vi Id.	.:.	viii	xx	v	xxi	x
xiii	A	v Id.	....	ix	xxii	vi	xxiii	xi
ii	b	iiii Id.	Sol in Tauro..	x	xxiiii	vii	xxv	xii
	c	iii Id.	....	xi	xxvi	viii	xxvii	xiii
x	d	Prid. Id.	....	xii	xxviii	ix	xxix	Jacob. i
	e	Idus.	....	xiii	xxx	x	xxxi	ii
xviii	f	xviii Kl.	Maii............	xiiii	ii King. i	xi	ii king. ii	iii
vii	g	xvii Kl.	....	xv	iii	xii	iiii	iiii
	A	xvi Kl.	....	xvi	v	xiii	vi	v
xv	b	xv Kl.	....	xvii	vii	xiiii	viii	i Pet. i
iiii	c	xiiii Kl.	....	xviii	ix	xv	x	ii
	d	xiii Kl.	Alphege.......	xix	xi	xvi	xii	iii
xii	e	xii Kl.	....	xx	xiii	xvii	xiiii	iiii
i	f	xi Kl.	....	xxi	xv	xviii	xvi	v
	g	x Kl.	....	xxii	xvii	xix	xviii	ii Pet. i
ix	A	ix Kl.	S. George.....	xxiii	xix	xx	xx	ii
	b	viii Kl.	....	xxiiii	xxi	xxi	xxii	iii
xvii	c	vii Kl.	*Mark Euang.*	xxv	Eccle. iiii	xxii	Eccle. v	i Joh. i
vi	d	vi Kl.	....	xxvi	ii king 23	xxiii	ii King 24	ii
	e	v Kl.	....	xxvii	iii king. i	xxiiii	iii King. 2	iii
xiiii	f	iiii Kl.	....	xxviii	iii	xxv	iiii	iiii
iii	g	iii Kl.	....	xxix	v	xxvi	vi	v
	A	Prid. Kl.	....	xxx	vii	xxvii	viii	ii, iii John

1578. APRIL.

1. In this first day, Noah opened the couer of the Arke. *Gene.* 8. 13. Also as vpon this day, Moses reared the Tabernacle. *Exod.* 40. 2, 17.

4. Christ, as vpon this day, which was eyght dayes after his resurrection, appeared to his disciples, Thomas also being present. *John* 20. 26.

6. Joshua and the Jewes camped before Jordan, the space of three dayes. *Joshua* 3. 1.

10. The Israelites as vpon this day, passe Jordan with a great multitude, the yeere before the Natiuitie of our Lord Jesus Christ 1457. *Joshu.* 3. 17. and 4. 1, 11.

11. Joshua circumcised the people nigh Jericho. *Joshua* 5. 3.

13. King Ahashuerosh as vpon this day, commanded all ye Jewes to be slaine. *Ester* 3. 11, 13.

14. The Israelites vpon this day kept passouer, and Man ceased. *Joshua* 5. 10, 12.

15. Moses, as on this day, brought the Israelites out of Egypt. *Exod.* 12. 37, 41.

16. As on this day, they departed from Succoth into the desert of Etham. *Exo.* 13. 20. *Nom.* 33. 6.

17. As on this day, they passed into the mountaines and daungerous places. *Exodus* 14. 2. *Nomb.* 33. 7.

18. As on this day they went through the red Sea. *Exod.* 14. 29. *Nomb.* 33. 8.

19. As on this day, they wander in the desert of Shur, and came to Marah. *Ex.* 15. 22. *Nom.* 33. 8.

¶ MAY HATH XXXI. DAYS.

Sunne {ryseth / falleth} houre {v mi. 48 / vii mi. 13}				Psalmes.	MORNYNG PRAYER.		EUENYNG PRAYER.	
					i Lesson.	*ii Lesson.*	*i Lesson.*	*ii Lesson.*
xi	b	Kalend.	*Philp & Jaco.*	i	Eccle. vii	Acte. viii	Eccle. ix	Judas i
	c	vi No.	....	ii	iii King. ix	xxviii	iii King. x	Rom. i
xix	d	v No.	Inuen. of ye	iii	xi	Math. i	xii	ii
viii	e	iiii No.	..........[cross	iiii	xiii	ii	xiiii	iii
	f	iii No.		v	xv	iii	xvi	iiii
xvi	g	Prid. No.	John Euang..	vi	xvii	iiii	xviii	v
v	A	Nonas.	....	vii	xix	v	xx	vi
	b	viii Id.	....	viii	xxi	vi	· xxii	vii
xiii	c	vii Id.	....	ix	iiii King. i	vii	iiii King. ii	viii
ii	d	vi Id.	....	x	iii	viii	iiii	ix
	e	v Id.	Sol in Gemini	xi	v	ix	vi	x
x	f	iiii Id.	....	xii	vii	x	viii	xi
	g	iii Id.	....	xiii	ix	xi	x	xii
xviii	A	Prid. Id.	....	xiiii	xi	xii	xii	xiii
vii	b	Idus.	....	xv	xiii	xiii	xiiii	xiiii
	c	xvii Kl.	Junii	xvi	xv	xiiii	xvi	xv
xv	d	xvi Kl.	....	xvii	xvii	xv	xviii	xvi
iiii	e	xv Kl.	....	xviii	xix	xvi	xx	i Cor. i
	f	xiiii Kl.	Dunstane......	xix	xxi	xvii	xxii	ii
xii	g	xiii Kl.	....	xx	xxiii	xviii	xxiiii	iii
i	A	xii Kl.	....	xxi	xxv	xix	i Esd. i	iiii
	b	xi Kl.	....	xxii	i Esd. iii	xx	iiii	v
ix	c	x Kl.	....	xxiii	v	xxi	vi	vi
	d	ix Kl.	....	xxiiii	vii	xxii	ix	vii
xvii	e	viii Kl.	....	xxv	ii Esd. i	xxiii	ii Esd. ii	viii
vi	f	vii Kl.	Augustine.....	xxvi	iiii	xxiiii	v	ix
	g	vi Kl.	....	xxvii	vi	xxv	viii	x
xiiii	A	v Kl.	....	xxviii	ix	xxvi	x	xi
iii	b	iiii Kl.	....	xxix	xiii	xxvii	Hester i	xii
	c	iii Kl.	....	xxx	Hester ii	xxviii	iii	xiii
xi	d	Prid. Kl.	....	xxx	iiii	Mark i	v	xiiii

1578. MAY.

1. As vpon this day, Moses and Aaron numbred the people of Israel, the second yeere after eir comming out of Egypt. *Nom.* 3 *and* 4 *Chapters.*

5. As vpon this day, Christ ascended into heauen, in the sight of his Apostles, and many others. *Mark* 16. 19. *Actes* 1. 9.

10. God commaunded Noah, as vpon this day, to carrie foode into the Arke for himselfe his oushold, and for such as were preserued with him. *Gene.* 6. 21.

14. Those that had not kept the feast of Passeouer the first day of the first moneth, kept it as pon this day of the second moneth. *Nomb.* 9. 11. and so did Hezekiah. 2 *Chron.* 30. 15.

15. As vpon this day, yᵉ Jewes kept their Whitsontide. And also as vpon the same day, God ent the Jewes Quailes for their foode. *Exod.* 16. 13. *Nomb.* 11. 31.

16. God, as vpon this day, rained yᵉ foode Man from heauen. *Exod.* 16. 13, 14, 15.

17. Noah, as vpon this day, at Gods commaundment entred the Arke. *Gen.* 7. 7, 11.

20. As vpon this day, yᵉ Israelites departed from Sinai. *Nomb.* 10. 11, 12.

22. As vpon this day, part of the Israelites, for their murmuring, were consumed with fire. *Nomb.* 11. 1.

27. Noah, as vpon this day, was commaunded by God, to go forth of the Arke. *Gene.* 8. 14, 16.

❡ JUNE HATH XXX. DAYS.

Sunne { ryseth / falleth } houre { iiii mi. 34 / viii mi. 26 }			Psalmes.	MORNYNG PRAYER.		EUENYNG PRAYER.	
				i Lesson.	*ii Lesson.*	*i Lesson.*	*ii Lesson.*
	e	Kalend.	i	Hester vi	Mark ii	Hes. vii	i Cor. xv
xix	f	iiii No.	ii	viii	iii	ix	xvi
viii	g	iii No.	Nichomede...	iii	Job i	iiii	Job ii	ii Cor. i
xvi	A	Prid. No.	iiii	iii	v	iiii	ii
v	b	Nonas.	Boniface.......	v	v	vi	vi	iii
	c	viii Id.	vi	vii	vii	viii	iiii
xiii	d	vii Id.	vii	ix	viii	x	v
ii	e	vi Id.	viii	xi	ix	xii	vi
	f	v Id.	ix	xiii	x	xiiii	vii
x	g	iiii Id.	x	xv	xi	xvi	viii
	A	iii Id.	Barnab apo...	xi	Eccle. x	Act. xiiii	Eccle. x	Act. xv
xviii	b	Prid. Id.	Sol in Cancro	xii	Job 17. 18	Mar. xii	Job xix	ii Cor. ix
vii	c	Idus.	Solstitium es-	xiii	xx	xiii	xxi	x
	d	xviii Kl.	Julii....[tiuum	xiiii	xxxii	xiii	xxiii	xi
xv	e	xvii Kl.	xv	24. xxv	xv	xxvi, 27	xii
iiii	f	xvi Kl.	xvi	xxviii	xvi	xxix	xiii
	g	xv Kl.	xvii	xxx	Luk. i	xxxi	Galat. i
xii	A	xiiii Kl.	xviii	xxxii	ii	xxxiii	ii
i	b	xiii Kl.	xix	xxxiiii	iii	xxxv	iii
	c	xii Kl.	Edwarde......	xx	xxxvi	iiii	xxxvii	iiii
ix	d	xi Kl.	xxi	xxxviii	v	xxxix	v
	e	x Kl.	xxii	xl	vi	xli	vi
xvii	f	ix Kl.	Fast	xxiii	xlii	vii	Prou. i	Eph. i
vi	g	viii Kl.	*John Baptist.*	xxiiii	Mala. iii	Mat. iii	Mal. iiii	Math. 14
	A	vii Kl.	xxv	Prou. ii	Luk. viii	Prou. iii	Ephe. ii
iiii	b	vi Kl.	xxvi	iiii	ix	v	iii
iii	c	v Kl.	xxvii	vi	x	vii	iiii
	d	iiii Kl.	Fast	xxviii	viii	xi	ix	v
xi	e	iii Kl.	*S. Peter apo..*	xxix	Eccle. xv	Act. iii	Eccle. xix	Act. iiii
	f	Prid. Kl.	xxx	Prou. x	Luke xii	Prou. xi	Ephe. vi

1578. JUNE.

1. The people of Israel, as vpon this day, came vnto yᵉ mount Sinai, which afterward was called the hill of Casius, and there taried almost a yeere, as apeareth, *Exod.* 19. 1. *Nomb.* 10. 11. *Deut.* 1. 19.

6. The Temple of Diana in Ephesus, which amongst all Panims Temples was the most magnificent and renouned, as vpon this day, was consumed with fire liiii yeeres before the Natiuitie of Jesus Christ.

20. Godfrey and Baldwine with their Christian armie, as vpon this day, ouercame the Persians at Antiochia, in a memorable conflict. *Benedic. de Aculf.*

23. The King Ahashuerosh, as on this day, sent forth a proclamation throughout all his countrey and prouinces, in yᵉ fauour of the Jewes, and against Haman and his conspiration, as apeareth, *Ester.* 8. 9. &c.

25. As on this day, was the conflict at Mersbrough, betweene the Emperour Henrie the fourth and Rodolfe duke of Sueuia, stickled forth by the Pope. *Anno* 1080.

27. After the flood had been fourtie dayes vpon the earth, the waters were so increased, that Noahs arke was lifted vp as vpon this day, aboue the earth. *Gene.* 7. 17.

¶ JULY HATH XXXI. DAYS.

Sunne {ryseth / falleth} houre {iii mi. 18 / viii mi. 42}			Psalmes.	MORNYNG PRAYER.		EUENYNG PRAYER.	
				i Lesson.	*ii Lesson.*	*i Lesson.*	*ii Lesson.*
xix	g	Kalend.	....	i	Pro. xii	Luk. xiii	Pro. xiii	Philip. i
viii	A	vi No.	Visitati. Mar.	ii	xiiii	xiiii	xv	ii
	b	v No.	....	iii	xvi	xv	xvii	iii
xvi	c	iiii No.	Martin........	iiii	xviii	xvi	xix	iiii
v	d	iii No.	....	v	xx	xvii	xxi	Coloss. i
	e	Prid. No.	....	vi	xxii	xviii	xxiii	ii
xiii	f	Nonas.	Dogge dayes.	vii	xxiiii	xix	xxv	iii
ii	g	viii Id.	....	viii	xxvi	xx	xxvii	iiii
	A	vii Id.	....	ix	xxviii	xxi	xxix	i Thes. i
x	b	vi Id.	....	x	xxxi	xxii	Eccle. i	ii
	c	v Id.	....	xi	Eccle. ii	xxiii	iii	iii
xviii	d	iiii Id.	....	xii	iiii	xxiiii	v	iiii
vii	e	iii Id.	Sol in Leone.	xiii	vi	John i	vii	v
	f	Prid. Id.	....	xiiii	viii	ii	ix	ii Thes. i
xv	g	Idus.	Swithune......	xv	x	iii	xi	ii
iiii	A	xvii Kl.	Augusti........	xvi	xii	iiii	Jerem. i	iii
	b	xvi Kl.	....	xvii	Jerem. ii	v	iii	i Tim. i
xii	c	xv Kl.	....	xviii	iiii	vi	v	ii, iii
i	d	xiiii Kl.	....	xix	vi	vii	vii	iiii
	e	xiii Kl.	Margaret......	xx	viii	viii	ix	v
ix	f	xii Kl.	....	xxi	x	ix	xi	vi
	g	xi Kl.	Magdalen.....	xxii	xii	x	xiii	ii Tim. i
xvii	A	x Kl.	....	xxiii	xiiii	xi	xv	ii
vi	b	ix Kl.	Fast	xxiiii	xvi	xii	xvii	iii
	c	viii Kl.	*James apostl*	xxv	Eccl. xxi	xiii	Eccle.xxiii	iiii
xiiii	d	vii Kl.	Anne........	xxvi	Jer. xviii	xiiii	Jer. xix.	Titus i
iii	e	vi Kl.	....	xxvii	xx	xv	xxi	ii, iii
	f	v Kl.	....	xxviii	xxii	xvi	xxiii	Phile. i
xi	g	iiii Kl.	....	xxix	xxiiii	xvii	xxv	Hebre. i
	A	iii Kl.	....	xxx	xxvi	xviii	xxvii	ii
xix	b	Prid. Kl.	....	xxx	xxviii	xix	xxix	iii

1578. JULY.

6. The **vi.** day of this moneth, the Josias of our age, Edward the sixt, King of England, dyed. *Anno.* 1553.

8. John Hus was burnt as on this day, at the councell holden at Constance for professing the Gospel of our Lord Jesus. *Anno* 1415.

9. As on this day, Jerusalem was besieged by the king of Babel, the space of eighteene moneths, and at length was taken. 2 *Kings* 25. 3. and Zedekiahs son slayne before his face, and after had his owne eyes put out. *Jeremi.* 39. 2, 7.

12. As on this day was the birth of C. Julius Cæsar, the first Emperour of Rome, of whome this moneth is so called.

15. About this time the great Sweat began in England. *Anno* 1551.

17. As on this day, Moses in his anger, being thereunto prouoked by the Idolatrie of the people, brake the two Tables of stone, which hee had receyued of the Lorde in the mount. *Exod.* 32. 19.

19. As on this day, the great hurt by fire began at Rome in Neroes reigne.

23. As on this day, Pope Alexander the third treadeth upon Frederick Barbarossa the Emperour.

27. As vpon this day, the Athenians receyved a great ouerthrewe in Sicilia, of the Syracusians.

❡ AUGUST HATH XXX. DAYS.

Sunne {ryseth / falleth} hour {vii mi. 34 / iiii mi. 26}				Psalmes.	MORNYNG PRAYER.		EUENYNG PRAYER.	
					i Lesson.	ii Lesson.	i Lesson.	ii Lesson.
viii	c	Kalend.	Lammas	i	Jer. xxx	John xx	Jere. xxxi	Heb. iiii
xvi	d	iiii No.	....	ii	xxxii	xxi	xxxiii	v
v	e	iii No.	....	iii	xxxiiii	Actes i	xxxv	vi
	f	Prid. No.	....	iiii	xxxvi	ii	xxxvii	vii
xiii	g	Nonas.	....	v	xxxviii	iii	xxxix	viii
ii	A	viii Id.	Transfigu	vi	xl	iiii	xli	ix
	b	vii Id.	The Name of	vii	xlii	v	xliii	x
x	c	vi Id.	............[Je.	viii	xliiii	vi	xlv, xlvi	xi
	d	v Id.	....	ix	xlvii	vii	xlviii	xii
xviii	e	iiii Id.	Laurence......	x	xlix	viii	l	xiii
vii	f	iii Id.	....	xi	li	ix	lii	Jacob. i
	g	Prid. Id.	....	xii	Lamen. i	x	Lamen. ii	ii
xv	A	Idus.	....	xiii	iii	xi	iiii	iii
iiii	b	xix Kl.	....	xiiii	v	xii	Ezech. ii	iiii
	c	xviii Kl.	Sol in Virgine[1]	xv	Ezech. iii	xiii	vi	v
xii	d	xvii Kl.	....	xvi	vii	xiiii	xiii	i Pet. i
i	e	xvi Kl.	Septembris ...	xvii	xiii	xv	xviii	ii
	f	xv Kl.	......	xviii	xxxiii	xvi	xxxiiii	iii
ix	g	xiiii Kl.	....	xix	Dani. i	xvii	Dani ii	iv
	A	xiii Kl.	....	xx	iii	xviii	iiii	v
xvii	b	xii Kl.	....	xxi	v	xix	vi	ii Pet. i
vi	c	xi Kl.	....	xxii	vii	xx	viii	ii
	d	x Kl.	Fast	xxiii	ix	xxi	x	iii
xiiii	e	ix Kl.	Bartho. apo...	xxiiii	Eccl. xxv	xxii	Eccl. xxix	i Joh. i
iii	f	viii Kl.	....	xxv	Dani. xi	xxiii	Dan. xii	ii
	g	vii Kl.	....	xxvi	xiii	xxiiii	xiiii	iii
xi	A	vi Kl.	....	xxvii	Osee. i	xxv	Ose, ii. iii	iv
	b	v Kl.	Augustine.....	xxviii	iiii	xxvi	v, vi	v
xix	c	iiii Kl.	Behead. of Joh	xxix	vii	xxvii	viii	ii, iii Jo.
viii	d	iii Kl.	....	xxx	ix	xxviii	x	Jude i
	e	Prid. Kl.	....	xxx	xi	Math. i	xii	Rom. i

[1 This and the following should each be three places higher.]

1578. AUGUST.

1. Aaron as vpon this day, being 123 yeeres olde, dyed vpon the mountaine Hor, 40 yeeres after the children of Israel's coming out of Egypt. *Nomb.* 20. 25, 28. and 33. 38, 39.

7. Nebuzar-adan, as on this day, setteth yᵉ citie and Temple of Jerusalem on fire. 2 *King* 25. 8, 9.

8. Henrie the 4. Emperour, as on this day dyed with sorowe, constrained thereunto by the Pope's iniuries.

10. Titus soldiours, as on this day, set the Citie and Temple of Jerusalem on fire, sithens which time neither of them haue euer bin reedified. *Joseph. lib. 6. Chap.* 26.

As on this day also, Ezra the Scribe entreth into Jerusalem with a great multitude of the Jewes, and is honorably receaued of those that about 50 yeeres before, came thither with Zerubbabel before the Incarnation of Christ, 596 yeeres. *Ezra.* 7. 9.

26. Darius being slaine Alexander, as vpon this day, obtaineth the Empire of Asia, and the same day, yᵉ monarchie was translated from the Persians vnto the Greekes. 1. *Macca.* 1. 1.

27. Religion, as on this day, was reformed, according to God's expresse truth, in the most renowned citie of Geneva. 1535.

29. The citie Buda in Hungarie, as on this day, yeelded vnto ᵗ*ʰᵉ* Turke in the yeere of our Lord God, 1526.

¶ SEPTEMBER HATH XXX. DAYS.

Sunne {ryseth/falleth} houre {v mi. 36 / vi mi. 24}		Kalend.		Psalmes.	MORNYNG PRAYER.		EUENYNG PRAYER.	
					i Lesson.	ii Lesson.	i Lesson.	ii Lesson.
xvi	f	Kalend.	Gyles..........	i	Ose xiii	Math. ii	Ose xiiii	Rom. ii
v	g	iiii No.	....	ii	Joel i	iii	Joel ii	iii
	A	iii No.	....	iii	Amos i	iiii	Amos i	iiii
xiii	b	Prid. No.	....	iiii	Amos ii	v	iii	v
ii	c	Nonas.	Dog days end	v	iiii	vi	v	vi
	d	viii Id.	....	vi	vi	vii	vii	vii
x	e	vii Id.	....	vii	viii	viii	ix	viii
	f	vi Id.	Nati. of Mary	viii	Abdias i	ix	Jonas i	ix
xviii	g	v Id.	....	ix	Jo. ii, iii	x	iiii	x
vii	A	iiii Id.	....	x	Miche i	xi	Miche ii	xi
	b	iii Id.	....	xi	iii	xii	iiii	xii
xv	c	Prid. Id.	....	xii	v	xiii	vi	xiii
iiii	d	Idus.	Sol in Libra..	xiii	vii	xiiii	Naum. i	xiiii
	e	xviii Kl.	Holy crosse..	xiiii	Naum. ii	xv	iii	xv
xii	f	xvii Kl.	Equinoctium.	xv	Abacuc i	xvi	Abac. ii	xvi
i	g	xvi Kl.	Autumnale....	xvi	iii	xvii	Soph. i	i Cor. i
	A	xv Kl.	Lambert	xvii	Soph. ii	xviii	iii	ii
ix	b	xiiii Kl.	....	xviii	Agge i	xix	Agge ii	iii
	c	xiii Kl.	....	xix	Zach. i	xx	Za. ii, iii	iiii
xvii	d	xii Kl.	.... Fast.	xx	iiii, v	xxi	vi	v
vi	e	xi Kl.	S. Mathewe...	xxi	Eccle. 35	xxii	Eccle. 38	vi
	f	x Kl.	....	xxii	Zach. vii	xxiii	Zach. viii	vii
xiiii	g	ix Kl.	....	xxiii	ix	xxiiii	x	viii
iii	A	viii Kl.	....	xxiiii	xi	xxv	xii	ix
	b	vii Kl.	....	xxv	xiii	xxvi	xiiii	x
xi	c	vi Kl.	Ciprian........	xxvi	Mala. i	xxvii	Mala. ii	xi
	d	v Kl.	....	xxvii	iii	xxviii	iiii	xii
xix	e	iiii Kl.	....	xxviii	Toby i	Mark i	Toby ii	xiii
viii	f	iii Kl.	S. Michael...	xxix	Eccle. 39	ii	Eccle. 44	xiiii
	g	Prid. Kl.	Hierom........	xxx	Toby iii	iii	To. iiii	xv

1578. SEPTEMBER.

2. Augustus Cæsar this day, ouerthrew Antonius and Cleopatra, in a battel by sea at Actium, 28 yeeres before Christ was borne. *Dion.*

7. Our Soueraigne Lady QUEENE ELIZABETH, was borne as vpon this day, at Greenewich. *Anno.* 1532 [1533].

8. Jerusalem was as vpon this day, sacked with fire and sworde, and vtterly rased, 73 yeeres after the birth of Christ : who prophesied the same 40. yeeres before. *Matth.* 24. 2, 34. *Joseph. lib.* 7. *chap.* 26.

13. Titus the Emperour, sonne to Vespasian, as vpon this day died, after Christes birth 83. yeeres.

14. Chrysostome being chased out of his Church of Constantinople, as vpon this day, died.

18. Domitian the Emperour as vpon this day, was slaine, by ye treason of his wife and seruaunts.

20. The noble Oratour L. Crassus, as vpon this day, died of a pleurisie. *Cicero. lib.* 3. *de Orat.*

23. Octauius Cesar, as vpon this day, was borne 60. yeeres before the Natiuitie of Christ. *Gel. lib.* 15 *chap.* 7.

24. Angelus Politian, as vpon this day, died, *Anno.* 1509.

25. As vpon this day, Nehemiah finished the walles of Jerusalem, 444. yeeres before Christ. *Nehe.* 6. 15.

30. As vpon this day, Pompeius surnamed the great, was borne, before Christ, 103. yeeres.

☾ OCTOBER HATH XXXI. DAYES.

Sunne { ryseth / falleth } houre { vi. mi. 35. / v. mi. 25.				*Psalmes.*	MORNYNG PRAYER.		EUENYNG PRAYER.	
					i Lesson.	*ii Lesson.*	*i Lesson.*	*ii Lesson.*
xvi	A	Kalend.	Remige........	i	Toby v	Mar. iiii	Toby. vi	1 Cor. xvi
v	b	vi No.	....	ii	vii	v	viii	2 Cor. i
xiii	c	v No.	....	iii	ix	vi	x	ii
ii	d	iiii No.	....	iiii	xi	vii	xii	iii
	e	iii No.	....	v	xiii	viii	xiiii	iiii
x	f	Prid. No.	Fayth.........	vi	Judit. i	ix	Judit. ii	v
	g	Nonas.	....	vii	iii	x	iiii	vi
xviii	A	viii Id.	....	viii	v	xi	vi	vii
vii	b	vii Id.	Dennis.........	ix	vii	xii	viii	viii
	c	vi Id.	....	x	ix	xiii	x	ix
xv	d	v Id.	....	xi	xi	xiiii	xii	x
iiii	e	iiii Id.	....	xii	xiii	xv	xiiii	xi
	f	iii Id.	Edwarde......	xiii	xv	xvi	xvi	xii
xii	g	Prid. Id.	Sol in Scorpio	xiiii	Wisd. i	Luk. di. i	Wisd. ii	xiii
i	A	Idus.	....	xv	iii	di. i	iiii	Galat. i
	b	xvii Kl.	Novembris....	xvi	v	ii	vi	ii
ix	c	xvi Kl.	Etheldrede ...	xvii	vii	iii	viii	iii
	d	xv Kl.	*Luke Euan...*	xviii	Eccle. li	iiii	Job i	iiii
xvii	e	xiiii Kl.	....	xix	Wisd. ix	v	Wisd. x	v
vi	f	xiii Kl.	.............•....	xx	xi	vi	xii	vi
	g	xii Kl.	....	xxi	xiii	vii	xiiii	Ephes. i
xiiii	A	xi Kl.	....	xxii	xv	viii	xvi	ii
iii	b	x Kl.	....	xxiii	xvii	ix	xviii	iii
	c	ix Kl.	....	xxiiii	xix	x	Eccle. i	iiii
xi	d	viii Kl.	Crispine.......	xxv	Eccle. ii	xi	iii	v
	e	vii Kl.	....	xxvi	iiii	xii	v	vi
xix	f	vi Kl.	Fast.	xxvii	vi	xiii	vii	Phil. i
viii	g	v Kl.	*Simon & Jude*	xxviii	Job 24, 25	xiiii	Job xlii	ii
	A	iiii Kl.	....	xxix	Eccl. viii	xv	Eccle. ix	iii
xvi	b	iii Kl.	....	xxx	x	xvi	xi	iiii
v	c	Prid. Kl.	Fast.	xxx	xii	xvii	xiii	Coloss. i

1578. OCTOBER.

1. The feast of Trumpets was kept this day. *Leuit.* 23. 24.
Also Pompeius and his armie, as vpon this day, was discomfited by Cesar.
4. The Jewes fast and mourne, as on this day, for the death of Gedaliah. *Jere.* 41. 1, 2.
10. As on this day the fast of reconciliation, the onely fast commaunded by God, was kept. *Leuit.* 23. 27.
11. As on this day was the first conflict of the Tigurines with yᵉ fiue Townes of Heluetia, wherein Zwinglius was slaine. *Anno.* 1532.
15. As on this day, the Jewish feast of Tabernacles was kept, lasting 7. dayes. *Leuit.* 23. 34.
17. As on this day, Noahs Arke, after 160. daies, rested on the mountaines Ararat, in Armenia. *Gene.* 8. 4.
21. As on this day, the Jewish great feaste of palmes was kept.
22. This day, yᵉ feast of holy conuocation was kept.
23. As on this day, the Jewes which returned from the captiuitie of Babylon, made a newe couenant with God. *Nehe.* 9. 1.
Also Titus, sonne to Vaspasian, after the destruction of Jerusalem, slaieth 3000. Jewes on the birth day of his brother Domitian. *An.* 73.
31. This day, in the yeere of our Lord God 1517. & CI. yeeres after yᵉ death of John Huss Martin Luther gaue his propositions in yᵉ Uniuersitie of Witemberg, against yᵉ Popes pardon.

❡ NOUEMBER HATH XXX. DAYES.

Sunne {ryseth}{falleth} houre {vii. mi. 34.}{iiii. mi. 26.}				Psalmes.	MORNYNG PRAYER.		EUENYNG PRAYER.	
					i Lesson.	*ii Lesson.*	*i Lesson.*	*ii Lesson.*
	d	Kalend.	*All Saintes* ...	i	Wisd. iii	He. xi, xii	Wisd. v	Apo. xix
xiii	e	iiii No.	....	ii	Eccl. xiiii	Lu. xviii	Eccl. xv	Coloss. ii
ii	f	iii No.	....	iii	xvi	xix	xvii	iii
	g	Prid. No.	....	iiii	xviii	xx	xix	iiii
x	A	Nonas.	....	v	xx	xxi	xxi	i Thess. i
	b	viii Id.	Leonarde	vi	xxii	xxii	xxiii	ii
xviii	c	vii Id.	....	vii	xxiiii	xxiii	¹xxv	iii
vii	d	vi Id.	....	viii	xxvii	xxiiii	xxviii	iiii
	e	v Id.	....	ix	xxix	John i	xxx	v
xv	f	iiii Id.	....	x	xxxi	ii	xxxii	ii Thess. i
iiii	g	iii Id.	S. Martin	xi	xxxiii	iii	xxxiiii	ii
	A	Prid. Id.	Sol in Sagit-	xii	xxxv	iiii	xxxvi	iii
xii	b	Idus.	Brice.... [tario	xiii	xxxvii	v	xxxviii	i Tim. i
i	c	xviii Kl.	Decembris....	xiiii	xxxix	vi	xl	ii, iii
	d	xvii Kl.	Machute	xv	xli	vii	xlii	iiii
ix	e	xvi Kl.	....	xvi	xliii	viii	xliiii	v
	f	xv Kl.	Hugh	xvii	xlv	ix	xlvi	vi
xvii	g	xiiii Kl.	*Init. reg.*	xviii	xlvii	x	xlviii	ii Tim. i
vi	A	xiii Kl.	.....[*Elizabet.*	xix	xlix	xi	l	ii
	b	xii Kl.	Edmund King	xx	li	xii	Baruc. i	iii
xiiii	c	xi Kl.	....	xxi	Baruc. ii	xiii	iii	iiii
iii	d	x Kl.	Cycelie	xxii	iiii	xiiii	v	Titus i
	e	ix Kl.	Clement	xxiii	vi	xv	Esay i	ii iii
xi	f	viii Kl.	....	xxiiii	Esay ii	xvi	iii	Phile. i
	g	vii Kl.	Katherine.....	xxv	iiii	xvii	v	Hebr. i
xix	A	vi Kl.	....	xxvi	vi	xviii	vii	ii
viii	b	v Kl.	....	xxvii	viii	xix	ix	iii
	c	iiii Kl.	....	xxviii	x	xx	xi	iiii
xvi	d	iii Kl.	*Fast.*	xxix	xii	xxi	xiii	v
v	e	Prid. Kl.	*Andrew Apo..*	xxx	Prou. xx	Actes i	Pro. xxi	vi

[¹ Note, that the begynnyng of the xxvi. chapter of Ecclesi. (vnto) But when one is, &c., must be read with the xxv. chapter.]

1578. NOUEMBER.

10. This day happened the woful slaughter of Varna, where Ladislaus king of Hungarie was slaine by the Turke *Anno.* 1444. Also as vpon this day Martin Luther was borne. *Anno.* 1483.

15. Jeroboam, after that he had turned the people from yᵉ obedience of Rehoboam their king vnto him self, deuised and ordained this day to be kept holy of the people, and because they should not goe vnto Jerusalem to worship, he caused two golden calues to be set vp, the one at Dan, and the other at Bethel, and so he & the people committed Idolatrie. 1 *Kings.* 12. 32, 33.

16. As vpon this daye Tiberius Cesar was borne, before the birth of Christ 39 yeeres.

17. As vpon this day, began most prosperously our most Soueraigne Ladye QUEENE ELIZABETH, to reigne ouer vs, *anno.* 1558. whom we beseech God long to continue in that gouernment.

18. Titus as vpon this day, vsed no lesse crueltie against the Jewes his prisoners, in the citie of Beryte in Syria, keeping the birth day of his father Vespasian, then he did on the birth day of his brother Domitian. *Joseph. Lib.* 7. *Chap.* 20.

¶ DECEMBER HATH XXXI DAYES.

Sunne {ryseth / falleth} -houre- {viii mi. 12 / iii mi. 48}				Psalms.	MORNYNG PRAYER.		EVENYNG PRAYER.	
					i Lesson.	ii Lesson.	i Lesson.	ii Lesson.
	f	Kalend.	......	i	Esa. xiv	Actes ii	Esay xv	Heb. vii
xiii	g	iiii No.	......	ii	xvi	iii	xvii	viii
ii	A	iii No.	......	iii	xviii	iiii	xix	ix
x	b	Prid. No.	......	iiii	xx, xxi	v	xxii	x
	c	Nonas.	......	v	xxiii	vi	xxiiii	xi
xviii	d	viii Id.	Nicholas.......	vi	xxv	di. vii	xxvi	xii
vii	e	vii Id.	......	vii	xxvii	di. vii	xxviii	xiii
	f	vi Id.	Concept Ma..	viii	xxix	viii	xxx	James i
xv	g	v Id.	......	ix	xxxi	ix	xxxii	ii
iiii	A	iiii Id.	......	x	xxxiii	x	xxxiiii	iii
	b	iii Id.	......	xi	xxxv	xi	xxxvi	iiii
xii	c	Prid. Id.	Sol in Capricor	xii	xxxvii	xii	xxxviii	v
i	d	Idus.	Lucie...........	xiii	xxxix	xiii	xl	i Pet. i
	e	xix Kl.	Januarii,.......	xiiii	xli	xiiii	xlii	ii
ix	f	xviii Kl.	......	xv	xliii	xv	xliiii	iii
	g	xvii Kl.	O Sapienc	xvi	xlv	xvi	xlvi	iiii
xvii	A	xvi Kl.	......	xvii	xlvii	xvii	xlviii	v
	b	xv Kl.	......	xviii	xlix	xviii	l	ii Pet. i
	c	xiiii Kl.	......	xix	li	xix	lii	ii
xiiii	d	xiii Kl.	Fast.	xx	liii	xx	liiii	iii
iii	e	xii Kl.	Thomas Apo..	xxi	Prou. 23	xxi	Prou. 24	i Joh. i
	f	xi Kl.	......	xxii	Esai. lv	xxii	Esay lvi	ii
xi	g	x Kl.	......	xxiii	lvii	xxiii	lviii	iii
	A	ix Kl.	Fast.	xxiiii	lix	xxiiii	lx	iiii
xix	b	viii Kl.	Christmas.....	xxv	Esay ix	Luk. xxii	Esay vii	Tit. iii
viii	c	vii Kl.	St. Stephen ...	xxvi	Prou. 28	Ac. 6, 7	Eccle. iv	Act. vii
	d	vi Kl.	Saint John....	xxvii	Eccle. v	Apoca. i	Eccle. vi	Apo. xxii
xvi	e	v Kl.	Innocentes	xxviii	Jer. xxxi	Act. xxv	Wisd. i	i Joh. v
v	f	iiii Kl.	... .	xxix	Esay lxi	xxvi	Esa. lxii	ii John i
	g	iii Kl.	......	xxx	lxiii	xxvii	lxiiii	iii Joh. i
xiii	A	Prid. Kl.	Syluester......	xxx	lxv	xxviii	lxvi	Jude i

1578. DECEMBER.

9. In the yeere of our Lord God, 1437—Sigismund King of Hungarie, and Emperour of Rome, as on this day dyed.

15. Antiochus Epiphnes, as on this day, placed the Idole of Jupiter vpon ye Altar of God in Jerusalem. 1 Macca. 1. 57.

16. Ezra as on this day, commaundeth ye Israelites to leaue their strange wiues. Ezra. 10. 11. and 1. Esdr. 9. 8, 9.

25. Christ borne as on this day, of the Virgin Marie, in the yeere from the worldes creation 4018.
Antiochus Epiphanes entred also as vpon this day into Jerusalem, with a great armie, and spoyled it. Joseph. lib. 12. chap. 6.
Also he caused sacrifice on this day to be made vpon the Altar, which was in the steade of the Altar of sacrifices, looke 1. Macca. 1. 62.

26. Steuen was stoned to death by the Jewes, for professing Christ, in the yeere after Christ his ascension. Acts. 7. 58, 59.

27. As vpon this day Saynt John the Euangelist, being of the age of lxxxix. yeeres, died at Ephesus, in the reigne of Traiane the Emperour, xxx. yeeres after the destruction of Jerusalem.

28. This day Herod slewe the Innocents, two yeeres after the birth of Christ, among whom he had thought to haue murthered Christ. Mat. 2. 16, 17, 18.

APPENDIX II.

A FOURME to be vsed in Common prayer twyse aweke, and also an order of publique fast, to be vsed euery Wednesday in the weke, duryng this tyme of mortalitie, and other afflictions, wherwith the Realme at this present is visited.

Set forth by the Quenes Maiesties speciall commaundment, expressed in her letters hereafter folowyng in the next page. xxx. July 1563.

By the Quene.

MOST Reuerende father in God, ryght trusty and ryght welbeloued, we grete you well. Lyke as Almyghtie God hath of his mere grace committed to vs, nexte vnder hym, the chiefe gouernement of this Realme and the people therein : So hath he of his lyke goodnes, ordered vnder vs sundry principall ministers, to serue and assist vs in this burden. And therefore consideryng the state of this present tyme, wherein it hath pleased the most hyghest, for thamendment of vs and our people, to visite certayne places of our Realme with more contagious sicknes than lately hath ben : For remedy and mittigation thereof, we thynke it both necessary and our bounden duetie, that vniuersall prayer and fastyng be more effectually vsed in this our Realme. And vnderstandyng that you haue thought and considered vpon some good order to be prescrybed therin, for the which ye require thapplication of our aucthoritie, for the better obseruation therof amongest our people, we do not onlye commende and allowe your good zeale therin ; But do also commaunde all maner our Ministers Ecclesiasticall or Cyuill, and all other our Subiectes, to execute, folowe, and obey such Godly and holsome orders, as you, beyng Primate of all Englande, and Metropolitane of this prouince of Cantorbury, vpon Godlye aduise and consideration, shall vniformely deuyse, prescribe, and publyshe, for the vniuersal vsage of Prayer, Fastyng, and other good deedes, duryng the tyme of this visitation by sicknes and other troubles.

Yeuen vnder our Signet, at our Manour of Richmond, the first day of August the fifth yere of our reigne.

To the moste Reuerende father in God our ryght trusty and ryght welbeloued, Tharchbyshop of Cantorbury and Primate of all Englande.

¶ The Preface.

WE be taught by many and sundry examples of holy Scriptures, that vppon occasion of perticuler punyshementes, afflictions, and

perylles, whiche God of his most iust iudgement hath sometymes
sent amonge his people, to shewe his wrath agaynst sinne, and
to call his people to repentaunce and to the redresse of theyr
lyues, the Godly haue ben prouoked and styrred vp to more feruencie and diligence in prayer, fastyng, and almesdedes, to a
more depe consideration of theyr consciences, to ponder theyr
vnthankfulnes and forgetfulnes of Gods merciful benefites towardes them, with crauyng of pardon for the tyme past, and to
aske his assistaunce for the tyme to come, to lyue more Godly,
and so to be defended and delyuered from all further peryls and
daungers. So king Dauid in the time of plague and pestilence,
which ensued vpon his vayne numbryng of the people, prayed vnto
God with wonderfull fervencie, confessyng his fault, desiryng God
to spare the people, and rather to turne his yre to hymwarde, who
had chiefely offended in that transgression. The lyke was done
by the vertuous kynges, Josaphat and Ezechias in theyr distresse
of warres and foreygne inuasions. So dyd Judith and Hester fall
to humble prayers in lyke perylles of theyr people. So dyd Daniell
in his captiuitie, and many other moe in theyr troubles. Nowe
therfore callyng to mynde, that God hath ben prouoked by vs to
visite vs at this present with the plague and other greuous diseases,
and partlye also with trouble of warres: It hath ben thought meete
to set foorth by publique order some occasion to excite and stirre
vp all godly people within this Realme, to pray earnestly and
hartely to God, to turne away his deserued wrath from vs, and to
restore vs aswell to the health of our bodyes by the holsomnes
of the ayre, as also to Godly and profytable peace and quietnes.
And although it is euery Christian mans duetie, of his owne deuotion to pray at all tymes : yet for that the corrupt nature of man
is so slouthfull and negligent in this his duetie, he hath nede by
often and sundry meanes, to be styrred vp and put in remembraunce of his duetie. For the effectuall accomplyshement wherof,
it is ordered and appoynted as foloweth.

Fyrst, that all Curates and Pastours, shall exhort theyr Parysshioners to endeuour them selues to come vnto the Churche, with
so many of theyr families as maye be spared from theyr necessary
busynes, (hauyng yet a prudent respecte in such assemblyes to
kepe the sicke from the whole, in places where the plague reigneth)
and they to resorte, not onely on Sundayes and holydayes : but
also on Wednesdayes and Frydayes, duryng the tyme of these
present afflictions, exhortyng them, there reuerently and Godly to
behaue them selues, and with penitent hartes to praye vnto God
to turne these plagues from vs, whiche we through our vnthankfulnes and synfull lyfe haue deserued.

Secondly, that the sayd Curates shall then distinctly and playnely
read the generall confession appoynted in the boke of Seruice,
with the residue of the Mornyng prayer, vsynge for both the
Lessons the Chapters hereafter folowyng.   That is to saye :

For the first Lesson, one of these Chapters, out of the olde Testament.

The 2. Kinges. Cap. 24. Leuiticus. 26. Deuteronom. 28. Hieremy. 18. vnto these wordes : Let vs. &c., and 22. 2. Para. Cap. 34. Esay. 1. Ezechiell. 18. and .19. Joell. 2. 2. Esdras. 9. Jonas the .2. and .3. Chapter together. Whiche Chapters would be read orderly on Sundayes, Wednesdayes, and Frydayes.

And for the seconde Lesson, one of these Chapters, out of the newe Testament.

Mathewe. 3. 6. 7. 24. 25. Luke. 13. Actes. 2. begynnyng at these wordes : Ye men of Israell, heare these wordes. To the ende of the Chapter. &c. Rom. 2. 6. 12. 13. Galath. 5. Ephesians 4. 5. 1. Tim. 2. Apoca. 2.

The order for the Wednesdayes.

¶ On Wednesdayes (which be the dayes appoynted for generall fast, in suche fourme as shall hereafter be declared) after the Mornyng prayer ended, as is aforesayde, the sayde Curates and Ministers shall exhort the people assembled, to geue them selues to theyr priuate prayers and meditations. For which purpose a pawse shalbe made of one quarter of an houre and more, by the discretion of the sayde Curate. Duryng which tyme, as good scilence shalbe kept as may be.

That done, the Letany is to be read, in the myddest of the people, with the additions of prayer hereafter mentioned.

Then shall folowe the ministration of the Communion, so oft as a iust number of Communicants shalbe therto disposed, with a Sermon, yf it can be, to be made by suche as he aucthorised by the Metropolitane or Byshop of the Diocesee, and they to entreate of suche matters especiallye as be meete for this cause of publique prayer : or els, for want of suche Preacher, to reade one of the Homylyes hereafter appoynted, after the readyng of the Gospell, as hath ben accustomed. And so the Minister commendyng the people to God with thaccustomed benediction, shall dimysse them.

If there be no Communion, then on euery of the sayde Wednesdayes after the Letary, the .x. Commaundments, the Epistle, Gospell, the Sermon or Homylye done : the generall vsuall prayer for the state of the whole Church shalbe read, as is set forth in the booke of Common prayer. After whiche shall folowe these two prayers :

Almyghtie God, the fountayne of all wysdome. &c.   And, Almyghtie God, which hast promysed. &c.   With the accustomed benediction.

¶ The Order for Frydayes.

¶ On Frydayes shalbe onely the Mornyng prayer, and the Letany, with the prayers nowe appoynted to be annexed to the same.

¶ Homylyes to be read in order on Wednesdayes.

1. First, an Homyly intituled, an Homyly concernyng the Justice of God in punyshyng of impenitent sinners. &c. Newly nowe set forth for that purpose.

2. The .viii. Homylye of the fyrst Tome of Homylies, entituled, Of the declynyng from God.

3. The .ix. Homyly of the same Tome, entituled : An exhortation agaynst the feare of death.

4. The Homyly of Fastyng, in the seconde Tome of Homylyes.

5. The Homyly of Prayer, in the same Tome.

6. The Homyly of Almes dedes, in the same Tome.

7. The Homyly of repentaunce, in the same Tome also.

When these Homylyes are once read ouer, then to begyn agayne, and so to continue them in order.

After the ende of the Collect in the Letany, whiche begynneth with these wordes : We humbly beseche thee, O father. &c. shall folowe this Psalme, to be sayd of the Minister, with the aunswere of the people.

¶ *The Psalme to be sayde in the Letany, before one of the prayers newly appoynted. Wherof one verse to be sayde of the Minister, and an other by the people, clarke, or clarkes.*

O come, let vs humble our selues, and fall downe before the Lord, with reuerence and feare.   1. Psal. 95.

For he is the Lorde our God : and we are the people of his pasture, and the sheepe of his handes.   2.

Come therefore, let vs turne agayne vnto our Lord ; for he hath smytten vs, and he shall heale vs.   3. Osee 6.

Let vs repent, and turne from our wickednes : And our sinnes shalbe forgeuen vs.   4. Actes 3.

Let vs turne, and the Lord wyll turne from his heauy wrath, and wyll pardon vs, and we shall not peryshe.   5. Jona. 3.

For we knowledge our faultes : and our sinnes be euer before vs.   6. Psal. 51.

We haue sore prouoked thine anger, O Lorde : thy wrath is waxed hotte, and thy heauy displeasure is sore kyndled agaynst vs.   7. Lament. 3.

Thou hast made vs heare of the noyse of warres, and hast troubled vs by the vexation of enemies.   8.

Thou hast in thine indignation stryken vs with greuous sicknes, and by and by we haue fallen as leaues beaten downe with a vehement wynde.   9. Esay 64.

In deede we acknowledge, that all punyshementes are lesse than our deservynges : But yet of thy mercy, Lorde correct vs to amendement, and plague vs not to our destruction.   10. Judith 8. Job 11. Sap. 11.

For thy hande is not shortened, that thou canste not helpe : neyther is thy goodnes abated, that thou wylt not heare.   11.

Thou hast promysed, O Lorde, that afore we crye thou wylt heare vs : whylest we yet speake thou wylt haue mercy vpon vs.   12. Esay 65.

For none that truste in thee shalbe confounded : neyther any that call vpon thee shalbe despised.   13.

For thou arte the only Lorde, who woundest, and doest heale agayne, who kyllest, and reuiuest, bryngest euen to hell, and bryngest backe agayne.   14. Toby 3. Job 5. Osee 6.

15. Our fathers hoped in thee, they trusted in thee, and thou dyddest
Psal. 22.   delyuer them.

16. *They called vpon thee, and were helped : they put theyr trust in
thee, and were not confounded.*

17. O Lorde, rebuke not vs in thine indignation : neyther chasten vs
Psal. 6.   in thy heauy displeasure.

18. *O remember not the sinnes and offences of our youth : but accord-
Psal. 25.   yng to thy mercy thynke thou vppon vs, O Lorde, for thy goodnes.*

19. Haue mercy vpon vs, O Lord, for we are weake : O Lorde heale
vs for our bones are vexed.

20. *And nowe in the vexation of our spirites, and the anguyshe of
Baruc. 3.   our soules, we remember thee, and we crye vnto the : Heare Lorde,
Jona. 2.   and haue mercy.*

21. For thine owne sake, and for thy holy name sake, inclyne thine
Dani. 9.   eare, and heare, O mercifull Lord.

22 *For we do not powre out our prayers before thy face, trusting in
our owne righteousnes : but in thy great and manyfolde mercies.*

23. Washe vs throughly from our wickednes : and clense vs from
our sinnes.

24. *Turne thy face from our sinnes, and put out all our misdedes.*

25. Make vs cleane hartes, O God : and renewe a ryght spirite
within vs.

26. *Helpe vs, O God of our saluation, for the glorye of thy name :
Psal. 79.   O delyuer vs, and be mercifull vnto our synnes for thy names sake.*

27. So we that be thy people, and sheepe of thy pasture, shall geue
thee thankes for euer, and wyll alwayes be shewyng foorth thy
prayse, from generation to generation.
Glory be to the father. &c.

¶ *After this Psalme, shalbe sayde by the Curate or Minister openly and
with an hygh voyce, one of these three prayers folowyng. And after that,
orderly the rest of the Collectes appoynted in the Letany.   At which
tyme the people shall deuoutly geue eare, and shall both with mynde and
speache to them selues, assent to the same prayers.*

¶ *A Prayer, conteynyng also a Confession of synnes.   Which is to be sayde
after the Letany, aswell vpon Sundayes, as Wednesdayes and Frydayes.*

O ALMYGHTIE, most iuste and mercifull God, we here acknowledge our selues moste vnworthy to lyfte vp our eyes vnto heauen ;
for our conscience doth accuse vs, and our synnes do reproue vs.
We knowe also that thou Lorde, beyng a iuste iudge, must needes
punyshe the synnes of them which transgresse thy lawe.   And
when we consider and examine all our whole lyfe, we fynde nothyng
in our selues, that deserueth any other thyng but eternall dampnation.   But because thou, O Lorde, of thy vnspeakable mercye,
hast commaunded vs in all our necessities to call onlye vpon thee,
and hast also promised, that thou wylt heare our prayers, not for
any our deserte (which is none) but for the merites of thy sonne

our onlye Sauiour Jesus Christe, whom thou hast ordeyned to be our only mediatour and intercessour : we lay away all confidence in man, and do flee to the throne of thy onlye mercye, by the intercession of thy only sonne our Sauiour Jesu Christe. And fiyrste of all, we do moste lament and bewayle, from the bottome of our hartes, our vnkyndnesse and vnthankfulnesse towardes thee our Lorde, consideryng, that besydes those thy benefytes which we enioy as thy creatures, common with all mankynde, thou hast bestowed many and singuler speciall benefites vpon vs, which we are not hable in harte to conceaue, muche lesse in wordes worthelye to expresse. Thou hast called vs to the knowledge of thy Gospell. Thou hast releassed vs from the harde seruitude of Sathan. Thou hast delyuered vs from all horrible and execrable Idolatry, wherein we were vtterly drowned, and haste brought vs into the moste clere and comfortable lyght of thy blessed worde, by the whiche we are taught howe to serue and honour thee, and howe to lyue orderly with our neyghbours in trueth aud veritie. But we, moste vnmyndfull in tymes of prosperitie of these thy greate benefites, haue neglected thy commaundmentes, haue abused the knowledge of thy Gospell, and haue folowed our carnall libertie, and serued our owne lustes ; and through our synfull lyfe haue not worshypped and honoured thee as we ought to haue done. And nowe, O Lorde, beyng euen compelled with thy correction, we do most humbly confesse that we haue synned, and haue most greuously offended thee by many and sundry wayes. And yf thou, O Lorde, wouldest now beyng prouoked with our disobedience, so deale with vs as thou myght, and as we haue deserued, there remayneth nothyng els to be loked for, but vniuersall and continuall plagues in this worlde, and hereafter eternall death and dampnation, both of our bodyes and of our soules. For yf we shoulde excuse our selues, our owne consciences woulde accuse vs before thee, and our owne disobedience and wickednes would beare witnesse agaynst vs. Yea, euen thy plagues and punyshementes, which thou dost nowe laye vppon vs in sundry places, do teache vs to acknowledge our synnes. For seying, O Lorde, that thou art iust, yea, euen iustice it selfe, thou punyshest no people without desert. Yea, euen at this present O Lorde, we see thy hande terrybly stretched out to plague vs and punyshe vs. But although thou shouldest punyshe vs more greuouslye then thou hast done, and for one plague sende an hundreth ; yf thou shouldest powre vpon vs all those the testimonies of thy most iust wrath, which in times passed thou powredst on thy owne chosen people of Israell : yet shouldest thou do vs no wronge, neyther could we denye but we had iustly deserued the same. But yet, O mercifull lord, thou art our God, and we nothyng but duste and ashes : Thou art our creatour, and we the worke of thy handes : Thou art our pastor, we are thy flocke : Thou arte our redeemer, and we thy people redeemed : Thou art our heauenly father, we are thy chyldren. Wherfore punyshe vs not, O Lorde, in thyne anger, but chasten vs in thy mercy. Regarde not the horror of our synnes, but the repentuance therof. Perfyte that worke whiche thou hast begonne in vs, that the whole worlde may know, that thou art our God and mercifull delyuerer. Thy people of Israell often tymes offended thee, and thou most iustly afflicted them : but as oft as they returned to thee, thou dyddest receaue them to mercy. And though theyr synnes were neuer so great, yet thou alwayes turned away thy wrath from them, and the punishment prepared for them, and that for thy couenaunt sake, whiche thou made with thy seruauntes, Abraham, Isaac, and Jacob. Thou hast made the same couenaunt with vs (O heauenly father), or rather a couenaunt of more excellencie and efficacie, and that, namely, through the mediation of thy deare sonne Jesus Chryste our Sauiour, with whose moste precious bloud it pleased thee that this couenaunt should be, as it were, wrytten, sealed, and confirmed. Wherfore, O heauenly father, we, now castyng away all confidence in our selues, or anye other creature, do flee to this most holy couenaunt and Testament, wherein our Lorde and Sauiour Jesus Chryst, once offeryng hymselfe a sacrifice for vs on the crosse, hath reconciled vs to thee for euer. Loke therfore, O mercifull God, not vppon the synnes which we continually commit : but vppon our mediatour and peace-maker, Jesus Chryst, that by his intercession thy wrath maye be pacified, and we agayne by thy fatherly countenance relieued and comforted. Receiue vs also into thy heauenly defence, and gouerne vs by thy holye spirite, to frame in vs a newnesse of lyfe, therein to laude and magnifie thy blessed name for euer, and to lyue euery of vs accordyng to the seuerall state of lyfe wherunto thou Lorde, hast ordeyned vs. And although we are vnworthy (O heauenly father), by meanes of our former foule lyfe, to craue any thyng of thee : yet because thou hast commaunded vs to praye for all men, we moste humbly here vpon our knees beseche thee, saue and defende thy holye Churche, be mercifull, O Lorde, to all common weales, Countres, Princes, and Magistrates, and especially to this our Realme, and to our moste gracious Quene and Gouernour Quene Elizabeth, increase the number of Godly Ministers, indue them with thy grace to be founde faithfull and prudent in their office, defende the Quenes Maiesties Councell, and all that be in aucthoritie vnder her, or that serue in any place by her commaundement for this Realme. We commende also to thy fatherly mercy all those that be in pouertie, exyle, imprisonment, sicknes, or any other kynde of aduersitie, and namely those whom thy hande nowe hath touched with any contagious and daungerous sicknes, whiche we beseche thee, O Lorde, of thy mercy (when thy blessed wyl is) to remoue from vs, and in the meane time graunt vs grace and true repentaunce, stedfaste fayth, and constant pacience, that whether we lyue or dye, we maye alwayes continue thyne, and euer prayse thy holye name, and be brought to the fruition of thy Godhead. Graunt vs these, and all other our humble petitions (O mercifull father) for thy deare sonnes sake, Jesus Chryste our Lorde. Amen.

Or els in the steade of the other, this Prayer may be vsed, and so to vse the one one day and the other another.

O ETERNALL and euerlyuing God, most mercifull father, whiche of thy great longsufferyng and pacience hast hytherto suffred and borne with vs most miserable offenders, who haue so long strayed out of thy way, and broken all thy lawes and commaundementes, and haue, neyther by thy manyfolde benefites bestowed vppon us vnworthy and vnthankfull synners, nor by the voyce of thy seruauntes and preachers, by continuall threatnynges out of thy holye worde, hytherto ben moued, eyther as thy chyldren, of loue to returne vnto thee our moste gracious father, eyther for feare of thy iudgementes, as humble and lowley seruauntes to turne from our wickednesse. And therefore, moste ryghteous iudge, thy pacience beynge (as it were) ouercome at the laste with oure obstinate vnrepentaunce, thou hast most iustly executed those thy terrible threates nowe partly vppon vs, by plaguyng vs so (with moste dreadfull and deadlye sicknes) (with troubles of warres) (with penury and scarcenes of foode and vyttayle), wherby great multitudes of vs are dayly afflicted and consumed. We beseche thee, O most mercifull father, that in thy wrath thou wylt remember thy old great mercies, and to correct vs in thy iudgementes, and not in thy iust anger, lest we be all consumed and brought to nought. Loke not so much vpon vs and vpon our deseruynges, O moste ryghteous iudge, to take iust vengeaunce on our synnes : but rather remember thy infinite mercies, O moste mercifull father, promysed to vs by thy dearely beloued sonne our Sauiour Jesus Christe, for whose sake, and in whose name, we do earnestly and humbly craue mercye and forgeuenes of our synnes, and delyueraunce from this horrible sicknes, being thy iust punyshment and plague for the same. And as thy holy worde doth testifie, that thy people of all ages, beyng iustlye plaged for theyr synnes, and yet in theyr distresse vnfaygnedly turnynge vnto thee, and suyng for thy mercye, obteyned the same : So lykewyse we, most worthely now afflicted with greuous and dreadfull plagues for our iniquities, pray thee, O most mercifull father, to graunt vs thy heauenly grace, that we maye lykewyse both truely and vnfaignedly repent, and obteine thy mercy, and delyueraunce from the same, which we beseche thee, O father of all mercies, and God of all consolation, to graunt vs, for the same Jesus Christes sake, our only Sauiour, mediatour and aduocate. Amen.

¶ Note to pray against any of these plages as they shall touch vs.

This Prayer may be sayde euery thirde day.

IT had ben the best for vs, O most ryghteous Judge, and our moste mercifull father, that in our wealthes and quietnes, and in the myddest of thy manyfolde benefites continually bestowed vppon vs most vnworthy synners, we had of loue harkened to thy voyce, and turned vnto thee our moste louyng and gracious father : For in so doing, we had done the partes of good and obedient louyng chyldren.   It had also ben well, yf at thy dreadfull threates out of thy holy worde continually pronounced vnto vs by thy seruauntes our preachers, we had of feare, as corrigible seruauntes, turned from our wickednes.   But alas we haue shewed hytherto our selues towardes thee, neyther as louyng chyldren (O moste mercifull father) neyther as tollerable seruauntes, O Lorde most myghtie. Wherfore nowe we feele thy heauy wrath, O most ryghteous Judge, iustly punyshyng vs with greuous and deadly sicknesse and plagues ; we do nowe confesse and acknowledge, and to our most iust punyshment do fynde in dede, that to be most true, whiche we haue so often hard threatned to vs out of thy holy scriptures, the worde of thy eternall veritie : that thou arte the same vnchaunge-able God, of the same iustice that thou wylt, and of the same power that thou canst punyshe the lyke wickednes and obstinacie of vs impenitent synners in these dayes, as thou hast done in all ages heretofore.   But the same thy holy Scriptures, the worde of thy trueth, do also testifie, that thy strength is not shortened but that thou canst, neyther thy goodnes abated but that thou wylt, helpe those that in theyr distresse do flee vnto thy mercyes, and that thou art the same God of all, ryche in mercy towardes all that call vppon thy name, and that thou dost not intende to destroy vs vtterly, but fatherly to correct vs ; who hast pitie vppon vs, euen when thou doste scourge vs, as by thy sayde holy worde thy gracious pro-mises, and the examples of thy saintes in thy holy Scriptures ex-pressed for our comfort, thou hast assurred vs.   Graunt us, O moste mercifull father, that we fall not into the vttermoste of all mischiefes, to become worse vnder thy scourge, but that this thy rodde maye by thy heauenly grace spedelye worke in vs the fruite and effecte of true repentaunce, vnfayned turnyng and conuerting vnto thee, and perfect amendement of our whole lyues, that, as we through our impenitencie do nowe moste worthely feele thy iustice punyshyng vs, so by this thy correction we may also feele the swete comfort of thy mercies, graciously pardonyng our synnes, and pitifully releassing these greuous punyshementes and dreadfull plagues.   This we craue at thy hande, O most mercifull father, for thy deare sonne our Sauiour Jesus Chrystes sake.   Amen.

¶ *A short meditation to be sayde of suche as be touched in affliction.*

Jerem. 14. O FATHER, doubtlesse our owne wickednes do rewarde vs : but do thou, O Lorde, accordyng to thy name.   Our oft transgressions and sinnes be many.   Agaynst thee haue we synned, yet art thou the comforter and helper of thy humble subiectes in the tyme of theyr trouble.   For thou O Lorde art in the myddes of vs, and thy name is called vpon vs.   Forsake vs not, O God, forsake vs not for the merites of thy only sonne our Sauiour Jesus Christ, to whom, with thee and the holy ghost, be all honor and glory. Amen.

¶ *Psalmes which may be song or sayd before the begynnyng, or after the endyng of Publique Prayer.*

1	2	3	4	5	6
13	15	25	26	30	32
46	51	67	79	84	91
102	103	107	123	130	143
147					

The Order for the generall Fast.

¶ It is moste euident to them that reade the Scriptures, that both in the olde Church vnder the lawe, and in the Primitiue Church vnder the Gospell, the people of God hath alwayes vsed generall Fastyng, both in tymes of common calamities, as Warre, Famine, Pestilence. &c. and also when any wayghtie matter, touchyng the estate of the Churche or the common wealth, was begon or intended. And it can not be denyed, but that in this our tyme, wherein many thinges haue ben reformed accordyng to the doctrine and examples of Gods worde, and the Primitiue Church, this part for fastyng and abstinence, beyng alwayes in the Scripture, as a necessary companion, ioyned to feruent prayer, hath ben to much neglected.

Wherefore, for some begynnyng of redresse herein, it hath ben thought meete to the Queenes Maiestie that in this contagious tyme of sicknes, and other troubles, and vnquietnes, accordyng to the examples of the Godly king Josaphat, and the kyng of Niniue, with others, a generall Fast should be ioyned with generall Prayer, throughout her whole Realme, and to be obserued of all her godlye Subiectes, in maner and fourme folowyng. 2 Par. 20. Jonas. 3.

Fyrst, it is ordeyned, that the Wednesday of euery weke shalbe the day appoynted for this generall Fast. 1.

Secondly, all persons betwene the age of .xvi. yeres and .lx. (sicke folkes and labourers in haruest or other greate labours, only excepted) shal eate but one only competent and moderate meale vpon euery Wednesday. In which sayd meale shalbe vsed very sober and spare diet, without varietie of kyndes of meat, dyshes, spyces, confections, or wynes, but only such as may serue for necessitie, comelynesse, and health. 2.

Item, in that meal it shalbe indifferent to eat fleshe or fysh, so that the quantitie be small, and no varietie or delycacie be sought. Wherein euery man hath to aunswere to God, yf he in such Godly exercyses eyther contempne Publique order, or dissemble with God, pretendyng abstinence, and doyng nothyng lesse. 3.

Item, those that be of wealth and habilitie, ought that daye to abate and diminishe the costlynesse and varietie of theyr fare, and encrease therwith theyr liberalitie and almes towardes the poore, that the same poore, whiche eyther in dede lacke foode, or els that which they haue is vnseasonable and cause of sycknes, may therby be relieued and charitably succoured, to be mainteyned in health. 4.

Last of all, this day, beyng in this maner appoynted for a day of generall Prayer and Fastyng, ought to be bestowed by them, which may forbeare from bodyly labour, in Prayer, studye, readyng or hearyng of the 5.

Scriptures, or good exhortations. &c. And when any dulnesse or wery-nesse shall aryse, then to be occupied in other godly exercyses : But no parte therof to be spent in playes, pastymes, or ydlenesse, muche lesse in lewde, wicked, or wanton behauyour.

When there is a Sermon, or other iust occasion, one of the Lessons may be omitted, and the shorteste of the three prayers appoynted in the Letany by this order may be sayd, and the longest left of.

Forasmuch as diuers Homylyes, appoynted before to be read in this fourme of Common prayer, are conteyned in the seconde Tome of Homylyes nowe lately set foorth by the Quenes Maiesties aucthoritie : Therefore it is ordered, that the Churchwardens of euery paryshe shall prouide the same seconde Tome or booke of Homylyes with all speede at the charges of the Paryshe.

APPENDIX III.

Thanksgeuing to God for withdrauing and ceasing the plage. 1563.

WEE yield the hartie thankes, O most mercifull father, that it hathe pleased the in thy wrayth to remember thy mercie, and partlie to mittigate thy severe rodde of this terrible plage, wher-with thowe hast hitherto most iustly scourged vs for our wickednes, and moste mercifully revoked vs from the same. Callinge vs (who in healthe and prosperitie had cleane forgotten bothe the and our selves) by sicknesse and adversitie to the remembrance bothe of thy iustice [1] and iudgmente and of our owne miserable fraylenes and mortalytie : and nowe leaste wee by the heavines of thyne indignation, shulde have utterly despeyred, comfortinge vs aigayne by the manifeste declaration of thy fatherly inclynation to all compassion and clemencie. Wee beseche the to perfecte the worke of thy mercie gratiously begone in vs : and forasmoche as trewe healthe is, to be sownde and [2] troow in that parte, which in vs is moste excellent, and like to thy godheade ; wee praye the throughly to cure and heale the woundes and diseases of our sowles,[3] grevously wounded and poysoned, by the [4] deyly assaults and in-fections of ye olde serpente Saitan, with the deadly plages of synne and wickednes : By [5] the which inwarde infection of our myndes [6] these outwarde diseases of our bodyes have by ye order of thy iustice, O Lord, issued and followed,[7] that wee by thy fatherly goodnes and benefytt, obteyninge perfecte health bothe of our myndes and bodies, maye render vnto the therefore contynewall and moste hartie thankes, and that, by flyenge from [8] sinne, wee

[1 terrible iustice. These notes shew the original readings of the manuscript copy.]
[2 and well att ease.]   [3 sickly sowles.]
[4 the great murtherer and old serpente.]   [5 from.]
[6 myndes, as it were out of a moste corrupte synke, these.]
[7 have issued and flowed.]   [8 of sin from henceforthe.

maye avoyde thyne anger[9] and plages, and ever hereafter, in innocencie and godlynesse of lyffe studienge to serve and please the, maye bothe by our wordes and works allwayes glorifye thy holly name. Which wee besech the to graunt vs, O father of mercies and godde of all consolation, for thy deare sonne, our only saviour and mediator, Jesus Christs sake.   Amen.

APPENDIX IV.

A FOURME to be vsed in common prayer, euery Sunday, Wednesday, and Fryday, through the whole Realme : To excite and stirre all godly people to pray vnto God for the preseruation of those Christians and their Countreys, that are nowe inuaded by the Turke in Hungary, or elswhere.

Set foorth by the most Reuerende father in God, Mathewe, Archbyshop of Canterbury, by the authoritie of the Queenes Maiestie.   1566.

The Preface.

WHERE as the Turkes the last yere moste fiercely assaylyng the Isle of *Malta*, with a great armie and nauye, by the grace and assistaunce of almightie God (for the whiche we with other Christians at that tyme by our hartie prayers made moste humble sute) were from thence repelled and dryuen, with theyr great losse, shame and confusion : they beyng inflamed with malice and desyre of vengaunce, do nowe by land inuade the kyngdome of Hungary (whiche hath of long tyme ben as a moste stronge wall and defence to all Christendome) farre more terribly and dreadfully, and with greater force and violence, than they dyd eyther the last yere, or at any tyme within the remembraunce of man : It is our partes, whiche for distaunce of place, can not succour them with temporall ayde of men, to assist them at the least with spirituall ayde, that is to say, with earnest, hartie, and feruent prayer to almightie God for them, desiring him, after the examples of Moses, Josaphat, Ezechias, and other godly men, in his great *Exod.* xvii. mercy to defende, preserue, and delyuer Christians, professyng his ii. *Para.* xx. holy name, and to geue sufficient myght and power to the Emper- iiii. *Reg.* xix. ours exellent Maiestie, as Gods principall minister, to represse the rage and violence of these Infidels, who by all tyrannye and crueltie, labour vtterly to roote out not onlye true religion, but also the very name and memory of Christ our only Sauiour, and all Chris-

[9 anger, and ever.]

tianitie. And forsomuch as if the Infidels, who haue already a great part of that most goodly and strong kyngdome in theyr possession, shoulde preuayle wholly agaynst the same (whiche God forbyd) all the rest of Christendome should lye as it were naked and open to the incursions and inuasions of the sayde sauage and moste cruell enemyes the Turkes, to the moste dreadfull daunger of whole Christendome, all diligence, hartinesse, and feruencie is so muche the more now to be vsed in our prayers for Gods ayde, howe farre greater the daunger and peryll is nowe, then before it was. And although it is euery Christian mans duetie, of his owne deuotion to pray at all tymes : yet for that the corrupte nature of man is so slouthfull and negligent in this his duetie, he hath neede by often and sundry meanes to be styrred up, and put in remembraunce of his duetie. For the effectuall accomplyshment wherof, it is ordred and appoynted as foloweth.

Fyrst, that all Parsons and Curates shall exhort theyr parysshioners to endeuour themselues to come vnto the Church, with as many of theyr famyly, as maye be spared from theyr necessary busynes : And they to resort thyther, not only vpon Sundayes and holydayes, but also vpon Wednesdayes and Frydayes, duryng this daungerous and peryllous tyme : exhortyng them there reuerently and godly to behaue themselues, and with penitent mindes, kneelyng on theyr knees, to lyft up theyr hartes, and pray to the mercyfull God to tourne from vs, and all Christendome, those plagues and punyshmentes, which we and they through our vnthankfulnesse and sinnefull lyues haue deserued.

Secondly, that the sayde Parsons and Curates shall then distinctlye and playnely reade the generall confession appoynted in the booke of Seruice, with the residue of the Mornyng prayer, vnto the first lesson.

Then for the first Lesson shalbe read one of the Chapters hereafter folowyng, or so muche therof as is appoynted.

Exod. xiiii. *Exod.* xvii. begynnyng at these wordes : *Then came Amelech and fought with Israell.* &c. *Iosue* x. Unto these wordes : *And layed great stones on the Caues mouth, which remayne vntyll this day. Iudges* vii. i *kyng* xvii. iiii *kyng* vii. iiii *kyng* xix. *The second of the Chronicles, or Paralepomenon* xx. Unto these wordes : *And his God gaue hym reste on euery syde. Act.* xii.

After that, insteade of *Te Deum laudamus,* that is to say : We prayse thee O God : shalbe sayde the li. Psalme : Haue mercy vpon me O God. &c.

Then immediatly after, vpon Wednesdayes and Frydayes, shalbe sayde the Crede. I beleue in God. &c. And after that the accustomed prayers folowyng, vnto the ende of the Mornyng prayer. And upon Sundayes, the seconde Lessons shalbe read, as they are ordinaryly appoynted, with the rest of the Mornyng prayer.

That done, the Letanie shalbe sayde in the myddes of the people, vnto the ende of the Collect in the same Letany, which beginneth with these wordes : *We humblye beseche thee O father.* &c.   And then shall folow one of these Psalmes in theyr order, to be sayde of the Minister accordyng too the order of the dayes, with the aunswere of the people.

¶ *The Psalmes.*

HEARE our prayer O Lord, consider our desire : harken vnto *Psal.* cxliii. vs for thy trueth and righteousnes sake.

Oh harken then to the voyce of our callyng, our kyng and our *Psal.* v. *God : for vnto thee wyll we make our prayer.*

O God, the Heathen are come into thine inheritaunce : thine *Psal.* lxxix. aduersaries roare in the middes of thy congregations, and set vp *& lxxiiii.* their banners for tokens.

They haue set fyre vpon thy holy places, and haue defiled the *Psal.* lxxiiii *dwelling place of thy name : and destroyed them euen vnto the grounde.*

The dead bodyes of thy seruauntes haue they geuen to be meate *Psal.* lxxix. vnto the fowles of the ayre : and the fleshe of thy saintes vnto the beastes of the lande.

Theyr bloud haue they shedde lyke water on euery syde of *Psal.* lxxix. *Hierusalem : and there was no man to bury them.*

And so we are become an open shame to our enemies : a very *Psal.* lxxix. scorne and derision vnto them that are rounde about vs.

Lord, howe long wylt thou be angry? shall thy gelousy burne *Psal.* lxxix. *lyke fyre for euer?*

O God, wherefore art thou absent from vs so long? why is thy *Psal.* lxxiiii. wrath so kyndled agaynst the sheepe of thy pasture?

Oh remember not our old synnes, but haue mercy vpon vs, and *Psal.* lxxix. *that soone : for we are come to great miserie.*

But thynke vppon the congregation : whom thou hast purchased *Psal.* lxxiiii. and redeemed of olde.

Helpe vs, O God, of our saluation, for the glory of thy name : O *Psal.* lxxix. *delyuer vs, and be mercyfull vnto our synnes, for thy names sake.*

Wherefore do the Heathen saye : Where is nowe their God? *Psal.* lxxix.

Make haste that thou mayst vtterly destroye euery enemie : *Psal.* lxxiiii. *which hath done euyll in thy sanctuarie.*

Aryse O God : mayntayne thyne owne cause : remember howe *Psal.* lxxiiii. the wicked man blasphemeth thee dayly.

Powre out thyne indignation vppon the Heathen that haue not *Psal.* lxxix. *knowen thee : and vpon the kyngdomes that haue not called vpon thy name.*

O let the vengeaunce of thy seruauntes bloud that is shedde : be *Psal.* xxxv. openly shewed vpon the Heathen in our syght.

Psal. lix.   *Delyuer vs from our enemies, O God : defende vs from them that ryse vp agaynst vs.*

Psal. lxxix.   Lette them be confounded and put to shame : let them be tourned backe and brought to confusion, that imagyne mischiefe agaynst vs.

Psal. lxxix.   *So we that be thy people, and sheepe of thy pasture, shal geue thee thankes for euer : aad wyll alwaye be shewyng foorth thy prayse jrom generation to generation.*

Glory be to the father, and to the sonne, and to the holy ghost. *As it was in the begynnyng, is nowe, and euer shalbe, worlde without ende.   Amen.*

Or this Psalme.

Psal. ii.   THE Heathen do furiously rage together, and the Kynges of the earth stand vp, and rulers take councell together : agaynst the Lorde, and agaynst his annoynted.

Psal. xi.   *The vngodly bende their bowes, and make redy theyr arrowes within the quyuer : that they may shoote at those that call vpon the name of the Lorde.*

Psal. xciiii.   They smite downe thy people, O Lorde : and trouble thyne heritage.

Psal. iii.   *Lord, howe are they encreased that trouble vs ! many are they that ryse agaynst vs.*

Psal. iii.   Many one ther be, that say of our soules : there is no helpe for them in theyr God.

Psal. x.   *The vngodly are so proude, that they care not for God : neyther is God in al their thoughtes, nor his iudgementes in theyr syght.*

Psal. x.   They haue sayde in theyr hartes tushe God hath forgotten : he hydeth awaye his face, and he wyll neuer see it.

Psal. xxv.   *For thy names sake, O Lorde, be mercyfull vnto our sinnes : for they are great.*

Psal. xxv.   Turne thee vnto vs and haue mercye vpon vs : for we are desolate and in great misery.

Psal. x.   *Stande not so farre of, O Lorde : neyther hyde thy face in the nedefull tyme of trouble.*

Psal. xxvii.   Harken vnto our voyce O Lorde, nowe when we crye vnto thee : aryse, O Lorde God, and lyft up thyne hande, and forget not thy people.

Psal. x.   *Wherefore should the wicked blaspheme God ? whyle he doth say in his hart, tushe, thou God carest not for it.*

Psal. x.   O take the matter into thy hande : thy people commit themselues vnto thee, for thou art theyr helper in theyr distresse.

Psal. x.   *Breake thou the power of the wicked and malicious : smyte all* our enemies vpon the cheeke bone, and breake the teeth of the *Psal.* iii. vngodly.

Rayne snares, fyre and brimstone, storme and tempest vpon *Psal.* xi. them : and let this be theyr portion to drynke.

Recompence thou theyr wyckednesse, and destroy them in their *Psal.* xciiii. *owne malice : yea, the Lord our God shall destroy them, and delyuer vs.*

And we shal geue thankes vnto the lorde accordyng to his great *Psal.* vii. mercies : and wyll praise the name of the lord the most hygh.

We will declare thy name vnto our brethren : in the myddes of *Psal.* xxii. *the congregation wyll we prayse thee, and magnifie thy saluation world without ende.*

Glory be to the father. &c.
As it was in the begynnyng. &c.

¶ *Or this.*

O LORD many doggs are come about vs : and the councell of *Psal.* xxii. the wicked layeth siege agaynst us.

Many Oxen do compasse vs : fat bulles of Basan close vs in on *Psal.* xxii. *euery syde.*

They gape vpon us with theyr mouthes : as it were rampyng *Psal.* xxii. and roaryng Lyons.

Our enemies are dayly in hande to swallowe vs vp : for they be *Psal.* lvi. *exceedyng many that fight against vs, O thou most hygh.*

O remember not the sinnes and offences of our youth and tymes *Psal.* xv. paste : but accordyng to thy mercye thinke vpon vs O Lorde for thy goodnes.

For thou, O Lorde, art our defender, thou art our health, and *Psal.* iii. *our saluation.*

O Lorde our God, in thee haue we put our trust : saue vs from *Psal.* vii. all them that persecute vs, and delyuer vs.

Lest they deuour our soules like Lions, and teare them in peeces : *Psal.* vii. *whyles there is none to helpe.*

Saue us from these Lyons mouthes : and from among the *Psal.* xxii. hornes of the Unicornes.

O delyuer not the soule of thy turtle doue vnto the multitude of *Psal.* lxxiiii. *the enemies : and forget not thy poore congregation for euer.*

And our prayses shalbe of thee in the great congregation : our *Psal.* xxii. vowes wyll we perfourme in the sight of them that feare thee.

And all the endes of the worlde shall remember themselues, and *Psal.* xxii. *be turned vnto the Lord : and al the kynredes of the nations shall worshyp before hym.*

Glory be to the father. &c.
As it was in the begynnyng. &c.

*After the Psalme, the prayer folowyng shalbe sayde by the Minister alone,
with a hygh voyce.   At saying wherof, the people shall deuoutly geue eare,
and shal both with mynd and speache to themselues assent to the same
prayer.*

The prayer.

ALMYGHTIE and euerlyuyng God our heauenly father, we thy
disobedient and rebellious chyldren, nowe by thy iust iudgement
sore afflicted, and in great daunger to be oppressed, by thyne and
our sworne and moste deadly enemyes, the Turkes, Infidels, and
miscreantes, do make humble suite to the throne of thy grace, for
thy mercie and ayde agaynst the same our mortall enemies.   For
though we do professe the name of thy only sonne Christ our
Sauiour, yet through our manifolde synnes and wickednesse we haue
moste iustly deserued so much of thy wrath and indignation, that
we can but say : O Lorde correct vs in thy mercie, and not in
thy furye.   And better it is for vs to fall into thy handes, then
into the handes of men, and especially into the handes of Turkes
and Infidels, thy professed enemies, who now inuade thyne inheritaunce.   Agaynst thee (O Lorde) haue we synned, and transgressed
thy commaundements : Agaynst Turkes, Infidels, and other enemies of the Gospell of thy deare sonne Jesus Christe haue we not
offended, but only in this, that we acknowledge thee, the eternall
father, and thy only sonne our redeemer, with the holy ghoste, the
comforter, to be one only true, almightie, and euerlyuyng God.
For yf we woulde denye and blaspheme thy most holy name,
forsake the Gospell of thy deare sonne, embrace false religion,
commit horrible Idolatries, and geue ourselues to all impure,
wicked, and abhominable lyfe, as they do, the deuyll, the worlde,
the Turke, and all other thyne enemies woulde be at peace with
vs, accordyng to the saying of thy sonne Christ : If you were of
the worlde, the worlde wold loue his owne.   But therefore hate
they vs, because we loue thee, therefore persecute they vs, because
we acknowledge thee God the father, and Jesus Christ thy Sonne,
whom thou haste sent.   The Turke goeth about to set vp to
extoll, and to magnifie that wicked monster and damned soule
Mahumet, aboue thy dearely beloued sonne Jesus Christ, whom
we in harte beleue, and with mouth confesse to be our only sauiour
and redeemer.   Wherfore awake O Lorde our God and heauenly
father, and with thy fatherly and mercyfull countenaunce loke
vpon vs thy chyldren, and all such Christians, as are now by those
most cruell enemies inuaded and assaulted, ouerthrowe and destroye thyne and our enemyes, sanctifie thy blessed name amonge
vs, which they blaspheme, establishe thy kingdome, which they
labour to ouerthrowe : suffer not thyne enemies to preuayle agaynste
those that nowe call vpon thy name and put theyr trust in thee,
least the Heathen and Infidels say, where is nowe theyr GOD ?   But
in thy great mercy saue, defende, and deliuer all thy afflicted

John xv.

Christians, in this and all other inuasions of these infidels, and geue to the Emperour thy seruaunt, and all the Christian army now assembled with hym, thy comfortable myght and courage, that we and they that delyght to be named Christians, may enioy both outwarde peace, and inwardly laude, prayse, and magnifie thy holy name for euer, with thy onlye sonne Jesus Christ, and the holye Ghost, to whom be all laude, prayse, glorie and empire for euer and euer.   Amen.

¶ This prayer to be said at Euenyng prayer, immediately after the Collect of the daye.

O LORDE God of hostes, most righteous iudge, and most mercyful Father : These dreadfull dangers and distresses wherin other Christian men our brethren and neyghbours doo now stande, by reason of the terrible inuasions of moste cruel and deadlye enemyes the Turkes, Infidels, and miscreantes, do set before our eyes a terrible example of our owne worthy[1] desertes, by our continuall sinnyng and offendyng against thy great maiestie and most seuere Justice: and do also put vs in remembraunce, here in this our Realm of England, of our most deserued thankes for our great tranquillitie, peace, and quietnes, whiche we by thy hygh benefite, and preseruation of our peaceable Prince, whom thou hast geuen vs, do enioye. Whyles others in the lyke or lesse offences then ours are against thy maiestie, are by thy righteous iudgementes so terribly scourged, this thy fatherly mercies do set foorth thy vnspeakable pacience whiche thou vsest towardes vs thy ingrate chyldren, as well in the same thy gratious benefites of suche our peace and tranquillitie, as in the wholsome warninges of vs by thy iuste punishments of others, lesse offenders then we be. For the whiche thy great benefytes bestowed vpon vs without al our deseruing, as we prayse thy fatherly goodnes towardes vs : so beyng stryken in our myndes with great dread of thy iuste vengeaunce, for that we do so lytle regarde the great ryches of thy fatherly goodnes, and pacence towardes vs : we most humble beseche thee to graunt vs thy heauenlye grace, that we continue no longer in the takyng of thy manyfold graces and goodnes in vayne. And vppon deepe compassion of the dreadfull distresses of our brethren and neighbours the Christians, by the cruell and most terrible inuasions of these most deadlye enemies the Turkes ; we do make and offer vp our moste humble and hartie prayers before the throne of thy grace, for the mitigation of thy wrath, and purchase of thy pitie and fatherly fauour towardes them : and not only towardes them, but to vs also by them; forsomuch as our daunger or safetie doth folowe vppon successe of them. Graunt them and vs thy grace, O most mercyfull Father, that we may ryghtly vnderstande, and

[1 un written in.]

vnfaynedlye confesse our synnes agaynst thy maiestie, to be the very causes of this thy iust scourge, and our miserie : graunt vs true and hartie repentaunce of all our synnes agaynst thee, that, the causes of thy iuste offence being remoued, the effectes of these our deserued miseries maye withall be taken awaye. Geue to thy poore Christians, O Lorde God of hostes, strength from heauen, that they, neyther respectyng theyr owne weakenes and paucitie, nor fearyng the multitude and fiercenes of theyr enemies, or theyr dreadfull crueltie, but setting theyr eyes and onlye hope and truste vpon thee, and callyng vppon thy name, who arte the geuer of al victorie, maye by thy power obteyne victorie agaynst the infinite multitudes and fiercenes of thine enemies, that al men vnderstandynge the same to be the acte of thy grace, and not the deede of mans myght and power, maye geue vnto thee all the prayse and glory: and specially thy poore Christians (by thy strong hand) beyng deliuered out of the handes of theyr enemyes, we for theyr and our owne safetie with them, may yelde and render vnto thee all laudes, prayses, and thankes, through thy Sonne, our Sauiour Jesus Christe, to whom with thee and the holy ghost, one eternall God, of most sacred maiestie, be all prayse, honour and glorie, world without ende.   Amen.

¶ *Or this Collect of the Letanye folowyng.*

O ALMIGHTIE God, King of all kinges, and gouernour of all thynges, whose power no creature is able to resiste, to whom it belongeth iustly to punishe sinners, and to be mercyful to them that truly repent : saue and delyuer vs (we humbly beseche thee) from the hands of our enemies. abate theyr pryde, aswage theyr malice, and confounde theyr deuises, that we beyng armed with thy defence, maye be preserued euermore from all perylles, to glorifie thee, which art the onely geuer of al victory, through the merites of thy onlye sonne Jesus Christ our Lorde.   Amen.

¶ *Psalmes which maye be songe or said before the begynnynge or after the endynge of publique prayer, or before and after Sermons.*

ii. iii. vii. x. xi. xxii. *vnto the ende of these wordes :*

In the myddes of the congregation wyll I prayse thee.

xxvii. xlvi. lii. lvi. lxx. lxxiiii. lxxxiii. lxxxxi. lxxxxiiii. cxxi. cxxiii. cxl.

IMPRINTED   AT   LON-
don in Powles Churchyarde by Ri-
charde Iugge, and Iohn Cawood,
Printers to the Queenes
Maiestie.

Cum priuilegio Regiæ Maiestatis.

APPENDIX V.

¶ *The Prayer.* 1569.

O MOST myghtie God, the Lorde of hoastes, the gouernour of all creatures, the only geuer of all victories, who alone art able to strengthen the weake against the myghtie, and to vanquishe infinite multitudes of thyne enemies with the countenaunce of a fewe of thy seruauntes callyng vppon thy name, and trusting in thee : Defend, O Lord, thy seruaunt and our gouernour vnder thee, our Queene Elizabeth, and all thy people committed to her charge. O Lorde withstande the crueltie of all those whiche be common enemies as wel to the truth of thy eternall worde, as to theyr owne naturall prince and countrey, and manifestlye to this crowne and Realme of England, which thou hast of thy diuine prouidence assigned in these our dayes to the gouernment of thy seruaunt our soueraigne and gratious Queene. O moste mercyfull father (if it be thy holy wil) make soft and tender the stonye heartes of all those that exalt them selues against thy truth, and seeke eyther to trouble the quiet of this Realme of Englande, or to oppresse the crowne of the same, and conuert them to the knoweledge of thy sonne, ye only sauiour of the worlde, Jesus Christe, that we and they may ioyntlye glorifie thy mercyes. Lyghten, we besche thee, their ignoraunt heartes, to embrace the trueth of thy worde : or els so abate theyr crueltie (O most mightie Lord) that this our Christian region with others that confesse thy holy gospel, may obtaine by thine aide and strength, suretie from all enemies, without shedding of christian blood, whereby all they whiche be oppressed with theyr tyrannie, may be releeued, and they which be in feare of theyr crueltie, may be comforted : and finally that all christian Realmes, and specially this Realme of England, may by thy defence and protection continue in the trueth of the Gospell, and enioy perfect peace, quietnes, and securitie : and that we for these thy mercies, ioyntly all together with one consonant heart and voyce, may thankfully render to thee all laude and prayse, that we knyt in one godly concorde and vnitie amongst our selues, may continually magnifie thy glorious name, who with thy sonne our sauiour Jesus Christe, and the holy ghost, art one eternal, almightie, and most mercifull God : To whom be all laude and prayse, worlde without ende. Amen.

H

APPENDIX VI.

¶ *A thankesgeuyng for the suppression of the last rebellion.*
1570.

O HEAUENLY, and most merciful father, the defendour of those that put theyr trust in thee, the sure fortresse of all them that flee to thee for succour : who of thy most iust iudgementes for our disobedience and rebellion agaynst thy holy worde, and for our sinfull and wycked lyuing, nothing aunswering to our holy profession, whereby we haue geuen an occasion that thy holye name hath ben blasphemed amongst the ignoraunt, hast of late both sore abashed the whole Realme and people of Englande with the terrour and daunger of rebellion, thereby to awake vs out of our dead sleepe of carelesse securitie ; and hast yet by the miseries folowyng the same rebellion more sharply punished part of our countreymen, and Christian brethren, who haue more neerely felt the same ; and most dreadfully hast scourged some of the seditious persons with terrible executions, iustly inflicted for theyr disobedience to thee, and to thy seruaunt their Soueraigne to the example of vs all, and to the warnyng, correction, and amendement of thy seruaunts, of thyne accustomed goodnesse turnyng alwayes the wyckedness of euyll men to the profite of them that feare thee : who, in thy iudgmentes remembryng thy mercye hast by thy assistaunce geuen the victorye to thy seruaunt our Queene her true nobilitie and faythfull subjectes, with so little, or rather no effusion of Christian blood, as also myght iustlye have ensued, to the exceedyng comfort of all sorrowfull christian heartes ; and that of thy fatherly pitie and mercyfull goodnesse only, and euen for thyne owne names sake, without any our desert at al.   Wherefore we render vnto thee most humble and heartie thankes for these thy great mercies shewed vnto vs, who had deserued sharper punishment ; most humbly beseching thee to graunt vnto all vs that confesse thy holy name, and professe the true and perfect religion of thy holye Gospell thy heauenly grace to shewe our selues in our liuing, accordyng to our profession : that we, truely knowyng thee in thy blessed word, may obediently walke in thy holy commaundmentes, and that we, being warned by this thy fatherly correction, do prouoke thy iust wrath agaynst vs no more; but may enioy the continuaunce of thy great mercyes towarde vs, thy right hande as in this, so in all other inuasions, rebellions, and daungers, continually sauing and defendyng our Churche our Realme our Queene and people of England : that all our posterities ensuyng, confessing thy holy name, professing thy holy Gospell, and leading an holye life, may perpetually praise, and magnifie thee, with thy onlye Sonne Jesus Christ our Sauiour, and

the holy ghost : to whom be all laude, praise, glory, and Empire
for euer and euer.   Amen.

APPENDIX VII.

A[1] FOURME of PRAIER WITH THANKES GIUING, to be vsed
euery yeere, the 17 of Nouember, beyng the day of the
Queenes Maiesties entrie to her raigne.   1576.

1. *Tim.* 2. *Chap. Verse* 1.

¶ I exhort you therefore, that first of all, prayers, supplications, inter-
cessions, and giuing of thanks be made for all men : for Princes, and for
all that are in authoritie, that we may liue a quiet and peaceable life, in
all godlynesse and honestie, for that is good and acceptable in the sight of
God our Sauiour.

A[2] fourme of prayer.

Morning prayer is to bee begun as in the booke of Common
prayer, vnto the ende of the psalme beginning, *O come let vs. &c.*

[1 The following extract from the Epistle to Whitgift, prefixed by Edmund Bunny to
his Form for the 17th of November, favours the notion, that Elizabeth made no express
provision for, at least, the religious celebration of that day.
"Whereas therefore euery yeere, when that day commeth, we resort to the Church
to giue thankes vnto God, and otherwise testifie that we haue good cause to reioyce
therein : the more that such doings of ours do witnes against vs, that it is but due
debt in vs, the more do I thinke it conuenient that order shoulde be taken for the continuance of the exercise begunne in your Graces Predecessors time [Grindal] : for the
better accomplishment whereof, especially in these partes where I am resident, I thought
it my duetie to make some triall of myself, to see how farre it would please the Lorde (of
his wonted mercies) to blesse me therein.   In which kinde of want, though my selfe be
not able to make any sufficient supplie ; yet, when I sawe howe to make a proffer
towards it, little though it were, I thought not good to let it slippe, not knowing whereunto by the goodnes of God (if it would please him to imploy some others thereabout that
are more able) it might be able to grow in the ende."]
[2 In, and from, 1578 the whole Service was printed according to the tenor of the fol-
following rubric.   This note shews how it then commenced.
An order for morning prayer, to be vsed the 17. of Nouember.
1 Tim. 2. vers. 1.
I exhort you therefore, &c., *as above.*
¶ You shall vnderstand, that euery thing in this booke is placed in order, as it shall be
vsed, without turning to and fro, sauing the three lessons taken out of the old Testament, of which you may chuse anie one, as you thinke best, for the first lesson at
this morning praier.   And in Cathedrall Churches, the minister may vse either of
the other two for the first lesson at euening praier.
¶ *First the Minister shall, with a loude voyce, pronounce some one of these three
sentences, as in the booke of common prayer.*
At what time soeuer a sinner doeth repent him of his sinne from the bottome of his   Ezech. 18.
heart, I will put all his wickednesse out of my remembrance, saith the Lord.
Rent your hearts and not your garments, and turne to the Lorde your God, because   Joel 2.
hee is gentle and mercifull, he is pacient, and of much mercy, and such a one that is
sorie for you afflictions.
If we say that we haue no sinne, we deceive ourselues, and there is no trueth in vs.
Dearely beloued brethren, &c.]

Then shall follow these special psalmes.

Psalmes xxi. lxxxv. cxxiiii.

¶ The first Lesson, taken out of the xvii. xviii. xix. and xx.
Chapters of the seconde Booke of Chronicles.

2 Chro. ch.
17. vers. a. 1.
3. &c.[1]
JEHOSAPHAT the sonne of Asa reigned ouer Juda. And the
Lorde was with him, because he walked in the former wayes of his
father Dauid, and sought not Baalim : But sought the Lorde God
of his father, and walked in his commaundementes, and not after
the doings of Israel. And ye Lord stablished the kingdome in his
hand, and all Juda brought him presents, so that he had abund-
ance of riches and honour. And he lift vp his heart vnto the
wayes of the Lord, and he put downe yet more of the high places
and groues out of Juda. In the thirde yeere of his reigne, he sent
to his lordes, euen to Benhail, Obadia, Zacharia, Nethanel, and to
Michaia, that they should teache in the cities of Juda : And with
them he sent Leuites, euen Semeia, Nethania, Zebadia, Asael,
Semiramoth, Jehonathan, Adonia, Tobia, and Tobadonia, Leuites ;
and with them Elisama and Joram, priests. And they taught in
Juda, and had the booke of the law of God with them, and went
about throughout al the cities of Juda, and taught the people.
And the feare of the Lord fel vpon al the kingdomes of the lands
that were round about Juda, and they fought not agaynst
Jehosaphat.

2 Chron. ch.
18. vers. 3. a.
& 31. e. &c.
And when Jehosaphat, taking part with Achab in his warres
against the king of Syria, was in great danger to be slaine, he cried
vnto the Lord, and the Lord helped him, and chased his enemies
away from him : but wicked Achab, king of Israel, was there slaine.

2 Chron. ch.
19. vers. a. 1.
4. &c.
And Jehosaphat came home againe in peace to Hierusalem, and
dwelt there. And Jehosaphat went out to the people from Beer-
seba to mount Ephraim, and brought them againe vnto the Lorde
God of their fathers. And he set iudges in the land, throughout
all the strong cities of Juda, citie by citie, and saide to the iudges,
Take heede what ye do : for ye execute not the iudgments of man,
but of God, which is with you in the iudgment. Wherefore now
let the feare of the Lord be vpon you, and take heed, and be doing
the thing that pleaseth him : for there is no vnrighteousnesse with
the Lord our God, that he should haue any respect of persons, or
take rewards. Moreover, in Hierusalem did Jehosaphat set of the
Leuites, and of the priests, and of the ancient fathers ouer Israel,
in the iudgement and cause of the Lord, and they returned again to
Hierusalem. And he charged them, saying, Thus shal ye do in
the feare of the Lord faythfully, and with a pure heart : What
cause so euer come to you of your brethren, that dwel in their
cities, betweene blood and blood, betweene lawe and commaund-

[1 These references are to the Bishop's Bible which, in its earlier editions, had
always both letters and figures, to mark the divisions of chapters.]

ment, betweene statutes and ordinances ; ye shall warne them that they trespasse not against the Lorde, and so wrath come vpon you, and your brethren : thus do, and ye shall not offende. And beholde, Amaria the high priest is among you in al matters of the Lord, and Zebadia the sonne of Ismael, a ruler of the house of Juda, for all the kinges matters : there be officers of the Leuites also before you, take courage to you therefore, and bee doing *manfully*, and the Lorde shalbe with such as be good.

After this there came an exceeding great armie of the Moabites and Ammonites agaynst Jehosaphat. And Jehosaphat feared, and set himself to seeke the Lorde, and proclaymed fasting thorowout all Juda. And he, with all Juda, and the inhabitants of Hierusalem praied, and fel before the Lorde, worshipping the Lorde. And the enemies fel out amongst themselues, and slue one another, vntil they were al destroyed. And Jehosaphat and his people had the spoyle of goodes, raiment, and iewelles, more then they coulde carie away. And they blessed the Lorde, and called the place the valley of blessing vnto this daye. And they returned to Hierusalem with great ioy and gladnesse. And the feare of God fell on the kingdomes of all landes, when they had hearde that the Lord fought agaynst the enemies of Israel. And so the Realme of Jehosaphat was in tranquillitie and his God gaue him rest on euery syde.

2 Chron. ch.
20. vers. a. 1.
2. 3.

a. 5. c. 18.
d. 22. &c.

The hystorie of King Hezekia, taken out of the fourth booke of Kings, the 18. 19. and 20. Chapters.

Or this may
be the first
Lesson.

HEZEKIAH the sonne of Ahaz reigned ouer Juda, and hee did that which is right in the sight of the Lorde, according to all as did Dauid his father. Hee putte awaye the high places, and brake the Images, and cut downe the groues, and allto brake the brasen serpent that Moses had made : for vnto those daies the children of Israel did burne sacrifice to it, and he called it Nehustan. He trusted in the Lorde God of Israel, so that after him was none like him among all the kings of Juda, neither were there any such before him. For he claue to the Lorde, and departed not from him, but kept his commaundementes which the Lorde commaunded Moses. And the Lord was with him, so that he prospered in all things which he tooke in hand : and he resisted the King of Assyria, and serued hym not. Therefore in the fourteenth yere of King Hezekia, did Sennacherib King of Assyria, come vp against al the strong cities of Juda, and tooke them. And he sent worde to King Hezekia by his captain Rabsakeh, who sayde, Tel Hezekia, thus sayth the great King, euen the King of Assyria, What confidence is this thou hast ? or on whome doest thou trust, that thou rebellest against me ? If ye say, Ye trust in the Lord our God, is not that hee, whose high places and whose aulters Hezekia hath put downe ? And Rabsakeh stoode, and cryed vnto the Jewes that stoode vpon the walles, with a loud voyce, saying, Heare the woordes of the

4 Reg. ch. 18.
vers. a. 1. 3.

4.

5.

6.

B. 7.

B. 13.

C. 17. 18.
C. 19.

E. 28.

29. great King, euen the King of Assyria, Thus sayth the King, Let
not Hezekia beguile you, for he shall not be able to deliuer you out
30. of my handes : Neither let Hezekia make you to trust in the Lorde,
saying, The Lord shall surely deliuer vs, and this citie shall not bee
32. giuen ouer into the handes of the King of Assyria.   Hearken not
vnto Hezekia, for he beguileth you, saying, The Lorde shall deliuer
33. vs.   Hath euery one of the gods of the nations deliuered his lande
34. out of the hande of the King of Assyria ?   Where is the God of
Hamath, of Arphad, and where is the God of Sepharuaim, Hena,
35. and Iua ? did they deliuer Samaria out of mine handes ?   And
what god is among all the gods of the nations, that hath deliuered
his land out of mine hand ?   Shal the Lord deliuer Hierusalem
out of mine hande ?

4 Reg. 19.   When king Hezekia heard of these wordes, he rent his clothes,
cha. ver. 1. a. and put on sackcloth, and came into the house of the Lorde, and
2.   sent Eliakim, which was the Steward of the householde, and Sobna
the Scribe, and the Elders of the priests clothed in sacke, to Isai
3.   the Prophet, the sonne of Amos : And they sayde vnto him, thus
sayeth Hezekia : This day is a day of tribulation, and of rebuke
4.   and blasphemie.   Peraduenture the Lorde thy God will heare all
the wordes of Rabsakeh, whom the King of Assyria his master
hath sent to raile on the liuing God, and to rebuke him with
woordes which the Lorde thy God hath heard : and lyft thou vp
5.   thy prayer for the remnant that are left.   So the seruaunts of King
6.   Hezekia came to Isai.   And Isai sayd vnto them, So shall you say
to your master. thus sayeth the Lorde, Be not afrayed of the wordes
which thou hast hearde, with which the yong men of the king of
B. 7.   Assyria haue rayled on me.   Beholde, I will put him in another
mind, and he shall heare tydings, and so returne to his owne land,
and I will bring to passe that he shall fall vpon the sword, euen in
9.   his own land.   And when Sennacherib had worde that Thirhaka,
King of Ethiopia, was come out to fight agaynst him, hee departed,
10.   and sent messengers vnto Hezekia, saying, Thus speake to Hezekia, king of Juda, saying, Let not thy God deceiue thee, in whom
thou trustest, saying, Hierusalem shal not be deliuered into the
11.   hande of the king of Assyria.   Beholde, thou hast heard what the
kings of Assyria haue done to al landes, how they haue vtterly
14.   destroyed them : and shalt thou escape ?   And Hezekia receiued
the letter of the hande of the messengers, and read it : and Hezekiah went vp into the house of the Lord, and layde it abrode be-
15.   fore the Lorde.   And Hezekia prayed before the Lord, and sayd,
O Lorde God of Israel, which dwellest betweene the Cherubims,
thou art God alone ouer all the kingdomes of the earth, thou hast
16.   made heauen and earth.   Lord, bow downe thine eare, and heare :
open Lord thine eyes (I beseech thee) and see, and heare the
wordes of Sennacherib which hath sent (this man) to rayle on the
17   liuing God.   Of a trueth Lord, the kings of Assyria haue destroyed
18.   nations, and their landes, and haue set fyre on their goddes : for

they are no goddes, but the worke of the handes of man, euen of wood and stone : and they destroyed them. Now therefore, O Lord our God, I beseeche thee, saue thou vs out of his hande, that all the kingdomes of the earth may knowe that thou onely art the Lord God. And Isai the sonne of Amos sent to Hezekia, saying, Thus saith the Lord God of Israel : That which thou hast prayed me concerning Sennacherib king of Assyria, I haue heard it. Wherefore thus saith the Lorde concerning the king of Assyria, He shal not come to this citie, nor shoote an arrowe into it, nor come before it with shielde, nor cast a bancke against it, but shall goe backe againe the way he came, and shal not come into this citie, sayth the Lord. For I will defend this citie to saue it, for mine owne sake, and for Dauid my seruants sake. And the selfe same night the angel of the Lord went out, and smote in the hoast of the Assyrians, an hundred foure score and fiue thousande ; and when the remnant were vp early in the morning, behold, they were al dead coarses. And so Sennacherib, king of Assyria, auoided and departed, and went againe and dwelt at Niniue. And as hee was in a temple worshipping Nisroch his God, Adramelech and Saresar, his owne sonnes, smote him with the sworde, and they escaped into the lande of Armenia, and Asarhaddon his sonne raigned in his stead. About that tyme was Hezekia sicke vnto death, and the prophet Isai the sonne of Amos came to him, and saide vnto him, Thus sayth the Lorde, Put thine householde in an order, for thou shalt dye, and not liue : and Hezekia turned his face to the wall, and prayed vnto the Lorde, saying, I beseeche thee (O Lorde) remember nowe howe I haue walked before thee in trueth, and with a perfect heart, and haue done that which is good in thy sight, and Hezekia wept sore. And afore Esai was gone out into the middle of the court, the worde of the Lord came to him, saying, Turne againe and tell Hezekia the captain of my people, Thus sayth the Lord God of Dauid thy father, I haue hearde thy prayer, and seene thy teares, and beholde, I will heale thee, so that on the thirde day thou shalt goe vp to the house of the Lorde. And I wil adde vnto thy dayes yet fifteene yeres, and I wil deliuer thee and this citie, out of the hand of the king of Assyria, and will defend this citie, for mine owne sake, and for Dauid my seruaunts sake. And Esai said, Take a lumpe of dried figs : and they tooke and laid it on the sore, and he recouered, and had exceding much honour and riches.

The summe of the historie of king Iosia, taken out of the fourth booke of the kings, the 22. and 23. Chapters, and the 2. of the Chronicles, the 34. Chapter.

Or this may be the first Lesson.

IOSIA raigned in Hierusalem, and he did that which was right in the sight of the Lord, and walked in the waies of Dauid his father, and bowed neither to the right hand nor to the left. In the

19.

20.

E. 32.

33.

34.
35.

36.
37.

4 Reg. 20.ch. vers. a. 1.

2.
3.

4.

5

6.

7.

2 Chron. ch. 34. vers. a. 1.
2.

eight yeere of his raigne, when he was yet a childe, he began to seeke after the God of Dauid his father : and in the twelfth yere he began to purge Juda and Hierusalem from the high places, groues, carued images, and images of metall.   And they brake downe the altars of Baalim, euen in his presence, and other images that were in greater honour then they, he caused to be destroyed : and the groues, carued images, and images of metall he brake, and made dust of them, and strawed it vpon the graues of them that had offred to them.   And he burnt the bones of the Priestes vpon the altars of them, and cleansed Juda and Hierusalem.   And in the eighteenth yere of his raigne, when he had purged the lande and the temple, he sent Saphan the Scribe to Helkia the high priest, that he should see the decayed places of the temple repaired with such money as the keepers of the porche of the house of the Lorde had gathered of the people.

And Helkia, as he was about the kings commaundement, founde in the temple the booke of the lawe of the Lorde and deliuered it vnto Saphan, who brought it vnto the king, and read in it before him.   When the king had hearde the words of the book of the law, he rent his clothes, and commanded Helkia the priest, with certaine others, saying. Goe ye, and enquire of the Lord for me, and for the people, and for all Juda, concerning the wordes of the booke that is founde, for great is the wrath of the Lord that is kindled against vs, because our fathers haue not hearkened to the wordes of this booke, to doe according to all that which is written therein for vs.

So Helkia the high Priest, with others, went vnto Hulda, the Prophetisse and they communed with her.   And she answered them ; Thus saith the Lorde God of Israel, Tell the man that sent you to me, Thus saith the Lorde, Beholde, I will bring euill vpon this place, and on the inhabiters thereof, euen al the wordes of the booke, which the king of Juda hath reade, because they haue for-saken me, and haue burnt incense to other gods, to anger me with al the workes of their handes : my wrath therfore is kindled against this place, and shall not be quenched.   But to the king of Juda, which sent you to aske counsell of the Lord, so shal ye say, Thus saith ye Lord God of Israel, Because thine heart did melte, and because thou hast humbled thy selfe before the Lorde, when thou heardest what I spake against this place, and against the in-habiters of the same, howe that they should be destroyed and accursed, and hast rent thy clothes, and wept before me, that I also haue hearde, sayth the Lorde.   Behold therfore, I will receyue thee vnto thy fathers, and thou shalt bee put into thy graue in peace, and thine eyes shall not see all the euill which I will bring vpon this place : And they brought the king worde againe.

And then the king sent, and there gathered together vnto him all the Elders of Juda and of Hierusalem.   And the Kyng went vp into the house of the Lorde, with all the men of Juda, and all

4.

5.
4 Reg. 22. ch.
vers. a. 3. 4.

a. 5. 6.
B. 8. 9. 10.

[B. 11. 12.]

[B. 13.]

14.
15.

16.

17.

18.
19.

20.

4 Reg. ch. 23.
vers. a. 1, 2.

the inhabiters of Hierusalem, with the Priests and Prophets, and all the people, both small and great : and he read in the eares of them all the wordes of the booke of the couenant, which was founde in the house of the Lord. And the king stoode by a piller, and made a couenant before the Lorde, that they shoulde walke after the Lorde, and keep his commaundements, his witnesses, and his statutes, with all their heart, and with all their soule, and make good the wordes of the saide couenant that were wrytten in the foresayde book : and all the people consented to the couenant. And the King commaunded Helkia, the hygh Priest, and the inferior Priestes, and the keepers of the ornaments, to bring out of the temple of the Lorde, all the vessels that were made for Baal, for the groues, and for all the hoast of heauen : and he burnt them without Hierusalem in the fieldes of Cedrone, and caried the ashes of them into Bethel. And he put downe the Priestes of Baal, whome the Kings of Juda had founded to burne incense in the high places and cities of Juda, that were rounde about Hierusalem, and also them that burnt incense vnto Baal, to the Sunne, to the Moone, to the Planets, and to all the hoast of heauen. And moreouer, all woorkers with spirites, and soothsayers, images, idolles, and all the abominations that were spyed in the land of Juda, and in Hierusalem : these did Josia put out of the waye, to performe the wordes of the lawe, which were written in the booke that Helkia the Priest found in the house of the Lorde. Like vnto him was there no king before him, that turned to the Lorde with all his heart, with all his soule, and all his might, according to al the lawe of Moses, neyther after him arose there any such as he.

3.

4.

5.

24.

25.

In Cathedral and Collegiate Churches, one of the former Lessons omitted at Morning prayer may bee read for the first Lesson at Euening Prayer.

Then, We praise thee, O God. &c.

The second Lesson. The xiii. to the Romanes.

Then the Psalme, O be ioyful. &c. *with the beleefe and the Lordes prayer, as is in the booke of Common prayer.*

Then shalbe sayde.

Minister. O Lord, shew thy mercie vpon vs.
People. And graunt vs thy saluation.
Minister. O Lorde, saue the Queene.
People. Who putteth her trust in thee.
Minister. Sende her helpe from thy holy place.
People. And euermore mightily defend her.
Minister. Let the enimies haue none aduauntage on her.
People. Let not the wicked approche to hurt her.
Minister. Indue thy ministers with righteousnes.
People. And make thy. &c. *as in the booke of Common prayer.*

Then the Collect for the Queene, beginning, O Lord our heauenly Father, high and mightie. *&c. as it is in the Letanie.*

It is ordered, that the Letanie shall not be omitted the seuenteenth day of Nouember, though it fall vpon Munday, Tuesday, Thursday, or Saterday. And that immediately after the collect beginning, We humbly beseech thee. *&c. this Psalme and prayer folowing be said.*

Psal.66.c.14. O COME hither, and hearken, all ye that feare God : and we will tell you what he hath done for our soules.

Psal. 59. a. 3. When men of power were gathered against vs, and lay in waite
& 71. b. 9. 10. for our soules : they tooke counsel together, saying, God hath forsaken them, persecute them, and take them, for there is none to deliuer them.

Psal. 22.b.12. Our enemies closed vs in on euery side : they gaped vpon vs
& 56. a. 1. 2. with their mouths, as it were ramping and roaring Lions, seeking to deuoure vs, and to swalow vs vp.

Psal.44.d.20. We were counted euen as sheepe appointed to be slaine : manye of vs were for thy sake killed all the day long.

Psal.107.a.4. And many went astray in the wildernes, wandring hungrie and
& 44. d. 22. thirstie in strange landes : our soules fainted in vs, and were brought low, euen vnto the very dust.

Psal.18.a.3.4. For why ? The snares and sorowes of death compassed vs : and the ouerflowinges of vngodlinesse made vs afraid.

Psal. 18. a. 5. Then we made our complaint vnto our God, and cryed vnto the
& 107. b. 12. Lorde in our trouble : and he heard the voyce of our prayer out of his holy temple, and deliuered vs out of our distresse.

Psal. 107.a.3. He gathered vs home againe out of the landes : from the East, and from the West, from the North, and from the South.

Psal.116.b.8. He delyuered our soules from death, our eyes from teares, and
& 4. a. 1. & our feete from falling : he hath set vs at libertie, he hath light our
18. d. 27. candle ; the lord our God hath made our darknesse to be light.

Psal.18.g.47. Wherefore we will giue thanks vnto thee, O Lorde, and sing
& 59. c. 16. prayses vnto thy name : we will sing of thy power, and prayse thy mercie betymes in the morning ; for thou hast beene our defence and refuge in the time of trouble.

Psal. 118. O giue thankes vnto the Lorde, for he is gracious : and his mercie endureth for euer.

Glory be to the father, and to the sonne, and to the holy ghost.

As it was in the beginning, is nowe, and euer shall be, worlde without ende. Amen.

Let us pray.

O [1] Lorde God, most mercifull Father, who as vpon this day, placing thy seruant our Souereigne and gracious Queene Elizabeth

[1 As an accompaniment to this prayer, may be added from the Bibl. Lans. 116. art. 24, ' The prayer for the Q. on her byrthe daye ' (September the 7th), though both its date and author are unknown :

O Lorde, the hope and strengthe of Israell, the onely planter and preseruer of Princes, and the rocke of sure defence for all that trust in thee : wee thine vnworthy seruants

in the kingdome, diddest deliuer thy people of England from daunger of warre and oppression, both of bodyes by tyrannie, and of conscience by superstition, restoring peace and true religion, with libertie both of bodies and mindes, and hast continued the same thy blessings, without all deserte on our parte nowe by the space of these * eighteen yeres : we who are in memorie of these thy great benefites assembled here together, most humbly beseech thy fatherly goodnesse to graunt vs grace, that we may in worde, deed, and heart, shew ourselues thankful and obedient vnto thee for the same : and that our Queene through thy grace may in all honour, goodnes, and godlines, long and many yeeres reigne ouer vs, and we obey and enioy her, with the continuance of thy great blessings, which thou hast by her thy minister powred vpon vs : This we beseech thee to grant vnto vs, for thy deare sonne Jesus Christes sake, our Lord and Sauiour.   Amen.

*Encrease this nomber, according to the yeeres of, her Maiesties reigne.

For the Epistle of the day, read i Pet. 2. beginning at the 11 *verse,* Dearely beloued, I beseeche you. *&c. to the* 18 *verse, ending with these wordes :* Fear God, honour the king.

For the Gospel, read Math. 22. beginning at the 16 *verse.* And they sent out vnto him their disciples with the Herodians. *&c. to the* 23 *verse,*

accepted in him, in whome thowe arte well pleased, do offer vp or sacrifice of praise and thankesgiuing for all the daungers wee haue escaped hauing soe iustlye deserued them, and for all the good thinges receiued, being so vnworthye of them. Among all other and aboue the reste, wth tearful hartes and humble handes lifted vp wth reuerence toward thy mercy seat, wee blesse and praise thy holy name, for that precious iewell of inestimable price, to witt the blessed spirit and being of thine humble seruant, our moste gratious Soverayn, whose sacred person according to thy word we doe reuerentlye repute and call the Breath of our nostrils, the Annoynted of the Lord, by whose breath we liue, and by whose Life we breathe. And now, Lorde, since it hathe pleased thee, in thy foreseeing prouidence, for the safety and comfort of so many thousands to giue to thine annoynted a princely birth and being, and by the right hand of Loue, by soe many dangers to lead the same along to that place of regall dignity, of wch thowe haste saide, Euen I haue sett my Kinge vpon my holy mount of Sion ; wee most humbly and earnestly entreat thy heauenly Maty that our woorkes may not impare thy woorkes, nor or sinnes impeach her safety. But [as] there is a plante wch thine owne right hand hath planted, so lett the eye of thy prouidence continually watch ouer her, and the arme of thy protection mightely defend her, that the Boars out of the forest, nor the Lyon out of the wood, nor any subtle Leopard out of the way of Ashur, may haue anie power to hurt the smallest Leafe of this thy princelye Plant. But so shadow her and compasse her wth the wings of thye Cherubims, that her highthe and State may be as the Cedars of Lebanon, her strength and long continuance as the Okes of Bashan, her perpetuall flourishing as the Palme tree, and her glorie as the Rose plantes in the Vale of Jericho. And lett those riuers that runne out of the Sanctuary, euermore flowe and ouerflowe round about her, as doth the Riuer Jordan at the tyme of haruest. And soe, O heauenly Father, to conclude our thankful prayer, we most humbly besech the in thy beloued, to pleade her cause with them that striue wth her, and to fight against those that fight against her, and by the sure and secret motions of thy most holy Spirit to saye vnto her Soule, I am thy Sauiour, Bless them that blesse her. Curse them that curse her. Lett the day of her birth be as the sweet influence of the Pleiades, and the day of their birth, as Arcturus and Orion. Lett the day of her birth be as the Sunn when he riseth in his mighte, and the day of their birth as the Moone in her way. Lett her rise. Lett them fall. Lett her flourish, Lett them perish. That the rude world may see and saye, thy promise is performed. Them that honor me, I will honor ; and they that despise me, shall be despised. Theis things, O heauenly Father, we besech thee graunte to vs and to thy whole Church, for Jesus Christ his sake or Lord and onely Saueour. Amen.]

ending with these wordes, They marueyled, and left him, and went their
way.

*The xxi. Psalme in Metre before the sermon, vnto the ende of the vii. verse.
And the c. Psalme after the sermon.*

Finis.

Imprinted at London by Christopher Barkar dwelling in Pater-
noster rowe, at the figure of the Tygres head.

APPENDIX VIII.

¶ A PRAYER for all Kings, Princes, Countreyes, and people,
which doe professe the Gospel : And especially for our
soueraigne Lady Queene Elizabeth, vsed in her Maiesties
Chappell, and meete to be vsed of all persons within her
Maiesties Dominions.

O LORD God of hostes, most louing and mercifull father, whose
power no creature is able to resist, who of thy great goodnesse
hast promised to graunt the petitions of such as aske in thy sonnes
name : we most humbly beseech thee to saue and defend all
Princes, Magistrates, kingdomes, countreyes, and people, which
haue receiued and doe professe thy holy word and Gospel, and
namely this Realme of Englande, and thy seruant Elizabeth our
Queene, whome thou hast hitherto wonderfully preserued from
manifolde perils and sundry dangers, and of late reuealed and
frustrated the trayterous practises and conspiracies of diuers
against her : for the which, and all other thy great goodnesse
towardes vs, we giue thee most humble and heartie thankes,
beseeching thee in the name of thy deare sonne Jesus Christ, and
for his sake, still to preserue and continue her vnto vs, and to giue
her long life and many yeeres to rule ouer this lande. O heauenly
Father, the practises of our enemies, and the enemies of thy
worde and trueth, against her and vs, are manifest and knowen
vnto thee. Turne them, O Lord, if it be thy blessed will, or ouerthrowe and confounde them for thy names sake : suffer them not
to preuaile : take them, O Lord, in their craftie wilinesse that they
haue inuented, and let them fall into the pit which they haue
digged for others. Permitt them not vngodly to triumph ouer vs :
discomfort them, discomfort them, O Lorde, which trust in their
owne multitude, and please themselues in their subtill deuices and

wicked conspiracies. O louing Father, wee haue not deserued the least of these thy mercies which we craue : for we haue sinned and grieuously offended thee, we are not worthy to bee called thy sonnes : we haue not bene so thankful vnto thee as we shoulde, for thy vnspeakable benefits powred vpon vs : we haue abused this long time of peace and prosperitie : we haue not obeyed thy worde : we haue had it in mouth, but not in heart ; in outward appearance, but not in deede : wee haue liued carelessly : wee haue not knowen the time of our visitation : we haue deserued vtter destruction. But thou, O Lorde, art mercifull, and ready to forgiue. Therefore wee come to thy throne of grace, confessing and acknowledging thee to be our onely refuge in all times of perill and daunger : and by the meanes of thy Sonne wee most heartily pray thee to forgiue vs our vnthankefulnesse, disobedience, hypocrisie, and all other our sinnes, to turne from vs thy heauie wrath and displeasure, which wee haue iustly deserued, and to turne our hearts truely vnto thee, that dayly we may encrease in all goodnesse, and continually more and more feare thy holy name : so shall we glorifie thy name, and sing vnto thee in Psalmes and Hymnes, and spirituall songs : and thy enemies and ours, shall knowe themselues to be but men, and not able by any meanes to withstande thee, nor to hurt those whome thou hast receiued into thy protection and defence. Graunt these things, O Lorde of power, and Father of mercy, for thy Christes sake, to whome with thee and thy holy spirite be all honour and glory for euer and euer. Amen.

¶ A prayer and thankesgiuing for the Queene, vsed of all the Knights and Burgesses in the High Court of Parliament, and very requisite to bee vsed and continued of all her Maiesties louing subiectes.

O ALMIGHTIE and most mercifull God, which dost pitch thy tents round about thy people, to deliuer them from the handes of their enemies, we thy humble seruants, which haue euer of olde seene thy saluation, doe fall downe and prostrate ourselues with praise and thankesgiuing to thy glorious name,who hast in thy tender mercies from time to time saued and defended thy seruant Eliza-beth, our most gracious Queene, not only from the hands of strange children, but also of late reuealed and made frustrate his bloody and most barbarous treason, who being her natural subiect, most vnnaturally violating thy diuine ordinance, hath secretly sought to shed her blood, to the great disquiet of thy Church, and vtter dis-comfort of our soules : his snare is hewen in pieces, but vpon thy seruant doeth the crowne florish. The wicked and bloodthirstie men thinke to deuoure Jacob, and to lay waste his dwelling-place : But thou (O God) which rulest in Jacob, and vnto the endes of

the worlde, doest dayly teach vs still to trust in thee for all thy
great mercies, and not to forget thy mercifull kindnes shewed
to her, that feareth thy name. O Lorde, wee confesse to thy glory
and praise, that thou only hast saued vs from destruction, because
thou hast not giuen her ouer for a pray to the wicked : her soule is
deliuered, and wee are escaped.   Heare us now, we pray thee,
(O most mercifull father) and continue foorth thy louingkindnesse
towards thy seruant, and euermore to thy glorie and our comfort
keepe her in health, with long life and prosperitie, whose rest and
only refuge is in thee, O God of our saluation.   Preserue her, as
thou art wont, preserue her from the snare of the enemie, from the
gathering together of the froward, from the insurrection of wicked
doers, and from all the traitorous conspiracies of those, which
priuily lay waite for her life.   Grant this, O heavenly father, for
Jesus Christs sake, our onely mediatour and aduocate.   Amen.

Io. Th.

A Prayer vsed in the Parliament onely.

O MERCIFULL God and Father, forasmuch as no counsell can
stande, nor any can prosper, but onely such as are humbly gathered
in thy name, to feele the sweete taste of thy holy spirite, we gladly
acknowledge, that by thy fauour standeth the peaceable protection
of our Queene and Realme, and likewise this fauorable liberty
graunted vnto vs at this time to make our meeting together :
Which thy bountifull goodnes we most thankefully acknowledging,
doe withall earnestly pray thy diuine Maiestie so to incline our
hearts, as our counsels may be subiect in true obedience to thy
holy worde and will.   And sithe it hath pleased thee to gouerne this
Realme by ordinary assembling the three estates of the same :
our humble prayer is, that thou wilt graffe in vs good mindes to
conceiue, free libertie to speak, and on all sides a ready and quiet
consent to such wholesome lawes and Statutes, as may declare vs
to be thy people, and this Realme to be prosperously ruled by thy
goode guyding and defence : so that we and our posteritie may
with chearefull hearts wayte for thy appearance in iudgement, that
art onely able to present vs faultlesse before God our heauenly
Father : to whome with thee our Sauiour Christ, and the holy
Spirit, bee all the glory both nowe and euer.   Amen.

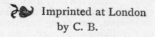

Imprinted at London
by C. B.

Cum priuilegio.

APPENDIX IX.

A Prayer of Thanksgeuing for the deliuerance of hir ma^tie from ye murderous intention of D. Parry. 1588.

O eternal God and mercifull father, we thy vnworthy Creatures most humbly doe confesse that wee are not able with owre tongues to vtter, nor in owre hartes to conceave, the exceading measure of thine infinite goodnes, graces, and fauours in this later age shewed to this Noble Realme, in that thou (O Lord) hast in most dangerous times, a few yeres past, by thy goodnes and prouidence, beyond expectation of man, directed and preserued the tender and noble parson of owre now Souereigne Lady Elizabeth, by thy grace, according to hir right, to cum to this kingdome and Roiall seate of hir noble father, and by hir, being thearein stablished, as thy deare beloved chosen servant,[1] to deliuer us thy people, that weare as Captiues to Babilon, out of Bondage and thraldome,[2] and to restore vs againe to the free fruition of the Gospell of thy Sonne owre Sauiour Christ; for the enioyeng wherof now these[3] manie yeres, wee doe confesse and acknowledge that beyond all owre desartes, yea trewly, O Lord, whan wee by owre daily vnthankefulness for[4] the benefitt of thy Gospell and by owre sinfull liues, contrarie to owre bold profession, haue most iustlie prouoked thee to withdrawe thy fauour from vs, thow, O Lord, with thy mercifull fauor and mightie power did[5] strength thy good blessed servant owre most gratious Quene, constantly against the roaring and threateninges of the mightie of the world, to persist in maintenaunce of vs hir subiectes and thy unworthie servants *to drawe owt owre daies* in all manner of prosperity, peace, and wealthe; But most singularlie, in a peaceable fredome, to enioie the blessed benefittes of thy holy worde, against the mightie roaring of Bulls and Tigres, the Enemies of thy Churche, dailie conspiring rownd abowte vs, and partly emongest owre selues against this Realme, and spetially against the Roiall person of owre blessed Quene thy humble servant and trewe Handmaide, whose Estate being in the expectacion of the nombre of wicked persons manie times in great and secrett dangers, yet thow Lord that art the Lord of Lordes, and king of kinges of thy heauenly goodnes hast alwaies preserued and defended hir by manie miraculous meanes : And as wee haue good cause to thinke, by manie other meanes, and at manie other times, than to vs are yet knowen,

[1 minister. These notes shew the readings of the uncorrected manuscript.]
[2 thraldome of the Enemies of thy trewe Churche.]
[3 now many.]   [4 of.]   [5 hast strengthened.]

but yet of late time wee haue fullie felt thy mervailous goodnes by the discouerie of sum Attemptes most apparantlie taken in hand against hir parson, by certaine wicked vnnaturall subiectes, the staie wherof onlie hath proceeded good Lord by thy most continuall tender and fatherly Care over hir, thy deare beloued Daughter and servant, and not by the witt, prouidence, or strengthe, of any wordlye Creature, as was most notably to bee seen the last yere to haue been attempted by one malitious and **Sommervile.[1]** furious parson resolutlie prepared, by persuasion of others, wicked Traitors, to haue committed a bloody fact uppon her parson, but mervilously by thy ordonance (o Lord God) discouered, by the trowbled desperat conscience of the very Malefactor, and so most happelie staied, for the which thy blessed fauor than showed, if wee weare not soe thankefull to thee, O Lord, as wee owght to haue been, yet, Lord God, wee are nowe most vrgentlie stirred upp to acknowledge owre most bownden dueties of praise and thankesgiuinge, by a verie late manifestacion of thy singuler fauor soe largelie aboue that former, as all wonderfull circumstances considered, wee maie compare it with anie Example of thy most wonderfull kindnes shewed to any Kinges or Nations of old time, *testified to us in thy Holy scriptures:* for Lord God what can be added to this thy secrett fauor nowe lastlie shewed to hir, whan neither she being the Quene of the whole Realme, nor wee being in nombre an exceeding multitude of hir subiectes, could imagin, or once thinke of the same, much lesse haue withstanded it,[2] in that a miserable wretched vnnatural borne subiect, A man in trewth of noe Religion (as nowe appeareth), vnder color seaking to be a diligent and most carefull servant to our gratious Quene, and pretending to discouer to hir, by his owne priuitie howe hir parson was in danger *of murdering,* and howe the same might be withstood, he himself did of longe time, euen whilest he had gotten creditt with hir Matie, and with hir Court, determin verie often most desperatlie and resolutelie to haue with his owne cursed hand distroied hir Matie sacred parson ; and if Lord thy mightie and vnsearcheable power had not at manie times diuerted his desperat Hart, and his bloodye hand, by reuerence of the Maiestie of hir parson, as by his owne voluntarie confession is declared ; Wee doe nowe perceiue, with trembling of our Hartes, that shee could not at sondrie times by the space of one whole yeare[3] and more haue escaped the danger of violence,[4] wickedly and reasolutelie by him intended. Wherefore wee nowe thy humble creatures, acknowledging our vnworthines of thes great graces, beeseche thee, O Lord, that thow wilt without regard of our former vnthankefulnes, shew thy mercie to vs, and continew thy blessinges over vs, that wee maie for thes so unspeakeable benefittes be more thankefull than wee haue been, not

[1 For an account of this man see page 265, note 2.]
[2 the same.]   [3 togeather.]   [4 violent death.]

onelie in wordes, but in deades also, according to the direction of thy Holy worde, *wheoof wee vnder the proteccion of our gratious Quene, by thy ordonance haue by the Ministerie of manie thy good servants had plentifull instrucion :* And wee doe firmelie hope in thy great goodnes, that our Soueraigne Lady the Quene thy humble servant, hauing soe notable proofes of thy spetiall prouidence in hir whole lief, besides thy vnknowen workes of favor towardes hir farre aboue that which thou showest to manie other Princes, shall by hir continuall thankefulnes, and by constancie in serving of thee, and maintaining of thy Holy Word, procure to hir self and vs the continuance of thes thy fauorable graces, still to preserue hir, from all manner of open or secrett perills, which the Enemies of thy word are knowen to entend against hir, whearebie hir yeares maie be prolonged, as farre as it maie please thee, to grawnt by the course of nature, to anie other prince in this worlde, for the main-tenance of the glorie of thy Sonne Jesus Christ, and of his Gospell, and for continuance of vs thy people hir naturall subiectes in the due feare and service of thee, and in owre naturall obedience to hir, wheareby wee and our posteritie maie enioie such peace, as wee haue had thes manie yeres, vnder hir. Maties gouernement, farre aboue anie like example, in anie age by past, either in this our naturall Cuntrie, or anie other within the limittes of Christendome : Grawnt this, grawnt this, O Heauenlie father for Jesus Christes sake, thy onelie Sonne owre Sauiour, to whome with thee and the Holie Ghost be geven all Honor and glorie, world withowt end. Amen.

APPENDIX X.

AN ORDER FOR PUBLIKE PRAYERS to be vsed on Wednes-dayes and Frydayes in euery Parish Church within the Prouince of Canterburie, conuenient for this present time : 1586.

Set forth by authoritie.

Imprinted at London by Christopher Barker, Printer to the Queenes most excellent Maiestie.

Cum gratia & Priuilegio.

Regiæ Maiestatis.

The Preface.

THE fatherly care and goodnesse, which Almightie God by his
Prophetes in many places declared vnto his people, neuer appeared
more abundantly toward any nation, then of late yeeres it hath
done toward this Realme of England. For when we were in
thraldome and captiuitie vnder the tyrannie of Rome, and carried
away with the false worshipping of God, he, by our gracious
Souereignne, deliuered vs : he planted the elect and chosen vine
of his gospel among vs, by law and authoritie : he raised vp
seruants to digge and delue about his vineyard that it might
prosper : he hath continually fenced vs from our enemies on all
sides, by his gracious and mightie prouidence : beyond the
reache of mans policie he hath reuealed their conspiracies, de-
feated their purposes, and made frustrate their counsels and
deuices : he hath erected a watch-tower of wise and godly
gouernment : he hath shed downe from heauen, and blessed vs
with his manifold graces, aswel of spiritual gifts, as of all plentie
of earthly creatures. And for these his manifolde benefites he
hath looked for some fruites at our handes according to our
dueties, that his name by our good doings might be glorified : but,
as the worlde seeth, and our owne consciences accuse vs, we haue
yeelded little other than sower and vnsauorie grapes, vnpleasant
vnto God, and mouing him to wrath towarde vs, that is, contempt of his word, worldlie securitie, infidelitie, hipocrisie, vsing
religion only for a shewe, and dishonoring the name of God and
profession of the Gospell in deede, with the practice of all maner
of wickednesse. Seeing therefore his mercie and goodnes wil not
allure vs, the Arme of his iustice will be stretched out against vs :
For he can abide nothing lesse than the contempt of his worde
and mercifull calling. Remember the wordes of God vttered by
[v. 13.] Jerémie the Prophet in the 7. Chapter, *Because you haue done all
these workes, and I rose vp early and spake vnto you, but when I
spake, you woulde not heare, neither when I called would ye
answere: Therefore will I do vnto this house, whereupon my Name
is called, wherein also ye trust, euen to the place which I gaue to
you and to your fathers, as I haue done to Silo ; and I wil cast
you out of my sight, as I haue cast out all your brethren, &c.* Let
vs therefore remember ourselues in time, and call vpon God with
earnest repentance, before he turne his face cleane from vs : let vs
Cap. lv.   followe the good counsell of the blessed Prophet Esay, *Seeke the
Lord while he may be founde, call vpon him while he is nigh vs :
let the wicked man forsake his wicked wayes, and the euill man his
naughtie cogitations, and returne vnto the Lord, and he will haue
mercie vpon vs. Let vs returne vnto God: for he is ready to for-*
[ii. 12.]   *giue.* Yea, God himselfe calleth vs by the Prophet Ioel : *Turn
vnto the Lorde* (saith he) *with all your heart, with fasting, with
weeping, and with mourning ; rent your hearts and not your*

clothes, and turne vnto the Lord your God: For he is gracious and merciful, slow to anger, and of great kindnes, and repenteth him of the euill that he hath purposed. Let vs therefore imbrace the mercie of God while it is offred : he hath not yet stretched out his arme against vs : only as a merciful father he hath shaken the rod of his iustice toward vs, to wake vs out of the deepe slumber of our securitie. The Lord God graunt, that in time we may take warning thereby, and not harden our hearts, and make stiffe our neckes against our gracious God ! These are therefore in the feare of God to charge the watchmen of the Lords citie, diligently and carefully to sounde the Trumpet in Sion, to gather the people together, to teach them in sackcloth and ashes to repent, to will them inwardly to rent their hearts, and not out-wardly their garments onely : sanctifie the congregation, assemble the elders, cal the yong ones, and euen those that sucke the breast. Let the bridegrome and his spouse, let them that liue in delicacie and pleasure of this life, in what state or condition so-euer they be, high or low, cast away their mirth and solace, and come and weepe and crie with bitter repentance before the mightie God, saying, Spare thy people (O Lord) and giue not thine heri-tage and beloued vineyard into reproch, that the wicked seed of Antichrist rule ouer it. Let not the enemies of thy truth say among themselues, Where is now their God, in whom they haue put their trust ? Then vndoubtedly will the Lord be ielous ouer this land, and spare his people, yea, the Lord wil answere, and say vnto his people, Beholde I wil send you corne, and wine, and oyle, and you shall be satisfied therewith, and I wil no more make you a reproch among mine enemies, and I wil remoue farre from you the Northerne armie, that is, the Antichristian power, and I wil driue him into a land barren und desolate, with his face toward the East sea, and his ende to the vttermost sea, and his stinke shal come vp, and his corruption shall ascende, because he hath exalted himselfe against the truth of God. Feare not (O land), but be glad and reioyce, for the Lord wil doe great things for thee. This godly admonition was giuen to the prince, priests, and people, with great zeale and earnestnes by Ioel the prophet, in the dayes of that good king *Ezechiah,* and is the only way to turne away the wrath of God from vs, and to obtaine the continuance of his gracious goodnes toward vs, and his diuine protection ouer vs in al our difficulties and distresses.

That therefore this admonition or exhortation may take the better effecte in mens hearts, it is ordered and streigtly charged, that in euery parish where there is a preacher allowed by the Ordinarie, that euery Sunday in some publike Sermon he shall put the people in remembrance of Gods exceeding benefites and bless-ings bestowed vpon vs these many yeres, and of our vnthankful receiuing and vsing of the same ; and exhort them to sincere and true repentance, and that in such sort, as they declare the inward affection of their hearts with the outward exercises of prayer, fastings and almes deedes, that the world may testifie and see that they truely returne to their Lord God.   In other places, where such sufficient and discreete preachers be not, the Ministers vpon the same days shal reade some part of these Homilies folowing, distinctly and reuerently, that the people may be moued thereby to the effect of that which is before mentioned.   Moreouer, vpon the Wednesdayes and Frydayes the Ministers in euery Parish shal say Diuine seruice morning and euening, in such sort as hereafter foloweth. At which Seruice one of euery house in the parish shall be present.   And if either the Ministers shalbe negligent in doing their dueties appoynted vnto them in this seruice, or the people disobedient in comming or resorting to this godly exercise, the Churchwardens and other discreete men of the Parish are required to complaine thereof vnto the Ordinary, that the slacknesse of eche partie may be corrected.   The people also at eche time of assemblie would be admonished to make their charitable contributions to the reliefe of the poore, at the least according to the order of the Statute.

The order of this booke.

First, the Confession, as it is in the Booke of Common prayer, with some one or two of the sentences of Scripture set before the same.

Then two or three of these Psalms following in order.

Psalm vi. x. xxv. ⎱   ⎰ xxxi. xxxiiii. xxxvii.
xxxviii. xli. li. ⎰   ⎱ cxii. cxliii. cxlv.

Then some one of these Chapters following : Esai. v. lviii. lix. lxv.   Ezechiel xvii.   Zechar. vii.   Joel i. ii.   Jonas iii.   Luke xvi. xxi.   Matthew xxv.   i John iii.

Then the Letanie with the prayer appoynted to be sayde in the time of dearth and famine : and the next Prayer following for the time of Warre.

And if there be a conuenient number of hearers vpon any of the workedayes in the Church, then one of these *Homilies* may be read, if there be no Sermon.

❧ An Homilie of repentance, and of true reconciliation vnto God.

THERE is nothing that the Holy Ghost doeth so much labour in, &c.

❧ An Homilie of fasting.

THE life which wee liue in this worlde, &c.

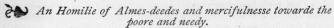 *An Homilie of Almes-deedes and mercifulnesse towarde the poore and needy.*

AMONGST the manifolde dueties that Almightie God requireth, &c.

The second part of the Sermon of Almes-deedes.

YE haue heard before (dearely beloued), &c.

The third part of the Homilie of Almes-deedes.

YE haue already heard two parts, &c.

APPENDIX XI.

A FOURME OF PRAYER, necessary for the present time and state.

Imprinted at London by the Deputies of Christopher Barker, Printer to the Queenes most excellent Maiestie. 1588.

The Preface

WE be taught by many and sundrie examples of holy Scriptures, that vpon occasion of particular punishments, afflictions and perils, which God of his most iust iudgement hath sometimes sent among his people, to shewe his wrath against sinne, and to call his people to repentance, and to the redresse of their liues, the godly haue bene prouoked and stirred vp to more feruencie and diligence in prayer, fasting and almes-deeds, to a more deepe consideration of their consciences, to ponder their vnthankfulnesse and forgetfulnesse of Gods mercifull benefits towards them, with crauing of pardon for the time past, and to aske his assistance for the time to come, to liue more godly, and so to be defended and deliuered from all further perils and dangers. So king Dauid in the time of plague and pestilence, which ensued vpon his vaine numbring of the people, prayed vnto God with wonderfull feruencie, confessing his fault, desiring God to spare the people, and rather to turne his ire to him-warde, who had chiefly offended in that transgression. The like was done by the vertuous kings Iosaphat and Ezechias in their distresse of wars and forrein inuasions. So did Iudith and Hester fall to humble prayers in like perils of their people. So did Daniel in his captiuitie, and many other moe in their troubles. Nowe therefore, calling to minde, that God hath beene prouoked by vs many and sundry wayes, and doth after a sort threaten vs with wars and inuasion : it behoueth vs to pray earnestly and hartily to God, to turne away his deserued wrath from vs, and as well to defend vs from the fiercenesse and furie of our enemies, (which combine and conspire together against vs,) as also from all other plagues and punishments, which our vnthankfulnesse and contempt of his worde hath iustly deserued. And although it is euery christian mans dutie, of his owne deuotion to pray at all times : yet for that the corrupt nature of man is so slouthfull and negligent therein, he hath need by often and sundry meanes to bee stirred vp, and put in remembrance of the same.

It is therefore meete and requisite : First, that all Curates and Pastors should exhort their Parishioners to endeuour themselues to come vnto the Church, with so many of their families as may bee spared from their necessary businesse, and they to resort not onely on Sundayes and Holidayes, but also on Wednesdayes and Fridayes, and at other times likewise during the time of these imminent dangers, exhorting them there reuerently and godly to behaue themselues, and with penitent hearts to pray vnto God to turne these plagues from vs, which wee through our vnthankfulnesse and sinnefull life haue deserued.

Secondly, that the sayd Curates then distinctly and plainly read the general confession appointed in the booke of Seruice, with the Letanie and residue of the Morning prayer, vsing according to their discretions some of the Psalmes and prayers hereafter folowing, and for the first lesson some of these Chapters : Exodus 14. Exodus 17. begin at the 8. verse. Iosua 10. vntill the 28. verse. Iudges 7. 1 Samuel 17. 2 Kings 7. 2 Kings 19. 2 Chron. 20. vnto the verse 30.

Finally, it is very requisite, that in their Sermons and exhortations they should mooue the people to abstinence and moderation in their diet, to the ende they might bee the more able to relieue the poore, to pray vnto God, to heare his holy worde, and to doe other good and godly workes.

❧ A [1] prayer for the forgiuenesse of sinnes. [1572.]

Psal. 95.   O COME, let us humble our selues : and fall downe before ye Lorde our maker, with reuerence and fear.

[1 In the summer of 1588, Christopher Stile 'Collected and gathered togither,' whilst John Wolfe printed, four Psalmes of Inuocation vpon God, To preserue her Maiestie and the people of this lande, from the power of our enemies.' They were followed by 'A Godly Prayer, Wherein is desired aide of God against his enimies, forgiuenesse of sinnes, and to turn his plagues, as well of the sword, as penurie, which be due for sinne, farre from this land.' The subioined passage from a copy in archbishop Harsnet's library, will shew the spirit of the publication : "We the people of England are thy people, O Lord, and thou art our God : we are thy flocke, and thou art our shepeheard : we are thy children, and thou art our Father. Be merciful vnto vs thy children : tender vs thy flocke, and defend vs thy English nation. Turne thy wrath vpon the nations that haue

Let vs repent and turne from our wickednesse, and turne againe Osee 6.
vnto our Lord : and our sinnes shall be forgiuen us. Acts 3.

Let vs turne, and the Lord will turne from his heauy wrath : he Jonas 3.
hath smitten vs, and he will heale vs, he will pardon vs, and we Osee 6.
shall not perish.

We acknowledge our faultes, O Lord : and our sinnes are euer Psal. 5[1].
before our sight.

We haue sore prouoked thine anger, O Lord : thy wrath is waxed Lamen. 51
hot, and thy heauie displeasure is sore kindled against vs. [5].

But rebuke vs not, O Lorde, in thine indignation : neither chasten Psal. 6.
vs in thy heauie displeasure.

Indeede we acknowledge that all punishments are lesse than our Judith 8.
deseruing : but yet of thy mercy, Lord, correct vs to amendment, Job 11.
and plague us not to our destruction. Sapi. 11.

O remember not the sinnes and offences of our youth, and times Psal. 25.
past, but according to thy mercie think vpon vs, O Lorde, for thy
goodnes.

Stande not so farre of, O Lorde : neither hide thy face in the Psal. 10.
nedefull time of trouble.

Turne thee vnto vs, and haue mercy vpon vs : for we are desolate Psal. 25.
and in great misery.

And nowe in the vexation of our spirites, and the anguish of oure Baruc. 3.
soules : we remember thee, and we cry vnto thee ; hear, Lorde, and Jonas 2.
haue mercie.

For we do not poure out our prayers before thy face, trusting in Dan. 9.
our own righteousnesse : but in thy great and manifolde mercies.

For thine own sake, and for thy holy names sake, incline thine Psal. 25.
eare and heare : and be merciful to our sinnes, for they are greate.

Helpe vs, O God of our saluation, for the glory of thy name : O Psal. 79.
deliuer vs, and saue vs for thy names sake.

So we that be thy people, and sheep of thy pasture, shal geue Psal. 79.
thee thankes for euer : and wyll be always shewing forth thy praise
from generation to generation.

Glory be to the father, &c.   As it was in the, &c.

A prayer to be deliuered from our enemies. [1572.]

O HEARKEN to the voyce of our prayer, our King and our God : Psal. 5.
for vnto thee do wee make our complaint.

not knowne thee, and that doe not call vpon thy name : and turne it we pray thee vpon
the Antechristians host, send forth thine angel stil to scatter them, as sometime thou
didst in the host of *Senacherib* for *Iudah* and *Hezechiah* in his time.   Let the blast of
the trumpets blowne by our Gedeon stil strike a terror in the harts of the Antechristian
Madianites, with their combined powers, and let be hard the sounding of thy host in the
aire to the amasing of the Spanish Assyrians, that they and theirs may be a pray for our
Elizabeth, and our English host : or sinke them in the sea, as thou didst *Pharao* and his
host in pursuing thy Israel, to bring them into their seruitude, that so our *Elizabeth* and
all her faithfull subiects may sing the songes of triumph to thy diuine maiestie, that
giuest victorie to Kinges."]

Psal. 22.   *O Lord, the counsaile of the wicked conspireth against vs : and our enemies are dayly in hand to swallow vs vp.*

Psal. 22.   They gape vpon vs with their mouths : as it were ramping and roaring lions.

Psal. 3.   *But thou, O Lord, art our defender : thou art our health and our saluation.*

Psal. 7.   We do put our trust in thee, O God : saue vs from all them that persecute vs, and deliuer vs.

Psal. 10.   *O take the matter into thy hande, thy people commit themselues vnto thee : for thou art their helper in their distresse.*

Psal. 7. & 22.   Saue vs from the Lions mouths, and from the hornes of the Unicornes : least they deuoure vs, and teare vs in pieces, while there is none to helpe.

Psal. 74.   *O deliuer not the soule of thy Turtle doue vnto the multitude of the enemies : and forget not thy poore congregation for euer.*

Psal. 59.   Deliuer vs from our enemies, O God : defende and saue vs from them that imagine mischiefe, and rise vp against vs.

Psal. 7.   *And we shal giue thanks vnto thee, O Lord, according to thy great mercies : and will praise the name of the Lord most high.*

Psal. 22   We wil declare thy name vnto our brethren : in the mids of the congregation will we prayse thee, and magnifie thy saluation world without ende.

Glorie be to the father, and to the sonne, and to the holy Ghost.

As it was in the beginning, is nowe, and euer shall be, world without ende.   Amen.

A prayer for deliuerance from enemies. [1572.]

Psal. 143.   HEARE our prayer, O Lorde, consider our desire : hearken vnto vs for thy trueth and mercies sake.

Psal. 3.   *Lorde howe are they increased that trouble vs : many are they that rise agaynst vs.*

Psal. 11.   The vngodly bende their bowes, and make readie their arrowes within the quiuer : that they may shoote at those that call vpon the name of the Lord.

Psal. 104.   *They smite downe thy people, O Lord : and trouble thine heritage.*

Psal. 79.   The dead bodies of thy seruants haue they giuen to bee meate vnto the foules of the aire : and the flesh of thy saintes vnto the beastes of the land.

Psal. 79.   *Their blood haue they shed like water on euery side of Hierusalem : and there was no man to burie them.*

Psal. 79.   And wee that liue are become an open shame to our enemies : a verie scorn and derision vnto them that are round about vs.

Psal. 74. & 79.   *O Lord, why is thy wrath such agaynst the sheepe of thy pasture?*

how long wilt thou be angry? shall thy iealousie burne like fire for euer?

Wherefore shoulde the vngodly say, Where is now their God? *Psal.* 79. there is now no more helpe for them in their God.

Oh remember not our old sinnes, but haue mercie vpon vs, and *Psal.* 79. *that soone : for wee are come to great miserie.*

O let the sorowfull sighing of the prisoners come before thee, *Psal.* 79. according to the greatnesse of thy power : preserue thou those that are appointed to die.

O Lord, thinke vpon the congregation of thy people, whome *Psal.* 74. *thou hast purchased and redeemed of olde : O deliuer vs and saue vs, for the glorie of thy name.*

And our prayses shall be of thee in the great congregation : our *Psal.* 22. vowes will we perfourme in the sight of them that feare thee.

And all the ends of the world shal remember themselues, and be *Psal.* 22. *turned vnto the Lord : and all the kindreds of the nations shall worship before him.*

Glorie be to the father, and to the, &c.
As it was in the beginning, is now, &c.

Prayers for true repentance and mercie. [1572.]

Moste mercifull father, who hast in thy holy worde, the worde of trueth, promysed mercy vnto sinners that doe repent and turne vnto thee, and hast by thy terrible examples of thy iust anger, being executed vpon people and countreyes round about vs, called vs, and most mercifully moued vs to repentance, and by thy patience and long suffering of vs hitherto hast graciously graunted vs time and space to repent : graunt also, we beseech thee, both to them and vs, grace truely to repent, and vnfeignedly to turne vnto thee with amendment of life, and to trust in thy mercies, and safely to rest vnder thy continuall protection from all enemies and euils, both bodily and ghostly, through our Sauiour Jesus Christ, who with thee and the holy ghost liueth and raigneth one God worlde without ende. *Amen.*

Another for the same.

We haue sinned Lorde we haue sinned grieuously, wee haue done vniustly, we haue liued wickedly ; wee are sorie therefore, O Lorde, yea, we are most sorie that we are no more sorie for our sins : but thou Lord God, father of all mercies, we humbly beseech thee, be not angry with vs for euer for our great and manifold sinnes, neither deale with vs according to our desertes, neither reward vs according to our wickednes ; but euen for thy selfe, O Lorde God, and for thy holy names sake, for thy most gracious assured promises made vnto penitent sinners in thy holy word, the worde of trueth, for thy infinite mercies which are in thy dearely beloued Sonne Jesu Christ our Sauiour, for his sake, for his death and precious blood, bee mercifull vnto vs sinners; and so we, who haue most grieuously offended thy diuine Maiestie, shal continually magnifie thy great and infinite mercie, through our sauiour Jesus Christ, to whom with thee and the holy ghost be all honour and glory, world without end. *Amen.*

Another prayer, to be deliuered from our enemies.

O LORDE God of hostes most louing and merciful father, we thy humble seruauntes prostrate our selues before thy diuine Maiestie: most heartily beseeching thee, to grant vnto vs true repentance for our sinnes past, namely for our vnthankfulnesse, contempt of thy word, lacke of compassion towards the afflicted, enuie, malice, strife and contention among ourselues, and for all other our iniquities. Lord deale not with vs as we haue deserued, but of thy great goodnesse and mercy doe away our offences, and giue vs grace to confesse and acknowledge, O Lord, with all humble and heartie thanks, the wonderfull and great benefits which thou hast bestowed vpon this thy Church and people of England, in giuing vnto vs without all desert of our part, not onely peace and quietnesse, but also in preseruing our most gracious Queene thine handmaid so miraculously from so many conspiracies, perils, and dangers, and in granting her good successe against the attempts of her aduersaries: for the which so wonderfull and great benefites we humbly beseech thee to stirre vp our dull mindes to such thankfulnesse and acknowledging of thy mercies as becometh vs, and as may bee acceptable vnto thee. We doe instantly beseech thee of thy gracious goodnesse to bee mercifull to thy Church militant here vpon earth, many wayes vexed and tormented by the malice of Satan and his members, and at this time, as it were, compassed about with strong and subtill aduersaries. And especially O Lord, let thine enemies know, and make them confesse that thou hast receiued England (which they most of all for thy gospell sake do maligne) into thine own protection. Set we pray thee (O Lord), a wall about it, and euermore mightily defend it. Let it bee a comfort to the afflicted, a helpe to the oppressed, a defence to thy Church and people persecuted abroad. And forasmuch as thy cause is now in hand, we beseech thee to direct and goe before our Armies both by sea and land, blesse and prosper them, and grant vnto them, O Lord, so good and honorable success and victories, as thou didst to Abraham and his company against the foure mightie kings, to Josua against the fiue kings and against Amalech, to Dauid against the strong and mightie armed giant Goliah, and as thou vsest to do to thy children, when they please thee. Wee acknowledge all power, strength, and victorie to come from thee: some put their trust in charets, and some in horses, but we will remember thy name, O Lord our God. Thou bringest the counsell of the heathen to nought, and makest the deuises of the people to be of none effect. There is no king that can be saued by the multitude of an host, neither is any mightie man deliuered by much strength. A horse is but a vain thinge to saue a man : therefore wee pray vnto thee, O Lord, thou art our helpe and our shield. O Lord, giue good and prosperous successe to all those that fight thy battell against the enemies of thy Gospell, shewe some token continually for our good, that they which hate vs may see it and bee confounded; and that we thy little and despised flocke may say with good King Dauid, Blessed are the people whose God is the Lorde Jehouah, and blessed are the folke that he hath chosen to be his inheritance. These and all other graces necessary for vs, graunt O heauenly Father, for Jesus Christes sake our onely mediatour and redeemer.

In the time of warre.

O Almightie God, King of all kings, and gouernor of all things, whose power no creature is able to resist, to whom it belongeth iustly to punish sinners, and to be mercifull to them that truly repent : saue and deliuer vs (we humbly beseech thee) from the handes of our enemies : abate their pride, asswage their malice, and confound their deuices, that wee being armed with thy defence, may be preserued euermore from all perils, to glorifie thee, which art the onely giuer of all victorie, through the merites of thy onely sonne Jesus Christ our Lord.

A prayer for the same. [1572.]

O most righteous God, and most mercifull father, who as well by the dreadfull plagues aud afflictions of nations round about vs, as by long suffering and sauing of vs, and by manifolde benefites bestowed vpon vs, hast shewed thy seueritie in punishing, or trying of them, and thy mercie in sparing and blessing of vs : we most humbly and heartily beseech thee, in thy iustice to remember thy mercie towardes them, and to saue them, and to graunt vnto vs grace not to despise the riches of thy patience and goodnesse towards vs, neither by hardnesse of heart and impenitencie to heape vpon ourselues vengeance in the day of vengeance ; but that wee being taught by the example of their punishment to feare thy iustice, and moued by thy long suffering and blessing of vs to loue thy goodnes, may by true repentance for our sinnes, and with all our soules, hearts, and minds, vnfeinedly turning vnto thee in newnesse of life, both escape thy wrath and indignation, and enioy the continuance and increase of thy fauour, grace, and goodnesse, through our sauiour, Jesus Christ, thy only sonne, to whom with thee and the holy Ghost, one God of most glorious maiestie be all honour and glory world without ende. *Amen.*

Another prayer for the same. [1572.]

O LORDE our God and heauenly father, looke down we beseech thee, with thy fatherly and mercifull countenance vpon vs thy people, and poore humble seruants, and vpon all such Christians as are any where persecuted, and sore afflicted for the true acknowledging of thee to be our God, and thy sonne Jesus Christ, whom thou hast sent, to be the onely Sauiour of the world : saue them, O mercifull Lord, who are as sheepe appointed to the slaughter, and by hearty prayer do call and crie vnto thee for thy helpe and defence, heare their crie, O Lord, and our prayer for them, and for our selues, deliuer those that be oppressed, defend such as are in feare of crueltie, releeue them that be in miserie, and comfort all that be in sorow and heauinesse, that by thy aide and strength they and we may obtaine suretie from our enemies, without shedding of Christian and innocent blood. And for that, O Lord, thou hast commaunded vs to pray for our enemies, we do beseech thee, not only to abate their pride, and to stay the furie and crueltie of such as either of malice or ignorance do persecute them which put their trust in thee, and hate vs, but also to mollifie their hard heartes, to open their blinded eyes, and to lighten their ignoraunt minds, that they may see and vnderstand, and truly turne vnto thee, and embrace thy holy word, and vnfeignedly bee conuerted vnto thy sonne Jesus Christ, the only sauiour of the world, and beleeue and loue his Gospel, and so eternally to be saued. Finally, that all Christian Realmes and specially this Realme of England, may by thy defence and protection, enioy perfect peace, quietnesse, and security, and all that desire to be called and accounted Christiaus may answere in deed and life to so good and godly a name ; and ioyntly all together in one godly concorde and vnitie, and with one consonant heart and minde, may render vnto thee all laude and praise, continually magnifying thy glorious name, who with thy sonne, our Sauiour Jesus Christ, and the holy Ghost, art one eternal, almightie, and most mercifull God, to whome be all laude and praise, world without end. *Amen.*

A Prayer.

BE [1] mercifull (O Father of all mercies) to thy Church vniversall, dispersed throughout the whole world : and grant that all

[1 There is considerable similarity, as to its tenor, between this prayer, and one of which Sancroft has preserved an early manuscript copy in his volume marked 3. 4. 30. What the archbishop deemed worth preserving, it has been thought right to reprint. The prayer, which is undated, commences somewhat abruptly.

Increase owr fayth, O Lord, and strengthen yt : graunt that we never distrust in thy mercies, nor decline from thy truth, nor fear the power of anie adversarie, nether anie vaine feare : but that we put owr whole trust and confidens in the, and depend vppon the wholie and onelie, not vppon man, nether anie kynde of creature. Mollifie owr hard hartes, work in vs true repentans : forgyve vs all owre synnes : clensse owr hartes and thowghtes frome all filthinesse, vanities, worldlinesse, and incline the same to thi lawes and testimonies. Continew, O Lord, thy most holie word and gospell in this realme of

they that confesse thy holy name, may agree in the truth of thy holy worde, and liue in godly concord and vnitie. And specially bee mercifull to such as are vnder persecution for the testimonie of their conscience, and profession of the gospell of thy Sonne our Sauiour Jesus Christ. Represse (O Lord) the rage and tyrannie of such as are bent to bloodshed, and mind nothing but murther : and saue and deliuer those silly soules, which (as sheepe) are appointed to the shambles and slaughter. And namely bee mercifull to thy Church and realme of England : to thy seruaunt our Souereigne and gracious Queene ELIZABETH, whose life (O Lord) long and long preserue from all the conspiracies and euils, which the craft and malice of the deuill, Antichrist, or other wicked men hath or can deuise against her (as hitherto most graciously thou hast done). Bee mercifull (O Lorde) to the Queenes most honourable Counsell, giuing them grace to counsel and to execute that which may be to thy honour and glory, to the edifying of the Church of thy sonne our Sauiour Jesus Christ, and to the benefit and safetie of the realme. Be mercifull also (O Lord) to the clergie, nobilitie, Judges, magistrates, people, and communaltie of this realm, granting to euery one thy heauenly grace, that they may in their vocation doe their dueties, to the honour and glory of thy name, the benefite of this church and realme, and to the saluation of their owne soules. Grant this (O Lord) to vs most vnworthy sinners for the worthines of thy deare sonne our Sauiour Jesus Christ, to whome with thee and the holy ghost bee all honour and glory world without ende. *Amen.*

A thankesgiuing and prayer for the preseruation of the Queene, and the Realme. [1572.]

O GOD, most mercifull father, who in thy great mercies hast both giuen vnto vs a peaceable princesse, and a gracious Queene, and also hast very often and miraculously saued her from sundry

England, graunt that we may trulie and thankfullie embrace yt : Convert the ennemies of yt (yf yt be thy wyll) dissipate there cownsailles, confound there devices. Preaserve Eliz. owr Quene, gyve her long life, and manie yeares to rule over vs. Govern her, O Lorde, and her whole counsail wt thy holie Spirite, that thorowt they may be directyd to thy glorie, and profyte and peace of this church and commonwealth. Gyve peace to thy church frome externall trobles and persecutions (yf yt be thy blessed wyll) and from domesticall discord and dissention : kepe yt frome the spoyler, frome oppression and wrong, and vs that be the ministers of yt, deal not wt vs as we have deservyd : but graunte that we may more fayfhfullie and more diligentlie walk in owr vocations, and do our duties then heatherto we have done. Discomforte, O Lord, confownd, or ells convert, all such as maling [malign] owr state wch are the ministers of thy word, desyer owr spoyle and seke our discreadite : all Simonites, wch bye and sell, or vnfytlie bestow livinges and offices ordeynyd for the ministers and preachers of thy word : all spoylers and oppressors of thy people, by what color and preatens soever they do yt : all vniust Judges and wickyd magistrates, wch take bribes and rewardes, and have respect of persons : and all such as hinder Justice and discorage those wch trulie and fayhfulli execute the same : all papists and haters of thy word and gospell. Finallie, O Lord, we vmblie besech the to graunt that those wch professe thy word and gospell may have the same, as well in hart as in mouthe, in dede as in outward apparens : for thy name sake and for thy Christes sake. Amen.]

great perils and daungers, and by her gouernement hast preserued vs and the whole Realme from manifold mischiefes, and dreadfull plagues, wherwith nations round about vs haue bene and be most grieuously afflicted : haue mercy vpon them, O Lorde, and graunt vs grace we beseech thee, for these thy great benefites, that we may be thankefull and obedient vnto thee, to flie from all things that may offende thee, and prouoke thy wrath and indignation against vs, and to order our liues in all thinges that may please thee ; that thy seruant our soueraigne Lady, and we thy people committed to her charge, may by thy protection be continually preserued from all deceipts and violences of enemies, and from all other daungers and euils both bodily aud ghostly, and by thy goodnesse may be mainteined in all peace and godlinesse : graunt this, O mercifull father, for thy dear sonnes sake our sauiour Jesus Christ, to whom, with thee and the holy ghost, one God immortall, inuisible, and onely wise, be all honour and glory for euer and euer.   Amen.

APPENDIX XII.

A PSALME AND COLLECT of THANKESGIUING, not vnmeet for this present time : to be said or sung in Churches.

At London.   Printed by the Deputies of Christopher Barker, Printer to the Quenes most excellent Maiestie.   1588.

A Psalme of Thankesgiuing.

Psal. 66. c. 14.[1]   O COME hither, and hearken, all yee that feare God, and we will tell you what he hath done for our soules.

Psal. 78. a. 4.   For we may not hide his benefites from our children, and to the generation to come, and to all people we will shew the prayses of the Lord, his power also, and his wonderful workes, that he hath done for vs.

Psal. 2. a. 1.   When the Kings and Rulers of the earth, and Nations round about vs, furiously raged, and tooke counsell together against God, and against his anoynted.

Psal 144.b.7.
Matt. 10. d. 22. & 24. b. 9. 10.
*Psal.*115.a.4.
Psal. 55. a. 3.   When men of another deuotion than we be, (*men bewitched by the Romish Antichrist*), men drowned in idolatries and superstitions, hated vs deadly, and were maliciously set against vs for our profession of the word of God, and the blessed Gospel of our Sauiour Christ.

Psal. 83. a. 3. 5.
The councill of Trent, and the holy league.   They cast their heads together with one consent, they tooke their common counsell and were confederate, and imagined mischiefe against thy people, O Lord God.

[1 See note to page 228.]

They secretly layd wayt, they priuily set snares and netts, they digged pittes for our soules, thinking that no man should see them. *Psal.* 35. b. 7. & 56. b. 6. & 64. a. 5. 6. & 83. b. 3.

They communed of peace, and prepared for most cruel warre : for they thinke that no faith nor trueth is to be kept with vs, but that they may feine dissemble, breake promise, sweare, and forsweare, so they may deceiue vs, and take vs vnwares, and oppress vs sodainely. *Psal.* 12. a. 1. 2. 3. & 14. b. 5. 6. *Psal.* 59. b. 7. c. 12. & 120. a. 2. & 140. a. 2. 3. b. 9.

And indeede innumerable multitudes of these most subtle and cruell enemies, and too mightie for vs, came sodainely vpon vs, by sea and by land, when we looked not for them. *Psal.* 3.a.1.2. *Psal.*22.c.12. 16. & 59. a. 3. & 69. a. 4.

They came furiously vpon vs, as it were roaring and ramping Lions, purposing to devoure vs, and to swallowe vs vp : they approached neare vnto vs, euen to eate vp our flesh. *Psal.*17.b.12. *Psal.*22.c.13. & 56. a. 1. 2. *Psal.* 27. a. 2.

They said in their hearts, Let vs make hauoc of them altogether, let vs roote them out that they be no more a people, and that the name of *England* may be no more had in remembrance. *Psal.* 74. b. 8. & 83. a. 4. *Israel.*

And surely their comming was so suddaine, their multitude, power, and crueltie, so great, that had we not beleeued verely to see the goodnes of God, and put our trust in his defence and protection, they might haue vtterly destroyed vs. *Psal.* 27.c.15. *Psal.* 55. a.3. *Psal.* 124. a. 1. 2. &c. *Psal.*94.c.17.

But though we had great cause to be afrayd, yet we put our whole trust in God : we cryed vnto the Lord in our trouble and distress ; we said, Helpe vs, O Lord our God, for vaine is the help of man. *Psal.* 56.a. 3. & 107. b. 6. & 108. c. 12.

We said, We commit ourselues wholly vnto thee ; according to the greatnes of thy power preserue vs, O Lord, who are appointed to die. *Psal.*60.c.11. 12. & 108. c. 12. 13.

And the Lord enclyned his eare and heard vs, and gaue courage to the hearts, and strength to the hands, of our captaines and souldiers, and put the enemies in feare. *Psal.* 81.b.7. & 18. d. 34. 35. 37. *Psal.* 48. a. 5. 6.

The Lord arose, and tooke the cause (*which indeede was his owne*) into his owne hands, and fought against them, that fought against vs. *Psal.* 10. c. 12. 14. *Psal.* 35. a. 1.

The Lorde scattered them with his windes, he confounded and disapointed their deuises and purposes of ioyning their powers together against us. *Psal.* 11. b.6. *Psal.*18.c.11.. 12. 13.

The Angel of the Lord persecuted them, brought them into dangerous, darke, and slipperie places, where they wandering long to and fro, were consumed with hunger, thirst, colde, and sickness : the sea swalowed the greatest part of them. *Psal.* 48. a. 6. & 83. c. 15. *Psal.* 35. a. 5. 6. *Exod.* 15. a. 4. 5.

And so the Lord repressed the rage and furie of our cruel enemies, intending nothing but bloodshed and murther, and turned the mischiefe which they purposed against vs vpon their owne heads ; and deliuered and saued vs who were as sheepe appointed to the shambles and slaughter. *Psal.* 7. c.15. 16. *Psal.* 35. b.8. *Psal.* 9. c. 15. 16. 17. 18. *Psal.* 9. b. 9. *Psal.*18.d.17. *Psal.*44.b.12. d. 22.

Psal. 64. b. 9.
Psal. 107. f.
42. 43.
Psal. 118. d.
23.
This was the Lords doing, and it is marueilous in our and in our enemies' sight, and in the eyes of all people ; and all that see it shall say, This is the Lords worke.

Psal. 74. c. 13.
Psal. 107. d.
22. 23. &c.
God is our king of olde : the helpe that is done by sea and by land, is his.

Psal. 144. b.
10.
David.
It is God that giueth deliuerance vnto Princes, and that rescueth our *QUEENE* from the hurtfull sword, and saueth her from all dangers and perils.

Psal. 107. a. 2.
We will therefore giue thankes, whom the Lord hath redeemed, and deliuered from the hand of the enemie.

Psal. 107. d.
21.
We wil confesse before the Lord, and prayse him for his goodnes : and declare the woonders that he doth for the children of men.

d. 22.
We will offer vnto him the sacrifice of thanksgiuing : and tell out his works with gladnesse.

Psal. 107. e.
32.
We will exalt him also in the Congregation of the people, and prayse him in the presence of the Elders.

Psal. 98. a. 1.
O sing vnto the Lord a new song : for hee hath done marueilous things.

a. 2.
With his owne right hand, and with his holy arme : hath he gotten himselfe the victorie.

Psal. 105. a. 1.
O giue thanks vnto the Lorde, and call vpon his name : tell the people what things he hath done.

a. 2.
O let your songes be of him, and prayse him : and let your talking be of all his wonderous workes.

a. 3.
Reioyce in his holy name : let the hearts of them reioyce that seek the Lord.

Psal. 35. b. 9.
And thou, my soul, be ioyful in the Lord : let it reioyce in his saluation.

b. 10.
All my bones shal say, Lord, who is like vnto thee, which deliuerest the oppressed from them that be too strong for them : yea, and them that are in distresse from them that seeke to spoile them.

Psal. 72. c. 18.
Blessed be the Lord God, euen the God of Israel : which onely doth wonderous things.

c. 19.
And blessed be the name of his maiestie for euer and euer : and all the earth shall be filled with the glory of his maiestie. Amen. Amen.

Glorie be to the Father, and to the Sonne : and to the Holy Ghost.

As it was in the beginning, is now, and euer shall be : world without end. Amen.

A [1] *Collect of thankesgeuing.*

WE cannot but confesse, O Lord God, that the late terrible intended inuasion of most cruell enemies, was sent from thee to

[1 In 1610 Thomas Sorocold, rector of St Mildred's in the Poultry, gave to the world a 'handfull of flowers, picked, sorted, and tyed up into a bundle,' entitled 'Supplica-

the punishment of our sinnes, of our pride, our couetousnesse, our excesse in meats and drinks, our securitie, our ingratitude, and our vnthankefulnesse towards thee, for so long peace, and other thy infinite blessings, continually powered vpon vs, and to the punishment of other our innumerable and most greeuous offences continually committed against thy diuine maiestie. And indeed our guiltie consciences looked for (euen a† that time) the execution of thy terrible iustice vpon vs, so by vs deserue. But thou O Lord God, who knowest all thinges, knowing that our enemies came not of iustice to punish vs for our sins committed against thy diuine maiestie (whom they by their excessive wickednesse haue offended, and continually do offend, as much or more than we), but that they came with most cruell intent and purpose to destroy vs, our cities, townes, countrie and people, and vtterly to root out the memorie of our nation from off the earth for euer ; and withall, wholly to suppresse thy holy word and blessed gospell of thy deere sonne our Sauiour Jesus Christ, which they (being drowned in idolatries and superstitions) do hate most deadly, and vs likewise, onely for the profession of the same, and not for any offences against thy diuine maiestie, or iniuries done to themselues. Where-fore it hath pleased thee, O heauenly father, in thy iustice to remember thy mercies towards vs, turning our enemies from vs and that dreadfull execution which they intended towards vs into a fatherly and most mercifull admonition of vs, to the amendment of our liues ; and to execute iustice vpon our cruell enemies, turn-ing the destruction which they intended against vs vpon their owne heads. For the which the same¦thy most gracious protection of vs, and all other thy graces, without all our desert, continually, and most plenteously powred vpon our Church, our QUEENE, our

tions of Saints.' The book contained also three prayers by Queen Elizabeth, 'carying in matter pithe, in stile maiestie, and in words true deuotion,' one of which will not be inappropriately placed here.

Queen Elizabeth's Prayer of Thanksgiving, for the overthrow of the *Spanish Navy*, sent to invade ENGLAND, *Anno* 1588.

MOST omnipotent Creator, Redeemer, and Conserver. When it seemed most fit time to thy worthy Providence to bestow the workmanship of this world's Globe : with thy rare judgment, thou didst divide into four singular parts the form of all this Mould, which aftertime hath termed Elements : all they serving to continue in orderly Govern-ment of all the mass. Which all, when of thy most singular bounty, and never yerst seen care, thou hast this year made serve for instruments to daunt our foes, and to confound their malice ; I most humbly, with bowed heart, and bended knees, do render my humblest acknowledgments, and lowliest thanks : And not the least, for that the weakest Sex hath been so fortified by thy strongest help, that neither my people need find lack by my weakness, nor Foreigners triumph at my ruin : Such hath been thy unwonted grace in my DAYS, as, though Sathan hath never made Holy-day in practising for my life and state, yet thy mighty hand hath overspread both with the shade of thy wings, so that neither hath been overthrown, nor received shame, but abide with blessing, to thy most glory, and their greatest ignominy. For which, Lord, of thy mere goodness, grant us grace to be hourly thankful, and ever mindful. And if it may please thee to pardon my request, give us thy continuance in my days of like goodness ; that my years never see change of such grace to me, but especially to this my kingdom : which, LORD, grant (for thy Son's sake) may flourish many ages after my end. Amen.]

I

Realme and people of England, we beseech thee, adde, and powre also the grace of gratitude and thankefulnesse into our hearts : that we neuer forgetting, but bearing in perpetuall memorie, this thy most mercifull protection and deliuerance of vs from the malice, force, fraud, and crueltie of our enemies, and all other thy benefits, most plenteously powred vpon vs, may inioy the continuance of thy fatherly goodnes towards our Church, our QUEENE, our Realme and people of England, and continually magnifie thy holy and most glorious name : which we doo beseech thee, O heauenly Father, to grant to vs most vnworthy sinners, for the woorthinesse of thy deere sonne our Sauior Jesus Christ, to whom with thee, and the Holy ghost, one God of most glorious maiestie, be all honour and glorie, world without end. Amen.

FINIS.

APPENDIX XIII.

CERTAINE PRAIERS to be vsed at this present time for the good successe of the French King, against the enemies of Gods true religion and his State.

Imprinted at London, by the Deputies of Christopher Barker Printer to the Queenes most excellent Maiestie. Anno Domini 1590.

A Prayer to be vsed in euery parish church at Morning and Euening prayer during the time of these present troubles in France.

O LORD God of hostes, most mightie and merciful Father, who in thy vnspeakeable wisedom and mercie, hast gathered vnto thy selfe a Church truly professing thy holy name and Gospell : We doe here most humbly acknowledge, that through our manifold sinnes and offences against thy heauenly maiestie, committed by vnthankfull receiuing of thy holy word, and by wicked led liues, we haue made ourselues vnwoorthie of the least of these and other thy singular blessings hitherto very aboundantly powred vpon vs. Neuerthelesse (O heauenly Father) with an assured confidence, relying vpon thy promises, we make bold to draw neere vnto the throne of thy grace, humblie crauing forgiueness of our sinnes, and the continuance of thy blessings vpon vs, and vpon all princes, countries and common wealths that haue receiued and do embrace thine holy Gospel, and that at this time fight thy battels against

the aduersaries of thy Gospell, and those that vphold the kingdome
of Antichrist. Therefore being cast downe in soule, we doe bewaile our iniquities, setting the bitter death and precious bloodshed of thy deare sonne Christ Jesus betwixt vs and thy iust wrath
conceiued against vs and them. Turne (O Lord) thy wrathfull
indignation from vs and them : And forasmuch as it is not for our
sinnes that our enemies in their purpose haue thus banded themselues against vs, but for the sincere profession of thy word and
Gospel : With thy mightie arme confound and bring to nought
the deuises, power, and strength of all such as set themselues
against ye same. Thou knowest (O Lord) how the heathen and
such as hold of superstitious vanities, euen at this present, in
France and elsewhere, doe rushe into thine inheritance to make
thy chosen Jerusalem, euen thy Church, a desolate heape of stones,
to lay waste thy holy sanctuarie, yea euen to giue vp the flesh of
thy deare children to the birdes of the aire, and the slaine carcasses
of thy Saints to the beasts of the field. Wherefore (most mightie
God of hostes) which art the Lord of glorie and power, that
canste arm the most base and meanest of thy creatures to the
ouerthrow of all the mightie of the world that bee enemies for thy
trueths sake : aduance thy selfe, like a mightie Giant, with a swift
and terrible iudgement against them ; frustrate the counsels of all
their Achitophels, breake them down with an iron rod like an
earthen vessell, send an hoste of Angels to scatter their armies,
confound them as thou diddest the host of the Assyrians, let thine
owne sword fight for thy seruants, and deuoure vp their enemies :
be thou as fire vnto them, and let them be as a stubble before
thee. Finally, let them be as *Oreb* and *Zeb*, yea like vnto *Zebah*
and *Salmanah*, and be made as dung on the face of the earth.
Send (good Lord) vpon them the spirite of feare and trembling,
that they may flee before the hoste of thine *Israel*, as chaffe before
the wind, to the ende they may bee discomfited and ouerthrowen
by thy mightie hand ; neither giue thy seruants (O Lord) to be a
praie vnto their teeth, or a by-word and reproch to such as hate
the true profession of thy Gospell. For we doe onely rest assured
vnder the shadow of thy wings. Protect in mercy as the apple of
thine eie, and mercifully powre vpon those armies that fight
against ye enemies of the Gospell, the spirit of wisedome, foresight,
counsel, strength, and courage, that, in full assurance of thine
heauenly helpe fighting for them, ten of them may chase an
hundred, and an hundred of them put to flight a thousand of
their aduersaries. Be thou (O Lorde) their continuall refuge and
strong rocke of defence, let thy holy Angels pitch their tents
round about them, that they may know thy holy hand both
stretched out for their helpe, and strongly set against their and
our enemies. Teach their hands to warre, and their fingers to
fight : prosper that which they take in hand, O prosper thou
their handie worke, and make them alwaies to reioice in thy

saluation and deliuerance ; that so all such as loue not the trueth of thy Gospel, hearing thereof, may bee discomfited, and that thy feare may fall vpon thine enemies to the perpetuall glory of thy holy name, and that we, escaping the rage and furie of those which seeke after our liues and the ouerthrow of thy trueth, may in thy holy Church here militant, and after in the Church triumphant in heauen, eternally sing praises to thee our heauenly Father, the onely giuer of all victorie. Grant these things for thy Sonne Christ Jesus sake, to whom with thee and the holy Ghost, three persons, and one eternall, immortall, inuincible, and onely wise God, be all honour, prayse, glory, and dominion, now and for euer. *Amen.*

A prayer.

O MOST mightie God and mercifull Father, forsomuch as thou hast promised to maintaine and defend the cause of thy Church so deerely purchased and redeemed, euen with the precious blood of thy deerely beloued Sonne : We thy humble seruants, confessing our owne vnworthinesse, through the infinite number of our wilfull transgressions, doe at this time prostrate our selues here before thy diuine maiestie, and wholy relying vpon thy promises, most heartily beseech thee through the merites of Jesus Christ our Sauiour, to protect and strengthen thy Seruants our brethren in *France*, that are now readie to fight for the glory of thy name. Thou knowest (O Lord) how the aduersaries that come to fight against them, haue entred into a league, and combined themselues together, neuer to desist vntill they haue destroied all such as professe thy Gospell, and laid the glory of thy *Sion* and *Temple* in the dust. And although both our and their offences doe most iustly deserue, that both they and we should bee deliuered to the edge of the sword : yet seeing that these conspirators and rebellers doe hate thy seruants onely for the cause of thy trueth, and that they are noted in the world for such as outwardly professe thy name, and the true doctrine of the Gospell of thy Sonne our Sauiour Christ ; Saue them in thy mercy (O heauenly Father) from the crueltie of their enemies, cast a feare and trembling into the hearts of their aduersaries, take the cause of thy Gospel into thine own hands : go before them, fight the battels of thy children, and subdue their enemies : so shal that proud generation haue no cause to insult ouer thy true Church, and ouer thy seruants, nor to say with thy old enemies, *Where is now their God?* And we thy penitent and most humble suppliants, that doe here at this time make intercession both for our brethren and for ourselues, will from henceforth declare thy name with cheereful hearts in the midst of the congregation ; we will euer praise thee and magnifie thy saluation, world without end. Graunt this (O mercifull Father) for thy· deare sonnes sake, our Lord and Sauiour Jesus Christ, to whom with thee and the holy Ghost, three persons and one God, bee all honour, glory, power and dominion, now and for euer. Amen.

Another.

O MOST mightie Lord God, the Lord of hostes, the gouernour of all creatures, the onely giuer of all victories, who alone art able to strengthen the weake against the mightie, and to vanquish infinite multitudes of thine enemies with the countenance of a fewe of thy seruants calling vpon thy name, and trusting in thee : Defend O Lord, thy seruant the most Christian king, the *French King,* and specially at this time giue him power to withstand the crueltie of all his enemies, as well forreners, as notorious rebels to his crowne and Realme, which thou hast of thy diuine prouidence assigned vnto him in these our dayes. O most mercifull Father, (if it be thy holy will) plucke downe those ambitious and rebellious heartes, that exalt themselues against their naturall Lord and King. Conuert them to the knowledge of their offences, that in so iust a cause for so noble a King, a friend to our soueraigne Lady & Queene, both these realmes may liue in amitie, and bee ioyned in strength to withstand the rage and crueltie of such as, not content with their own, aspire to depriue others of their kingdomes. Abate therefore their crueltie, (O most mightie Lorde,) that such Christian Regions as desire the peace of thy Church, may obtaine by thy aide and strength surety from their enemies without shedding of Christian and innocent blood, whereby all they that be oppressed with their tyrannie may bee releeued, and all which be in feare of their cruelty may be comforted. And finally, that all Christian Realmes, and specially this Realme of England, may by thy defence and protection enioy perfect peace, quietnesse, and security. And that we for these thy mercies ioyntly altogether, with one consonant heart and voyce, may thankfully render to thee all laude and prayse, and in one godly concorde and vnitie amongst our selues may continually magnifie thy glorious name, who with thy Sonne our Sauiour Jesus Christ, and the holy Ghost, art one eternal, Almighty, and most mercifull God, to whom be all laud and prayse, worlde without end. Amen.

APPENDIX XIV.

An Order for Prayer and Thanksgiuing (necessary to be vsed in these dangerous times) for the safetie and preseruation of her Maiesty and this realme.

Set forth by Authoritie.

LONDON.

Printed by the Deputies of Christopher Barker, Printer to the Queenes most excellent Maiestie. 1594.

An admonition to the Reader.

There haue bene sundry, but *heathen men* (as *Plato* and others), being no better instructed then the lame reache of reason coulde guide them, nor any clearer enlightened, then by the dimmed glimpse of nature, who neuertheles arriued thus farre, as to know and acknowledge that God, who is aboue all, extendeth his carefull prouidence ouer all, and especially in preseruation of Kingdomes, and of other politique societies, and of their Gouernours and Rulers. *For that which may bee knowen of God, is manifest* (saieth Saint Paul) *among them: for God hath opened it vnto them. For his inuisible thinges beeing vnderstoode by his woorkes through the creation of the worlde, are seene: that is, both his eternall power and Godhead, so that they are without excuse.* Then howe much more must all *Christians*, to whome the *Daystarre* hath in greater brightnesse and measure appeared, and the treasures of *God* the *Father* in his sonne *Christ Jesu* bene opened, acknowledge this his prouidence, and reuerently adore and magnifie that good *God*, which to the heape of all other his mercies towardes them addeth this blessing and protection of *Magistracie* and gouernment, whereby men liue peaceably with all honesty in this life !

But if euer any nation, yea, if all the nations in the worlde besides, haue cause with thankefulnesse to acknowledge this kinde of benefite, surely wee the people of *England* haue most iust and abundant occasion, of all others, to performe this duetie vnto God. First, for placing ouer vs our most gratious dread Soueraigne Ladie *Queene Elizabeth*, by whose happie gouernement wee haue so long breathed from the burden of intolerable miseries of *scarcity, bloodshed,* and spirituall *bondage,* vnder which afore wee laye grouelong, and pitifully groned. Then, for preseruing these her Realmes and dominions so long in the true profession of the Gospel, and in peace and tranquillitie notwithstanding the sundrie priuie conspiracies and open hostilities practised, both inwarde and outwarde, for the interruption of our quiet repose and holy profession. Thirdly, for protecting so long and so often her sacred royall

Rom. 1. ver. 19, 20.

person from the cruell and bloodie handes of such and so many seuerall detestable and treacherous Conspirators. And likewise for the Lordes prouident and watchfull eye ouer her and vs, and for the woonderfull happie discoueries of so manifolde cruell designements so closely plotted against her innocent life, and so dangerously against her *Highnesse* Realmes and dominions. Which mischieuous deuises as they haue all flowed from none other fountaine, than from that citie of seuen hills, the *See of Rome*, and seate of the *Beast*, not in regarde of any desert of ours, but because wee haue abandoned the cuppe of spirituall abhominations, wherewith these haue long intoxicated the Kings of the earth : So haue they beene continually proiected, caried forwarde, and managed by idolatrous *Priestes* and *Jesuites* his creatures, the very loathsome *Locusts* that crawle out of the bottomlesse pitte. Howebeit they haue beene and are mightily seconded by certaine (*Potentates* of the earth,[1]) who doe nothing els but serue themselues of that idolatrous *Romish religion*, as of a Maske and stalking-horse, therewith to couer the vnsatiable ambition, wherewith they are possessed, of vsurping [2] other mens *kingdoms*. For if we will first particularly cast our eyes vpon the variable conspiracies that haue beene entred into but against her Highnesse realmes : shal we not find the treason of the two *Pooles*,[3] of *Felton*,[4] and of the late Duke of *Northfolk*;[5] of *Throgmorton*,[6] of

Apocal. 13. & 17.

[1 The two other editions mentioned in the next note have not these four words, "*Potentates* of the earth."]

[2 There exist three editions of this Order, but only one has the following long enumeration of conspirators. The other two (which are in the University library, Cambridge, and at Lambeth) differ from each other merely in the arrangement of the type, and in the number of pages, one containing C in fours, the other D iii. In both the Admonition goes on thus, " of vsurping the *kingdoms* of other Princes.
Which their most dangerous and desperate plots and enterprises, God of his great mercie hath hitherto most happily discouered to his infinite glorie, and our vnspeakeable comfort. So that it may aptly, &c."]

[3 In Ocotber, 1562, Arthur Pole, and his brother Edmund, (great grandsons of George, duke of Clarence, Edward the fourth's brother,) with others, were apprehended on a charge of conspiring, by means of a French army landing in Wales, to depose Elizabeth, and set on the throne Mary, queen of Scots, who was to marry Edmund, and create Arthur duke of Clarence They were tried on the 26th of February, 1563, but, though found guilty, were all pardoned. Carte, Vol. III. p. 408. Zurich Letters, second edition, p. 172.]

[4 Pope Pius V., he who even desired to 'shed his blood in an expedition against England,' issued, February the 25th, 1570, a bull, excommunicating the heretic Elizabeth, and absolving her subjects from their oaths of allegiance. This bull one John Felton affixed to the gates of the bishop of London's palace in St Paul's church-yard, May the 25th, and on the 8th of August was hanged for his offence before the same gates. Camden, p. 428. Foulis, p. 433. Zurich Letters, pp. 341, 349.]

[5 Thomas Howard, duke of Norfolk, a protestant since he 'knew what religion meant,' the pupil of John Foxe, the martyrologist, to whom he left 'Twenty pound a yeare,' was beheaded on Tower hill, the 2nd of June, 1572, five months after condemnation, for a second time intending to marry Mary, queen of Scots, and thereby further her designs on the English throne. Camden, pp. 437-440. Wright's Elizabeth, Vol. I. pp. 402, 406. Zurich Letters, p. 320. Two warrants for his execution had first been signed and revoked. Lingard, Vol. VIII. pp. 89, 90.]

[6 John Throckmorton of Norwich was hanged the 30th of August, 1570, for having endeavoured, about a month before, to raise a rebellion in the county, in order, amongst other things, to set the duke of Norfolk at liberty on his first imprisonment. Camden, pp. 428, 429. Zurich Letters, p. 342. Perhaps, however, the Throckmorton alluded to

Englefield,[1] of *Paget*, of *Shelly*, and *Stanley*,[2] and *Yorke*,[3] and of all the seminary *Priestes*,[4] and *Jesuites*, to haue beene tickled vp by Romish busses and practices, and to haue bene caried forward by their own gross dotage vpon that absurd religion?

As for those other attempts against her dominions, which haue not staied themselues in the bare termes of conspiracie only, but haue also broken further into open rebellion and hostilitie; they likewise haue no less beene blown vp by that broode of *Massing Priests*, being vnnaturall subiects (for the most part) of these *kingdomes*. For was not *Moreton*[5] a Priest sent from the *Popes* own side to stirre vp the two Earls and others vnto the Northern rebellion? Did not *Saunders*[6] second his bookish treasons euen

was rather Francis, a gentleman of Cheshire, apprehended November the 7th, 1583, and put to death at Tyburn in the usual manner the 10th of July, 1584, nearly two months after conviction, because he had striven to bring about an invasion of England by the Catholic powers, so that Mary might be delivered from prison, and Elizabeth deposed. Thomas lord Paget, engaged in the same plot, fled into France. Camden, pp. 497, 498. The ship, wherein this nobleman escaped, William Shelley provided, who, being thus connected with the conspiracy, was cast into prison, and in 1586 condemned for treason. Ibid., pp. 504, 553. Lingard, Vol. VIII. p. 188.]

[1 Sir Francis Englefield had been one of queen Mary's privy council, and her master of the horse; but, retiring on the accession of Elizabeth to Flanders, was taken into the pay of Spain, of which court he became a great favourite. Strype's Annals, Vol. I. pp. 370-374; Vol. II. p. 27. In 1594 he was still engaged in plotting against Elizabeth. Camden, p. 576.]

[2 Though a Roman catholic, Sir William Stanley was by the earl of Leicester left in charge of Deventer in Holland, which city having betrayed to the Spaniards in the beginning of 1587, 'upon a principle of conscience,' he thenceforth became a pensioner or Philip the second. Carte, Vol. III. p. 599. Lingard, Vol. VIII. p. 264, note.]

[3 Rowland Yorke, 'a Man of a loose and dissolute Behaviour,' whom the earl of Leicester had appointed governor of a fort near Zutphen, not only turned traitor himself, but was the cause why his neighbouring commander, Sir William Stanley, did the same. Soames's Elizabethan Religious History, pp. 350-353.]

[4 The English clergy, who had withdrawn from their own country on account of religion, were formed into a society after the manner of a college, first at Douay, in 1568, then, on being banished from the Netherlands in 1575, at Rheims, and in 1579 at Rome. Camden, p. 476. These establishments, whose members are not to be confounded with the Jesuits, were called Seminaries, being designed 'to nourish and bring up persons to become seedmen in the tillage of sedition.' Stow, p. 1266. Fuller, Book ix. p. 84. Ranke's History of the Popes, Book v. chap. 7.]

[5 In 1569 Pius V. sent Dr Nicholas Morton, a Yorkshireman, from Rome into the northern parts of England, to stir up a rebellion there, by declaring on his authority (in anticipation of his famous bull) to the two principal Catholic nobles, the earls of Northumberland and Westmoreland, that Elizabeth was a heretic, and thus had no right to the kingdom. Soames, pp. 107, 108.]

[6 Nicholas Saunders (more truly *Slanders*—Fuller, Book ix. p. 169), 'that indefatigable writer, as well as warrior,' besides other treatises, put out one, *De visibili Monarchia Ecclesiæ*; and also another, *De Origine et Progressu schismatis Anglicani*; whose errors and falsehoods have been amply exposed by Burnet, at the end of the first two volumes of his History of the Reformation. Strype's Whitgift, p. 47. Zurich Letters, p. 418. 'D. Sanders, a lewde scholler and subiect of *England*, a fugitiue and a principall companion and conspirator with the traitors and rebels at *Rome*, was by the *Popes* speciall commission a commaunder, as in forme of a Legate, and sometime a treasorer or paymaster for those warres: which D. Sanders, in his booke of his Church Monarchie, did afore his passing into *Ireland* openly by writing gloriously allowe the foresaid Bull of *Pius Quintus* against her Maiestie, to be lawfull.' See a Tract published in 1583 to prove that the executions of Priests by Elizabeth were 'for Treason and not for Religion.' Saunders, being sent by Gregory XIII. to Ireland with a consecrated banner, landed, about the 1st of July, 1579, at Smerwick, in Kerry, in company with a small body of soldiers under James Fitzmaurice, whose brother, the earl of Desmond, 'the Pope's great champion,' he soon persuaded to rebel. Camden, pp. 472, 495. Foulis, p. 390. Ellis's Letters, Second Series, Vol. iii. pp. 92-97.]

with banner displaied, and by commotion in *Ireland?* And doth
not that *carnall arch-traitor Allen*[1] proclaime to the worlde vnto
his owne euerlasting reproch, that he and others excited the *King
of Spaines* inuincible *Nauy* (vainly so surnamed) by inuasion to
haue conquered his owne natiue countrie, and to haue swallowed
vs all vp? Yea, and in all those their latter hidden, hellish and
dampnable designs against her Maiesties own persone and life,
such *Priestes* haue also bene the principall stirrers and agents
vnder their vnholy father. *Somerfield*[2] and *Arden*, were not they
drawen into that action by *Hall* the Priest? *Parry* by Cardinal
Como, and by certaine English fugitive Priestes at *Millaine* and
Paris, and also by *Allens* traitorous writings? *Babington*[3] and
all the other bloudy conspirators, his complices, by *Ballard* the
Priest? So *Lopez*[4] his late purposed empoisoning is said to
haue bene first plotted and sette forward in *Spain* by *Parsons*[5]
the Jesuit Friar. And *Patrick o'Cullen*,[6] *Laton, Kale, Poule
Wheele*,[7] and sundry others very lately were animated by *Holt,
Hart, Sherwood*,[8] and other priestes, the detestable instruments
of the Bish. of *Rome*, and of the king of *Spaines* most dishonor-
able intended executions.

[1 William Allen, generally called the cardinal of England, died at Rome, October the 16th, 1594. It was, doubtless, in allusion to his ecclesiastical dignity, that the Admonition styles him "*carnall*," a species of wit not uncommon in the sixteenth century. He retired from the kingdom very soon after Elizabeth's accession. 'His learning and piety were very great, and he laboured very vsefully for the defence of the Catholic religion against the Heretics.'. Du Pin's Eccles. Hist. of the 16th century, Vol. II. p. 152. Ranke, Book v. chap. 12.]

[2 Somerfield is clearly an error for Somer*ville*. This 'furious yong man of War-wickeshire' (see p. 240), with Arden, his father-in-law, their two wives, and Hall, a priest, were arraigned on December the 16th, 1583, and condemned for conspiring against the queen's life. Somerville strangled himself in prison, Arden was hanged and quartered in Smithfield on the 20th of December, and the rest were spared. Stow, p. 1176.]

[3 Babington and Ballard and twelve others were hanged as conspirators on the 20th and 21st of September 1556. It was on the charge of having had a hand in this plot that the Queen of Scots was put to death.]

[4 Dr Roderigo Lopez, a Portuguese, suspected to be a Jew, but outwardly a Christian, and the queen's domestic physician, was tried on the last day of February 1594, at Guildhall, for contriving her majesty's destruction by poison, and on June the 7th hanged at Tyburn. Stow, pp. 1274, 1278.]

[5 Parsons, 'a turbulent, insidious, and intriguing Jesuit,' resided sometimes at Rome, sometimes in Spain. He came to England in disguise with Campion, in 1580, charged 'by speciall authoritie to execute the sentence of the bul' of 1570. Foulis, pp. 679-688.]

[6 Patrick o'Cullen, an Irish fencing-master, bribed, like many others, by the traitorous fugitives in the Netherlands, to destroy the queen, was tried at Westminster for that offence on March the 1st, 1594, and hanged at Tyburn on the following day. Camden, p. 577.]

[7 Nothing has been found respecting *Laton, Kale*, and *Poule Wheele*. Were they among those enumerated by Bacon, Vol. i. p. 538?]

[8 In 1585 Elizabeth commanded all Jesuits, and priests belonging to seminaries, of whom some were condemned, and others in danger of the law, 'to quit England within forty days, under pain of being dealt with as traitors; in the same manner as the protestant preachers had been driven out of the dominions of so many catholic princes.' Ranke, Book v. chap. 12. Among these was 'John Heart, the most learned of them all.' Camden, p. 497. Holinshed (p. 1380) prints a document, signed on the 3rd of February by this man and others. acknowledging that their deportation to Normandy had been managed with great kindness and courtesy.]

These and some other complots we see how desperately they haue bene attempted, yet (thanked be God) are not achieued : how perilously plotted, but are not perfected : how secretly deuised, yet most happily hithertoe discouered to Goddes infinite glorie, and our vnspekeable comfort.   So that it may aptly bee verified, that her Maiesties life hath all this while bene susteined *in manu altissimi*, and that vnder the shadowe of his wings shee hath not miscaried.   A llwhich whosoeuer hee bee that will attentiuely weigh and consider, and cannot see the very finger of God mightily working herein by his prouidence and mercy, no doubt, hee is insensible blockish : who seeth, and will not acknowledge it, is wilfully malicious : but who acknowledgeth, and also tasteth of the sweete blessings that are enioyed thereby, and is not most heartily thankefull to God therefore, is extremely impious, and doth but adde this vngratefulnes vnto the masse of all his other wickednes, euen vnto his own greater damnation.   Let euery of vs therefore who haue good will to *Sion*,[1] turne from our wicked waies, and from the euil that is betwixt our hands, and incessauntly with heart and voyce yeelde most humble and hearty thankes to God our deliuerer.   But let it not be for a day or two onely, whiles the intended wound doeth (as it were) present it selfe fresh and greene before the eyes of our mindes ; but continually, euen so long as wee may iustly imagine the same deuill in his impes still to rage and to bee prest to deuoure vs ; so long as *our habitation is amongst the Tents of Mesech*, and our *soules amongst Lions, who hunt after our liues*, and doe greedily seeke to *giue our Dearling to the dogge, and to lay our honour in the dust* : to the intent, that (if it be so Gods good will) our ioy may long and long bee redoubled and trebled vnto vs vnder the happy gouernment of so gracious a *Soueraigne*.   Which our bounden duetie that it may the more frequently and fruitfully be performed of vs ; it hath bin thought meete to publish this forme of praier for the continuance of Gods mercies towardes vs, and of thankesgiuing for his vnspeakable goodnesse in detecting so many conspiracies, and auerting so great mischiefes intended against vs.   Which duetie of praying and thankesgiuing there is no doubt but euery true hearted *English* man and faithfull *Subiect* will both priuately and publikely from the bottome of his heart performe.

Psalme 20.   *Psalme* 27.   *Psalme* 33.
Psalme 21.   *Psalme* 31.   *Psalme* 91.

Prayers for the preseruation of the Queenes Maiestie.

ALMIGHTY and euerlasting God, Creator and Gouernor of all the world, by whom *Kings* do beare rule, and vnder whose prouidence they are wonderfully and mightily oftentimes protected from

[1 Instead of, *Sion*, each of the other editions has, " the trueth of the Gospel."]

many fearefull dangers, by which the malice of *Satan* and his wicked impes do seek to intrap them : We giue vnto thy heauenly maiestie most humble and heartie thanks, for that it hath pleased thee, of thine infinite mercy and goodnes in *Christ Jesu*, so wonderfully to vphold, deliuer and preserue thine *Hand-maid*, our most dread and Soueraigne Queene *Elizabeth*, so many and sundry times, from the cruell and bloody treacheries of desperate men, who addresse themselues to all wickednes ; and at this time especially, wherein her innocent life was shotte at by diuers wicked designements of bloodthirsty wretches and traytors. And we doe most humbly, and from the bottom of our hearts, pray and beseech thee in *Christ Jesu*, to continue this thine vnspeakable goodnes towards her and this realme, and euermore to defend and protect them. O Lorde dissipate and confound al practises, conspiracies, and treasons, against her, against this realm of *England*, and against the trueth of thine *holy word* here taught and professed. Smite our enemies *Psal.* 2. [3]. (good Lord) vpon the cheek-bone, breake the teeth of the vngodly, frustrate their counsels, and bring to nought all their deuises. Let them fall into the pit, that they haue prepared for vs : Let a sudden *Psal.* 7. destruction come vpon them vnawares ; and the net that they haue *Psal.* 35. laid for others priuily, let it catch themselues, that they may fal into their own mischiefe. Let them bee ashamed and confounded *Psal.* 40. together, that seeke after her life to destroy it. Let them be driuen backeward and put to rebuke, that wish vs euill : so that the whole world and all posteritie may see and know, how mightily with thy *Psal.* 91. fatherly care and prouidence thou watchest ouer and defendest those, which put their trust in thee, and are in the hand of the most highest, and dwel vnder the shadow of the almighty : And that those which seeke thee may be ioyfull and glad in thee, and *Psal.* 40. all such as loue thy *Saluation* may say alway, *The Lord bee praised.* Graunt this (O most louing and mercifull father) for thy deare sonnes sake, *Jesus Christ* our Lord and onely *Sauiour*. Amen.

Another.

O ALMIGHTIE and eternal God, creator and gouernour of the whole worlde, vnto whom all power belongeth ouer all creatures both in heauen and earth, who spake the word, and they were made, commaunded, and al things were created, and by whom alone it is, that not only all *Kings* and *Princes* do rule and gouern the people committed to their charge, but are likewise by thy diuine prouidence and mighty protection (so long as it seemeth best to thy godly wisedome defended and deliuered, euen in the midst of all their perils and dangers, out of the hands of all their enemies : We yeeld vnto thee most humble and hearty thanks, for that it hath pleased thy gratious goodnes according to thine accustomed fauour towards her, still to preserue and defend thy welbeloued *Hand-maid* and our most gracious *Queene Elizabeth,* from all the wicked conspiracies, traiterous attempts, and deuilish deuises, which either the foreign and professed enemies abroad, or els her most vnloyal, desperate, and rebellious *Subiects* at home, were able at any time to deuise and practise against her. But specially (O Lord) at this time, as iust occasion is offered vnto vs all, we all euen from the bottome of our hearts praise thy holy name, and giue thee most hearty and vnfeined thanks for his thy late and most happy deliuery of her *Maiesties* most royall person from all those manifolde treasons, which were most wickedly inuented and cruelly attempted against her : most humbly beseeching thee, of thine infinite goodnesse and mercie, stil to continue thy fatherly protection ouer her, daily to encrease and multiply thy heauenly blessings and graces vpon her. Be thou euer vnto her (*O Lorde God* of hostes) euen a strong rock and tower of defence against the face of al her enemies, which either openly abrode, or secretly at home, go about to bring her life vnto the graue, and lay her honour in the dust. Disclose their wicked Counsels, and make frustrate all their deuillish practises in such sort, as that all the world may learne and know, that there is no counsell, no wisedome, no pollicy against the Lord. And if it be thy wil (*O Lorde*), either giue them grace in time to see howe in vaine they still kicke against the prickes, and doe seek to depose her whome thou doest exalt, and so acknowledge and repent them of these their sinnes, and thus conuert them in thy mercy : or els in thy iudgements (if with the wilful, obstinate, and reprobate sinners, they still harden their hearts and wil not repent) let all the enemies (*O Lord*), let all the malicious and deadly enemies of thine annointed seruaunt, and our most gracious Queene *Elizabeth*, perish together. Let them fall into the ditch which they haue digged for others, and be taken in their owne nets : but let her Maiesty (*O Lord*) euer escape them, that all the world may see how deare and precious in thy sight the life of this thine anointed is, who doth not so much as imagine this euil against them, that thus continually thirst after her blood. Wherfore (*O Lord* our God, king of kings and Lord of all Lords, vnto whose eyes al things are open, and from whom no secrets are hid, who only knowest al the deuises and thoughts of men, and searchest out the depth of their hearts) thou knowest (*O Lorde*) that nothing at any time hath bin more deare vnto thine annonynted *Hand-maid Elizabeth* our Queene, then the publike good and benefit of thy Church, and the godly peace and vnity of all good *Christians* among themselues. Wee beseech thee therefore of thy great goodnes (*O Lord*) still to looke downe from heauen, and behold her with thine eye of pitie and compassion, daily with thy mightie power and stretched out arm to saue and deliuer her from all her enemies, preserue and keepe her as the apple of thine own eye, and grant vnto her (O most mercifull father) a long, prosperous, and happie reigne ouer vs, and prolong her dayes as the dayes of heauen heere vpon earth, that she may be an olde mother in *Israel,* and see her desire vpon all thine and her enemies, though in number neuer so many, or in power neuer so mightie. And finally, after this life, giue vnto her euerlasting life, through *Jesus Christ* thine onely sonne and our onely *Sauiour.*

Another.

O MOST gracious God and our most louing and merciful father, which hast not only created vs, and all things by thy power, but hast also continued our preseruation by thy holy prouidence, therein working wonderfully, reuealing things hidden and secret, as thou doest discouer the bottoms and foundations of the deepe : how can wee woorthilye praise thy goodnes, or sufficiently declare thy louing kindnesse, which thou hast at all times shewed vnto vs thy seruaunts in the land of the liuing? we magnifie thy glorious name : thou hast a mightie arme ; strong is thy hand, and high is thy right hand, yea, thy wisedome is infinite. The prowd haue risen against thee, O Lord, and against thine annointed, our Soueraign vnder thee, and against thy people that call vpon thy name : but thou hast cast them downe from time to time, and scattered them abroad, for thy mercie endureth for euer. They haue taken wicked counsels together, saying, None shal be able to espie it : but thou hast opened them, and brought them out of darknes into light, for thou art God alone which destroyest the wisedom of the wise, and castest away the vnderstanding of the prudent, therefore do we worship thee and praise thy holy Name, reioycing continually in thy strength and thy saluation, for thou art the glorie of our power, and by thy fauor and louing kindnesse are wee preserued. Our shield and defence belongeth to thee (O Lord of hostes), and our gracious Prince to thee, O thou Holie one of Israel. And because thou hast loued her for thy names sake, and the glorie of thy kingdome vpon the earth, and vs also thy people to whom thou hast giuen her and many excellent blessings together with her righteous gouernment, thou hast also many times preserued and kept her, as the apple of thine eye, from the mis-chieuous imaginations and cruell handes of thine and her enemies, and from the secret practises of those that haue indeuoured to rise vp against her. Thou (O Lord) hast preserued her Honour from the ignominy, her life from the crueltie, and her Crowne from the tyranny of the wicked, her estate from ruine, her peace from dis-turbance, her kingdome and her people from being a prey to the malignant. The foote of pride hath come against vs, but the hand of iniquitie hath not cast vs downe. Therefore do we reioyce before thee, and be glad in thee, yea our songs doe wee make of thy name, O thou most Highest, and will be euer setting foorth thy praise and thy glorie, thy might and thy mercie from one generation to another. Only, O Lord, forsake vs not in the time of our age, vntil we haue shewed thy strength to this generation, and thy power to all that are yet for to come. And albeit if thou

Lord, in thy displeasure do mark among vs all what is done amisse, there is none that can abide it, yet forsake vs not, nor leaue vs, O God of our saluation.   Giue courage and constancie to our Soueraigne to perseuere in perils : prudence and wisedome to her Counsill wisely to foresee and discouer the subtil sleights and dangers of all enemies : faithfulnes and fortitude to the Nobles of the land, duty and obedience to vs all that are vnder her.   Forgiue also, we most humbly pray thee thorow thy fatherly kindnes in Iesus Christ, the multitude of our sinnes and transgressions against thy diuine maiestie, and thy commaundments, and according to the multitude of thy mercies doe away all our offences, that the light and candle of thy seruaunt *Elizabeth*, our gracious Queene and Gouernor, which is our life in the light of thy countenance, and the breath of our nosethrils, bee not put out, but may still shine and burne bright, illumined by the beames of thy heauenlie grace. Protect her (O Lord), we still beseech thee in safetie saue her in maiestie keepe her in peace, guide her in counsell, and defend her in danger : blesse her, Lord, in al temporal and celestial blessings in Christ, that she may still blesse thee : for in death no man remembreth thee, and who shall giue thee thankes in the pit? Detect and reueale still the foundations and buildings of all treasons and conspiracies, both at home and abroad ; and herein (O Lorde) either conuert the wicked hearts and secret conceits from their wicked imaginations, or confound their deuises, and make them as the vntimely fruit that they neuer see the sunne. Say (O Lord) to her soule as sometime thou diddest to *Abraham* the father of the Faithfull, I am thy buckler and thy exceeding great rewarde : and, as thou diddest sometime to the soule of thy seruant *Dauid*, I am thy saluation, with my holie oile haue I annointed thee.   Therefore my hand shall hold thee fast, and mine arme shall stablish thee.   The enemy shall not be able to do thee violence, the sonne of wickednes shall not hurt thee.   I will beate downe thy foes before thy face, and plague them that hate thee. Heare Lord, and saue us O King of heauen, when wee call vpon thee, and so shall wee all both Prince and people, dwell stil vnder the shadow of thy wings, protected by thy power, and preserued by thy prouidence, and ordered by thy gouernance, to thy euerlasting praise, and our vnspeakable comfort in Iesus Christ, to whom with thee, O Father and God of al consolation, and the holy spirit of sanctification, be al honor and glory both nowe and for euer.   Amen.

APPENDIX XV.

A [1] Prayer made by the queene at the departure of the fleet.

Moste omnipotent: Maker and guider of all our worldes masse, that onely searchest and fadomeste the bottome of all our hartes conceites, and in them seest the trewe originall of all our actions intended : thou that by thy foresight doest trewly discerne, how no mallice of reuenge, nor quittans of iniurie, nor desyre of bloodshede, nor greedines of lucre, hath bredd the resolution of our now sett out Armie, but a heedefull care and warie watche, that no neglecte of foes, nor over suertie of harme, might breede ether daunger to vs, or glorie to them : These beinge groundes, thou that didest inspyre the mynde, we humbly beseche with bended knees, prosper the wourke, and with beste forewyndes guyde the iourney, speede the victorie, and make the returne the aduancement of thy glorie, the tryumphe of there fame, and suertie to the Realme, with the leaste losse of Englishe bloude. To these deuout petitions Lorde geue thou thy blessed graunt.[2]

[1 'The queen composed two prayers, one for her own use, the other to be daily used in the fleet during the expedition. The former may be seen in Birch, ii. 18, with a letter to Essex from Sir Robert Cecil.' Lingard, Vol. VIII. p. 324. It has been printed also (under different titles, and not without variations), in Sorocold and Strype, the latter (Annals, Vol. IV. p. 216.) supposing it to belong to 1595, if not to 1594, whilst Sorocold, who lived so much nearer the time, with more correctness refers it expressly to 1596.]

[2 The two prayers, which follow, are unconnected with the object of this volume : still, as being attributed to Elizabeth, their insertion, appears allowable. The first is her prayer just before proceeding to her coronation, the 14th day of January, 1559 Holinshed (p. 1180), and Heylin (Elizabeth, p. 106), have printed it. The second, which exists in the Bibl. Lans. 116. art. 26, indorsed 'the Q. prayer after a progress, Aug. 15 [1574], being then a Bristow' [Bristol], is likewise in the State Paper Office (Domestic Elizabeth), whence the present copy was procured. Zurich Letters, p. 480.

Her highness, being placed in her chariot within the Tower of London, lifted up her eyes to heaven, and said :

O Lord almighty, and everlasting God, I give thee most hearty thanks, that thou hast been so merciful unto me, as to spare me to behold this joyful day. And I knowledge, that thou hast dealt as wonderfully with me, as thou didst with thy true and faithful servant Daniel the prophet, whom thou deliveredst out of the den, from the cruelty of the greedy raging Lions : even so was I overwhelmed, and only by thee delivered. To thee therefore be only thanks, honour and praise for ever. Amen.

The Queenes Prayer.

I render unto Thee (O mercifull and heavenly Father) most humble and hearty thanks for thy manifold mercies so abundantly bestowed upon me, as well for my creation, preservation, regeneration, and all other thy benefites and great mercies exhibited in Christ Jesus, but especially for thy mightie protection and defence over me, in preserving me in this long and dangerous journey, as also from the beginning of my life unto this present hower, from all such perills as I should most justly have fallen into for mine offences, haddest Thou not, O Lord God, of thy great goodness and mercy preserved and kept me. Continue this thy favorable goodness toward me, I beseech Thee, that I may still likewise be defended from all adversity both bodily and ghostly : but specially, O Lord, keep me in the soundness of thy faith, fear, and love, that I never fall away from Thee, but continue in thy service all the daies of my life. Stretch forth, O Lord most mightie, thy right hand over me, and defend me from mine enemys, that they

APPENDIX XVI.

A PRAYER OF THANKESGIUING, and for continuance of good
successe to her Maiesties Forces.

O[1] LORD God of Hosts, everlastenge and most mercifull
Father, wee thine unworthie creatures do yeld unto thy devine
maiestie all possible praise and humble[2] thankes for thine infinite
benefits,[3] which thou hast of longe time plentifullie poured uppon
thine Handmaiden and humble servant, our Sovereigne Lady the
Quene, and uppon hir[4] whole realm, and vs hir Subiects the people
of this Kingdome : And namelie (O Lord,) for that gratiouslie re-
spectinge vs in the merittes of thy deare sonne our Saviour, and
by his intercession passing ouer and forgivinge our manifold
sinnes,[5] thou hast this present Sommer so fauourablie conducted
the Roiale Navie and Armie sent to the seas[6] by our Gracious
Quene not for any other wordly respects, but for defence of this
Realme, and vs thy people, ageynst the mighty preparations of our
Enemyes threatning our ruin, by savelie directinge them vnto
places appointed, and by strengthning[7] the Gouuernors and
Leaders of the same with counsell and resolution, and blessinge
them with notable victories both by Sea and Land, wheareby the
insolencies[8] and pride of our Enemies, which soughte our Conquest
and subversion, is by thes late victories notablie daunted,[9] repulsed,
and abased. Grawnt vnto vs (most mercifull father) the grace[10]
with due thankefulnes to acknowledge thy[11] fatherlie goodnes
extended uppon us by the singular favor shewed to thy Servant[12]
and Minister our Soveraine Ladie and Quene. And for thy holie

never prevayle against me. Give me, O Lord, the assistance of thy Spiritt, and comfort
of thy Grace, truly to know Thee, intirely to love Thee, and assuredly to trust in Thee.
And that as I do acknowledge to have received the Government of this Church and
Kingdome at thy hand, and to hold the same of Thee, so graunt me grace, O Lord, that
in the end I may render up and present the same unto Thee, a peaceable, quiett, and
well ordered State and kingdome, as also a perfect reformed Church, to the furtherance
of thy Glory. And to my subjects, O Lord God, graunt, I beseech thee, faithfull and
obedient hearts, willingly to submit themselves to the obedience of thy Word and Commandments, that we altogether being thankfull unto Thee for thy benefitts received, may
laud and magnifie thy Holy Name world without end. Graunt this, O mercifull
Father, for Jesus Christes sake our only Mediatour and Advocate. Amen.]

[1 The following notes will point out the original readings of the author's manuscript ; such corrections thereof, as first suggested themselves, being placed within
brackets.]   [2 hartie.]

[3 spirituall and temporall, wch by the medeation of thy sonne or lord Jesus Christ or
Redemer thou hast.]

[4 her subiects.]   [5 and transgressions.]
[6 seas, for defence of this Realme and vs thy people, by savelie directinge.]
[7 enduinge the Gouuernors and Leaders wth Counsell and Courage.]
[8 pride, and mightenes of that nation of Spaine, wch hateth vs mortallie and seeketh
most greedelie or Conquest.]   [9 and abassed to or [great] comfort.]
[10 of hartie and unfeined repentance to the amendment of or liues past, and wth
due.]   [11 all thy.]
[12 or Soueraine Ladie the [and noble] Queene.]

Name [1] continue thes thy wonderfull blessinges [2] still uppon us, to defend us against our Ennemies, and [3] blesse us with thy graceful hand to the endlesse praise of thy holie name, and to our lasting joy. [4] And direct our Armies by thy providence and favorable support, to finish thes late victories to the honnour of our Soverain [5] and safty of hir Realme, that hath most carefullie made the same hable to overmatche hir Ennemies : so as the Noble men, [6] and all others serving in the same Navie and Armie under theire charge, [7] maie with much honnour, triumphe, and savetie retorne home to theire Cuntries, and give thee dewe thanks for thy spetiall favours marvelouslie shewed to them in preservinge of them [8] all this Sommer tyme from all contagion and mortaletie by sword or sicknes, notwithstandinge theire force and violence most manfullie exercised against their Ennemies, to the vanquishinge of [9] great Nombers both by Sea and Land, and to the destruction of their most mightie Shippes, [10] that hertofor have attempted to invade this realm, and of their Fortes and Castles, and waste of their notable substances of their riches, [11] without hurting any person that did yeelde, or of any women or children, or Religious persons, to whom all fauour was shewed that they did require. All which prosperous successes wee doe most iustlie acknowledge [12] (O Lord) to haue proceaded only from thy speciall fauour, to whome with thy sonne and holie Ghost, be all honor [13] and praise. Amen.

Set foorth by authoritie.
Imprinted at London by the Deputies of
Christopher Barker,
Printer to the Queenes most excellent Maiestie.

Anno Domini. 1596.

[1 sake, for thy Gospell, and thine eternall sonnes sake continue.]
[2 vppon vs, to defend vs [still] against.]
[3 and to blesse vs with continuance of peace to the endlesse.]
[4 perpetual comfort. And for this purpose wee beseeche thee gratious Lord for vs and or Armies [whersoevr by sea or land] to continewe still thy fauor, as in great mercie thou diddest in old time promise to be to thy people of Israele, that is, be thou an heauie Ennemy to such as [contemn thy power and] for thy sake are or Ennemies, and afflict them [wt repentance or correction] whoe seeke to afflict vs for or trewe honoringe of thee and thy sonne Jesus Christ. And direct or Armies yet [contynuyng] vppon the seas by thy prouidence.]
[5 noble Quene, and hir Realme.]   [6 with all the sayd Nauie.]
[7 and or valiant Countriemen seruing them thearein, maie.]
[8 from all mortallitie by.]
[9 of such as did withstand, and yt of such only as did mightily inuade and withstand them with force both.]
[10 shippes, fortes, and Castles.]   [11 riches. All wch.]
[12 to haue proceaded from thy fauor.]
[13 praise, glorie and dominion nowe and for euer.]

K

APPENDIX XVII.

CERTAINE PRAYERS set foorth by Authoritie to be vsed for the prosperous successe of her Maiesties Forces and Nauy.

Imprinted at London by the Deputies of Christopher Barker, Printer to the Queenes most excellent.   1597.

MOST mighty God and mercifull Father, as hitherto of thyne infinite goodnes thou hast very miraculously protected thy humble Seruant, our Soueraigne Lady and Queene, and all vs her subiects the people of her Dominions, from many dangerous conspiracies, malicious attempts, and wicked designements of her and our very obstinate and implacable enemies : Forasmuch as they stil continewing their malice, and preparing their Forces to assaile vs both by Land and Sea, thou (O Lord), to withstand their furie hast stirred vp the heart of thine Anoynted, our Soueraigne, to send out some of her Forces for our defence : we thine vnworthy seruants doe most humbly beseech thee, through the merites of our Sauiour Christ, so to conduct them, encourage them, and defend them with thy strong and mightie arme, as that whatsoeuer they shall attempt and take in hand for defence of this Realme against her enemies, may prosper and haue most happy successe. Direct and leade them (O Lord) in safetie, strengthen their Gouernours and Leaders with sound counsell and valiant resolution. Blesse their conflicts with notable victories both by Sea and Land : preserue them from all contagion and mortalitie either by sworde or sicknesse, and giue vnto them (O Lord) if it be thy blessed will, such an honourable and happy returne, as may tend to our defence by confusion of our enemies, to the renowne and comfort of our Soueraigne, to the benefite of thy Church, to the good of this Kingdome, and to the prayse and glory of thy most mighty Name, through Jesu Christ our Lord : To whome with thee and the holy Ghost bee ascribed all honour, power, and dominion, both nowe and for euer.   Amen.

O MOST mightie GOD, and Lorde of Hostes, which reignest ouer all the Kingdomes of the world, who hast power in thine hand to saue thy chosen, and to iudge thine Enemies, and in all ages hast giuen great and glorious Victories vnto thy Church, with small handfuls ouerthrowing great multitudes and terrible Armies : Let thine eares be now attent vnto our prayers, and thy mercifull eye vpon this Realme and kingdome.   And as of thine vnspeakable goodnes thou hast blessed vs with infinite and extraordinary bless

ings, all the yeres of her Maiesties most happy reigne ouer vs, and
of late hast also myraculously deliuered vs from sundry the bloody
practises of our very implacable enemies : So now we humbly beseech thee (O mercifull Father) to ayde vs with thy mighty Arme
in this our present iust cause, waging warre not in pride, nor ambition of mind, or any other worldly respect, but onely for the
necessary defence of Religion, our liues, and Countrey. Be mercifull therefore, O Lord, to our present Forces, and passing ouer
both their transgressions and ours, prosper them both by Sea and
land. Giue our Leaders and companies the strength of Unicornes,
the hearts of Lyons, armes of steele, hands of iron, and feete of flint,
to beate and tread downe all thine enemies and ours. Let thine
helpe from aboue at this time strengthen our Nauy and Army, thy
mercie overshadowe them, thy power as a wall of fire enuyron
them, thy wisedome direct them, thy prouidence secure them, thine
holy Angels garde them, thy Sonne our Lorde Jesus Christ stand
vp for them, and thy Justice confound, and Maiestie ouerwhelme
all aduersarie power exalting it selfe against this land and thy
Gospel. That all the world may know, that it is thy fauour that
prospereth, thy blessing that preserueth, and thine arme that ouer-
cometh in the day of battell. So we that be thy people and sheepe
of thy folde, shall sing vnto thy glorye the songs of prayse and
thankesgiuing, and magnifie thy goodnesse in the midst of thine
holy Temple for euer, through Jesus Christ our Lord, our onely
Sauiour and Mediatour. Amen.

O ALMIGHTIE Lorde God of Hostes, it is thine owne gracious
promise, that when thy people shall go out to battell against their
enemies, by the way y^t thou shalt send them, and shall call vpon
thee for thy holy helpe, that then thou (Lord) wilt heare their
prayers in heauen, and iudge their cause : In assured trust of this
thy good promise, we present this our supplication before thee. O
Lorde iudge thou our cause, iudge thou betweene vs and our cruell
enemies. Thou seest Lorde, that they first inuaded vs, and so doe
still continue, and not wee them : that they first conspired to root
vs out, that we might be no more a people of *English* birth, and
that then though thou from heauen diddest shew thy selfe, in
scattering their proud forces, to be displeased with their attempt,
yet notwithstanding by mightie preparations at this present they
seeke our ruine still. That which armeth vs, is neither desire of
enlarging our owne borders, nor thirst of blood, nor rauine of
spoyle, but onely our owne iust defence, onely to breake the power
of our enemies, and to turne away the battell from our owne gates ;
For that if we sit still, and suffer them to gather strength, they
will suddenly make a breach vpon vs, and destroy the mother with
the children. This they seeke, O Lord, and as thou seest, that
the heart of thine Anointed in all her actions is vpright before thee,
so mainteine thou our right, and be enemie to our enemies. Great

is their malice (as thou Lord seest), and great is yᵉ mischiefe they
intend against vs. Let not the wicked haue their desire : O Lord,
let not their mischieuous imaginations prosper, least they be too
proude. And albeit our many and grieuous iniquities may testify
against vs, and iustly deserue, that thou shouldest make the
enemies sword the auenger of thy couenant which wee haue
broken ; Yet deale thou with vs according to thy mercy, O Lord.
We haue sinned, Lord, doe thou vnto vs what seemeth good in
thine eyes : onely at this time wee pray thee to succour vs, and
not make vs a scorne and derision to our oppressors. The rather
O Lord, for that wee put not our trust in any strength of our owne,
but our eyes looke onely to thee. We know, Lord, the battel is
thine, and that with thee it is nothing to saue with many, or with
few : For that, except thou command the winds, we can not stirre,
and except thou blesse with counsell aud courage, wee shall not
preuaile, and all these are in thine handes to giue or to withholde.
Helpe vs, O Lord God, for we rest on thee, and in thy Name go
we foorth against these mightie preparations. O Lorde thou art
our God, let not man preuaile against thee : let thine arme rise up,
and put on strength to preserue vs nowe as of olde, euen the same
arme that was mightie for vs and against them in their former
pride and furie.

Wherefore from thy holy Sanctuarie, O Lorde, open thine eyes
and behold, incline thine eare and heare the prayer of thy seruants.
Goe foorth, O Lord, with our Hostes, by Sea and by land. Send
forth the windes out of thy treasures to bring them to the place
appointed. Take all contagious sicknesse from the middest of
them, O Lord the strength of our saluation. Couer their heads in
the day of battell. Send thy feare before thy seruants, and make
their enemies to flee and fal before them. Let thy faith (Lord)
make them valiant in battell, and put to flight the Armies of
Aliens. And by this shall we know, O Lorde, that thou fauourest
vs, in that our enemie doeth not triumph ouer vs, and shall
alwayes confesse to the prayse of thy Name, that it was thy hand,
and that it was thou, Lord, the shield of our helpe, and sword of
our glory, that hast done these great things for vs, and euermore say, Praysed be the Lorde, that hath pleasure in the prosperitie of his seruants. Heare vs, O Lord for the glorie of thy
Name, for thy louing Mercie, and for thy trueth sake, euen for the
merits and intercession of our Lord Jesus Christ. Amen.

O ETERNALL God, in power most mightie, in strength most
glorious, without whom the Horse and Chariot is in vaine prepared against the day of battell : vouchsafe (wee beseeche thee)
from thy high throne of Maiestie to heare and receiue the heartie
and humble prayers, which on bended knees wee the people of
thy pasture, and sheepe of thy handes, doe in an vnfayned ac-
knowledgment of thy might and our owne weakenesse powre out

before thee on the behalfe of our Gracious Soueraigne, and on the behalfe of her Armies, her Nobles, her Valiants, and men of warre : who by thee inspired haue put their liues in their hands, and at this time doe oppose themselues against the malice and violence of such, as beare a mortall hate at thy Sion, and doe dayly conspire and rise vp against it, euen against the Church, thine Annointed, and the people of this her Land.   Arise then (O Lord) and stand vp, we pray thee, to helpe and defend them : be thou their Captaine to go in and out before them, and to lead them in this iourney : teache their fingers to fight, and their hands to make battaile.   The Generall and Chieftaines bless with the spirite of wisdome, counsell, and direction ; the Souldiers with mindes ready to performe and execute.   Gird them all with strength, and powre out vpon them the spirite of courage : giue them in the day of battell heartes like the hearts of Lions, inuincible and fearelesse against euill, but terrible to such as come out against them.   Where the enemie doeth rage, and danger approache, be thou (O Lord) a rocke of saluation, and a tower of defence vnto them.   Breake the enemies weapons : As smoke vanisheth, so let their enemies be scattered, and such as hate them, flie before them.   Thou seest (O Lord) the malice of our aduersaries, howe for thy Name, which is called on ouer us, and for the trueth of thy Gospell wherein we reioyce, they beare a tyrannous hate against vs, continually vexing and troubling vs, that fain would liue in peace.   Styrre vp therefore (O Lord) thy strength, and auenge our iust quarrell : turne the sword of our enemy vpon his owne head, and cause his delight in warre to become his owne destruction.   As thou hast dealt with him heretofore, so now scatter his Forces, and spoile bis mighty Ships, in which he trusteth ; so shall we the people of thine inheritance, giue praise vnto thy Name, and for thy great mercy giue thankes vnto thee in the great Congregation : yea, the World shall know, and the Nations shall vnderstand to the praise of thy glory, that thou alone defendest them that trust in thee, and giuest victorie vnto Princes.   Heare vs (O Lord our strength) in these our prayers, for Jesus Christ his sake.   Amen.

O ALMIGHTY God, which onely doest great woonders, shewe foorth (wee pray thee) at this time the power of thy might, and the glorie of thy strength, by preseruing our Armies at Sea and Land, from death and sicknesse, and all perils on the Sea, and by helping them in the day of battell against the rage and violence of the Aduersarie.   Thou seest (O Lord) that not for any worldly respects, but for the defence of this Realme, and the peace of thy Church in it, this iourney is vndertaken, to abate and withstand the pride, and to daunt the insolencies of our enemies, who conspire and bandie themselves against vs, breathing out wrath and vtter subuersion.   Arise therefore, wee pray thee, (O Lord of

Hostes) vnto our helpe, and let our enemies feele that thou still defendest our iust cause, and in ye day of battell doest fight for vs. Not in our owne sword, nor in the arme of our owne flesh, doe we put our trust ; but our trust is in the multitude of thy mercies, and in the strength of thy mightie Arme, who art God alone. Blesse therfore the Chieftaines and Leaders of our bands with ye spirit of wisedome, counsell, and magnanimitie, and the Souldiers with courage and fortitude, to stand vndaunted and without feare in the day of battell. But as for their enemies, and such as come out against them, cast a feare and astonishment vpon them, that they may fal, and couer their faces with shame and confusion. That all the worlde may knowe, that thou (O God) resistest the proude and wicked men, and that thou auengest the cause of such us put their trust in thee. Heare us, O God of Hostes, euen for Christ his sake our only Sauiour and Redeemer. Amen.

O GOD, most glorious, the shielde of all that trust in thee, who alone doest sende Peace to thy people, and causest Warre to cease in all the worlde, consider the dayly troubles of thy seruants, and beholde the malice of our Aduersaries, who for thy Names sake, which is called on ouer us, and for the truth of thy Gospel wherin we reioyce, do conspire and band themselues against vs, breathing out wrath and vtter subuersion. Many a time hath their wrath bene kindled, so that they would haue swallowed vs vp quicke : but by thy power their purpose hath bene frustrated, their counsels preuented, their preparations ouerthrowen, and we deliuered. Yet, O Lorde, their heart is set against vs, still to vexe and trouble vs that faine would liue in peace. But for the quiet of thy Church, and that thine enemies may knowe thee to be a God of mercy, cause them to returne at last, and not any longer to hate those whome thou hast loued : Make them to see that their plotts and designements are against them, who for vs fightest against them, drowning their ships, and casting downe their strong-holdes in which they doe trust ; that thy Name may be glorified in the day of their conuersion. But if they shall still harden their hearts, and will not vnderstand either our defence, or their owne calamitie to come of thee : Make voyde their deuises, disclose their counsels, discouer their secret complots, that in the snare, which they haue layd for vs, their owne feete may be taken. Finally, O Lord, whensoeuer they prepare themselues to bat-taile, take the defence of our iust cause into thine hand : Break their Nauies, disperse their Armies, and cast vpon them a feare and astonishment, that they may tremble at thy presence, and flye before they be pursued : Graunt this O Lord our strength euen for Christ his sake.   Amen.

O ETERNALL God, Lorde of the whole World, and guide of Sea

and land, who by thy mightie power sortest to what effect thou wilt the Councels and actions of all men : gratiously vouchsafe to blesse and order vnto happy issue the late begunne worke of our gratious Soueraigne in the hand of her Nobles and men of warre, nowe sent out by Seas, to withstande the Enemies of her life, her people, and thy Church. As Guide and Generall of the iourney, let it please thee (mightie Lorde of Hostes) to goe in and out before them, with best fore-windes and streightest course to speede and prosper them in the way. And when thou hast brought them to the appointed place, in a pillar of fire giue light to direct their steps, and in a pillar of a Cloude defend them. Put vpon them thy spirit of counsell and fortitude, and vnder the banner of thy power and protection let the worke be effected. Courage and imbolden them in the day of conflict, to stand vndaunted and without feare. Make way and opportunitie for them to attempt with aduantage, and for thy Names sake graunt (O glorious God) to their puissant attempts happy successe in battell, to their battell a ioyfull victorie, and to their victorie a safe and triumphant returne. So will we yᵉ people of thine inheritance, which nowe pray for the blessing of thy grace vpon them, praise thy Name for euer, and together with them ascribe both cause and glory of the worke, not to our owne strength, but vnto thy power, who alone giuest victory in the day of battell : and for thy great mercies will giue thanks vnto thee in the midst of the Congregation. Hear vs O Father, euen for Christ his sake. Amen.

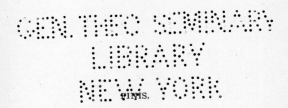

GEN. THEO. SEMINARY
LIBRARY
NEW YORK.

TURNBULL AND SPEARS, PRINTERS, EDINBURGH.

2 M.—D.—11/93.